Fairchild C-82 Packet

ALSO BY SIMON D. BECK

The Aircraft-Spotter's Film and Television Companion (McFarland, 2016)

Fairchild C-82 Packet
The Military and Civil History

SIMON D. BECK

McFarland & Company, Inc., Publishers
Jefferson, North Carolina

LIBRARY OF CONGRESS CATALOGUING-IN-PUBLICATION DATA

Names: Beck, Simon D., 1972– author.
Title: Fairchild C-82 Packet : the military and civil history / Simon D. Beck.
Description: Jefferson, North Carolina : McFarland & Company, Inc., Publishers, [2017] | Includes bibliographical references and index.
Identifiers: LCCN 2017041854 | ISBN 9781476669755 (softcover : acid free paper) ∞
Subjects: LCSH: Fairchild aircraft—History. | Transport planes—United States—History. | Airplanes, Military—United States—History.
Classification: LCC TL686.F19 B43 2017 | DDC 358.4/483—dc23
LC record available at https://lccn.loc.gov/2017041854

BRITISH LIBRARY CATALOGUING DATA ARE AVAILABLE

**ISBN (print) 978-1-4766-6975-5
ISBN (ebook) 978-1-4766-2864-6**

© 2017 Simon D. Beck. All rights reserved

No part of this book may be reproduced or transmitted in any form or by any means, electronic or mechanical, including photocopying or recording, or by any information storage and retrieval system, without permission in writing from the publisher.

Front cover photographs: *top* the prototype Fairchild XC-82 Packet s/n: 43-13202 (Fairchild); *bottom* C-82A Jet-Packet 1600 N6887C (United States Air Force).
Back cover photograph: a C-82A crash test conducted by the NACA during 1952 (courtesy NASA Glenn Research Center, Cleveland, Ohio)

Printed in the United States of America

*McFarland & Company, Inc., Publishers
Box 611, Jefferson, North Carolina 28640
www.mcfarlandpub.com*

To the memory of Captain Wendell W. Levister, Sr.,
and to all those, both military and civil, who built, flew
and serviced the C-82 Packet from Hagerstown

Acknowledgments

An undertaking such as this has required the expertise, assistance and kindness of many people in donating their time, their memories, and in many cases their photographic collections. The author would like to extend a sincere and grateful acknowledgment to the following persons and organizations, without whose help this book would not have been possible. In alphabetical order they are: Adell and William Aldrich for background *Phoenix* movie material; Fred Austin for C-82 data; Michael Bernhard for photographic assistance; Martin Bernsmuller for Brazil C-82s; Ed Bertschy; Jacob Chakko for Steward-Davis data; Eddie Coates; John Davis for his brilliant help covering many of the Latin American C-82s; Ray Deacon; Roger Deere of the WPAFB Museum; Archie DeFante, USAF Archivist, Maxwell AFB; the late Stanley Epstein for Steward-Davis background; Rufus Escalanti; Jaime Escobar for Colombian C-82s; the Federal Aviation Administration; James H. Farmer; Roberto Gaineddu; Robert Gorman for Steward-Davis data; Dan Hagedorn; the Hagerstown Aviation Museum, Maryland; Wilhelm Hell; Paul J. Holsen II for Honduran data; William Hopkins; Betsy Kemper; Gary Killion; Dick Lansman for Steward-Davis data; William T. Larkins; John LaSalandra; the late Captain Wendell Levister for his memories of N4834V; the late Chuck Lunsford for 60th TCG history; Jim Moffett for XC-82 help; Jonathan Oglin for Bolivian histories; Milo Peltzer for C-82 materials; the National Museum of the U.S. Air Force; Bruce Orriss; Michael Prophet for use of his C-82 photo collection; Rob Raine of AMARC, Tucson, Arizona; Gordon Reid for his notes taken at Long Beach in 1967; Angelo Romano; Sergio Luis dos Santos for Brazil C-82s; Wally Soplata; LaDonna Springer for data on the N74127 crash; the late Bob Thayer for his memories at Steward-Davis; Alicia Thomas of the Yuma County Library for newspaper help; Dan Thompson for background on Steward-Davis; Reynaldo Tinoco for Mexico C-82s; Jean-Pierre Trevor for making his father Elleston Trevor's photo collection available; Rick Turner; Richard Vandervord; Johan Visschedijk; Aad van der Voet; Andre van Loon; Ron Vidor for *Phoenix* movie help; Captain Bob West; John Wegg; Rebecca Whaley-Wiant for use of her father Ted Whaley's photographic collection; Nick Williams; Hans-Joachim Wirtz; Roger Wyckoff; plus the many others who gave their time and assistance in the making of this book—I thank you all.

Table of Contents

Acknowledgments	vi
Preface	1
Abbreviations	3
Introduction: C-82 Development History	5

SECTION ONE

The Airplane	17
Mission	24
Specifications	27
Serial Number List	29
Variants	32
Steward-Davis Jet-Packet	41
Jet-Packet Variants	53
The Flight of the Phoenix	57

SECTION TWO

Military Operators	71

SECTION THREE

Civil Operators/Owners	111

SECTION FOUR

Production Histories	150

Appendix I: Civil Registration to Serial Number Cross-References	291
Appendix II: C-82 Retirement Bases/Civil Sales and NACA Assignments	294
Appendix III: Unknown Identities and Dispositions	299
Appendix IV: Conversions and Unique Packets	301
Appendix V: Attrition	303

Appendix VI: Accidents	304
Appendix VII: Existing Aircraft	308
Appendix VIII: Civil C-82A Checklist	309
Postscript: Sebring C-82 Packets	312
Bibliography	313
Index	315

Preface

The first Fairchild C-82 Packet flew in prototype form in 1944. In 1945 the first production example was delivered to the USAAF. The last example was retired from regular civil service in Alaska in 1984. It has now been many decades since the first Packet twin-boomers entered service, but their history has largely gone unrecorded, and subsequently forgotten, in the annals of aviation history.

During my research into Fairchild Aircraft in general, and with a keen interest in the motion picture *The Flight of the Phoenix* (1965), a film that featured the C-82 Packet as a main backdrop and integral part of the story, I realized that there has never been a complete, dedicated history written for this aircraft, which was really the first practical, end-loading cargo design to gain full production status with regular military service. Its design set the standard for cargo aircraft that exists to this day in the form of the C-130 Hercules and C-17 Globemaster III.

Most previously published material on the C-82 only notes the aircraft in minor notations alongside other aircraft types.

I've researched the C-82 Packet since 2004, and by 2013 I had enough materials gathered to write this book solely focused on the military and civil history of this aircraft. My research has revealed an interesting and often colorful record of military assignments, humanitarian missions, civil adventures and final dispositions that have not seen the light of day for many, many decades. Most of the people who flew or worked with this aircraft, in any form or capacity, are no longer with us, but I hope this book will be an enduring testimony to their memory.

Dates are presented as "month dd yyyy" in the narrative text and captions
but presented as "dd mon yy" in the technical sections.

Abbreviations

AAC—Alaskan Air Command
AACS—Airways & Air Communications Service
AAF—Army Air Field
AB—Air Base
acc—accepted
ADC—Air Defense Command
AF—Air Force
AFB—Air Force Base
AFE—(U.S.) Air Force in Europe
AFS—Air Force Station
AMC—Air Materiel Command
ARD—Air Research & Development Command
ARS—Air Rescue Service
ATC—Air Transport Command
ATSC—Air Technical Service Command
avble—available
A1C—Airman 1st Class
A2C—Airman 2nd Class
BAS—Base Unit
bku—broken up
BOC—Brought on charge
CAA—Civil Aeronautics Administration (1940–1958/to FAA)
CAB—Civil Aeronautics Board (1940–1967/to NTSB)
CAF—Continental Air Force
canx—canceled
Capt—Captain
CNC—Continental Air Command
Cpl—Corporal

cvtd—converted
d/b/a—doing business as
del—delivered
depl(s)—deployment(s)
depmnt—depot maintenance
de-reg—de-registered
des—designated
DFI—dropped from inventory
FAA—(i) Federal Aviation Agency (1958–1966)
 (ii) Federal Aviation Administration (1966–present)
ff—(date of) first flight
FMS—Foreign Military Sales
GP—Group
hp—horsepower (engine power)
IARC—Individual Aircraft Record Card
lb—pounds (weight)
lbst—pounds static (thrust)
Lt—Lieutenant
Maj—Major
MAP—Municipal Airport (Civil)
MATS—Military Air Transport Service
MNT/mnt—Maintenance
MSgt—Master Sergeant
MSU—Maintenance & Supply
NEAC—Northeast Air Command
nfd—no further details
NTSB—National Transportation Safety Board (1967–present)
ntu—not taken up
PFC—Private First Class

PGC or NPGC—(Air) Proving Ground Command
re-des—redesignated
reg—(civil) registration
re-reg—(civil) re-registered
RES—Air Rescue
ret—retired
retd—retained
rsved—reserved
SAC—Strategic Air Command
SAR—Search & Rescue
S-D—Steward-Davis
Sgt—Sergeant
s/n—serial number
SOC—Struck off charge
SQ—Squadron
SSgt—Staff Sergeant
TAC—Tactical Air Command
TC—Air Training Command
TCG—Troop Carrier Group
TCSq—Troop Carrier Squadron
TCWG—Troop Carrier Wing
tranmnt—transient maintenance
TSgt—Technical Sergeant
u/c—undercarriage
unk—unknown
USAAF—United States Army Air Force
USAF—United States Air Force
USAFE—United States Air Force in Europe
UT—Unit
wfu—withdrawn from use
WG—Wing
w/o—written-off
WPAFB—Wright-Patterson Air Force Base

Introduction:
C-82 Development History

The Fairchild Engine and Airplane Corp. achieved outstanding success during World War II with its PT-19, PT-23 and PT-26 series of monoplane primary-trainer designs named the Cornell. Although during this period it was not quite in the same league as aviation giants Boeing, Douglas, Lockheed, North American or Grumman, the company did establish itself as a major military manufacturer in the postwar years. Fairchild did this through its entry into the "big plane" market with the C-82 Packet, C-119 Flying Boxcar and C-123 Provider, the last two achieving a well-earned place in the annals of USAF service. Fairchild continued to develop aviation technologies into the 1960s and 1970s, all the while producing such diverse aircraft as the F-27 and FH-227 Friendship, the PC-7 Turbo-Porter, and the classic A-10 Thunderbolt II close-air support aircraft. The last A-10 was delivered in 1984, then, after 62 years, due in part to changing economic times, Fairchild left the aircraft manufacturing business altogether in 1987. Its various aviation interests were eventually diluted down and absorbed into other aerospace companies.

It all began with a wealthy, innovative New York State–born American businessman named Sherman M. Fairchild (April 7, 1896–March 28, 1971), who at 29 years of age inherited his father's multi-million-dollar estate of companies and stock. This gave Sherman the ability to pursue his own desire of becoming an entrepreneur, something he had been gravitating toward in prior years. He already owned and held patents on several inventions, chief among them an aerial camera and its associated shutter mechanism. Nurturing this technology, he founded the Fairchild Aerial Camera Corp. in 1920 to manufacture and sell his cameras. The company was later renamed Fairchild Camera & Instrument.

Sherman then began renting airplanes and hiring pilots to demonstrate his cameras; this venture became Fairchild Aerial Surveys in 1921. After seeing the results of the extreme conditions of high-altitude flying on the crews doing his aerial photography work, Sherman sought an aircraft with an enclosed, heated cabin. When he learned no such aircraft existed, and by now having inherited family wealth, he formed the Fairchild Airplane Manufacturing Corp. in 1925 and built the first aircraft dedicated to aerial photography—the Fairchild FC-1. Facilities were soon built at Farmingdale, Long Island, New York, and Fairchild entered into the aircraft manufacturing business with resounding success. It should also be remembered that in the pre–Depression era of the late 1920s, Fairchild was, for a time, the second largest producer of aircraft in the world.

Fairchild Airplane's subsequent famous association with Hagerstown, Maryland, began with a small aviation company formed in that town in 1925—the Kreider-Reisner

The prototype Fairchild XC-82 Packet s/n: 43-13202 (msn: 10001) (Fairchild).

Aircraft Co. In 1929 Fairchild purchased a controlling interest in this company and began building new manufacturing facilities at Hagerstown Airfield, a location that would later become the center of the Fairchild aviation business.

Unfortunately, the ravages of the Great Depression of late 1929 decimated the Fairchild empire, with Sherman losing control of many of his companies to a financial conglomerate known as AVCO (Aviation Corp.). Luckily, he still had a major stake in Kreider-Reisner at Hagerstown, where he consolidated his aircraft business to form the Fairchild Aircraft Co. in 1931. Maintaining its high quality of workmanship in aircraft design and manufacture, Fairchild clawed its way back and in 1936 was reorganized under a corporate umbrella known as the Fairchild Engine and Airplane Corp. headquarterd in New York. Its two aviation subsidiaries were the Fairchild Aircraft Division, located in Hagerstown, Maryland, and the Ranger Engineering Division of Farmingdale, New York, specializing in the manufacturing of Ranger piston engines.

With the outbreak of World War II, the Fairchild plant, supported by a healthy workforce from nearby Hagerstown, was well established to produce aircraft for the war effort. Their main product became the famous Fairchild PT-19 Cornell, a single-engined primary trainer, which was first flown in military guise in 1940. A fleet of 6,748 were built by Fairchild (along with licensed manufacturers like Aeronca) up until 1944, with a further 1,883 built in Canada and Brazil. A lesser-known Fairchild product during this period was the AT-21 Gunner, of which 179 were built. With a firmly established plant, a reliable workforce and a good history of aeronautical expertise, Fairchild was well placed to tackle a larger project.

The bulk cargo role has always been a specialized one for the aviation community. The mainstay of freight/paratroop operations during World War II were catered to by the legendary Douglas C-47 Skytrain and Curtiss C-46 Commando. Both were great aircraft in their own right, but they were built as prewar civil passenger aircraft with a sloping deck and side-entry doors. So when a USAAF requirement from General Henry H. "Hap" Arnold was issued in 1941 for a dedicated cargo aircraft, Fairchild's vice-president Richard S. Boutelle responded with a submission by their chief designer Armand J. Thieboldt. He had made sketches of what would become the Fairchild Model 78 in November 1941. It was to be of all-wood construction in order to preserve precious metals for proven designs already in production. A mock-up was completed by the spring of 1942, and Army representatives were favorably impressed with the design presented to them. Then, as the tides of war changed in late 1942, the Army Air Force canceled the wood design requirement and allowed an all-metal construction technique.

On August 6, 1942, Fairchild received contract AC-30435 to build one static test airframe and two flyable prototypes with the USAAF designation XC-82. It would be the largest airframe yet built by the eager plant at Hagerstown, Maryland. The twin-boom design, with engineering drawings, was then finalized, tooling and assembly jigs were built, and construction on a prototype was begun. Power would be provided by two Pratt & Whitney R-2800 Double Wasp radial engines, each rated at 2,100 hp. Competing for the same contract were three other prototypes, the Budd RB-1 Conestoga, the Curtiss-Wright YC-76 Caravan, and the Waco YC-62. Just over two years later, and after Fairchild had beaten competition for the same contract from the competing manufacturers, the first prototype was ready to fly.

At 6:18 p.m. on Sunday, September 10, 1944, a red-letter date in the history of the

XC-82 s/n: 43-13202 (msn: 10001), showing the twin boom design (National Museum of the United States Air Force).

Two views of the XC-82 under construction in the Fairchild plant at Hagerstown Airport, Maryland (Fairchild).

company, the prototype Fairchild XC-82 (s/n: 43-13202) took to the air at Hagerstown Airfield, witnessed by 6,000 factory employees who turned out for the event. The flight lasted 18 minutes, the crew returning with encouraging results. Further flight tests were so positive that the Army issued Fairchild with contract AC-124 on September 28, 1944, for an order of 100 production C-82A aircraft. At the same time the requirement for the second flyable XC-82 (c/n: 10002) prototype was canceled. The new airplane was on track with a future that would put the manufacturer into the league of a "big planemaker."

The formal name of Packet was assigned by the USAAF on November 10, 1944, in honor of the 19th-century British "packet sailing ships." However, the nickname of Flying Boxcar soon came into more common and popular use with the aircrews and in the media—it was even printed on the prototype during demonstration tours. This name came about because the internal cargo hold volume of the C-82 was equal to that of a railway boxcar—2,598 cubic feet. No doubt Flying Boxcar does indeed have a more appealing ring to it.

By late 1944 an anticipated invasion of Japan (Operation Downfall) was set to take place in 1945. The U.S. Army, seeing the urgent need for the new twin-boom cargo/paratroop transport in the proposed Japanese invasion, issued contract AC-7179 on December 19, 1944, to North American Aviation Inc. at Dallas, Texas, for the licensed manufacture

The prototype XC-82 featured an informal nose art logo promoting the new aircraft as *The Flying Boxcar* (Fairchild).

of up to 1,000 aircraft under the designation C-82N. However, with the war abruptly ending due to the use of the atomic bombs, Packet production was drastically cut—only three of the 1,000 C-82Ns ordered were completed before the contract was canceled. Fairchild was allowed to continue production with their 100-plane order, and with additional contract orders, eventually delivered 220 of the type by October 1948.

During 1946, the USAAF began to re-equip their transport and troop carrier groups with the C-82 Packet. The 62nd and 316th Troop Carrier Groups (TCG) were the first to integrate the aircraft into their ranks. The 64th, 313th, 314th and 375th TCGs would soon follow with frontline service lasting until mid–1953. The 60th TCG in West Germany was also a substantial user of the aircraft with deployments into Africa and the Middle East. Later, as the Fairchild C-119 Flying Boxcar, a revised and more powerful version of the C-82, began to arrive in numbers, the Packet was relegated to Continental U.S. assignments such as base and unit support duties with the fighter groups of Air Defense Command.

It was also found that Fairchild's twin-boomer was well suited to the search and rescue role with its long endurance and ability to air-drop cargoes. Consequently, 37 of the type served in the Air Rescue Service under MATS from 1947 to 1953, both in the U.S. and abroad in Europe.

Overall, the Packet's military service was relatively uneventful, but two events the airplane made a worthy contribution to were the Berlin Airlift and Operation Haylift. Five Packets were assigned to the Berlin Airlift from September 1948 to September 1949, providing much-needed heavy equipment and supplies, beyond the capacity of the C-47 or C-54, for the rebuild of Berlin. Many Packets were supplied for Operation Haylift, catering to the desperate requirement by ranchers for airdrops of hay to stranded cattle during the destructive snowstorms of 1949 in the rural U.S. Northwest. The operation

C-82A s/n: 45-57783 (msn: 10153) in formation with three other Packets (National Museum of the United States Air Force).

Large-scale paratroop exercises with the United States Army were a mainstay of the C-82's stateside military duties (National Museum of the United States Air Force).

ran from January 23 to February 17, 1949, with C-82 crews dropping 4.2 million pounds of hay, saving up to 300,000 cattle.

Although the plane was keenly ordered by the USAAF toward the end of World War II when a pure cargo type was in dire need for the war effort, design limitations were going to be inevitable in order to meet deadlines and get the C-82 into military service.

Even though initial tests were outstanding, the aircraft had been ordered into production before thorough flight tests could be completed with the XC-82. These limitations became quite apparent in postwar service; crews noted there was a lack of forward visibility from the flight deck, especially during airdrops and the flare on landing, when the runway could disappear altogether from view. Other problems were that the boom structure could become weakened by repeated heavy landings and the undercarriage on occasion gave trouble, becoming stuck in flight or collapsing while on the ground.

The most serious flaw with the C-82, however, was its inherent poor single-engine performance and poor directional control in a single-engine situation. In some instances, directional control on a single-engine could be so poor, the pilot could lose control of the aircraft altogether. At a full weight of 54,000 pounds on one engine, a C-82 is unable to maintain any sort of level flight at all, losing 78 ft/min. This shortcoming would cause the Packet to develop a less than favorable reputation in air force service, so much so that a redesign of the aircraft was initiated in early 1947 as the XC-82B.

By the time the last Packets had been retired from service in 1955, the USAF had lost 53 to accidents and incidents, amounting to nearly a quarter of the Packet fleet delivered to the USAF! At least 18 of these were due to a single-engine loss or poor single-engine handling.

The XC-82B featured a redesigned fuselage with many other improvements. Most important was the addition of two 2,650 hp Pratt & Whitney R-4360 Major Wasp engines in place of the C-82's 2,100 hp R-2800 Double Wasps. Redesignated as the XC-119A by

Excellent publicity photograph depicting the Packet's capabilities. Aircraft from top to bottom are s/n: 44-23024 (msn: 10068), s/n: 45-57793 (msn: 10163) and s/n: 45-57738 (msn: 10108) (National Museum of the United States Air Force).

the USAF, the new model made its first flight on December 17, 1947, from Hagerstown, Maryland. Further refinements during production, including a wider fuselage for greater cargo capacity, saw the aircraft go on to a very successful future with both the USAF and USMC, as well as several foreign military forces, as the C-119 Flying Boxcar.

XC-119A s/n: 45-57769 (msn: 10139) on a test flight. Note the "Fairchild Packet C-119A" branding on the nose (National Museum of the United States Air Force).

A total of 1,185 C-119 aircraft were delivered by 1955, the success of which meant the end of USAF service for the C-82. Retirements began in mid–1953 as deliveries of Fairchild's much-improved Boxcar began to enter USAF service in sufficient numbers. The last regular C-82s were retired into storage at Davis-Monthan AFB in early 1955, with subsequent civil purchases taking place from August 1955 through March 1956.

The Packet's civil career, then, began in 1955 with sales made to both U.S. aviation operators and many in Latin America. In total 140 of the 224 C-82 Packets built, nearly 63 percent of the total, found their way into civil service in one form or another, a high percentage when compared to other ex-military types. Thirty of these were written-off in crash tests by the civilian agency NACA during the early 1950s, leaving 110 that actually entered some sort of civilian ownership as cargo aircraft from 1955.

Miami-based companies like L.B. Smith Aircraft Corp. of Florida did several initial modifications, stripping military gear and installing civil equipment, reportedly somewhat improving aircraft performance through weight reductions. The first civil operator to put the C-82A into service was Guest Aerovias of Mexico in 1955 with their two Packets XA-LIK (msn: 10128) and XA-LIL (msn: 10117).

The most significant civil operator of the C-82 by far was the California company Steward-Davis Inc. They acquired the C-82 civil CAA type certificate plus all spares from the Air Force in 1955 and set about improving the Packet's performance through the installation of an auxiliary jet engine mounted on the top of the fuselage. Such conversions were known as the Jet-Packet and came as either the model 1600, 3200 or 3400, depending on the size of the jet installation. TWA famously operated a C-82 in Europe as a "Flying Repair Station" for 17 successful years. The C-82 was even immortalized on the big screen with its appearance in the motion picture *The Flight of the Phoenix* (1965), the twin-boom design essential to the film's storyline. In fact, this movie did more for the C-82's legacy than anything else in the aircraft's entire military or civil career!

Although there were many C-82 owners and operators throughout the U.S. and South America from the mid–1950s through the mid–1970s, most Packets enjoyed only a limited service life, and many merely ended their days parked in corners of airfields only to later be scrapped. By the 1980s a few were still flying in Alaska; Northern Air Cargo Inc. operated two C-82A Packets, N4752C and N4753C, up to 1984. By the 1990s,

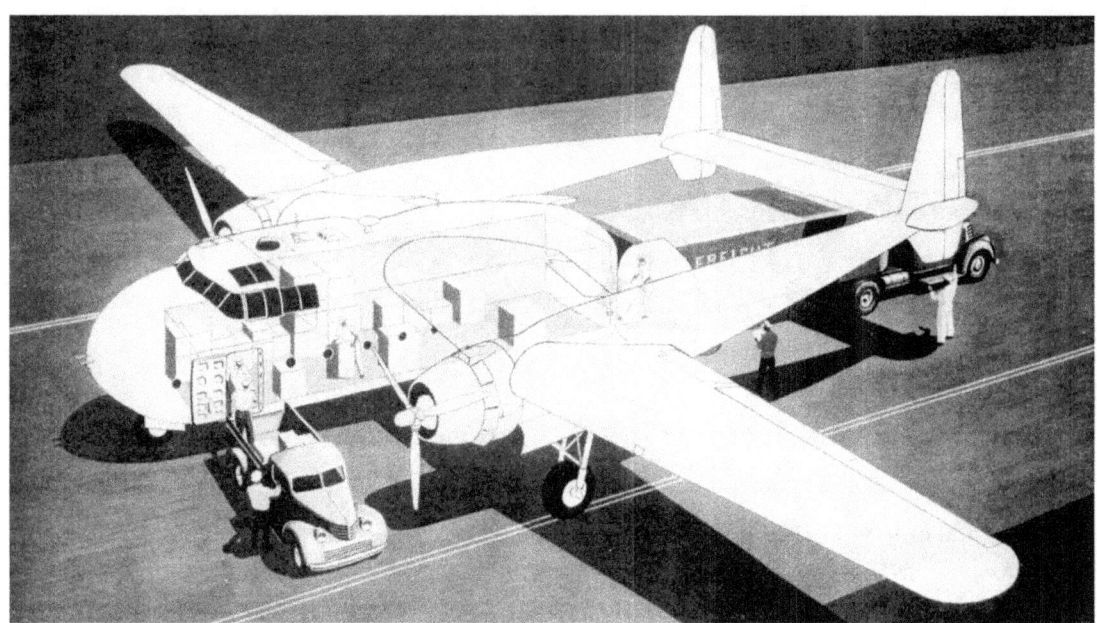

Top: An artist's impression of a civil Fairchild Packet. The manufacturer had hoped to find a civil market for the Packet in the postwar years (Fairchild). *Bottom:* A C-82A crash test conducted by the NACA in 1952 (courtesy NASA Glenn Research Center, Cleveland, Ohio).

Top: When C-82A aircraft entered civil service they had all military equipment and markings removed as in this example of C-82A N74810 (msn: 10150) (Peter J. Marson Collection). *Bottom:* C-82A Jet-Packet 1600 N6887C (msn: 10059) was converted to a Flying Repair Station in 1965 by Steward-Davis. It then salvaged aircraft in Mexico such as this 1968 Cessna 185E N2262T (Ivan Marks Collection).

Hawkins & Powers Aviation Inc. of Wyoming operated the last flyable C-82, N9701F, albeit only on a limited basis. This aircraft made the last ever C-82 flight on October 15, 2006, when it returned home to Hagerstown, Maryland, for preservation with the Hagerstown Aviation Museum.

The Fairchild C-82 Packet's lasting contribution to aviation history is that it was the first practical, purpose-built design for the carriage of bulk cargo to enter regular service. An aircraft had long been sought that would ease the loading and unloading of cargo, and the C-82 was the first to accomplish this by utilizing a high-mounted wing with an end-loading capability onto a low and level fuselage deck. In subsequent years this design layout has become the accepted norm by which all pure cargo aircraft were designed. These include Fairchild's more refined twin-boom model, the C-119 Flying Boxcar, plus many other cargo types such as the Fairchild C-123 Provider, British Bristol B170 Freighter, French Nord N2500 NorAtlas, DHC-2 Caribou and more modern types like the Lockheed C-130 Hercules, C-141 Starlifter, C-5 Galaxy and Boeing C-17 Globemaster III.

If anyone could summarize the Fairchild C-82 Packet's history, it would be, and is today, remembered for these three factors:

1. The first practical, purpose-built, end-loading cargo aircraft to be built in number and designed from the outset for the carriage of outsized cargoes. The direct end-loading design remains today the standard cargo plane layout seen on major cargo types.
2. The outstanding humanitarian contributions in times of crisis, especially for the Berlin Airlift of 1948–1949, Operation Haylift in 1949, and other similar tasks both in military and civil fields.
3. Its starring role in the classic Hollywood aviation film *The Flight of the Phoenix* (1965).

Too late for service in World War II and obsolete even before the Korean War, overshadowed by the superior C-119 Flying Boxcar and suffering a hindering design flaw in its single-engine performance, the twin-boomer never saw combat service and only had a limited civil life. Some may say the Fairchild C-82 Packet had a fairly obscure service history, but as can be seen from the pages of this book, no doubt it was sometimes a very colorful one, and one that left a lasting impression on cargo aircraft design that endures to this day.

C-82A s/n: 48-575 (msn: 10210) of the 316th TCG (National Museum of the United States Air Force).

Section One

The Airplane

Fairchild The Fairchild Engine and Airplane Corp., Aircraft Division, Hagerstown, Maryland, USA.

C-82 USAAF designation system first introduced in 1924 using a Type Letter followed by a number to identify an aircraft. In this case the 82nd Cargo design to be accepted by the air force since 1924.

Packet Official name for the aircraft, named in honor of the 18th- and 19th-century British Packet ships, known for their speed and efficiency. Unofficially known as the Flying Boxcar, which became official with the more refined C-119 series.

FA Two-letter code used by the air force to identify the manufacturer and build plant. In this case, the code indicated Fairchild's Hagerstown plant. North American-produced aircraft carried the code NT, meaning the North American plant in Dallas, Texas.

Model 78 The 78th aircraft design undertaken by Fairchild. License-built North American aircraft carried the Charge Number NA-135.

CQ Buzz Number Designation. C is for Cargo and Q is for Fairchild. This was followed by a dash, then the last three digits of the serial number.

Design Layout

A twin-engined, twin-boom, land monoplane with a high-mounted, cantilevered wing, tricycle undercarriage and of all-metal construction. The flight-deck is located on an upper level forward of the wings. The nose section houses the nose gear and accessories. Cargo is loaded through two hinged clamshell doors at the rear, which then close to form the rear of the fuselage. Each clamshell door has an inward-opening door for paratroop jumps. Access is via a door on the port side of the forward fuselage or through the rear clamshell doors. Some aircraft have inward-opening paratainer doors on the fuselage deck. Three emergency exits are located on the flight-deck roof and two on the roof at the rear of the aircraft forward of the clamshell doors.

Structure

Fuselage

All-metal semi-monocoque structure which is assembled from seven main parts: main section, two sides, upper front and upper rear sections, nose section and rear (cargo

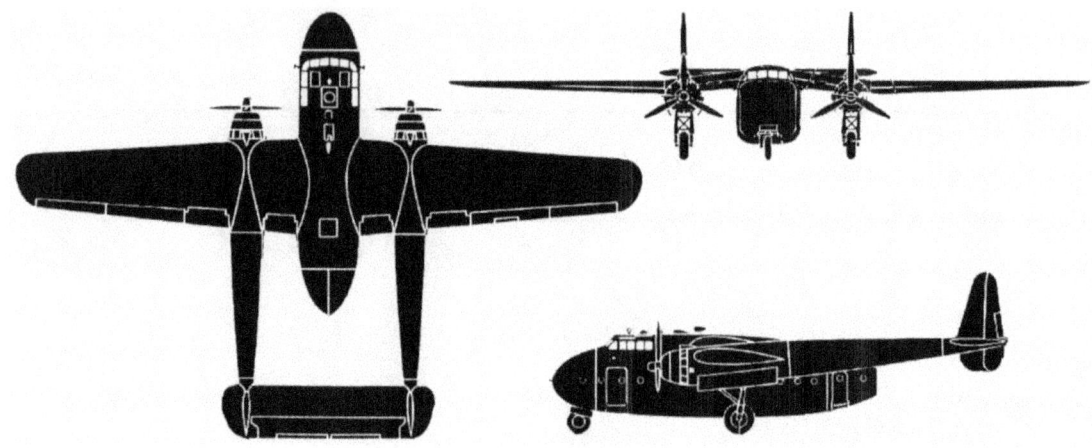

Source: Fairchild.

door) section. A tension-field structure of aluminium metal construction consists of Alclad vertical frames, longitudinal stringers and longitudinal transverse beams with an Alclad skin. General metals used in construction are 24ST Alclad with higher-strength aluminium (75ST) used in high-stress sections. Cargo floor is three-ply Douglas fir plywood sheets, aluminium-covered. Fuselage spacing frames are 35 inches. Fourteen portholes run the length of the fuselage with an extra one on the rear paratroop exit doors.

Wings

The fuselage is attached to the wing center section by 16 large bolts. All-metal wings are constructed in three main sections: the cantilevered center section, which carries the engine nacelles, and two outer wings with detachable tips. The outer wings consist of three main sections: leading edge, inter-spar section and trailing edge. Wings are of a two-spar structure with inter-spar torsion box (in three sections); they are cantilevered with an inverted gull design that allows shorter main gear struts. Construction is built-up I-section front and rear spars of extruded T-section top and bottom booms with plate-webs and rolled vertical stiffeners. Ribs of pressed light alloy and built-up web-beams. Span-wise stringers and stressed Alclad skin. Undersurfaces of the wings are reinforced by corrugated sheets beneath the outer skin.

Booms/Tail Section

Booms are all-metal construction of cylindrical shape tapered to an aft oval-section at the tail end. Forward sections connect to the rear engine nacelles on main wing center-section. They are of semi-monocoque construction with pressed light-alloy channel-section frames, top-hat section longitudinal stringers and light-alloy skin. Rear section of booms are bolted to forward section at leading edge of tailplane. The booms are joined at the rear by the horizontal stabilizer, which has the elevator attached. Twin vertical stabilizers and the horizontal stabilizer are of all-metal construction each with two spars, pressed chord-wise ribs and stressed metal skin. Both booms, vertical and ventral fins, rudders and outboard stabilizers are designed as left-right interchangeable to simplify field repairs.

Two views of a typical C-82A flight deck. Seen here is Brazilian civil C-82A PP-CEK (msn: 10147) (Steward-Davis).

Accommodation

Crew accommodation consists of the following:

One Pilot—left side of flight-deck.
One Copilot—right side of flight-deck.
One Navigator—seated behind copilot facing starboard.
One Radio Operator—seated centrally facing aft and behind navigator.
One Loadmaster/Crewman—seated in cargo-hold.

Flight Controls

All primary control surfaces are fabric-covered with trim tabs and are direct cable-controlled. There are two aileron sections on the outboard trailing edge of each outer wing of pressed channel-spar and tail-rib construction with metal leading edges and fabric-covered surfaces. Inboard ailerons droop when flaps are lowered. One large elevator on rear stabilizer and two rudders on rear vertical stabilizers are one-piece metal frames and single-spar construction. Each has metal leading edges with fabric surfaces. Flaps are an electrically driven NACA two-segment slotted design with two on each wing, one

A C-82A flight deck photographed during the Berlin Airlift in Europe (George Kemper via Betsy Kemper).

inboard and outboard of each boom, all are metal-covered. Maximum flap depression is 40 degrees.

ENGINES AND PROPELLERS

Engines are two Pratt & Whitney R-2800 Double Wasp 18-cylinder radials each rated at 2,100 hp at sea level with a single-stage, two-speed turbo-supercharger. Engines are air-cooled with cowl flaps on the nacelles. Air induction is via an air scoop on top of the nacelles. Engines are electrically started and are mounted by six bolts to a bracket design that is anchored via four bolts to the nacelle structure. The XC-82 Packet prototype was fitted with the R-2800-34 engine; the first ten C-82A aircraft (s/n: 44-22959/44-22968), were powered by the R-2800-22. All subsequent C-82A were powered by the R-2800-85, with the first ten aircraft later upgraded to this standard. Propellers are three-bladed Hamilton Standard 33E60 propellers 15 feet 2 inches (4.63 meters) in diameter; they are of the constant speed, full-feathering, hydromatic type. Ground clearance is 2 feet 10 inches (64 cm).

	R-2800-22	*R-2800-34*	*R-2800-85*
Specification Number:	N-1801	N-1801	A-8104-A
Engine Series:	C Series	C Series	C Series
Rating: Take-off:	2,100 hp @ 2,800 rpm	2,100 hp @ 2,800 rpm	2,100 hp @ 2,800 rpm
Rating: Military:	2,100 hp @ 2,800 rpm (@ 1,000 ft)	2,100 hp @ 2,800 rpm (@ 3,000 ft)	2,100 hp @ 2,800 rpm (@ 3,000 ft)
Rating: Normal:	1,700 hp @ 2,600 rpm (@ 7,000 ft)	1,700 hp @ 2,600 rpm (@ sea level)	1,700 hp @ 2,600 rpm (@ 7,300 ft)
Displacement:	2,804 cu.inches	2,804 cu.inches	2,804 cu.inches
No. of Cylinders:	18	18	18
Block Weight:	2,359 lb	2,359.5 lb	2,375.5 lb
Compression Ratio:	6.75: 1	6.75: 1	6.75: 1
Blower Ratio (Low):	7.29: 1	7.29: 1	7.29: 1
Blower Ratio (High):	9.45: 1	9.45: 1	9.45: 1
Prop. Reduction Ratio:	.450: 1	.450: 1	.450: 1
Bore:	5.75 inches	5.75 inches	5.75 inches
Stroke:	6.0 inches	6.0 inches	6.0 inches
Spline:	SAE 60A	SAE 60A	SAE 60A
Magnetos:	DF-18LN	DF-18LN	S-18LG-P1
Carburetion: (Bendix/Stromberg)	PR-58E1-1	PR-58E1-1	PR-58E2-2
Crankshaft Rotation:	Clockwise	Clockwise	Clockwise
Fuel Grade (Octane):	100/130	100/130	100/130

LANDING GEAR

The landing gear consists of two single-tire main wheels, each mounted on two oleo shock-absorber struts, which retract into the booms behind the engines. The nose gear is a single-tire arrangement on a half-fork oleo shock-absorber strut which retracts into the nose section and is non-steerable, with taxiing achieved through braking and engine power. Main tires are Hayes Industries 56-inch diameter smooth contour type and nose tire is a Goodyear 44-inch smooth contour type. The landing gear system is electrically raised and lowered.

Fuel and Oil System

Four collapsible bladder-type fuel cells are installed on the C-82, two in each wing, with one outboard and inboard of each boom. The inboard tanks are each made up of four interconnecting cells, and the outboard tanks are each made up of six interconnecting cells. A cross-feed system is installed so any tank can feed any engine port or starboard. The total average fuel capacity for the C-82A variant is 2,641 U.S. gallons (15,648.54 lb). Fuel grade is 100/130 octane (Fuel Spec. No. MIL-F-5572).

A 55 U.S. gallon oil tank is behind the firewall of each engine; oil cooling is via an elliptical air intake on the inboard leading edge of each wing. 1100 oil grade (Oil Spec. No. MIL-O-6082). Aircraft s/n: 44-22959/44-22988 have a reserve oil tank of 69.5 U.S. gallons located in the fuselage.

Volume to Weight Conversion:
Specific Gravity of 100/130 Octane Fuel is 0.71

Serial Numbers	Fuel Tanks	Sub-Total	Total Capacity	Total Weight
44-22959/44-22988	2 Inboard	741 U.S. gal each		
	2 Outboard	676 U.S. gal each	2,834 U.S. gal	16,792.11 lb
44-22989/44-23058 &	2 Inboard	642 U.S. gal each		
45-57733/45-57738	2 Outboard	602 U.S. gal each	2,488 U.S. gal	14,741.98 lb
45-57739/45-57832 &	2 Inboard	669 U.S. gal each		
48-568/48-587	2 Outboard	631 U.S. gal each	2,600 U.S. gal	15,405.61 lb
45-25436/45-25438	2 Inboard	765 U.S. gal each		
	2 Outboard	753 U.S. gal each	3,036 U.S. gal	17,989.02 lb

Electrical System

All systems on the C-82, except the brakes, are electrically operated. The system is a 24 volt DC installation that is grounded through the aircraft structure. It is made up of a single 24 volt/34 amp/hour AN3150, Type G-1 storage battery; a 1,000 VA, 400-cycle, 3-phase inverter; two 200 amp engine-driven generators; two reverse current relays and two voltage regulators. There is also provision for an external power supply.

Hydraulic (Braking) System

The braking system is hydraulically operated with two 1,000 psi cross-connected accumulators, one in each boom. Hydraulic reservoir and associated equipment are housed in the nose section.

Oxygen System

A conventional low-pressure demand oxygen system was provided for the five crew members and a separate continuous-flow oxygen system was provided for up to 43 passengers/troops in the main cabin. Four Type J-1 cylinders were under the cargo deck for the continuous system and eight Type G-1 steel cylinders located in the rear main cabin ceiling for the demand crew system.

Anti-Icing/Heating and Ventilation Systems

Four primary heat exchangers (via two air scoops side-mounted on each engine nacelle) are connected to the engine exhaust system and provide hot air for wing anti-icing. Hot air is piped out along the main wing leading edges and ducted down the booms for anti-icing of the horizontal and vertical stabilizer leading edges.

A secondary heat exchanger is located on the inside fuselage roof behind the flightdeck, which provides heating and ventilation to the fuselage interior and defogging for the windows. Heat is extracted from the primary heat exchanger system and mixed with fresh air gathered from a small air scoop on the top of the fuselage.

COMMUNICATIONS AND NAVIGATION EQUIPMENT

The following radio and navigation gear was carried by C-82 aircraft:

Interphone	AN/AIC-2
Interphone	AN/AIC-3
Glide Path Receiver	AN/ARN-5
VHF Command	AN/ARC-3
VHF Command	SCR-274N
Radio Beacon Receiver	AN/APN-2 (s/n: 44-22959 through 45-57737)
Radio Beacon Receiver	AN/APN-12 (s/n: 45-57738/45-57832)
LORAN	AN/APN-9
Glide Path Receiver	AN/ARN-5A
Automatic Radio Compass	AN/ARN-7
Manual Radio Compass	AN/ARN-11
Liaison	AN/ARC-8
Localizer	RC-103
Marker Beacon	RC-193
IFF	SCR-695B
Radio Set	AN/APS-10 (s/n: 45-57783/45-57832)

Much of this equipment was removed when aircraft went into civil service. The autopilot is an A-10 electrically operated unit consisting of a Gyro Flux Gate transmitter.

ONBOARD EQUIPMENT

The following equipment was carried onboard C-82 aircraft:

- 42 folding canvas seats along fuselage cabin sides.
- Monorail aerial delivery rack for up to 10 paratainers.
- Two 16-foot-long loading ramps.
- Two under-fuselage support jacks.
- 86 cargo tie-down fittings at 20-inch intervals.
- Block and tackle fitting.
- One three-step entrance ladder.
- One lavatory in nose compartment.
- Drinking water cylinder.
- Three fire extinguishers.
- One crash axe.
- Pyrotechnic pistol with 12 cartridges.
- First aid kits.
- One 7-man life raft.
- Engine and cabin covers.
- Mooring fittings.

A spacious flight deck was one of the notable aspects of the C-82 Packet (Fairchild).

Mission

Cargo Carrier

The cargo deck is 38 feet in length, 8 feet in width and 8 feet high. Cargo is loaded through two truck-bed height clamshell doors at the rear of the fuselage. The C-82 can lift a variety of freight for military operations, including the following equipment:

>   75 mm M3A1 howitzer
>   75 mm M2A3 howitzer
>   37 mm M-4 gun
>   37 mm antitank gun and motor carriage
>   40 mm M-2 antiaircraft gun and carriage
>   105 mm M2A1 gun
>   155 mm howitzer
>   T-8 caisson
>   10-wheel 2.5-ton truck
>   quarter-ton truck
>   small and large aircraft engines on cradles

When equipped with special loading ramps, the C-82 can lift the following equipment:
>   T-9E1 light tank
>   3 inch antiaircraft gun and carriage

Section One—Mission 25

75 mm gun and halftrack
90 mm antiaircraft gun
M-14 tank

Outsized cargoes can see the removal of the clamshell doors with cargo protruding from the rear if need be. This made for a very frosty ride for the loadmaster and anyone else on the cargo deck! The removal of the clamshell doors also allowed the aerial delivery of large cargoes to the battlefield via a parachute system. Small cargoes could be air delivered via a paratainer door on the cargo deck floor. Paratainers are cylindrical containers that are parachute-attached, containing fresh ammunition or various supplies for soldiers on the battlefield. Aircraft s/n: 44-22959 thru 45-57737 were equipped with a ten-paratainer setup on a rack directly above the doors. Aircraft s/n: 45-57738 and subsequent used a monorail system that allowed up to 15 paratainers of 350 lb each to be delivered. Paratainer doors could only be opened at airspeeds of 150 mph or less.

Top: A 10-wheel, 2.5-ton truck being loaded into the XC-82 prototype (National Museum of the United States Air Force). *Bottom:* C-82A s/n: 44-22987 (msn: 10031) performing a cargo drop with the clamshell doors removed (National Museum of the United States Air Force).

Troop/Paratroop Carrier

One of the main tasks of the C-82. Up to 42 troops or paratroops could be transported, occupying folding seats along the fuselage sides. Paratroops could exit the aircraft via two paratroop doors built into the rear clamshell doors, or with the doors removed jump directly out.

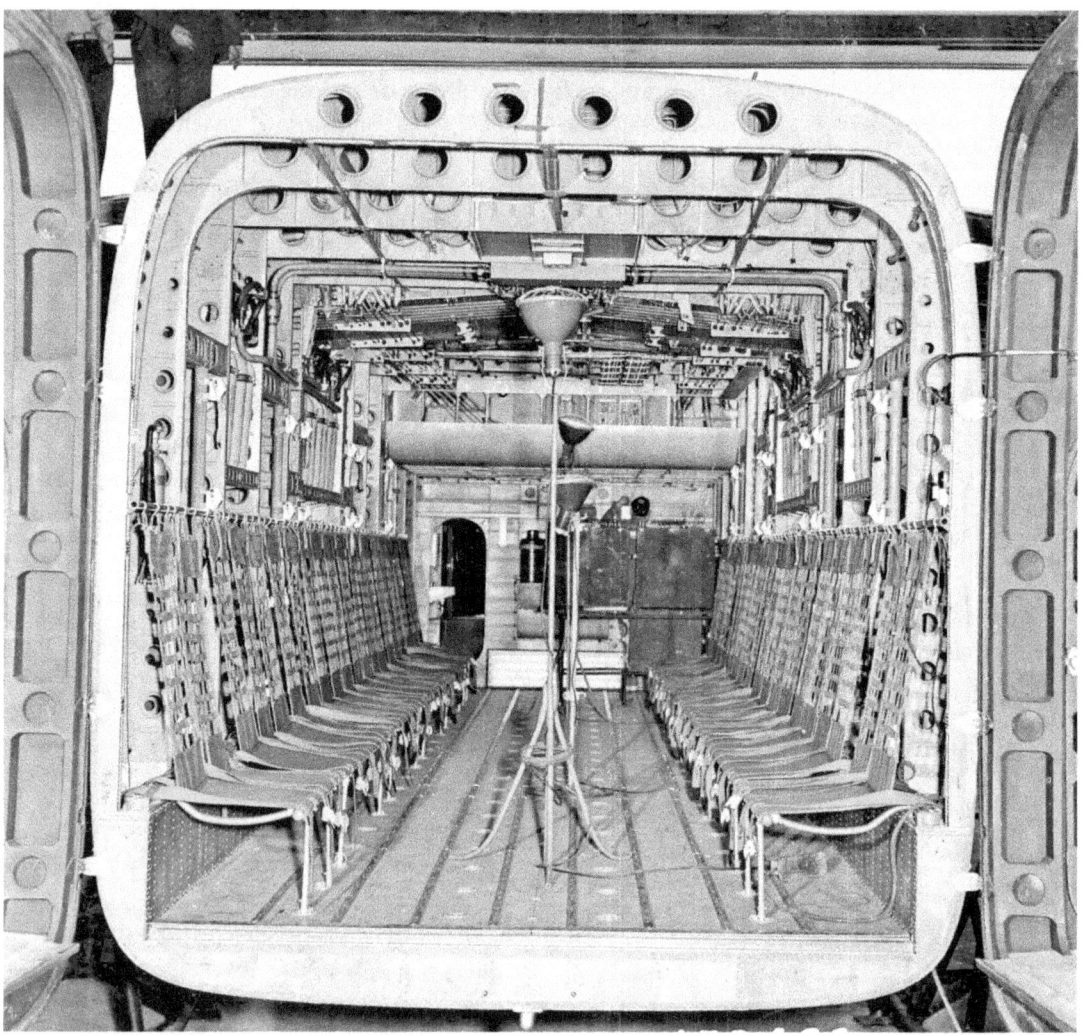

Paratroop/passenger seats in their deployed position (National Museum of the United States Air Force).

Air Ambulance

The following combinations of patients could be carried in the air ambulance role:

40 seated patients and 2 attendants
40 seated patients and 13 litter patients and 2 attendants

22 seated patients and 22 litter patients and 3 attendants
34 litter patients and 5 attendants

Patient litters set up in a C-82A cargo hold (National Museum of the United States Air Force).

Glider Tow

One 15,000 lb glider, or two gliders not more than 15,000 lb, can be towed. Aircraft s/n: 44-23034 and subsequent can tow a 30,000-lb glider. The twin-glider configuration was found to be too much strain on the tail booms, so this practice was later abandoned. The single glider attachment point was then relocated to the main fuselage on the C-82A, these modifications being done by Fairchild in Hagerstown.

Specifications

Dimensions

Overall Length:	77 feet 1 inch	23.50 meters
Overall Width:	106 feet 6 inches	32.46 meters
Overall Height:	26 feet 4.25 inches	8.03 meters
Fuselage Length:	55 feet 2.75 inches	16.83 meters
Fuselage Width:	10 feet 4 inches	3.15 meters
Fuselage Height: (from ground on u/c)	13 feet 6 inches	4.12 meters

A C-82A takes off towing a Waco CG-15A glider, s/n: 45-5276, during tests carried out at Wright-Patterson Air Force Base in November 1951 (National Museum of the United States Air Force).

Cargo Hold Length:	38 feet 5 inches	11.71 meters
Cargo Hold Width:	8 feet 0 inches	2.44 meters
Cargo Hold Height:	8 feet 5 inches	2.57 meters
Cargo Hold Height: (under flight-deck)	6 feet 3 inches	1.92 meters
Cargo Hold Deck Area:	308 sq. feet	28.61 sq. meters
Cargo Hold Volume: (usable freight volume)	2,598 cu. feet	73.57 cu. meters
Total Internal Volume:	3,529 cu. feet	99.93 cu. meters
Main Cabin Door Height:	5 feet 7 inches	1.70 meters
Main Cabin Door Width:	2 feet 11 inches	0.89 meters
Boom Length: (from wing trailing edge)	36 feet 9.5 inches	11.21 meters
Horizontal Stabilizer Width: (including tips)	36 feet 4 inches	11.07 meters
Vertical Stabilizer Heights: (including ventral fins)	16 feet 6 inches	5.03 meters
Propeller Diameters:	15 feet 2 inches	4.63 meters
Wheel Base:	26 feet 6 inches	8.08 meters
Main Wheel Track Width:	28 feet 0 inches	8.53 meters

Wing and Tail Specifications

Overall Wing Area:	1,400 sq. feet	130.06 sq. meters
Total Aileron Area:	112 sq. feet	10.41 sq. meters
Total Flap Area:	100 sq. feet	9.29 sq. meters
Total Fin Area:	113.2 sq. feet	10.52 sq. meters
Total Rudder Area: (including tabs)	85.6 sq. feet	7.95 sq. meters
Total Tailplane Area:	219 sq. feet	20.35 sq. meters
Total Elevator Area: (including tabs)	91 sq. feet	8.45 sq. meters
Wing Loading: (at max weight 54,000 lbs.)	38.57 lb/sq. foot	188.33 kg/sq. meter
Aspect Ratio:	8.1	
Taper Ratio:	2:1	
Main Wing Chord (root):	17 feet 10 inches	5.44 meters
Main Wing Chord (tip):	8 feet 11 inches	2.72 meters
Main Wing Section (root):	NACA 2418	
Main Wing Section (tip):	NACA 4409	
Main Wing Thickness (root):	18%	
Main Wing Thickness (tip):	9%	

Weights

39 C-82 Packets built to a 50,000 lb max weight.
184 C-82 Packets built to a 54,000 lb max weight.

Serial Numbers	*Max Take-off Weight*	*Max Landing Weight*
44-22959/44-22968 & 45-25436/45-25438	50,000 lb (22.68 metric tons)	42,000 lb (19.05 metric tons)
44-22969/44-22993 & 44-23004	50,000 lb (22.68 metric tons)	47,200 lb (21.41 metric tons)
44-22994/44-23003 & 44-23005/44-23058 & 45-57733/45-57832 & 48-568/48-587	54,000 lb (24.49 metric tons)	50,000 lb (22.68 metric tons)

Empty Airframe Weight:	28,000 lb	12,700.59 kg
Max Zero Fuel Weight: (at max weight 50,000 lb)	47,200 lb	21,409.56 kg
Operational Airframe Weight: (60% of max take-off weight)	32,500 lb	14,741.75 kg
Max Fuel/Payload Weight: (40% of max take-off weight)	21,500 lb	9,752.24 kg
Max Take-off Weight:	54,000 lb	24,493.99 kg

Performance

Performance specifications vary widely depending on the conditions figures are based on. Most data presented below is quoted directly from the USAF C-82 Handbook.

Service Ceiling:	**21,200 feet**	**6,462 meters**
Sea level at 54,000 lb max weight		
Take-off Distance:	3,960 feet	1,207 meters
Initial Climb Rate: (at 136 mph)	620 ft/min	998 m/min
Landing Distance: (at 42,000 lb)	1,600 feet	488 meters
At 50,000 lb/5,000 ft/182 mph		
Range (max. fuel):	2,590 statute miles	4,168 kilometers
Range (max. payload):	224 statute miles	361 kilometers
At 45,000 lb		
Cruising Speed: (at 10,000 ft)	218 mph	351 km/hr.
Max Speed: (at 17,500 ft)	248 mph	399 km/hr
At 50,000 lb		
Gliding Speed:	110–120 mph	177–193 km/hr
Stall Speed: (flaps up/gear down)	94 mph	151 km/hr
Stall Speed: (flaps/gear down)	86 mph	138 km/hr

Serial Number List

Contract	*Requesting*	*Date Issued*
W33-038 AC-30435	2 XC-82	August 6, 1942
W-535 AC-30435	1 XC-82 mock-up	August 1942
W33-038 AC-124	100 C-82A	September 28, 1944
W33-038 AC-7179	1000 C-82N	December 19, 1944
W33-038 AC-124	100 C-82A	May 28, 1945
W33-038 AC-124	20 C-82A	March 30, 1948

Type	*Manufacturer s/n*	*Military s/n*	*Total*
XC-82	10001	43-13202	001
XC-82	10002	-	(1 canx)
C-82A	10003/10102	44-22959/44-23058	
C-82A	10103/10202	45-57733/45-57832	
C-82A	10203/10222	48-568/48-587	220
C-82N	135-49496/135-49498	45-25436/45-25438	003
C-82N	135-49499/135-50495	45-25439/45-26435	(997 canx)
			224

With the rear clamshell doors removed, aerial freight drops were a C-82 specialty. Aircraft from front to back are s/n: 44-23055 (msn: 10099), s/n: 44-23046 (msn: 10090), s/n: 44-23050 (msn: 10094) and s/n: 45-57824 (msn: 10194) (George Kemper via Betsy Kemper).

Block Number Mystery

Introduced during 1941 by the USAAC, the block number system was a way of tracking minor equipment and modifications to an aircraft on the production line. Minor changes might be radio types, small design improvements or procedural changes. Since these changes were applied to a batch, or block, of aircraft on a factory line, they became known as "block numbers." Sometimes they were allocated consecutively as -1, -2, etc., but this was later changed to five-digit gaps as -1, -5, -10, etc., with the numbers between left for post-factory or field changes.

In early 1946 Fairchild allocated the following block numbers for C-82 production listing a total of 15 blocks ("7" was allocated twice due to a serial number change):

Block No.	Manufacturer s/n	Airplane No.	Military s/n	Total
1	10003/10012	1/10	44-22959/44-22968	10
2	10013/10032	11/30	44-22969/44-22988	20
3	10033/10047	31/45	44-22989/44-23003	15
4	10048/10062	46/60	44-23004/44-23018	15
5	10063/10077	61/75	44-23019/44-23033	15
6	10078/10092	76/90	44-23034/44-23048	15
7	10093/10102	91/100	44-23049/44-23058	10
7	10103/10107	101/105	45-57733/45-57737	5
8	10108/10122	106/120	45-57738/45-57752	15
9	10123/10137	121/135	45-57753/45-57767	15
10	10138/10152	136/150	45-57768/45-57782	15
11	10153/10167	151/165	45-57783/45-57797	15
12	10168/10182	166/180	45-57798/45-57812	15
13	10183/10197	181/195	45-57813/45-57827	15
14	10198/10202	196/200	45-57828/45-57832	5
1	135-49496/135-49498	1/3	45-25436/45-25438	3

These allocations were subsequently changed to a five-digit gap sequence, but this is where the C-82 Block Number mystery begins. The full sequence has never been published, so definitive confirmation cannot be verified. Unfortunately these numbers were never recorded on the aircraft data-plates, but only as a printed stencil located below the flight-deck. With time, these stencils wore off, leaving no way of verifying the block number of any given C-82.

The following table presents, for the most part, a speculative C-82 Block Number sequence based on the following evidence:

- The first 105 deliveries (msn: 10003/10107) are known and confirmed, which are blocks **-1/-30**.
- It is known that s/n: 45-57807 was a **C-82A-60-FA**, with s/n: 45-57814 and 45-57818 both being **C-82A-65-FA**. However, this means that the five-digit gaps don't line up with the earlier confirmed allocations, so another block number batch must have been created somewhere between msn: 10108 and 10167 at some point after 1946.
- The 1954 C-82A Handbook states that aircraft s/n: 45-57753/45-57761 had a different Starter Mesh Switch installed and that aircraft from s/n: 45-57762 and subsequent had a different one again. These nine C-82As (indicated by the * in the following table) could be the missing batch that would allow the completion of the five-digit block sequence. All other serial number batches mentioned in the handbook link up accurately with other known blocks.
- It is unclear if the requirement for 20 more C-82A Packets, ordered in 1948, were built to **Block 70** standard or whether there were additional allocations (Block 75 etc.) within this batch.
- Only three C-82N variants were built and are known to be **Block 1**.

Designation	Manufacturer s/n	Military s/n	Sub-Total	Total
XC-82-FA	10001	43-13202	1	001
XC-82-FA	10002	-	1	-
C-82A-1-FA	10003/10012	44-22959/44-22968	10	
C-82A-5-FA	10013/10032	44-22969/44-22988	20	
C-82A-10-FA	10033/10047	44-22989/44-23003	15	
C-82A-15-FA	10048/10062	44-23004/44-23018	15	
C-82A-20-FA	10063/10077	44-23019/44-23033	15	
C-82A-25-FA	10078/10092	44-23034/44-23048	15	
C-82A-30-FA	10093/10102	44-23049/44-23058	10	
C-82A-30-FA	10103/10107	45-57733/45-57737	5	
C-82A-35-FA	10108/10122	45-57738/45-57752	15	
C-82A-40-FA	10123/10131	45-57753/45-57761	9 *	
C-82A-45-FA	10132/10137	45-57762/45-57767	6	
C-82A-50-FA	10138/10152	45-57768/45-57782	15	
C-82A-55-FA	10153/10167	45-57783/45-57797	15	
C-82A-60-FA	10168/10182	45-57798/45-57812	15	
C-82A-65-FA	10183/10197	45-57813/45-57827	15	
C-82A-70-FA	10198/10202	45-57828/45-57832	5	
C-82A- -FA	10203/10222	48-568/48-587	20	220
C-82N-1-NT	135-49496/135-49498	45-25436/45-25438	3	003
C-82N- -NT	135–49499/135–50495	45-25439/45-26435	997	-
				224

Due to the speculative nature of the above table, only confirmed block numbers have been noted in other parts of this book.

Variants

XC-82

Twin-engined, twin-boom cargo/troop transport. Two were originally ordered, but after the favorable maiden flight of the first prototype XC-82 (USAAF s/n: 43-13202) on September 10, 1944, the second was canceled, with a production order following a short time later. After a period of flight tests, the aircraft was then assigned to Pope Field as a ground trainer in November 1946; oddly, it wasn't formally delivered to the USAAF until April 1948. It was declared surplus and scrapped after October that same year.

XC-82 s/n: 43-13202 (msn: 10001). Note the more rounded nose, as compared with production C-82A aircraft (National Museum of the United States Air Force).

C-82A

The main variant developed from the prototype for the USAAF. Production ran from 1945 to 1948 to fill an immediate need for a cargo/troop transport aircraft in the postwar years. The first production C-82A, from a contract for 100 (s/n: 44-22959/44-23058) issued on September 28, 1944, first flew on May 30, 1945, with delivery to the USAAF on June 11, 1945. Many improvements were incorporated into the production run, the main one being the introduction of upgraded R-2800-85 engines, starting from the eleventh airframe (msn: 10013). From the fourth airframe (msn: 10006), a slightly longer (14.75 inches) and more contoured nose was used, taking the overall length from 75 feet 10.25 inches up to 77 feet 1 inch. The fourth production airframe also featured a bare metal finish, as opposed to the previous three deliveries in U.S. Army olive drab. Provision was also made for glider-towing from lugs on the ends of the booms.

A second order for 100 (s/n: 45-57733/45-45-57832) aircraft was let on December 19, 1944; 53 of this run were assigned to the USAF in Europe from 1948 to 1953. Due to stability problems with the C-119B variant during flight testing, an additional 20 C-82A airframes (s/n: 48-568/48-587) were ordered as a stopgap measure on May 28, 1948, with

C-82A s/n: 48-585 (msn: 10220) in typical basic C-82 markings (National Museum of the United States Air Force).

the last of this batch being delivered to the USAF in October 1948. The C-82A numbers delivered by year are 6 during 1945, 76 during 1946, 82 during 1947, and 56 during 1948. The C-82A is the only variant later made available to civilian operators.

EC-82A

Nine conversions were made to C-82A aircraft at various intervals from 1948 to 1954. Most of these were directly assigned to the 2750th Air Base Group for test and experimental duties at Wright-Patterson AFB, Ohio. The "E" suffix letter in the late 1940s and 1950s stood for Exempt from normal operations. S/n: 44-22962 and 44-23004 were the most utilized EC-82A conversions during this period, the latter taking part in extensive tests concerning a snow-ski–fitted undercarriage. These tests, taking place in Alaska and Canada from 1948 to 1950, were deemed unproductive due to take-off performance being hindered by the drag-inducing ski fittings. S/n: 45-57746 and 45-57757 were the tracked undercarriage prototypes (see: *Tracked Undercarriage Conversions* for details). Three were also converted for test support duties with the 6520th Test Support Wing in Massachusetts. The following table details EC-82A test assignments:

USAF s/n	Cvtd Period	Assignments	Remarks
44-22962	1948–1951	2750th AB GP, WPAFB Ohio.	Experimental, test duties.
	1951–1952	ARD HQ, WPAFB Ohio.	Experimental, test duties.
	1952	6502nd Parachute Dev Test GP, El Centro NAS California.	Experimental, test duties.
	1952–1954	Fairchild Aircraft, Maryland.	**Group A** developments.
44-23004	1949–1951	2750th AB GP, WPAFB Ohio.	Snow ski u/c tests.
	1951–1952	ARD HQ, WPAFB Ohio.	Experimental, test duties.
	1952–1953	Armament Test HQ, Eglin AFB Florida.	Test support duties.

USAF s/n	Cvtd Period	Assignments	Remarks
	1953–1954	6520th Test Support WG, Hanscom AFB Massachusetts.	Test support duties.
44-23014	1948–1949	2750th AB GP, WPAFB Ohio.	Experimental, test duties.
44-23034	1948–1951	2750th AB GP, WPAFB Ohio.	Experimental, test duties.
45-57746	1949	2750th AB GP, WPAFB Ohio.	Tracked u/c prototype.
	1949–1950	3203rd MSU GP & 3200th Proof Test GP, Eglin AFB Florida.	Hot climate testing.

Top: EC-82A s/n: 44-23004 (msn: 10048) during snow-ski undercarriage tests. *Bottom:* EC-82A s/n: 45-57746 (msn: 10116) converted as the track-undercarriage prototype (both photographs, National Museum of the United States Air Force).

Section One—Variants

USAF s/n	Cvtd Period	Assignments	Remarks
45-57749	1952–1954	6520th Test Support SQ, Hanscom AFB Massachusetts.	Test support duties.
45-57757	1949–1950	2750th AB GP, WPAFB Ohio.	Tracked u/c prototype.
	1950	5064th Cold Weather Materiel Testing UT, Ladd AFB Alaska.	Cold climate testing.
45-57795	1948–1949	2750th AB GP, WPAFB Ohio.	Experimental, test duties.
	1948–1949	3203rd MSU GP & 3200th Proof Test GP, Eglin AFB Florida.	Experimental, test duties.
45-57802	1954	6520th Test Support WG, Hanscom AFB Massachusetts.	Test support duties.

JC-82A

Four C-82A (s/n: 45-57740, 45-57791, 45-57796, 45-57818) conversions were made for service with the 513th Troop Carrier (Special) Group during the Berlin Airlift. The "J" prefix stands for Temporary Modification. These conversions were required for the carriage of outsized cargoes into and out of Berlin during September 1949.

SC-82A

37 C-82A Search and Rescue conversions were made for MATS service from 1947 to 1953. Each was equipped with rescue gear which could be dropped through the belly paratainer doors. The "S" prefix in the late 1940s stood for Search and Rescue. One extra C-82A (s/n: 45-57762) was assigned to the 7th Rescue Squadron in West Germany, but appears not to have been converted because it was assigned for a period of only two days.

USAF s/n	Cvtd Period	USAF s/n	Cvtd Period	USAF s/n	Cvtd Period
44-22963	1947–1949	44-23011	1947–1953	45-57734	1950–1953
44-22966	1947–1949	44-23015	1950–1953	45-57736	1950–1953

SC-82A s/n: 44-22978 (msn: 10022) at Hamilton Air Force Base, California, during 1949. The typical SC-82A rescue livery were yellow fuselage and boom bands with black edges. Some SC-82A, however, were simply marked RESCUE, stenciled by the crew entry door (National Museum of the United States Air Force).

USAF s/n	Cvtd Period	USAF s/n	Cvtd Period	USAF s/n	Cvtd Period
44-22971	1947–1949	44-23019	1948–1951	45-57737	1950–1953
44-22972	1949–1950	44-23021	1950	45-57762	1950 (not cvtd)
44-22973	1949–1950	44-23027	1950–1953	45-57799	unk–1952
44-22976	1949–1950	44-23029	1951–1953	45-57827	1951–1953
44-22978	1948–1949	44-23030	1950–1953	45-57828	1950–1953
44-22979	1949–1950	44-23033	1950–1953	45-57829	1950–1953
44-22982	1949–1950	44-23036	1950–1953	45-57830	1948
44-22983	1949–1950	44-23041	1950–1953	45-57831	1948–1949
44-22984	1949–1950	44-23057	1950–1953	48-568	1950–1953
44-22986	1949–1950	44-23058	1950–1953	48-574	1949–1953
44-22990	1949–1950	45-57733	1950–1953		

XC-82B

One C-82A (s/n: 45-57769) was factory converted as a prototype to improve on the single-engine performance and other shortcomings experienced in the C-82A design during tactical USAF missions. The immediate change was a redesigned and wider streamlined fuselage with the flight-deck relocated to the nose of the aircraft, as opposed to the "upper-deck" recessed position on the C-82. Many technical refinements were made thanks to a peacetime pace that allowed previous design errors, made under wartime haste, to be worked out. The much-needed power boost and single-engine performance was solved with the addition of two 2,650 hp Pratt & Whitney R-4360 Major Wasp engines in place of the C-82s 2,100 hp R-2800 Double Wasps.

The changes were extensive enough for the XC-82B prototype to be redesignated as the **XC-119A** (Fairchild Model 105A), the first flight being made on December 17, 1947. After test flights were undertaken, it was delivered to the USAF in June 1948, redesignated as the **C-119A**. The prototype proved be to a winning formula that eventually saw 1,185

The XC-119A s/n: 45-57769 (msn: 10139) takes off on a test flight powered by two 2,650hp Pratt & Whitney R-4360 Major Wasp radial engines (National Museum of the United States Air Force).

of the type built from 1949 to 1955 as the C-119 Flying Boxcar. 45-57769 was assigned ground duties at Chanute AFB, Illinois, in January 1951, then declared surplus and dropped from the inventory in December that year. It was later scrapped.

C-82N

License-built version by North American Aviation Inc., identical to the C-82A but with minor internal changes. The first delivery was in 1945, painted in U.S. Army olive drab, but the remaining two were delivered in a bare-metal finish. The remaining order of 997 were canceled on VJ Day. None of them ever entered regular USAAF service, with all soon assigned as ground instructional airframes during 1946, the first two being scrapped by 1947. Technically, the Series Suffix Letter should have, at the time, been "B" as the C-82B. Why "N" was chosen out of sequence is unclear, but most likely it was to denote North American. Assigned USAAF s/n: 45-25436/45-25438.

This C-82N s/n: 45-25437 (msn: 135–49497) was at one point earmarked for museum preservation, but this was later dropped and the aircraft scrapped (National Museum of the United States Air Force).

ZC-82N

The third C-82N (s/n: 45-25438) was redesignated as obsolete ("Z") in 1948 for ground duties at Keesler AFB, Mississippi. Finally scrapped in 1951.

TRACKED UNDERCARRIAGE CONVERSIONS

During the late 1940s the USAF began looking into various ways of operating aircraft off unprepared airstrips. One of these tests adopted the use of a tracked undercarriage design in place of a conventional wheeled undercarriage.

One C-82A (s/n: 45-57746), was assigned to Fairchild Aircraft at Hagerstown, Maryland, in October 1947 on bailment for modification of a tracked landing gear. The system was initiated by Fairchild designer Alfred A. Gassner and consisted of a tank-like chassis on the end of the u/c struts with sprocket-style wheels driving a rubber tread belt fitted over the top. Modifications were also made to the hydraulic braking system, with each new tracked unit having disc brakes attached to the sprocket wheels. The two main tracked units each had four disc brakes with the nose unit having two.

The C-82A tracked u/c prototype first flew during 1948 and the program initially looked quite promising, with 18 further C-82A aircraft (s/n: 45-57747/45-57764) assigned on bailment to Fairchild at the beginning of 1949. Although the 1954 C-82 flight manual states that s/n: 45-57749, 45-57755, 45-57756, 45-57761, 45-57762 and 45-57764 were never converted from this batch, IARCs clearly show that all 18 were in fact at the Fairchild factory from March 1949. It appears, however, that these six aircraft were actually retrofitted back to a wheeled u/c before the flight manual was revised in October 1949.

C-82A s/n: 45-57746 and 45-57757 were redesignated for tracked u/c tests as EC-82A prototypes with '746 going to Eglin AFB in Florida for hot climate tests and '757 assigned to the 5064th Cold Weather Materiel Testing Unit in Alaska for cold climate testing in snow conditions. The "E" prefix in the late 1940s stood for Exempt from normal operations.

The other 17 tracked u/c conversions were assigned to various test duties during 1949 (see following table), but were not given the EC-82A redesignation. Shortcomings in the design soon became apparent, with the rubber treads becoming bogged with mud and debris on soft airstrips. They even clogged on conventional dirt airstrips with grass, and during crosswind landings the rubber belts would be blown off their sprocket wheels by the slipstream.

By late 1949 the 17 tracked u/c conversions had been retrofitted back to standard wheeled units and the program was canceled altogether in December 1949. The two EC-82A prototypes continued on until April 1950 until they were also retrofitted. Of the total, three of these aircraft were later w/o in accidents, eight were wfu to Ogden Air Materiel Area at Hill AFB in 1950 for project duties and subsequently scrapped. The last eight were sold to civil operators.

USAF s/n	Cvtd Period*	Remarks	Disposition
45-57746	8 Feb 49–6 Oct 50	EC-82 prototype.	To Ogden 1950. Scrapped.
45-57747	7 Mar 49–27 Aug 49	—	Wfu 1953. Civil sale XA-LIL.
45-57748	7 Mar 49–late 49	WPAFB for tests.	To Ogden 1950. Scrapped.
45-57749	7 Mar 49–22 Jul 49	Listed as not cvtd.	Wfu 1954. Civil sale N2064A.
45-57750	7 Mar 49–late 49	Tested with 314th TCG.	To Ogden 1950. Scrapped.
45-57751	7 Mar 49–23 Jul 49	—	To Ogden 1950. Scrapped.
45-57752	7 May 49–23 Aug 49	—	W/o 1950.
45-57753	7 Mar 49–31 Aug 49	—	To Ogden 1950. Scrapped.
45-57754	7 Mar 49–10 Sep 49	—	To Ogden 1950. Scrapped.
45-57755	7 Mar 49–19 Sep 49	Listed as not cvtd.	Wfu 1953. Civil sale N5109B.
45-57756	7 Mar 49–27 Jun 49	Listed as not cvtd.	Wfu 1953. Civil sale N75885.
45-57757	7 Mar 49–12 Apr 50	EC-82A prototype.	To Ogden 1950. Scrapped.
45-57758	7 Mar 49–2 Sep 49	—	Wfu 1953. Civil sale XB-YOA.
45-57759	7 Mar 49–31 Aug 49	—	To Ogden 1950. Scrapped.
45-57760	7 Mar 49–10 Sep 49	—	W/o 1950.
45-57761	7 Mar 49–13 Jun 49	WPAFB for tests. Listed as not cvtd.	W/o 1951.
45-57762	7 Mar 49–21 Jun 49	Listed as not cvtd.	Wfu 1953. To unk civil owner.
45-57763	7 Mar 49–late 49	Tested with 314th TCG.	Wfu 1954. Civil sale N4830V.
45-57764	7 Mar 49–13 Jun 49	Listed as not cvtd.	Wfu 1953. Civil sale N74039.

*Dates are only best estimates based on IARC findings.

Top: The second EC-82A s/n: 45-57748 (msn: 10118) with tracked undercarriage. *Bottom, left and right:* Two views of the rollers on the tracked undercarriage design tested on 19 C-82A aircraft (three photographs, National Museum of the United States Air Force).

GROUP A UPGRADES

Twenty-five C-82A Packets were upgraded during 1953 with flight-deck communications and electronic equipment and designated as **Group A** aircraft by the USAF. Fourteen of these upgrades were carried out by the Aircraft Engineering & Maintenance Co. (AEMCO) at Oakland Intl. Airport, who also completed an overhaul of each aircraft. It appears that s/n: 44-22962 was used as a prototype and was never assigned to any subsequent units. Other upgrades were completed at various AFBs. Most of the Group A upgraded C-82As were assigned to air defense fighter groups for support duties and are all within the last 16 C-82As to be retired in 1955.

The 1954 revised C-82 flight manual lists s/n: 45-57768 as a Group A upgrade, but the IARC cards for this aircraft don't support this. It's the author's opinion this is a printing error, which is actually meant to be s/n: 45-57767, a C-82A that was assigned to AEMCO in 1953, then on to an air defense group.

USAF s/n	In	Out	Upgraded at	New Assignment
44-22962	12 Jun 52	n/a	Fairchild Aircraft	Group A prototype
44-23001	1953	15 Sep 53	Robbins AFB	501st Air Defense GP
44-23004	13 Feb 53	25 Sep 53	Hill AFB	6520th Test Support WG
44-23005	14 May 53	21 Oct 53	Robbins AFB	501st Air Defense GP
44-23006	1953	21 Oct 53	Robbins AFB	501st Air Defense GP
44-23009	14 May 53	10 Jan 54	Robbins AFB	501st Air Defense GP
44-23015	12 Jul 53	28 Apr 54	AEMCO	501st Air Defense GP
44-23027	3 Jul 53	5 Jan 54	AEMCO	567th Air Defense GP
44-23033	1 Aug 53	1 Feb 54	AEMCO	1st AACS INST&MNT SQ then 567th Air Defense GP
44-23046	21 Jul 53	19 Jan 54	AEMCO	521st Air Defense GP
44-23055	1953	unk	Hill AFB	—
44-23057	26 Jun 53	1 Dec 53	AEMCO	3rd Air Materiel SQ then 568th Air Defense GP
45-57734	18 May 53	6 Jan 54	AEMCO	1800th AACS WG
45-57744	14 Apr 53	4 Sep 53	AEMCO	521st Air Defense GP
45-47749	9 Dec 53	1954	Hill AFB	—
45-57767*	17 Apr 53	1 Aug 53	AEMCO	501st Air Defense GP
45-57777	5 May 53	9 Feb 54	AEMCO	521st Air Defense GP
45-57802	1953	1954	Eglin AFB	6520th Test Support WG
45-57806	14 Apr 53	7 Feb 54	AEMCO	567th Air Defense GP
45-57811	21 Apr 53	3 Jan 54	AEMCO	567th Air Defense GP
45-57812	14 Apr 53	Late 53	AEMCO	521st Air Defense GP
45-57828	5 Jun 53	15 Dec 53	AEMCO	1st AACS INST&MNT SQ
48-569	21 Jul 53	6 Jan 54	AEMCO	567th Air Defense GP
48-574	16 Dec 53	unk	Elmendorf AFB	5039th MNT GP
48-581	29 Jul 53	unk	Elmendorf AFB	5039th MNT GP

*Incorrectly listed in the 1954 C-82 flight manual as 45-57768.

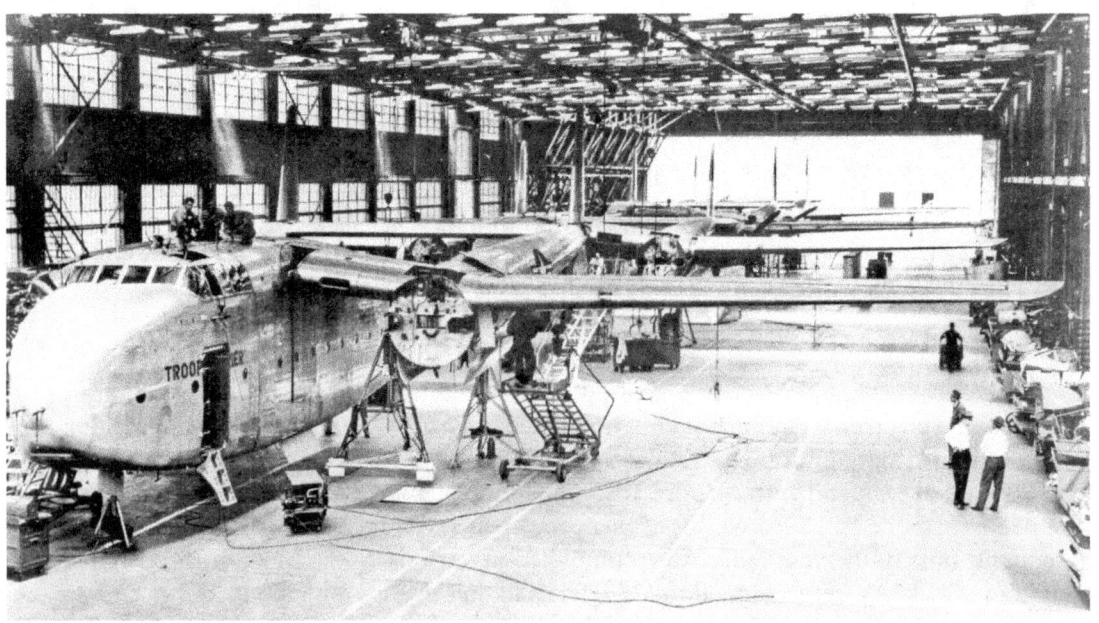

C-82A Packets going through upgrades at AEMCO in Oakland, California, during 1953 (National Museum of the United States Air Force).

Steward-Davis Jet-Packet

Steward-Davis would come to play a significant role in the civil history of the C-82 Packet. Founded at Compton Airport, Gardena, California, in 1946 by aviation businessmen Herb Steward and Stanley Davis as a small charter airline, they soon expanded into the testing and overhauling of military surplus radial engines for resale into a flourishing postwar airliner market. By 1950 Stan Davis had left the company, to be replaced by Dan Thompson, whose forte was in promotion and advertising; the "Davis" part of the company name, however, was retained. Herb and Dan then set about expanding the business, providing aircraft and engine servicing, overhauls and conversions. They acquired aircraft Type Certificate No. 785 for the Consolidated PBY-5A Catalina and eventually converted over ten "Cats" with upgraded Wright Cyclone R-2600 engines, modified tail fin, faired nose and other civilian improvements, and marketed them as the Steward-Davis Super Catalina. They are also known to have modified and overhauled a Northrop F-15A Reporter (reg: N5093V) and several Sikorsky S-51 helicopters for export to Mexico.

Steward-Davis workhorse C-82A N6985C (msn: 10090) being loaded for a cargo flight (Rebecca Wiant Collection).

When the U.S. Navy's McDonnell FH-1 Phantom fighter was declared surplus and retired in 1953, Herb acquired the type certificate plus all spares and manufacturing rights to the Phantom's power plant, the Westinghouse J30-W turbojet. Westinghouse itself was a well-established American corporation giant that got into the jet engine business in 1945 when it established the Westinghouse Aviation Gas Turbine Division. Their first product was the Westinghouse 19XB turbojet with the military designation J30-W, which was, in fact, the first American-designed turbojet to run. It later developed into the J34-WE (civil designation: 24C), for such aircraft as the U.S. Navy's F2H Banshee. However, when their new J40-WE failed with the next naval fighter, the F3H Demon, the Westinghouse engine division was crippled, suffering a terrible loss of reputation. By 1955 they had been forced out of the aviation business altogether, which created an opportunity for Steward-Davis to also acquire the rights to the J34-WE turbojet.

The Westinghouse J34-WE engine used in Jet-Pak 3400 conversions (National Museum of the United States Air Force).

Steward-Davis began selling and overhauling the J30 and J34 for various military and civil operators worldwide, including customers in Australia, France, India, Japan and the Netherlands. In particular, from 1953, the J34 engine had found a niche market as an auxiliary jet-pod on the Lockheed P-2 Neptune, then in service with many air forces around the globe. As well as providing spare parts, Steward-Davis also manufactured new replacement components for these engines.

A very tidy Steward-Davis C-82A Jet-Packet 3200 N5095V (msn: 10071) during 1957 (José Villela G.).

By 1955, the C-82A Packet had been officially retired by the USAF, who then put up for tender the surplus airframes to civilian operators. Herb Steward saw the amazing potential his Westinghouse turbojet engines could have in overcoming the Packet's greatest weakness—single-engine performance. Fully loaded, a C-82 will lose 78 feet per minute on one engine, and even at full power on the good engine, it is unable to maintain level flight. A Jet-Pak using the J30 or J34 could be utilized to assist take-offs, reducing runway distance; it could then serve as an auxiliary engine for greater power in addition to the two radial engines, or as an "emergency stand-by" power source in case of a radial engine failure.

An aerial photograph of the Steward-Davis C-82 program. Up to 33 C-82 Packets are in this picture taken over Long Beach Airport, California, on February 23, 1959 (Rebecca Wiant Collection).

Steward-Davis applied for, and was awarded, Civil Aeronautics Administration (CAA) Type Certificate No. AR-15 on July 7, 1955, for the C-82 Packet. A type certificate basically certifies an aircraft for civil operation and outlines all the performance, weight and restrictions the aircraft is allowed to operate under. Fairchild themselves, and the USAF from 1955, had ceased all association and support with the C-82 Packet, and so Steward-Davis became the sole type certificate holder for the aircraft. They were also the sole worldwide parts, sales and service agents, having also acquired the massive stores of brand-new, crated spares from USAF inventories. The company would go onto supply C-82 operators with spares throughout the continental U.S., Alaska and Latin America into the 1970s.

The "restricted" part of the type certificate issued to Steward-Davis stated, however, that the C-82 could only operate over congested areas up to a maximum weight of 43,560 lb, which restricted payloads. With congested (populated) areas building up around the flight paths into airports, it became imperative to get an auxiliary jet-powered C-82 Packet up and running so the type certificate could be amended to allow maximum weight flights up to 54,000 lb.

C-82A Jet-Packet 3200 N5095V (msn: 10071) demonstrating flight on the twin Jet-Pak alone in this publicity photograph taken in the late 1950s (Rebecca Wiant Collection).

The overall proposal saw a J30-W engine installed in a pod (Jet-Pak) mounted on a pylon which was bolted to the dorsal wing center section, mid-fuselage on a C-82A. It offered operators not only the safety of engine-out performance but also enabled the take-off run to be greatly reduced—up to 25 percent in some cases. Plumbing refinements were made to the fuel system, which luckily still used the same 100/130 octane gasoline to power the J30-W as it did to power the piston engines, so no additional fuel tanks were required. The entire assembly weighed around 860 lb (390 kg). Controls for the turbojet were installed on the flight-deck with Jet-Pak startup accomplished via modifications to the hydraulic system connected to a jet-starter unit. Jet-Paks required 1 minute to 1 minute 45 seconds to start up and accelerate to full power.

Jet-Paks—Normal Specifications

J30: single-stage turbine/ten-stage axial-flow compressor/electric starter motor.
J34: two-stage turbine/eleven-stage axial-flow compressor/24 volt electric starter motor.

	J30-W	J34-WE-34	J34-WE-36
Civil Designation:	19XB-2B	24C	24C
Overall Length:	7.84 feet	10.16 feet	9.29 feet
Overall Width:	1.59 feet	2.33 feet	2.25 feet
Overall Height:	1.59 feet	3.24 feet	2.89 feet
Unit Weight:	692 lb	1,233 lb	—
Compression Ratio:	3.80:1	3.85:1	4.35:1
Power Rating:	1,560 lbst	3,250 lbst	3,400 lbst

The Jet-Packet 3200 (msn: 10071) under construction at Gardena, California, during 1956 (Steward-Davis).

	J30-W	J34-WE-34	J34-WE-36
Fuel Octane Grade:	100/130	100/130	100/130
Oil Pressure:	80 lb/sq. inch	80 lb/sq. inch	80 lb/sq. inch
Exhaust Gas Temperature:	1,220 deg. F.	1,025 deg. F.	1,025 deg. F.

Left and above: Two views of the Jet-Pak framework used to support the jet engines on C-82A N5095V (msn: 10071) (Steward-Davis).

The conversions were branded and marketed as the Steward-Davis C-82 Jet-Packet 1600, 3200 or 3400, with the first flight taking place in November 1956, using a J30-W engine, and operational services beginning in June 1958. The FAA type certificate was amended on May 12, 1961, for full weight J30-engined C-82 operations over congested areas. After a period of further development, the FAA type certificate was amended again on 23 July 1963, for J34-engined C-82 operations.

 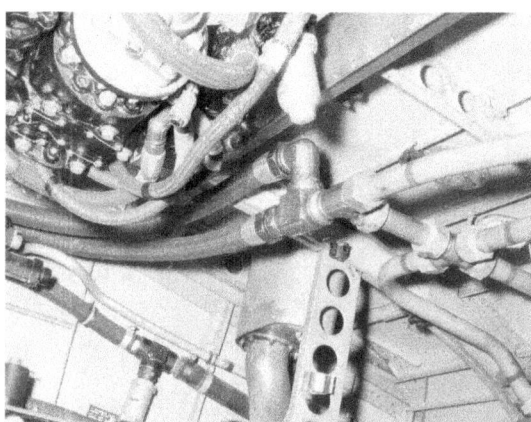

Left: Detail view of Jet-Pak engine plumbing and accessories. *Right:* Interior detail of Jet-Pak plumbing inside the aircraft fuselage directly underneath the pylon mounting point (both photographs, Steward-Davis).

Restricted Type Certificate AR-15

Type	Engine	Issue Date	Weight Restrictions
C-82A	unmodified	July 7, 1955	43,560 lb over congested areas. 50 to 54,000 lb over uncongested areas.
Jet-Packet 1600	J30-W	May 21, 1961	50 to 54,000 lb over any area.*
Jet-Packet 3400	J34-WE	July 23, 1963	50 to 54,000 lb over any area.*

*Jet engine must be operating over congested areas; otherwise, weight restriction of 43,560 lb applies.

It was noted during test flights that there were some vibrations coming from jet-wash over the rear horizontal stabilizer. To remedy this, the outer horizontal stabilizer tips were removed and small, streamlined tail-cone extensions were added onto the ends of the booms; this modification became one of the distinguishing features of a Jet-Pak conversion. Another modification was the addition of a rudder servo control tab to decrease rudder force and reduce the single-engine minimum control speed.

J34-WE engines were later developed to incorporate intake duct-doors, which stopped the engine from windmilling during periods of non-operation. Steward-Davis also made various modifications to the C-82A aircraft itself, namely the engines, flaps (from fabric to metal skin) and fuel systems. The main landing gear was often replaced with lighter Douglas DC-4 units with the hydraulic system modified to raise and lower them rather than the original electrical system—this also saved weight. Hydraulic nose-wheel steering was also a common addition. These modifications were marketed as the Jet-Packet 1600A/1600B or Jet-Packet 3400A/3400B, depending on the level of modifications and options chosen by a customer.

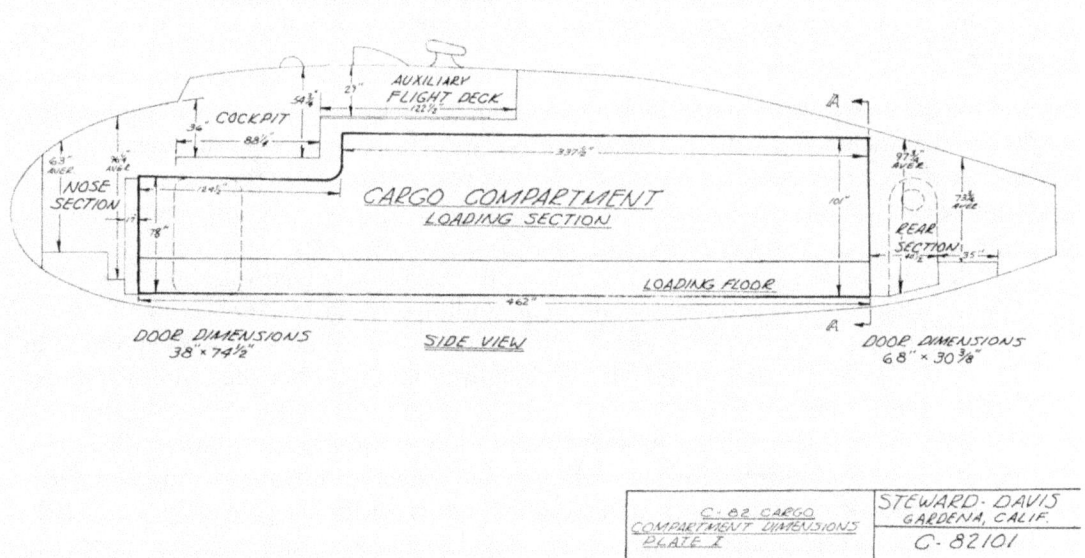

A Steward-Davis schematic noting the fuselage space for the C-82 Packet (Steward-Davis).

The USAF evaluated a Jet-Packet 1600, N6887C, in late 1961 as a follow-up to the FAA flight tests which had seen the C-82 type certificate amended the previous May. A series of five flights took place with the final report written by a USAF test pilot and engineer. They concluded that the Jet-Packet design, overall, performed as required and was

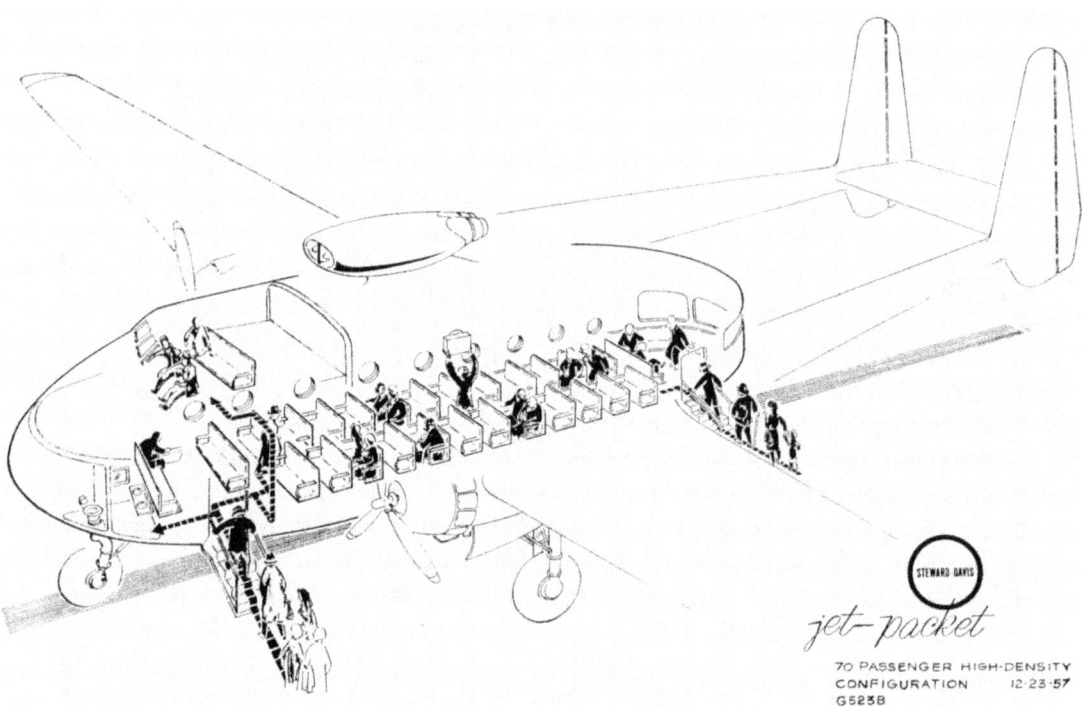

An interesting schematic by Steward-Davis depicting a C-82 civil airliner configuration dated December 23, 1957. Note the flight-deck seating, twin Jet-Pak and panoramic windows on the clamshell doors—something actually built for one C-82 exported to Mexico, XB-KOI (msn: 10154) (Steward-Davis).

safe for the operations intended for it. However, they also pointed out several limiting factors that included: (1) there was no significant decrease in take-off distance with the Jet-Pak running—a result of jet-wash over the rear horizontal stabilizer appearing to reduce elevator effectiveness at take-off; (2) large control inputs were still required during flight handling; (3) stall warnings in all flight configurations were inadequate; (4) several Jet-Pak controls were not properly laid out, including a lack of guards on some switches; (5) nose-wheel shimmy was detected on some landings. The last factor was a well-known Packet fault that had never been cured until the twin nose-wheeled C-119G appeared in 1953. It isn't known if Steward-Davis ever followed up on any of the report's findings published in November 1961.

With the C-82 type certificate amended to allow full weight flights using the J30-W engine, the Jet-Packet program was seemingly building a healthy momentum. Steward-Davis created a holding company named New Frontier Airlift Corp. in early 1961 to help market the C-82 Jet-Packet models. From sales brochures at the time, they appear to have operated mainly in a leasing capacity offering various lease options to customers, with special consideration given to those wishing to operate in developing countries. They were headquartered on a floor in the iconic Luhrs Building in Phoenix, Arizona, under the leadership of company President Henry A. Smith. Documentation from 1963 shows several further business partners were involved in the venture, all being grouped under a company named the International Corporate Services of California. The business structure is outlined as follows:

International Corporate Services

New Frontier Airlift Corp., Arizona	Cargo Aircraft—C-82 supplier.
Steward-Davis Inc., California	Aerial Trucking—C-82 logistics, pilots, servicing.
Northshore Goldfields Ltd., Canada	Resource Development.
Lawa Goudvelden N.V., Surinam	Gold Dredging.

C-82A Jet-Packet 1600 N6887C (msn: 10059) while on Jet-Pak evaluation at Edwards Air Force Base, California, on September 2, 1961 (United States Air Force).

C-82A Jet-Packet 1600 N6887C (msn: 10059) in Lawa Goudvelden livery, which it carried from 1961 to 1965. Lawa was an investor in the Jet-Packet program (Rebecca Wiant Collection).

Apparently some of the financing for New Frontier came from the Canadian mining company North Shore Goldfields Ltd. One of its employees, Arthur Hunter, was, according to some at Steward-Davis, involved in dealings at New Frontier. The Dutch gold mining company Lawa Goudvelden, it appears, was also a financier; Steward-Davis painted their C-82 N6887C in Lawa livery in 1961.

All existing Steward-Davis C-82 aircraft were re-registered to New Frontier during 1961–62, as were newly acquired Packets when they were purchased. Many Packets were obtained from sales agents like Samuel C. Rudolph of California and Smock & Jenner Inc. of Ohio—both had purchased numbers of C-82s directly off the air force for civil resale. New Frontier had C-82 airframes stored at Long Beach, California; Phoenix, Arizona; and Miami, Florida, all with the intent of being upgraded to Jet-Packets and subsequently sold. Since most of its C-82 operations were already there, Steward-Davis shifted its headquarters to roomier facilities at Long Beach Airport in 1962.

JET-PACKETS have proven their ability in South, Central and North America...are slashing timetables and costs for others. *Why not investigate how much time and money a JET-PACKET can save you?*

Steward-Davis Jet-Packet sales brochure circa 1963 (Steward-Davis).

As ambitious and promising as the Steward-Davis Jet-Packet program was, it soon became apparent there just wasn't a large enough market for a specialized, outsized cargo aircraft of the like, and in the numbers being proposed by Steward-Davis. The Packet was an airplane that had fallen between the cracks—too late for service in World War II, obsolete by the Korean War, and considered too outdated by many for civilian service, even with the Jet-Pak. Plus, it was too late to the market, having to then compete with other high-capacity cargo aircraft that were by now turbo-prop powered or even jet-powered.

Only six firm Jet-Packet sales are known to have been made—N4829V to M&F Inc. in Alaska; N5095V and N6990C to the Rivaereo Co. in Chile; N5102B to the Tanana Investment Corp. in Alaska; N9701F for TWA Airlines in Europe and PP-CEK for Cruzeiro do Sul in Brazil. Steward-Davis retained ownership of three for lease operations and as sales demonstrators—N6887C, N6985C and N74127. The remaining, unconverted C-82 Packets of New Frontier Airlift Corp. sat parked up on airport aprons or airfields, slowly decaying, until finally, in 1970, New Frontier went bankrupt and was dissolved. Their stock of C-82 twin-boomers were subsequently scrapped, the final ones being dispatched in 1972.

Aerial view of Steward-Davis's C-82 Long Beach storage area around late 1965. Aircraft present are N136E, N4833V, N53228, N6887C, N6985C, CP-393, XA-LOJ and XA-LOK (Steward-Davis).

Steward-Davis survived the demise of the C-82 Jet-Packet, but their aviation projects became somewhat less prolific, concentrating instead on smaller contracts in support of larger aircraft companies, with the business finally closing in 1990 when Herb Steward retired. The APU technologies section of the company was brought out by businessman Stan Epstein, who continued on as Steward-Davis International Inc. in Van Nuys, California. Although carrying the old name, it was, in fact, a completely different company. It finally closed in 2008 when Epstein retired.

Retired Steward-Davis employee Bob Thayer, who was a longtime engineer for the company, had this to say about Steward-Davis in a 2009 correspondence with the author:

C-82A N6887C (msn: 10059) on the job, this time salvaging a Cessna 195 N4324V at Bahia De La, Mexico, during April 1969 (Rebecca Wiant Collection).

Steward-Davis was perhaps one of the most uniquely diversified aircraft companies in the world. They were the type certificate holder for the C-82 Packet, PBY Catalina, Westinghouse J30, J34, Boeing 502 and T50 engines; held around fifty other type certificates; modified and serviced aircraft for celebrities like Elton John, Ray Charles, Elvis Presley, John Travolta and the Sheik of Abu Dabi; installed an auxiliary power unit into the "Air Force One" 707, s/n: 27000, now in the Ronald Reagan Library; modified the North American Thrush aircraft; Northrop F-15 aircraft and Guppy aircraft for AeroSpace Lines; produced the nine "Val" dive-bombers for the film *Tora! Tora! Tora!* (1970); converted a Turbo Commander aircraft into a flight inspection aircraft for the South Korean Government and developed internal folding air-stairs for Boeing airliners. I could go on, but these are some of the highlights.

Bob also remembers Herb as being a good boss: "Although Herb was only six years my senior, I looked upon him as a father figure. My favorite memory of Herb was one

Superb view of C-82A Jet-Packet 1600 N6887C (msn: 10059) (Rebecca Wiant Collection).

day when he was leaning against the door jam of my office and said in a very matter of fact voice, 'You know, Thayer, when I was a child I wanted to grow up to be a genius, and I did,' then he turned and walked away." Bob and his wife Betty worked at Steward-Davis right up until the company closed.

Jet-Packet Variants

JET-PACKET 1600

The main conversion marketed by Steward-Davis got underway in 1956. The term "1600" is derived from the 1,600 lbst of thrust generated by the Westinghouse J30-W jet engine installed in a jet-pod on the dorsal center section of the fuselage. S-D branded the J30 installation as the J1600 Jet-Pak. The C-82 type certificate was amended on May 12, 1961, for full-weight flights over congested areas. Additional modifications were offered on the Jet-Packet 1600A, with upgrades to the landing gear, brakes, hydraulic, flap, fuel and emergency systems. Engines were also upgraded to R-2800-85AM2H or similar. The Jet-Packet 1600B upgrade featured 2,400 hp R-2800-CB16 radials. There were four conversions:

N5102B	10152/45-57782	To Jet-Packet 1600A.
N6887C	10059/44-23015	To Jet-Packet 1600A/owned by S-D.
N6990C	10045/44-23001	Exported to Chile.
PP-CEK	10147/45-57777	Exported to Brazil.

C-82A Jet-Packet 1600 N6887C (msn: 10059) at Long Beach, California, during 1963 while on flights to Surinam in support of gold dredging operations with Dutch company Lawa Goudvelden (Ed Coates Collection).

JET-PACKET 3200

One of the first conversions undertaken by Steward-Davis saw the installation of a twin J30 jet-pod—the "3200" is derived from the twin 1,600 lbst of thrust from the two Westinghouse J30 engines. It's also notable for the addition of prop spinners. The first flight was in 1957, followed by some notable appearances in aviation publications of the day promoting S-D's new C-82 workhorse. For reasons unknown, no other "3200" development was undertaken and only one was ever converted:

    N5095V   10071/44-23027   Later to N8009E.

The one and only C-82A Jet-Packet 3200 N5095V (msn: 10071) at Torrance MAP, California, in 1960. Note the tail boom extensions and prop-spinners (Ed Coates Collection).

C82A Jet-Packet 3400 N4829V (msn: 10073) at Steward-Davis, Long Beach, California, in 1963 (Ed Coates Collection).

Jet-Packet 3400

This was the second main conversion marketed by Steward-Davis and featured the installation of a Westinghouse J34 in a jet-pod on the dorsal center section of the fuselage. It was also marketed as the Jet-Packet Model II. The "3400" is derived from the 3,400 lbst of thrust delivered by the J34 turbojet engine. S-D branded the J34 installation as the J3400 Jet-Pak (for the J34-WE-34) and J3402 Jet-Pak (for the J34-WE-36 with flapper doors). The first flight was in October 1962 with the C-82 type certificate amended on July 23, 1963, for full-weight flights over congested areas. Additional modifications were offered on the Jet-Packet 3400A, with upgrades to the landing gear, brakes, hydraulic, flap, fuel and emergency systems. Engines were also upgraded to R-2800-85AM2H or similar. The Jet-Packet 3400B upgrade featured 2,400 hp R-2800-CB16 radials. There were three conversions:

N4829V	10073/44-23029	To Jet-Packet 3400A.
N6985C	10090/44-23046	Owned by S-D.
N9701F	10184/45-57814	To Jet-Packet 3400B.

Skytruck Mk. I

This conversion was an attempt to reduce the C-82 airframe's basic operating weight and so enable it to carry higher payload weights. S-D also branded this version as the Jet-Packet Model III with conversion work starting in June 1963 and the first flight taking place on February 26, 1964. With the installation of the J3400 Jet-Pak, the basic operating weight has been reduced to 30,335 lb, allowing a payload max weight of 23,665 lb (at a max weight of 54,000 lb), but a max take-off weight has been quoted as high as 60,000 lb. Other modifications were leading edge hot-air de-icing and alcohol propeller de-icing systems. Only one conversion was completed, but it crashed in Mexico in late 1964:

N74127	10177/45-57807	Owned by S-D.

C-82A Skytruck Mk. I N74127 (msn: 10177) at Long Beach, California, during 1964. Note the Steward-Davis logos and large tail beacon. This aircraft crashed in Mexico in late 1964, killing both pilots (Ed Coates Collection).

A Skytruck Mk. II prototype was also at one time under development, but no conversion was ever made.

Skypallet

The Skypallet was a one-off experiment to create a "skycrane" design that would shorten turnaround times on the ground and also permit loads of up to 30,000 lbs to be lifted. The conversion had the cargo deck floor of a C-82 removed and a hydraulic hoist

Top: Steward-Davis Skypallet conversion N4828V (msn: 10085) (Andre Van Loon Collection). *Bottom:* The removable cargo deck floor on the Steward-Davis Skypallet N4828V (msn: 10085) (Steward-Davis).

installed on the inside fuselage roof. Palleted cargo would be readied and the bellyless C-82 would taxi in and hoist up the cargo without the crew having to leave the flight-deck. Design work was started in 1963 with the single prototype, N4828V (10085/44-23041), to be ready for flight in 1965. However, there's no evidence it ever flew. The Sky-pallet was designed as an option that could supplement either a Jet-Packet 1600, 3400 or Skytruck conversion.

The Flight of the Phoenix

It's not often in the annals of aviation history that a motion picture has such a profound effect on an individual aircraft type that it becomes a synonymous part of that aircraft's written history. Just as the Avro Lancaster became cinematically famous for its appearance in *The Dam Busters* (1955) and the Grumman F-14 Tomcat in *Top Gun* (1986), the same could not be truer for the Fairchild C-82 Packet as featured in the Hollywood motion picture *The Flight of the Phoenix* (1965).

This production was based on the critically successful bestselling 1964 novel of the same name by British author Elleston Trevor, a noted writer of crime and thrillers. It tells the story of a twin-boom freight plane that crashes in the Sahara Desert and the efforts of the survivors to build a flyable airplane, the *Phoenix*, from the wreckage before they succumb to thirst and exhaustion.

The movie featured leading stars such as James Stewart, Richard Attenborough, Peter Finch, Hardy Kruger and Ernest Borgnine under the direction of Robert Aldrich. The finished movie was dedicated to Hollywood stunt pilot Paul Mantz, who lost his life during filming when the *Phoenix* airplane he built, based on but not built from a C-82 boom, crashed on July 8, 1965. Although marred by this incident, the film went on to have modest success during its 1966 exhibition and remains today a classic aviation film for the original storyline and high-tension drama.

A twin-boom airplane design was essential to the story as one of the booms, of course, had to serve as the "new fuselage" on the *Phoenix*. The aircraft utilized for the story was the C-82 Packet, but is referred to in the novel as a Salmon-Rees Skytruck Mk. IV, in all likelihood a fictional

The front cover of the UK first edition of *The Flight of the Phoenix* showing the twin-boom design required for this intriguing story of survival (courtesy Penguin Random House UK).

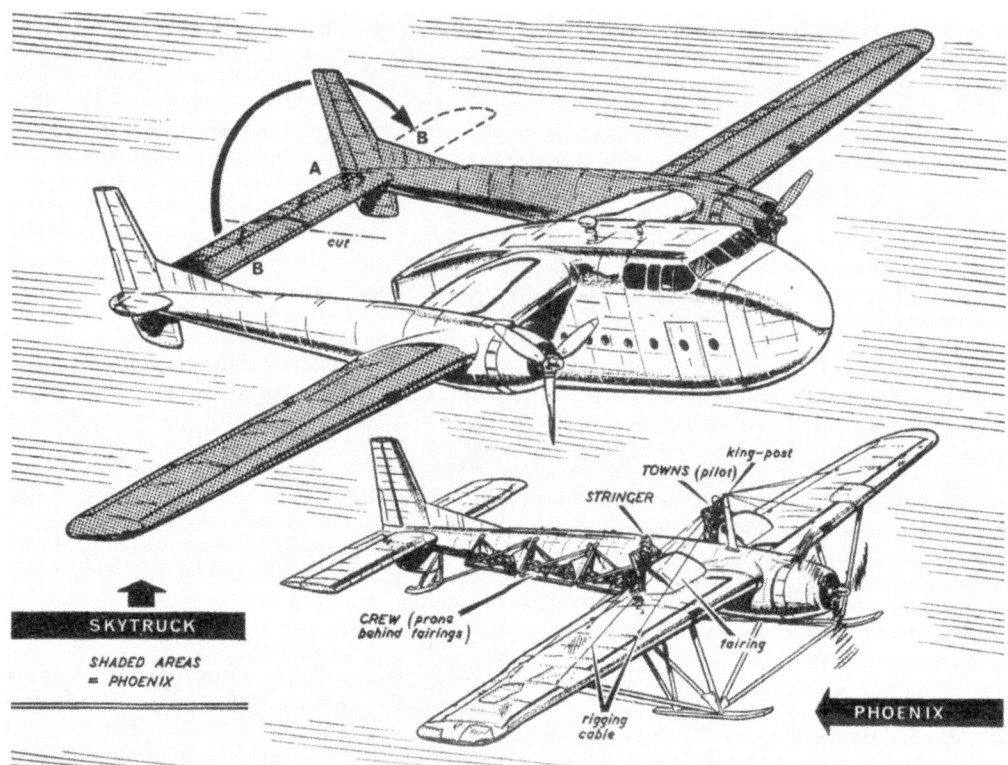

The Skytruck/Phoenix diagram as featured in the UK editions of the novel. Note the addition of dorsal fins and squared vertical stabilizer tips (courtesy Jean-Pierre Trevor).

British civil conversion of the C-82 Packet. The novel describes the airplane as a twin-boom "passenger-conversion freighter" and commonly just refers to it as the "Skytruck."

The film version follows suit with the "Skytruck" designation, avoiding any references to "Fairchild" or the military designation of "C-82." This might stem from the fact that during the 1960s aircraft manufacturers and operators didn't like their products being associated with what was termed "air-disaster stories" at a time when air travel was a new and growing industry, especially in the jet-set arena. This resulted in many novels and films resorting to the creation of fictional aircraft names and manufacturing companies in order to avoid scaring potential airline customers.

It was obvious to the film's production company, the Associates and Aldrich Company, that a twin-boom aircraft was going to be required in order to remain true to the storyline. By 1965, however, the Fairchild C-82 Packet was slowly fading from the skies over the United States. Steward-Davis Inc. at Long Beach Airport were one of the last bastions of the type that were able to provide all that was needed in order for the filmmakers to tell their story. Negotiations between the Associates and Aldrich Co. and Steward-Davis Inc. were finalized on February 18, 1965, with a contract that would require Steward-Davis to provide the following C-82 aircraft and parts:

One C-82A aircraft for flying scenes.
C-82A-15-FA/s/n: 44-23015/c/n: 10059/civil reg.: N6887C
A complete and flyable aircraft for lease to Fox Studios with pilots and crew for

Top: C-82A N53228 (msn: 10080) was used for the night scenes in *The Flight of the Phoenix* (1965) shot at Fox Studios in Culver City. It's quite obvious where the pilot's side canopy has been cut out for camera access during filming (James H. Farmer). *Bottom:* The Buttercup Valley filming site with C-82A N4833V (msn: 10075) (John LaSalandra).

various aerial photography sequences over Imperial Valley plus a take-off shot to be performed as a touch-and-go on Pilot Knob Mesa West of Yuma. Rental with crew costed out at $465.00 dollars per hour plus fuel and oil expenses.

One C-82A fuselage for wreck scenes/on-location day-exteriors.
C-82A-20-FA/s/n: 44-23031/c/n: 10075/civil reg.: N4833V
Fuselage only to be leased and transported to the sand dunes in Buttercup Valley 17 miles west of Yuma.

One C-82A fuselage for wreck scenes/studio-based night-exteriors.
C-82A-25-FA/s/n: 44-23036/c/n: 10080/civil reg.: N53228
Fuselage only to be leased and transported to Stage 6 at Fox Studios in Century City as a duplicate to the exterior set built outside Yuma.

One C-82A fuselage for interior filming.
A C-82A fuselage to be cut up for the pre-credit onboard flying scenes. Fuselage sections to be transported to Fox Ranch in Malibu.

C-82A equipment.
C-82A starboard engine assembly, ramps, ladders, landing gear components, tires and various other parts from Steward-Davis' spares inventory including window and glass sections.

C-82A N6887C (msn: 10059) painted in fictional "Arabco Oil Co." livery for flying duties on *The Flight of the Phoenix* (1965) (Ed Bertschy).

Why were so many aircraft required if there was only one aircraft depicted in the story? The answer is quite simply the old business phrase—time and money. Once a motion picture goes into production, the cost outlays are in the tens of thousands of dollars per day, even way back in the 1960s. There were four different settings required for the "Skytruck" during filming: flying scenes; daytime wreck scenes; nighttime wreck scenes; and onboard interiors requiring the cutting up of a fuselage for camera access. By having these four required elements in place simultaneously, the film's schedule

C-82A N4833V (msn: 10075) soon after the fuselage was returned to Long Beach Airport after filming for *The Flight of the Phoenix* (1965). Note the missing window glass, something evident in the final minutes of the movie. Bottom: C-82A N53228 (msn: 10080) soon after the fuselage was returned to Long Beach Airport after filming on *The Flight of the Phoenix* (1965) (both photographs, Andre Van Loon Collection).

becomes far more cost-effective, enabling the studio to shoot the necessary scenes without waiting for a single fuselage to be shipped from here to there, then be readied for filming. This results in a more streamlined flow to the production that avoids lengthy and expensive breaks in filming.

It was noted in the *Hollywood Reporter* on March 23, 1965, that the three rented C-82 fuselages had been delivered to Fox Studios in preparation for filming. It was here

A whole construction crew was required to handle the multitude of C-82 aircraft parts at the Yuma sand dunes filming location (John LaSalandra).

The "Arabco Oil Co." logo as seen on C-82A N4833V (msn: 10075) (G. Pat Macha).

that the three fuselages were painted in identical Arabco Oil Co. markings and livery to each play their assigned roles in the movie. Flyable C-82A N6887C was also painted in the same manner, presumably at Long Beach Airport. Interestingly, the movie livery carried no registration markings of any kind apart from the Arabco Oil Co. logos on the nose.

On April 22, the fuselage of C-82A N4833V was

transported to the filming site in Buttercup Valley outside Yuma. Roads into the site had to be built to take the heavy trucks and cranes required to shift the aircraft parts into position.

Back at Long Beach, the remaining wing and boom components of N4833V and N53228 were a peculiar sight. Both were left fully assembled, resting on their main under-

Both photographs: Fox Studios cameraman Ron Vidor surveys the Yuma filming set. Vidor filmed pilot Paul Mantz's death when his *Phoenix* airplane crashed on July 8 (Ron Vidor).

carriage, but each with its fuselage section missing. This meant they were now tail-heavy with no fuselage for counterbalance. To remedy this, both aircraft were balanced with lengths of rope attached to lead weights.

Dick Lansman, an ex–Steward-Davis employee who helped remove the fuselages for transport to the filming locations, remembers that one weekend someone broke into the airfield and stole the lead weights, letting the tail-heavy booms fall back onto the tarmac. Some damage was undoubtedly done to the ventral fins.

On June 29, a Certificate of Airworthiness was issued by the FAA giving approval for C-82A N6887C to commence aerial filming. The C-82 Jet-Packet's total airframe time at the start of filming was 1,858.22 hours; the engines were recorded as s/n: 55259 with 90.23 hours since overhaul and s/n: P26510 with 537.09 hours since overhaul. Total flight time logged during filming was less than 14.00 hours.

Steward-Davis's Airworthiness Certificate application for C-82A N6887C (msn: 10059) (Federal Aviation Administration).

July 1, 1965, was slated as the first official day of filming for the movie's second unit, also known as the aerial unit, based out of Yuma International Airport. The aerial unit work was contracted to Tallmantz Aviation Inc., a well-known company within the film industry, run by veteran Hollywood stunt pilots Paul Mantz and Frank Tallman. Aircraft to be utilized were the Tallmantz scratch-built Phoenix P-1 N93082; C-82A Packet N6887C; a Tallmantz B-25 Mitchell camera-plane—either N1203 or more likely N1042B;

Paul Mantz's personal aircraft, a Piper PA-23 Apache N3131P; and a Beechcraft Bonanza. Both of these last two were used for off-camera support duties.

Steward-Davis employee Bob Thayer arrived to act as the FAA coordinator during the shoot. Bob recalls, "FAA coordination was one of my tasks. It was necessary to obtain FAA clearance for multiple flight shots, especially below limits with a restricted category aircraft." Bob also remembers seeing Paul Mantz the day before he was killed: "The three-quarter scale model single-boom was built by Tallmantz and was somewhat unstable even with Paul Mantz as pilot. The evening before he crashed, we had dinner together in Yuma."

The Skytruck crew were pilot Earl Bellotte, an ex–USAF C-82 pilot who was occasionally hired by Steward-Davis as a freelancer for C-82 operations. He would later move to Alaska to work for Bob Schlaffly flying PB4Y-2 Privateers. Ironically, Bellotte would subsequently work alongside another pilot, Bob West, who would later go on to acquire the same film piloting role Bellotte had in 1965—flying the C-119 Flying Boxcar for the 2004 *Flight of the Phoenix* remake.

The copilot, according to Thayer, was Steward-Davis employee Ted Whaley, who had earned his multi-engined rating while working on the Jet-Packet program. However, research carried out by the author has shown that he possibly wasn't the copilot. After Ted's daughter Rebecca was located in Long Beach, California, she very kindly made her father's logbook available to the author for study. It shows Ted did indeed fly N6887C, and other Steward-Davis C-82s, many times, but there's no entry at all for any flights undertaken by him from March 1965 through to December 1965. Rebecca also pointed out that Ted often spoke of his flying activities at Steward-Davis, but she cannot recall a single instance when he ever talked about a "Phoenix movie shoot" in Yuma.

One possibility is that the copilot may actually have been fellow Steward-Davis pilot Don Dinoff, a very experienced flyer and, to some degree, a warbird collector. Dinoff would later go on to fly one of the Japanese replicas for *Tora! Tora! Tora!* (1970).

C-82A Jet-Packet 1600 N6887C (msn: 10059) with a rather shabby livery during 1966 (Andre Van Loon Collection).

Aerial photography of the C-82 Packet has been recorded as taking place on five separate days. The first was on Saturday, July 3, when the Tallmantz B-25 camera-plane arrived in Yuma. At this point the Phoenix P-1 was giving much trouble, which resulted in continued cancellations of filming. While the Phoenix was undergoing modifications on this day, Paul Mantz and Tallmantz pilot Frank Pine departed with the C-82 for a session of air-to-air photography over Imperial Valley. The B-25 was piloted by Pine, with Mantz directing the action likely from the copilot's seat. All flying shots were done from the left-hand side of the C-82, so the flow of action on-screen was always right to left.

On July 6, filming in Buttercup Valley was canceled for a third time due to mechanical problems with the Phoenix P-1. With a free afternoon on the schedule, Paul Mantz and Frank Pine again departed Yuma in the B-25 camera-plane along with the C-82 at 1:30 p.m. for two flights of aerial filming over Imperial Valley. They finished at 5:30 p.m. that evening.

July 13 saw more aerial photography with the B-25 camera-plane and C-82, this time over the northern end of Imperial Valley, filming the Skytruck "nosing-up to climb over the sandstorm." This session was done by another Tallmantz crew, as by now Mantz himself had already been killed in the Phoenix P-1 crash of July 8.

The most prominent and exciting scene featuring the C-82 Skytruck is the opening shot of the film when it roars past the camera while taking off from a dirt airstrip. The airstrip itself was a Hollywood creation and not based on any existing runway in the

A rare photograph of the flight deck on C-82A N4833V (msn: 10075) taken by *The Flight of the Phoenix* novelist himself, Elleston Trevor, during his visit to the Yuma sand dunes in May 1965. Actor James Stewart sat here for some scenes filling out a logbook (Elleston Trevor via Jean-Pierre Trevor).

Yuma area. The take-off is really an illusion—the C-82 only performed touch-and-go passes before the cameras, as the airstrip was graded dirt and not of a standard to support large aircraft. At least two passes were made for the film cameras; however, it remains unclear whether this scene was completed before or after Mantz's death on July 8.

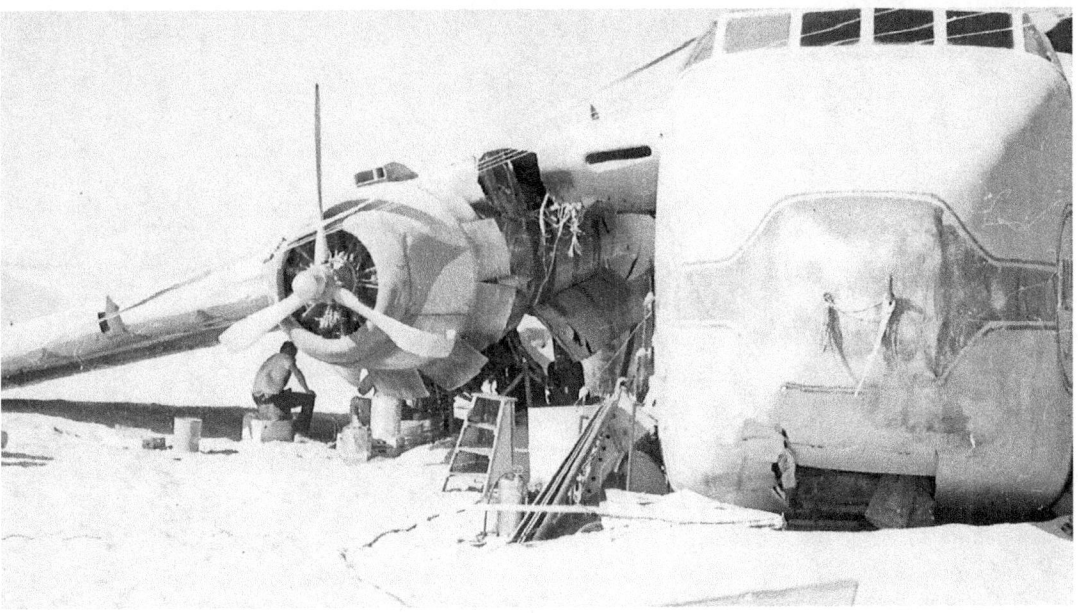

Top: The wings and booms used on the Yuma location film set were from an R4Q-1 wreck obtained out of Tucson, Arizona, and the vertical stabilizers were scratch-built fakes. *Bottom:* C-82A N4833V (msn: 10075) set up at the Yuma sand dunes set in May 1965. The wings and booms, however, came from a former USMC R4Q-1 Packet, BuNo. 126580 (both photographs, Elleston Trevor via Jean-Pierre Trevor).

Other scenes with the C-82 were shot on Saturday, July 10, and Monday, July 12, when it performed overhead fly-bys for part of a camel sequence that was later cut from the film during editing. The "Skytruck shadow" across the dunes was also shot on July 12 by filming out the side door of the aircraft as it skimmed over the sand dunes.

In terms of the C-82 flying scenes, including the "C-82 ground shadows," there are only 11 individual shots, running less than a minute in total, contained in the final cut of the film. Afterward, C-82A N6887C was refitted with its Jet-Pak 1600 and continued in regular service with Steward-Davis until 1970. The fuselages of N4833V and N53228 were reunited with their wings and booms at Long Beach Airport in late 1965. Both were later scrapped sometime in 1970.

A fourth, unidentified C-82 fuselage was used for the pre-credit onboard flying scenes. It was required to be cut up into sections and moved to Fox Ranch located in Malibu, California, where initial filming was started in late April 1965. The flight-deck was one section for scenes with James Stewart and Richard Attenborough, and the cargo hold section was another for the rest of the cast. Both sections were gimble-mounted so they could be rocked around to simulate the wind buffeting of the sandstorm. Steward-Davis employee Bob Thayer remembers that the aircraft used was never registered as a flying aircraft and was a dummy airframe for testing Jet-Packet components. The author has conducted his own research into identifying the airframe used, and through a series of eliminations, seems to have narrowed it down to a few strong possibilities. The flight-

Filming the in-flight sandstorm scenes required some real Hollywood trickery. Here film crews are using giant wind fans and fuller's earth to recreate a Saharan sandstorm at Fox Studios Malibu Ranch, California, in April 1965. A real C-82A fuselage was used, but the wings and engines are plywood mock-ups (Elleston Trevor via Jean-Pierre Trevor).

Top: A film crew member's visiting family pose with the non-flying Phoenix built from a Fairchild R4Q-1 Packet, BuNo.126580 (John LaSalandra). *Bottom: The Flight of the Phoenix* novelist Elleston Trevor and his wife on a visit to the Yuma set during May 1965. C-82A N4833V (msn: 10075) was used as the main outdoor set piece (Elleston Trevor via Jean-Pierre Trevor).

deck layout of the main instrument, overhead and center panels shows the airframe to definitely be within the 44-22989 through 45-57737 serial number range. Through a series of further eliminations, based on each aircraft status in 1965, the C-82 most likely used it seems was either Steward-Davis–owned N7884C (s/n: 44-23013) or N5116B (s/n: 44-23045), the latter purchased by Steward-Davis as a derelict from Swensair Parts, Florida, in 1962.

The *Phoenix* aircraft themselves were firstly the wings and booms from a former USMC Fairchild R4Q-1 BuNo. 126580 (msn: 10549), purchased from a scrap yard in Tucson, Arizona. These parts were used for the airplane-build sequences and engine-start scenes with the actors. The flyable *Phoenix* was a scratch-built one by Tallmantz Aviation Inc. registered as the Phoenix P-1, N93082, and flown by veteran Hollywood stunt pilot Paul Mantz. The last *Phoenix* was a North American O-47A N4725V (s/n: 38–284), loaned by the Air Museum of California in order to complete the flying scenes after the Mantz aircraft tragically crashed during filming on July 8, 1965.

Section Two

Military Operators

United States of America

Since the Fairchild C-82 Packet was originally ordered for service by the USAAF, they were, of course, the single largest military operator of the aircraft.

It should be noted here that during the C-82 Packet's ten-year service period, from 1945 to 1955, the American Air Force went through one of the biggest structural and organizational changes it has ever seen. During 1946, structural developments saw the introduction of Major Commands (MAJCOM) within the USAAF. Each of these oversaw a certain specific air mission, namely tactical, strategic, air defense, materiel, transport and support elements. Various command refinements and unit renaming took place throughout the late 1940s and early 1950s, which is a large reason why there are so many unit listings for the C-82 Packet. Another factor is the high number of assignments for depot and transient maintenance of individual aircraft.

The most significant change overall was that the United States Army Air Force (USAAF), so named on June 20, 1941, became independent of the U.S. Army on September 18, 1947. Renamed the United States Air Force (USAF), it entered into the jet age as the world's largest, and by no small margin, most powerful air force.

Production C-82A Packet deliveries to the USAAF began in June 1945, some of the early aircraft initially going to the 4000th AAF Base Unit at Wright Field for trials and flight tests. Others went to similar base units for tests and integration during 1945. Proper frontline service entry began with deliveries to the 62nd and 316th Troop Carrier Groups in 1946, which were the largest users of the aircraft with a combined service period from 1946 to 1951 and overall troop carrier service up to 1953.

The primary mission of this new aircraft was in troop/cargo transport including paratroops, air ambulance duties and glider towing. It was found the Packet's long flight-time endurance on full tanks made it ideal for the search and rescue mission, so 38 aircraft were assigned to the Air Rescue Service from 1947 to 1953. Later, as frontline service of the C-82 was starting to wind down, secondary duties were assigned, such as air base and unit support with various groups and fighter wings within Air Defense Command (ADC) and Strategic Air Command (SAC).

Although there were a large number of unit assignments during the C-82 Packet's military service, there were actually only a handful of groups the aircraft had a significant role to play in its primary mission of troop and cargo carrier. The following table summarizes the most prominent Air Force C-82 units based on the troop and cargo

As many as 32 C-82A Packets can be counted at this air base somewhere in the United States (National Museum of the United States Air Force).

transport mission, unit service period, and total number of aircraft that were assigned overall.

Major Commands: **Tactical Air Command (TAC)**
USAF in Europe (USAFE)
Primary Mission: Troop Carrier/Cargo Transport

Units	Period	Inventory
60th Troop Carrier Group	1948–1953	53
62nd Troop Carrier Group	1946–1950	105
64th Troop Carrier Group	1952–1953	44
313th Troop Carrier Group	1947–1948	43
314th Troop Carrier Group	1948–1951	98
316th Troop Carrier Group	1946–1951	119
375th Troop Carrier Group	1950–1952	51

Major Command: **Military Air Transport Service (MATS)**
Primary Mission: Search and Rescue (SAR)

Units	Period	Inventory
Multiple **Air Rescue Service** Squadrons	1947–1953	38

Major Command: **Strategic Air Command (SAC)**
Primary Mission: Unit & Base Support

Units	Period	Inventory
55th Strategic Reconnaissance Group (including **7th Geodetic Squadron**).	1949–1953	16
91st Strategic Reconnaissance Group	1949–1950	12

Major Command:	**Air Defense Command (ADC)**	
Primary Mission:	Unit & Base Support	
Units	**Period**	**Inventory**
325th Fighter (All-Weather) Wing	1950	8
501st Air Defense Wing	1953–1955	6
521st Air Defense Wing	1953–1955	7
567th Air Defense Wing	1954–1955	5

Paratroop training exercises and unit support deployments were a major role for the C-82 troop carrier groups during their primary service period both abroad and within the Continental United States.

A trio of 4th TCSq C-82A Packets (Elton Schlimmer via Marvin Schlimmer).

The following are some of the operations undertaken, or partaken in, by C-82 units, a few are historically notable for their humanitarian contribution, a mission the C-82 excelled at:

Project Comet

Twenty-nine Lockheed P-80A Shooting Stars of the 412th Fighter Group were assigned the task of flying from California to Washington, D.C., from May 15 to 27, 1946, to evaluate any problems encountered on long-range deployments and to promote America's need for a strong air force to the public. Six C-82A Packets from the 36th TCSq, 316th TCG were assigned as support aircraft. Although the overall mission was a success, the Packet's performance was questioned, with several mechanical faults dogging parts of the mission.

Operation Combine

C-82 Packets assigned to drop 82nd Airborne paratroops at Lawson Field, Georgia, during October 1947.

Operation Yukon

62nd TCG Packets from McChord AFB transported troops and supplies as part of a joint U.S. Army mission to Alaska in January 1948.

Operation Assembly

62nd TCG Packets from McChord AFB deployed to Pope AFB in April 1948 to assist in airdrop and paratroop maneuvers with the 82nd Airborne Division.

Operation Vittles

Vittles was the unofficial code name given for the famous Berlin Airlift operation staged into and out of Tempelhof Airport in Berlin during the late 1940s. The political history of post–World War II Germany falls outside the scope of this book, but essentially the Berlin Blockade began on April 1, 1948, when Soviet forces blocked road and rail access into West Berlin, depriving the civilian population of food, materials and fuel. The only way in or out was via air, and so the Berlin Airlift was initiated on June 26, 1948, led by the USAF with help from the RAF and several other Commonwealth air

The crew of the first C-82A s/n: 45-57818 (msn: 10188) to arrive at Wiesbaden for the Berlin Airlift. *From left to right:* **Staff Sergeant Joseph McRae; Staff Sergeant Edward Baldwin; Sergeant James Astin; 1st Lieutenant Thad Brannon (co-pilot); 1st Lieutenant George Kemper, Jr. (pilot); and 1st Lieutenant Joseph Carlin (navigator) (George Kemper via Betsy Kemper).**

forces. In total, over 278,000 flights over a fifteen-month period brought in essential supplies including much-needed sacks of coal—mainly on Douglas C-47 and C-54 aircraft. The huge success of the operation forced the Soviets to withdraw, and the blockade was lifted on May 12, 1949, with the airlift finishing on September 30, 1949. The politically divided East and West Germany had been formally established on May 23, 1949.

A total of 53 C-82A Packets were assigned to the 60th TCG with the USAF in Europe (USAFE) from 1948 to 1953. Five were formally assigned to Berlin Airlift operations, namely s/n: 45-57740, 45-57785, 45-57791, 45-57796 and 45-57818. However, '785 crashed at Tempelhof AB on December 14, 1948, due to a landing accident, and it appears s/n: 45-57810 was then assigned as a replacement aircraft. Notably, these five aircraft were among the first Packets to arrive in Europe and were crewed by ten pilots, five radio operators and seven engineers led by 1st Lt (later Captain) George A. Kemper Jr. Most other C-82 Packets for the 60th TCG arrived during 1949.

C-82A s/n: 45-57810 being engine serviced during the Berlin Airlift (George Kemper via Betsy Kemper).

The Berlin Airlift C-82s were all assigned from the 316th TCG at Greenville AFB and all followed common units and dates during the airlift as outlined below:

45-57740 (CQ-740)
60th TCG	Erbenheim (Wiesbaden AB) Germany	16 Sep 48
7160th AB GP	Erbenheim (Wiesbaden AB) Germany	6 Oct 48
7165th AB GP	Erbenheim (Wiesbaden AB) Germany	22 Dec 48 & 17 Mar 49
60th AB GP	Wiesbaden AB West Germany	1 Jun 49
513th TCG (JC-82A)	Rhein-Main AB West Germany	22 Sep 49–1 Oct 49

45-57785 (CQ-785)
60th TCG	Erbenheim (Wiesbaden AB) Germany	16 Sep 48
7160th AB GP	Erbenheim (Wiesbaden AB) Germany W/o Tempelhof 14 Dec 48	6 Oct 48

45-57791 (CQ-791)
60th TCG	Asmushausen Germany	14 Sep 48
7160th AB GP	Erbenheim (Wiesbaden AB) Germany	6 Oct 48

45-57791 (CQ-791) (**continued**)

7165th Composite GP	Erbenheim (Wiesbaden AB) Germany	22 Dec 48 & 17 Mar 49
60th AB GP	Wiesbaden AB West Germany	1 Jun 49
513th TCG (**JC-82A**)	Rhein-Main AB West Germany	19 Sep 49–1 Oct 49

45-57796 (CQ-796)

60th TCG	Erbenheim (Wiesbaden AB) Germany	14 Sep 48
7160th AB GP	Erbenheim (Wiesbaden AB) Germany	6 Oct 48
7165th Composite GP	Erbenheim (Wiesbaden AB) Germany	22 Dec 48 & 17 Mar 49
60th AB GP	Wiesbaden AB West Germany	1 Jun 49
Middletown Air Materiel Area (**JC-82A**)	Olmsted AFB Pennsylvania	12 Sep 49

45-57810 (CQ-810)

7165th Composite GP	Erbenheim (Wiesbaden AB) Germany	22 Feb 49 & 17 Mar 49
60th TCG	Erbenheim (Wiesbaden AB) Germany	8 Mar 49
60th AB GP	Wiesbaden AB West Germany	1 Jun 49
513th TCG (not cvtd)	Rhein-Main AB West Germany	19 Sep 49–1 Oct 49

45-57818 (CQ-818)

60th TCG	Erbenheim (Wiesbaden AB) Germany	14 Sep 48
7160th AB GP	Erbenheim (Wiesbaden AB) Germany	9 Oct 48
7165th Composite GP	Erbenheim (Wiesbaden AB) Germany	22 Dec 48 & 17 Mar 49
60th AB GP	Wiesbaden AB West Germany	1 Jun 49
513th TCG (**JC-82A**)	Rhein-Main AB West Germany	19 Sep 49–1 Oct 49

The C-82s flew all kinds of outsized cargoes into Berlin that other types could not, such as earth-moving and construction equipment, generators, jeeps and cars. Outbound

The C-82A crews assigned to the Berlin Airlift. *Last names front row left to right:* Mathis, Moen, Stewart, Gillam, Kemper Jr., Tibbs, Pendleton, Brown, Yancey and Watkins. *Last names back row left to right:* Astin, Young, McRae, King, Coleman, Martin, Baldwin, Russell, Davis, Stiverson and Bevan (George Kemper via Betsy Kemper).

flights carried civilian automobiles owned by Berlin residents who left the city at the start of the blockade. Each Packet could carry two cars with the 100 or so left behind airlifted out within the period of a week. The JC-82A conversions were a temporary modification to four aircraft during a two-week assignment to the 513th TCG. It's not clear what was carried, but it appears to have involved the removal of the rear clamshell doors with modifications to the cargo hold area.

One of the C-82s was hired as a movie camera-ship for filming C-54 Skymaster transports on landing approaches into Tempelhof for the 20th Century–Fox film *The Big Lift*, shot in Berlin during 1949 and released in the U.S. during 1950.

A C-82A copilot takes a break during Berlin Airlift missions (George Kemper via Betsy Kemper).

C-82A s/n: 45-57800 (10170) during a winter in West Germany while assigned to the 60th TCG. The C-82 performed well in cold weather conditions (George Kemper via Betsy Kemper).

Operation Haylift

In January 1949 a fierce snowstorm ravaged the northwest U.S., which reached as far inland as Nebraska. Stranded cattle were in dire need of feed, with many dying from starvation and the freezing temperatures. Seventeen C-82As from the 62nd TCG at McChord AFB and 10 from the 316th TCG at Greenville AFB were provided for emergency distribution of hay. From January 24 to February 17 some 4.2 million lb of hay was airdropped from C-82 aircraft saving some 300,000 head of cattle. Haylift was a real baptism of fire for the C-82 Packet, which had to operate out of high-altitude airfields—NAS Fallon (elevation 4,000 ft) and Ely Airfield (elevation 6,000 ft)—and deal with well below freezing temperatures, a lack of facilities, extreme weather and mountainous terrain. Hay bales weighing 100 lb each were dropped from the aircraft via the paratroop doors at the rear of the fuselage, or through the belly paratainer doors. Since they knew the terrain better than anyone, local ranchers were employed on the flight-deck of many C-82s to act as "navigators" during the airdrops; for some it was their first time on an aircraft of this size! The livestock industry was so impressed and appreciative of the help rendered by the Air Force that each C-82 crew member received a personalized certificate from Governor Vail Pittman of Nevada. Each certificate was stamped with the State of Nevada Seal and signed by Pittman himself. Known Haylift C-82 identities include: 45-57750, 45-57751, 45-57774, 45-57776, 45-57778, 45-57820, 48-573 and 48-579.

Operation Portrex

A massive American joint-forces exercise undertaken prior to the Korean War in the Caribbean area around Puerto Rico from February 25 to March 11, 1950. Many C-82 Packets from the 316th TCG were stationed out of Guantanamo Bay, Cuba, during March 1950 to provide paratroop support. Portrex is an abbreviation for "Puerto Rico Exercises."

Operation Umbrella

C-82s from the 60th TCG doubled as incoming bombers to help test fighter air defenses.

Project Redhead

Two 60th TCG C-82s flew trans–Atlantic resupply fights for a three-month period in 1952 keeping a deployed B-50 and KB-29 group serviced in England.

Operation Coldspot

Ten 64th TCG C-82s were deployed in this operation as unit support aircraft for the 366th Fighter-Bomber Wing in 1953.

The layout detailed on the subsequent pages covers every unit, wing, group or base unit the C-82 Packet was assigned to within the USAF. This data has been deciphered, consolidated and analyzed from Air Force Individual Aircraft Record Cards (IARC) obtained by the author.

As can be noted from the full listed unit histories, the C-82 was assigned to many air base groups and AF base units under many major commands. These unit assignments, in most cases, are related to depot or transient maintenance, repairs or salvage, and so are not classified in the normal sense as unit assignments in which the C-82 was serving in its primary mission. It has, however, been noted where "out of the ordinary" duties were assigned on any of these particular units, such as flight tests or training.

In an attempt to bring some order to the multitude of various commands and sub-commands, the following layout has been adopted for this section:

1. Major commands (MAJCOM) are listed in alphabetically as headings in bold.
2. Within each Major Command are the relevant Groups, Wings, Units and Air

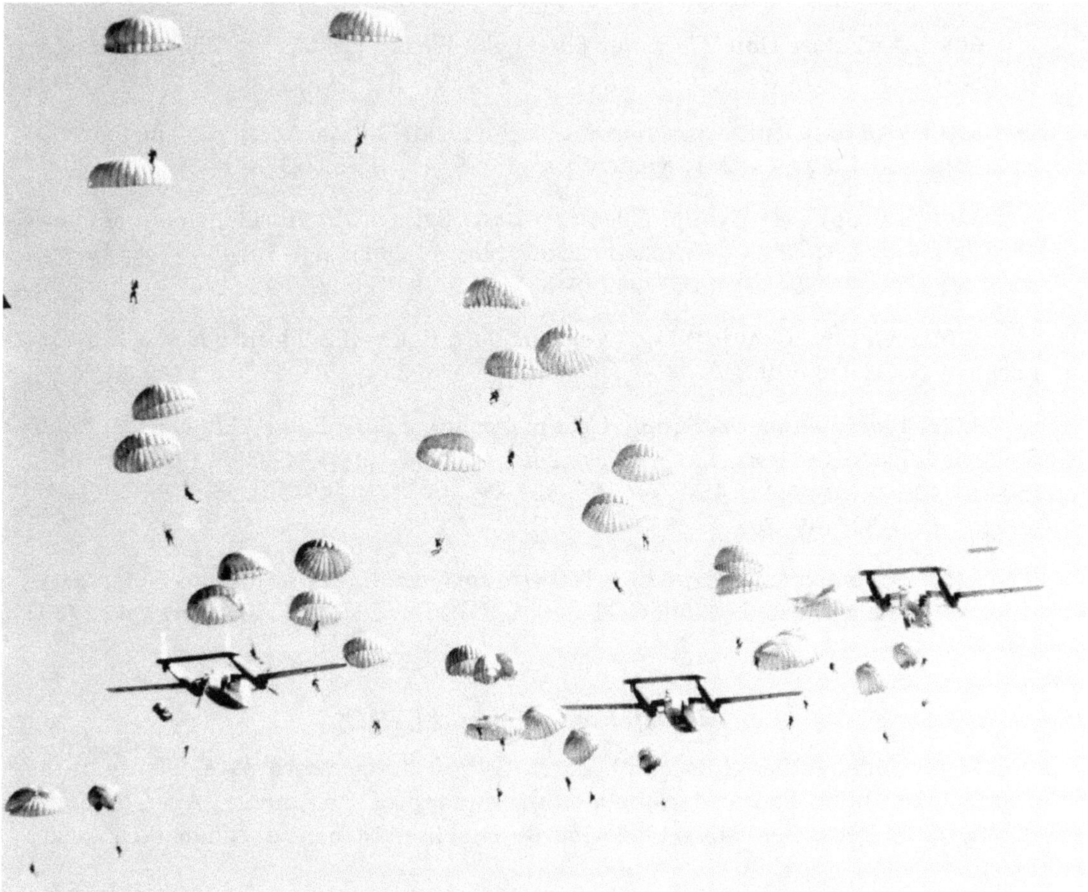

Top: Five C-82A Packets from the 4th TCSq/62nd TCG during an army exercise in December 1948 (Elton Schlimmer via Marvin Schlimmer). *Bottom:* A C-82 paratroop exercise with the United States Army (National Museum of the United States Air Force).

Base Groups that C-82 aircraft were assigned too. Squadrons have also been noted were applicable.
3. "Notes" are added, where relevant, describing unit histories, deployments and unit redesignations. Histories are only covered, in most cases, for the period the C-82 was in service with that particular unit.
4. C-82 serial numbers are listed with 2-digit year dates and relevant notes in brackets.

AAF Proving Ground Command (PGC)

Major command established for the testing of aircraft weapons systems. Named as such 8 March 1946. Renamed Air Proving Ground Command (APGC) 10 July 1946. Renamed Air Proving Ground (APG), losing major command status under the Air Materiel Command (AMC) 1 June 1948. Renamed Air Proving Ground Command (APGC) 20 December 1951.

605th AF Base Unit: *Operating Base:* Eglin AFB, Florida; *C-82 Assignments:* 44-23015 (47), 45-57743 (47).

609th AAF Base Unit: *Operating Base:* Eglin Field, Florida; *C-82 Assignments:* 44-23015 (47), 45-57743 (47).

611th AAF Base Unit: *Operating Base:* Eglin Field, Florida; *Notes:* Assigned for special projects and tests; *C-82 Assignments:* 44-23015 (47), 45-57743 (47).

3200th Proof Test Group: *Operating Base:* Eglin AFB, Florida; *Notes:* Some as EC-82A for tests.; *C-82 Assignments:* 44-23007 (48), 44-23055 (50–51), 45-57738 (48–49), 45-57746 (EC-82A 49–50), 45-57754 (49–50), 45-57795 (EC-82A 48–49).

3201st Air Base Group/Wing: *Operating Base:* Eglin AFB, Florida; *Notes:* Test support and associated duties; *C-82 Assignments:* 45-57802 (49–51), 45-57821 (49–51).

3203rd Maintenance & Supply Group: *Operating Base:* Eglin AFB, Florida; *Notes:* Some as EC-82A for tests; *C-82 Assignments:* 44-23007 (48), 44-23051 (49), 44-23055 (50–51), 45-57738 (48–49), 45-57746 (EC-82A 49), 45-57754 (49–50), 45-57795 (EC-82A 48–49), 45-57802 (49–50), 45-57821 (49–51).

3210th Chemical and Ordnance Test Group: *Operating Base:* Phillips Field, Maryland; *Notes:* Redesignated 6570th COT GP (ARD) 1 Dec 52; *C-82 Assignment:* 45-57802 (51–52).

Air Defense Command (ADC)

Major command established 21 March 1946 to oversee aerospace defense of the continental United States. Became a sub-command of Continental Air Command (CNC) from 1 December 1948 to 1 July 1950. Re-established as a major command 1 January 1951.

2nd Fighter-Interceptor Squadron: *Operating Base:* McGuire AFB, New Jersey; *Notes:* C-82s assigned as support aircraft. Assigned F-86 Sabres in 1954; *C-82 Assignments:* 44-23015 (54), 44-23057 (54).

4th Fighter-Interceptor Wing: *Operating Base:* Langley AFB, Virginia; *Notes:* C-82 assigned as support aircraft. Assigned F-86 Sabres. Wing reassigned to New Castle Airport, Delaware, 8 Sep 50; *C-82 Assignment:* 48-587 (50).

35th Air Division: *Operating Base:* Dobbins AFB, Georgia; *Notes:* Assigned for unit support duties; *C-82 Assignment:* 44-23015 (54–55).

56th Fighter-Interceptor Wing: *Operating Base:* Selfridge AFB, Michigan; *Notes:* C-82s assigned as support aircraft. Assigned F-86 Sabres in 1950; *C-82 Assignments:* 44-22986 (50), 45-57737 (50).

56th Maintenance & Supply Group: *Operating Base:* Selfridge AFB, Michigan; *Notes:* Associated to the 56th Fighter-Interceptor WG; *C-82 Assignment:* 44-22986 (50).

78th Fighter-Interceptor Wing: *Operating Base:* Hamilton AFB, California; *Notes:* Redesignated as such 20 Jan 50. Assigned F-51D Mustang, F-84 Thunderjet and F-89 Scorpion. Four C-82s as support aircraft; *C-82 Assignments:* 44-23025 (50), 44-23033 (50; 52), 45-57736 (51), 48-569 (50).

78th Maintenance & Supply Group: *Operating Base:* Hamilton AFB, California; *Notes:* Associated to the 78th Fighter-Interceptor GP; *C-82 Assignments:* 44-22979 (49), 44-22983 (49), 44-22990 (49).

81st Fighter-Interceptor Wing: *Operating Base:* Moses Lake AFB, Washington; (Renamed Larson AFB, WA, 2 May 50); *Notes:* C-82s assigned as support aircraft. Assigned F-86 Sabres in 1950; *C-82 Assignments:* 44-23016 (50), 44-23017 (50).

130th AAF Base Unit: *Operating Base:* Offutt Field, Nebraska; *C-82 Assignment:* 44-22964 (46).

131st AAF/AF Base Unit: *Operating Base:* Offutt Field, Nebraska; *C-82 Assignments:* 44-22964 (47), 45-57805 (48).

141st AF Base Unit: *Operating Base:* McChord AFB, Washington; *C-82 Assignment:* 44-23011 (48).

325th Fighter (All-Weather) Wing: *Operating Base:* McChord AFB, Washington; *Notes:* Eight C-82s assigned as support aircraft. Assigned F-82 Twin Mustang and F-94 Starfire fighters in 1950; *C-82 Assignments:* 44-23025 (50), 44-23038 (50), 44-23058 (50), 45-57738 (50), 45-57739 (50), 45-57776 (50), 45-57815 (50), 48-580 (50).

401st AAF Base Unit: *Operating Base:* Hamilton Field, California; *C-82 Assignment:* 44-22978 (46–47).

501st Air Defense Group: *Operating Base:* O'Hare Intl. Airport, Illinois; *Notes:* Six C-82s as support aircraft. Assigned F-86 Sabres 1953–1955; *C-82 Assignments:* 44-23001 (53–55), 44-23005 (53–55), 44-23006 (53–55), 44-23009 (54), 44-23015 (54), 45-57767 (53–55).

519th Air Defense Group: *Operating Base:* Suffolk AFB, Virginia; *Notes:* C-82s as support aircraft. Assigned F-86 Sabres in 1954; *C-82 Assignments:* 44-23009 (54), 44-23057 (54).

521st Air Defense Group: *Operating Base:* Sioux City MAP, Iowa; *Notes:* Seven C-82s as support aircraft. Assigned F-51D Mustang and F-86D Sabre fighters 1953–1955; *C-82 Assignments:* 44-23009 (54–55), 44-23015 (54), 44-23046 (54–55), 44-23057 (54–55), 45-57744 (53–54), 45-57777 (54–55), 45-57812 (53–55).

567th Air Defense Group: *Operating Base:* McChord AFB, Washington; *Notes:* Five C-82s as support aircraft. Assigned F-86D Sabre and F-94 Starfire fighters 1954–1955; *C-82 Assignments:* 44-23027 (54–55), 44-23033 (54–55), 45-57806 (54–55), 45-57811 (54–55), 48-569 (54).

568th Air Defense Group: *Operating Base:* McGuire AFB, New Jersey; *Notes:* C-82s as support aircraft. Assigned F-86D Sabres in 1954; *C-82 Assignments:* 44-23009 (54), 44-23057 (54).

2471st Air Repair Squadron: *Operating Base:* O'Hare Intl. Airport, Illinois; *C-82 Assignment:* 45-57824 (48).

4103rd AAF Base Unit: *Operating Base:* Jackson AAF, Mississippi; *C-82 Assignment:* 44-23018 (46–47).

4131st AAF Base Unit: *Operating Base:* Offutt Field, Nebraska; *C-82 Assignment:* 44-22964 (46–47).

4681st Air Base Squadron: *Operating Base:* Grenier AFB, New Hampshire; *C-82 Assignment:* 44-23023 (52).

4702nd Defense Wing: *Operating Base:* Hamilton AFB, California; *C-82 Assignment:* 44-23033 (52).

4708th Defense Wing: *Operating Base:* Selfridge AFB, Michigan; *C-82 Assignment:* 45-57737 (52).

4750th Training Group: *Operating Base:* Yuma AFB, Arizona; *C-82 Assignment:* 44-23001 (54).

Air Materiel Command (AMC)

Previously known as Air Technical Service Command (ATSC). Established 9 March 1946 incorporating R&D, procurement, supply and maintenance. The R&D section was separated 2 April 1950 as the Air Research and Development Command (ARDC).

8th AF Reserve Flying Training Squadron: *Operating Base:* Fairchild Aircraft, Maryland; *C-82 Assignment:* 44-23016 (47).

300th AF Base Unit: *Operating Bases:* San Diego, California; Fairchild Aircraft, Maryland, Farmingdale Air Field, New York; *Notes:* Forty-one aircraft assigned prior to delivery. Ferrying assignments; *C-82 Assignments:* 45-57782 (47), 45-57783 (47), 45-57784 (47), 45-57786 (47), 45-57787 (47), 45-57788 (47), 45-57789 (47), 45-57791 (47), 45-57792 (47), 45-57793 (47), 45-57794 (47), 45-57795 (47), 45-57796 (47), 45-57797 (48), 45-57798 (48), 45-57800 (48), 45-57802 (48), 45-57803 (48), 45-57804 (48), 45-57805 (48), 45-57806 (48), 45-57807 (48), 45-57808 (48), 45-57809 (48), 45-57810 (48), 45-57811 (48),

45-57812 (48), 45-57813 (48), 45-57814 (48), 45-57815 (48), 45-57816 (48), 45-57817 (48), 45-57818 (48), 45-57819 (48), 45-57820 (48), 45-57821 (48), 45-57823 (48), 45-57824 (48), 45-57825 (48), 45-57828 (48), 45-57829 (48).

414th Air Force Base Unit: *Operating Base:* Fairchild Aircraft, Maryland; *C-82 Assignment:* 45-57827 (48).

428th Base Complement Squadron: *Operating Base:* Kirtland Field, New Mexico; *C-82 Assignment:* 44-23018 (47).

2704th Aircraft Storage & Disposition Group: *Operating Base:* Davis-Monthan AFB, Arizona; *Notes:* Designated as such 1 Aug 59. Previously the Arizona Aircraft Storage Branch (AASB). The NASA C-82 was retired here in 1961. Commonly known as "The Boneyard"; *C-82 Assignment:* 44-23056 (ret 61).

2750th Air Base Group/Wing: *Operating Base:* Wright-Patterson AFB, Ohio; *Notes:* Fourteen aircraft assigned for experimental and test duties; *C-82 Assignments:* 44-22962 (EC-82A 48–51), 44-22981 (49), 44-23001 (52), 44-23004 (EC-82A 49–51), 44-23005 (54), 44-23014 (EC-82A 48–49), 44-23033 (50), 44-23034 (EC-82A 48–51), 45-57737 (51–52), 45-57746 (EC-82A 49–52), 45-57748 (49–50), 45-57757 (EC-82A 49–50), 45-57761 (49), 45-57795 (EC-82A 48–50).

2753rd Aircraft Storage Squadron: *Operating Base:* Pyote AFB, Texas; *Notes:* Aircraft w/o en route; *C-82 Assignment:* 45-57818 (53).

2845th Air Force Depot Wing: *Operating Base:* Griffiss AFB, New York; *C-82 Assignment:* 44-23001 (54).

3040th Aircraft Storage Squadron: *Operating Base:* Davis-Monthan AFB, Arizona; *Notes:* Designated as such 28 Aug 48. Became the Arizona Aircraft Storage Branch (AASB) in 1956. The last 14 USAF serving C-82s were retired here in 1955. Commonly known as "The Boneyard"; *C-82 Assignments:* 44-23001 (ret 55), 44-23005 (ret 55), 44-23006 (ret 55), 44-23009 (ret 55), 44-23015 (ret 55), 44-23027 (ret 55), 44-23033 (ret 55), 44-23046 (ret 55), 44-23057 (ret 55), 45-57767 (ret 55), 45-57777 (ret 55), 45-57806 (ret 55), 45-57811 (ret 55), 45-57812 (ret 55).

4000th AAF/AF Base Unit: *Operating Base:* Wright Field & Patterson Field, Ohio (Renamed Wright-Patterson AFB 13 Jan 48); *Notes:* Fifteen aircraft assigned for experimental and test duties; *C-82 Assignments:* 44-22962 (46–48), 44-22963 (47), 44-22973 (46), 44-22989 (47), 44-23000 (46), 44-23004 (47–49), 44-23008 (47), 44-23014 (46–48), 44-23034 (46–48), 44-23056 (47), 45-57742 (47–48), 45-57766 (47), 45-57785 (47), 45-57795 (48), 45-57820 (48).

4006th AAF Base Unit: *Operating Base:* Miami Airport, Florida; *C-82 Assignment:* 44-22995 (46).

4105th AAF/AF Base Unit: *Operating Base:* Davis-Monthan Field, Arizona; *Notes:* Designated as such 15 Nov 45. Redesignated as 3040th Aircraft Storage Depot 28 Aug 48. One C-82N was retired here in 1946. Commonly known as "The Boneyard"; *C-82 Assignment:* 45-25437 (ret 46–49).

4112nd AAF Base Unit: *Operating Base:* Olmsted Field, Pennsylvania; *C-82 Assignments:* 44-22964 (46), 44-22970 (46), 44-22977 (46–47).

4117th AAF/AF Base Unit: *Operating Base:* Robins Field/AFB, Georgia; *Notes:* In for depot maintenance; *C-82 Assignments:* 44-22973 (47), 44-23055 (48), 45-57796 (48).

4120th AAF Base Unit: *Operating Base:* Freeman Field, Indiana; *Notes:* C-82N ground instructional airframe; *C-82 Assignment:* 45-25437 (46).

4121st AF Base Unit: *Operating Base:* Kelly AFB, Texas; *C-82 Assignments:* 44-23018 (47–49), 45-57809 (48–49).

4127th AF Base Unit: *Operating Base:* McClellan AFB, California; *C-82 Assignments:* 44-22973 (47–48), 44-23000 (47–48), 44-23009 (47–48), 44-23025 (47–48), 45-57798 (48), 45-57826 (48).

4135th AF Base Unit: *Operating Base:* Hill AFB, Utah; *C-82 Assignment:* 45-57782 (48–49).

4136th AAF/AF Base Unit: *Operating Base:* Tinker Field/AFB, Oklahoma; *C-82 Assignments:* 44-22983 (46–47), 44-23039 (48), 45-57766 (47).

4140th AAF Base Unit: *Operating Base:* Patterson Field, Ohio; *C-82 Assignment:* 44-23000 (46).

4152nd AAF Base Unit: *Operating Base:* Clinton County Field, Ohio; *Notes:* Serving as part of the All Weather Flying Center (AWFC); *C-82 Assignments:* 44-22989 (47), 44-23008 (47).

Middletown Air Materiel Area: *Home Base:* Olmsted AFB, Pennsylvania; *Notes:* Air Force maintenance, overhaul, repair and modification center for aircraft and engines. Twenty-nine C-82s went in for depot maintenance 1949–1953; *C-82 Assignments:* 44-22968 (49), 44-22974 (49), 44-22977 (49), 44-22985 (49), 44-23009 (54), 44-23015 (51), 44-23021 (49), 44-23024 (49), 44-23027 (49), 44-23031 (49), 44-23033 (49), 44-23037 (49), 44-23038 (49), 44-23040 (51–52), 44-23043 (49), 44-23045 (49), 44-23046 (46), 44-23048 (53), 44-23053 (49), 44-23054 (49), 44-23056 (47), 45-57735 (49; 50), 45-57745 (51–52), 45-57793 (53), 45-57795 (52), 45-57796 (JC-82A 49), 45-57798 (49), 48-572 (49), 48-578 (53).

Mobile Air Materiel Area: *Home Base:* Brookley AFB, Alabama; *Notes:* Air Force maintenance, overhaul, repair and modification center. Eleven C-82s went in for transient maintenance 1949–1953; *C-82 Assignments:* 44-22963 (49), 44-23013 (50), 44-23029 (49–50), 44-23041 (51; 52), 44-23051 (50; 51), 45-57749 (50), 45-57783 (49), 45-57789 (49), 45-57809 (49), 45-57819 (52–53), 45-57821 (51–52).

Northern Air Materiel Area: *Home Base:* Inglewood, California; *Notes:* Air Force maintenance, overhaul, repair and modification center. One C-82 in for transient maintenance 1954; *C-82 Assignment:* 45-57767 (54).

Ogden Air Materiel Area: *Home Base:* Hill AFB, Utah; *Notes:* Major Air Force maintenance, overhaul, repair and modification center for aircraft and engines. Forty-six C-82s went through for various maintenance requirements with 39 of these for retirement (ret) and storage; *C-82 Assignments:* 44-22962 (ret 54), 44-22981 (ret 53–54), 44-22992 (49), 44-23000 (49), 44-23004 (53; ret 54), 44-23011 (51; ret 53–54), 44-23018 (ret 53–54), 44-23019 (training 50; ret 51–54), 44-23023 (ret 53–54), 44-23026 (ret 53–54), 44-23029 (ret 53–54), 44-23030 (ret 53–54), 44-23031 (ret 54), 44-23041 (ret 53–54), 44-23046 (54), 44-23047 (ret 53–54), 44-23055 (ret 53–54), 44-23058 (ret 53–54), 45-57733 (ret 53–54), 45-57734 (ret 54–55), 45-57736 (51; ret 53–54), 45-57737 (ret 53–54), 45-57746 (50–51; ret 52–54), 45-57747 (project 50–52), 45-57748 (ret 50–54), 45-57749 (ret 54–55), 45-57750 (ret 50–54), 45-57751 (ret 50–54), 45-57753 (ret 50–54), 45-57754 (ret 50–54), 45-57757 (ret 50–54), 45-57758 (49; 50–52), 45-57759 (ret 50–54), 45-57763 (50; ret 54), 45-57777 (54), 45-57780 (ret 54), 45-57782 (49), 45-57802 (51; ret 54–55), 45-57819 (ret 53–54), 45-57827 (ret 53–54), 45-57828 (ret 54–55), 45-57829 (ret 53–54), 45-57830 (52; ret 53–54), 45-57832 (ret 53–54), 48-568 (ret 53–54), 48-575 (ret 53–54).

Oklahoma Air Materiel Area: *Home Base:* Tinker AFB, Oklahoma; *Notes:* Air Force maintenance, overhaul, repair and modification center. Nineteen C-82s went in for maintenance 1949–1954; *C-82 Assignments:* 44-22969 (49), 44-22984 (49), 44-23001 (54), 44-23005 (50; 54), 44-23007 (53), 44-23026 (51; 53), 44-23027 (54), 44-23031 (53–54), 44-23033 (54), 44-23046 (54), 44-23055 (associated to Boeing Wichita Kansas 52–53), 44-23057 19(54), 45-57749 (53), 45-57767 (54), 45-57793 (50), 45-57806 (55), 45-57811 (55), 45-57812 (53; 54; 55), 48-586 (53).

Sacramento Air Materiel Area: *Home Base:* McClellan AFB, California; *Notes:* Air Force maintenance, overhaul, repair and modification center for aircraft and engines. Seventeen C-82s in for transient and depot maintenance; *C-82 Assignments:* 44-22977 (49), 44-23030 (50), 44-23033 (51), 44-23037 (49), 44-23038 (49–50; 50–51), 44-23041 (50), 45-57733 (50), 45-57736 (50), 45-57744 (49), 45-57772 (49), 45-57776 (49), 45-57777 (49), 45-57778 (49), 45-57815 (50), 45-57816 (49), 45-57828 (49), 48-578 (50).

San Antonio Air Materiel Center/Area: *Home Base:* Kelly AFB, Texas; *Notes:* Major Air Force maintenance, overhaul, repair and modification center for aircraft and engines. One hundred and four C-82s went through for various maintenance requirements with 75 of these for retirement (ret) and storage; *C-82 Assignments:* 44-22967 (49), 44-22973 (49), 44-22984 (49), 44-22992 (49), 44-23005 (49), 44-23007 (ret 53–54), 44-23008 (ret 53–54), 44-23012 (ret 53–54), 44-23013 (ret 53–54), 44-23015 (52; 53), 44-23017 (ret 53–54), 44-23018 (49), 44-23025 (ret 53–54), 44-23030 (52), 44-23032 (ret 53–54), 44-23034 (ret 53–54), 44-23037 (ret 53–54), 44-23038 (ret 53–54), 44-23039 (ret 53–54), 44-23040 (52; ret 53–54), 44-23041 (50), 44-23043 (ret 53–54), 44-23045 (ret 53–54), 44-23048 (ret 53–54), 44-23049 (ret 53–54), 44-23050 (ret 53–54), 44-23051 (ret 53–54), 44-23052 (51; ret 53–54), 44-23053 (ret 53–54), 44-23054 (ret 53–54), 44-23055 (51–52), 44-23057 (50), 44-23058 (50–51), 45-57733 (52–53), 45-57734 (50), 45-57735 (ret 53–54), 45-57737 (50), 45-57739 (50), 45-57740 (ret 53–54), 45-57741 (ret 53–54), 45-57744 (53), 45-57745 (ret 53–54), 45-57747 (ret 53–54), 45-57755 (ret 53–54), 45-57756 (ret 53–54), 45-57758 (ret 53–54), 45-57762 (ret 53–54), 45-57764 (ret 53–54), 45-57765 (ret 53–54), 45-57766 (53; ret 53–54), 45-57767 (53), 45-57768 (53), 45-57770 (ret 53–54), 45-57771 (ret 53–54), 45-57773 (ret 53–54), 45-57774 (ret 53–54), 45-57775 (ret 53–54), 45-57776 (ret 53–54), 45-57777 (53), 45-57778 (ret 53–54), 45-57780 (53), 45-57782 (ret 53–54), 45-57783 (ret 53–54), 45-57784 (ret 53–54), 45-57786 (ret 53–54), 45-57787 (ret 53–54), 45-57788 (ret 53–54), 45-57789 (ret 53–54), 45-57790 (ret 53–54), 45-57792 (ret 53–54), 45-57793 (ret

53–54), 45-57794 (ret 53–54), 45-57795 (ret 53–54), 45-57800 (ret 53–54), 45-57803 (ret 53–54), 45-57804 (ret 53–54), 45-57806 (53), 45-57807 (ret 53–54), 45-57808 (ret 53–54), 45-57809 (49), 45-57810 (ret 53–54), 45-57811 (53), 45-57812 (53), 45-57814 (ret 53–54), 45-57815 (ret 53–54), 45-57817 (ret 53–54), 45-57822 (ret 53–54), 45-57824 (ret 53–54), 45-57825 (ret 53–54), 45-57828 (51), 45-57829 (stored 53), 48-569 (51), 48-571 (ret 53–54), 48-573 (ret 53–54), 48-574 (51; 52; 53), 48-576 (ret 53–54), 48-577 (ret 53–54), 48-578 (ret 53–54), 48-580 (ret 53–54), 48-583 (ret 53–54), 48-584 (ret 53–54), 48-585 (ret 53–54), 48-586 (ret 53–54), 48-587 (ret 53–54).

San Bernardino Air Depot: *Home Base:* Norton AFB, California; *Notes:* Renamed Aircraft Repair Depot in 1951. Air force maintenance, overhaul, repair and modification center. Eight C-82s in for maintenance; *C-82 Assignments:* 44-22967 (49), 44-23057 (54), 45-57734 (54), 45-57749 (48), 45-57806 (54), 45-57827 (51), 45-57831 (49), 48-577 (49).

Warner-Robins Air Materiel Area: *Home Base:* Robins AFB, Georgia; *Notes:* Major Air Force maintenance, overhaul, repair and modification center for aircraft and engines. Seventy-three C-82s went through for either transient or depot maintenance; *C-82 Assignments:* 44-22963 (49–50), 44-22966 (49–50), 44-22970 (49), 44-22975 (49), 44-22980 (49), 44-22981 (49), 44-22987 (49), 44-22989 (49), 44-22990 (50), 44-22992 (49), 44-22993 (49), 44-22996 (48–49), 44-23001 (52–53), 44-23005 (stored 52–53), 44-23006 (stored 52–53), 44-23007 (51), 44-23008 (49; 51), 44-23009 (stored 52–54), 44-23011 (49–1950), 44-23012 (51), 44-23013 (49; 51), 44-23015 (49), 44-23016 (49), 44-23018 (51), 44-23023 (51), 44-23025 (51–52), 44-23026 (49), 44-23030 (48–49), 44-23031 (51), 44-23032 (49–50; 51), 44-23034 (51; 53), 44-23037 (51), 44-23039 (51), 44-23040 (49), 44-23043 (49–50; 51; 53), 44-23045 (51), 44-23046 (51), 44-23047 (51), 44-23048 (49; 51), 44-23050 (50; 52), 44-23051 (49; 52), 44-23052 (51–52), 44-23053 (51), 44-23054 (51), 44-23055 (51), 45-57735 (50), 45-57737 (51), 45-57738 (51), 45-57749 (51), 45-57772 (50), 45-57786 (49), 45-57788 (51), 45-57795 (51), 45-57803 (49), 45-57805 (50–51), 45-57815 (51), 45-57822 (51), 45-57824 (49), 48-568 (50), 48-569 (51–52), 48-571 (51), 48-573 (51–52), 48-574 (51), 48-576 (51–52), 48-577 (51), 48-578 (51), 48-580 (51), 48-581 (51), 48-583 (51), 48-584 (51–52), 48-585 (51–52), 48-586 (51), 48-587 (51–52).

Air Research and Development Command (ARD)

Started as Research and Development Command on 23 January 1950 under AMC. Established as a separate major command 2 April 1950. Redesignated as such on 16 September 1950. Devoted to R&D of new weapons systems.

4901st Support/Air Base Wing: *Operating Base:* Kirtland AFB, New Mexico; *C-82 Assignments:* 44-23046 (54), 45-57777 (55).

6502nd Parachute Development Test Group: *Operating Base:* El Centro NAS, California; *Notes:* EC-82A for test duties; *C-82 Assignment:* 44-22962 (52).

6520th Test Support Squadron: *Operating Base:* (Laurence G.) Hanscom AFB, Massachusetts; *Notes:* Became 6520th Test Support WG Dec 52. All three were EC-82A; *C-82 Assignments:* 44-23004 (53–54), 45-57749 (52–54), 45-57802 (54).

Air Research and Development HQ: *Operating Base:* WPAFB, Ohio; *Notes:* Renamed Wright Air Development Center 22 Jun 51; *C-82 Assignments:* 44-22962 (EC-82A 51–52), 44-23004 (EC-82A 51–52), 45-57815 (52).

Armament Test Headquarters: *Operating Base:* Eglin AFB, Florida; *Notes:* Renamed Air Force Armament Test Center 1 Feb 53; *C-82 Assignments:* 44-23004 (EC-82A 52–53), 45-57802 (52–54).

Rome Air Development Center: *Operating Base:* Griffiss AFB, New York; *Notes:* Air Force maintenance, overhaul, repair and modification center. One C-82 in for transient maintenance in 1952. Also an air force research center; *C-82 Assignment:* 45-57814 (52).

Air Technical Service Command (ATSC)

Established to oversee supply and maintenance duties. Named as such 1 July 1945. Renamed as Air Materiel Command (AMC) 9 March 1946.

4000th AAF Base Unit: *Operating Base:* Wright Field & Patterson Field, Ohio; *Notes:* Continued as the 4000th under Air Materiel Command (AMC); *C-82 Assignments:* 44-22959 (46), 44-22960 (45-47), 44-22961 (46–47), 44-22963 (46), 45-25436 (C-82N 45-46).

4121st AAF Base Unit: *Operating Base:* San Antonio Air Materiel Center, Kelly Field, Texas (Renamed Kelly AFB Jan 48); *Notes:* Continued as the 4121st under Air Materiel Command (AMC); *C-82 Assignment:* 45-25438 (C-82N 45-46).

4152nd AAF Base Unit: *Operating Base:* Lockbourne & Clinton County Field, Ohio; *Notes:* Continued as the 4152nd under Air Materiel Command (AMC). Serving as part of the All Weather Flying Center (AWFC); *C-82 Assignment:* 44-22968 (46–47).

4806th AAF Base Unit: *Operating Base:* Fairchild Aircraft, Maryland; *C-82 Assignment:* 44-22959 (45).

4862nd AAF Base Unit: *Operating Base:* Fairchild Aircraft, Maryland; *C-82 Assignment:* 44-22959 (45-46).

Aircraft Production Division: *Operating Base:* Dayton Field, Ohio; *C-82 Assignment:* 44-22961 (45-46).

Air Training Command (TC)

Major command established 1 July 1946 to oversee Air Force training duties.

415th Technical Training Wing: *Operating Base:* Lowry AFB, Colorado; *C-82 Assignment:* 45-57733 (51).

2002nd AAF Base Unit: *Operating Base:* Stewart Field, New York; *Notes:* Pilot training; *C-82 Assignment:* 44-22980 (46).

2621st AF Base Unit: *Operating Base:* Barksdale AFB, Louisiana; *C-82 Assignments:* 45-57745 (48), 45-57827 (48).

3010th AF Base Unit: *Operating Base:* Williams AFB, Arizona; *C-82 Assignment:* 44-23030 (48).

3320th Technical Training Wing: *Operating Base:* Amarillo AFB, Texas; *C-82 Assignments:* 44-23046 (54), 45-57777 (54), 45-57812 (53).

3345th Technical Training Wing: *Operating Base:* Chanute AFB, Illinois; *C-82 Assignments:* 45-57767 (54), 45-57769 (XC-119A 51).

3380th Technical Training Wing: *Operating Base:* Keesler AFB, Mississippi; *Notes:* Some in for ground instructional duties; *C-82 Assignments:* 44-23044 (48–49), 45-25438 (ZC-82N 48–49), 45-57741 (53), 45-57797 (48–49).

3415th Technical Training Wing: *Operating Base:* Lowry AFB, Colorado; *C-82 Assignments:* 44-22984 (49–50), 44-23027 (54).

3500th Pilot Training Wing: *Operating Base:* Reese AFB, Texas; *C-82 Assignment:* 44-23026 (53).

3525th Pilot Training Wing: *Operating Base:* Williams AFB, Arizona; *C-82 Assignments:* 44-23004 (52), 44-23015 (51).

3605th Navigator Training Wing: *Operating Base:* Ellington AFB, Texas; *C-82 Assignments:* 44-23015 (52), 45-57733 (52).

3605th Observer Training Wing: *Operating Base:* Ellington AFB, Texas; *C-82 Assignment:* 45-57733 (52).

3704th AAF Base Unit: *Operating Base:* Keesler Field, Mississippi; *Notes:* Training and technical unit. C-82N used for ground instruction; *C-82 Assignments:* 44-22967 (46–48), 44-23044 (47–48), 45-25438 (ZC-82N 46–48).

3750th Technical Training Wing: *Operating Base:* Sheppard AFB, Texas; *Notes:* C-82N used for ground instructionl *C-82 Assignment:* 45-25438 (ZC-82N 49–51).

Air Transport Command (ATC)

Established 20 June 1942 for the deployment and transport of cargo, supplies and personnel to the war zone. Renamed as the Military Air Transport Service (MATS) 1 June 1948 with the Air Rescue Service also being reassigned to MATS. Unless otherwise noted all Air Rescue Service assignments are SC-82A conversions.

62nd AAF Base Unit: *Operating Bases:* Westover Field, Massachusetts; McChord Field, Washington; *C-82 Assignments:* 44-22966 (47), 44-22978 (47–48), 44-23011 (47–48), 44-23019 (46–47).

503rd AAF Base Unit: *Operating Base:* Gravelly Point Field, Washington, D.C.; *C-82 Assignment:* 44-22977 (46).

520th Air Transport Squadron: *Operating Base:* Westover AFB, Massachusetts; *C-82 Assignment:* 45-57783 (48).

550th AAF Base Unit (HQ Ferrying Division); *Operating Base:* Cincinnati, Ohio; *C-82 Assignment:* 44-22977 (46).

554th AAF Base Unit (4th Ferrying Group): *Operating Base:* Memphis, Tennessee; *Notes:* Thirty assigned for ferrying duties; *C-82 Assignments:* 44-22969 (46), 44-22970 (46), 44-22972 (46), 44-22973 (46), 44-22974 (46), 44-22976 (46), 44-22978 (46), 44-22979 (46), 44-22980 (46), 44-22981 (46), 44-22982 (46), 44-22983 (46), 44-22984 (46), 44-22985 (46), 44-22986 (46), 44-22987 (46), 44-22988 (46), 44-22990 (46), 44-22991

(46), 44-22992 (46), 44-22994 (46), 44-22995 (46), 44-22996 (46), 44-22997 (46), 44-22999 (46), 44-23001 (46), 44-23002 (46), 44-23003 (46), 44-23005 (46), 44-23006 (46).

555th AAF Base Unit (5th Ferrying Group): *Operating Base:* Dallas, Texas; *C-82 Assignments:* 44-22965 (46), 44-22973 (46).

1100th AF Base Unit: *Operating Base:* McClellan AFB, California; *C-82 Assignments:* 44-22977 (47–48), 44-22981 (47–48), 44-22996 (47–48), 44-22997 (47–48).

1103rd AAF Base Unit: *Operating Base:* Morrison Field, Florida; *C-82 Assignment:* 44-22966 (46–47).

1377th AAF/AF Base Unit: *Operating Base:* Westover Field/AFB, Massachusetts; *C-82 Assignments:* 44-23034 (47), 45-57739 (47), 45-57783 (48), 45-57811 (48).

1383rd AF Base Unit: *Operating Base:* Goose Bay, Labrador, Canada; *C-82 Assignment:* 45-57811 (48).

1455th AAF/AF Base Unit: *Operating Base:* East Base Field, Montana; *Notes:* Base became a part of the adjacent Great Falls AFB, Montana 26 January 1948. To MATS redesignated as 517th Air Transport WG 1 June 1948. Unit also stationed at Fort Nelson, Canada; *C-82 Assignments:* 44-23027 (47–48), 45-57767 (48), 45-57782 (48), 45-47809 (48), 45-57810 (48).

1504th AAF Base Unit: *Operating Base:* Fairfield-Suisun Field, California; *C-82 Assignment:* 45-57738 (47).

3520th Combat Crew Training Wing: *Operating Base:* Wichita AFB, Kansas; *C-82 Assignment:* 45-57832 (51).

Cincinnati Ferrying Division: *Operating Base:* Cincinnati, Ohio; *Notes:* Twelve assigned to be ferried to AAF assignments; *C-82 Assignments:* 44-22965 (46), 44-22966 (46), 44-22967 (46), 44-22969 (46), 44-22970 (46), 44-22971 (46), 44-22972 (46), 44-22974 (46), 44-22976 (46), 44-22977 (46), 44-22978 (46), 44-22979 (46).

Air Rescue Service (ARS)
5TH AIR RESCUE SQUADRON—Operating Bases: Westover Field, Massachusetts; MacDill Field, Florida; *Notes:* Squadron later reassigned to MATS; *C-82 Assignments:* 44-22966 (47–48), 44-22963 (47–48), 44-22971 (47–48), 44-23011 (47–48).

8TH AIR RESCUE SQUADRON—Operating Bases: Hamilton AFB, California; McChord AFB, Washington; *C-82 Assignments:* 44-22978 (48), 44-23011 (48), 44-23019 (48).

9TH AIR RESCUE SQUADRON—*Operating Base:* Selfridge AFB, Michigan; *Notes:* Squadron later reassigned to MATS; *C-82 Assignment:* 44-22971 (48).

Air University (AU)

Established as a major command 29 November 1945. Named as such 12 March 1946 for educational, research and training duties.

3800th Air University Wing: *Operating Base:* Maxwell AFB, Alabama; *Notes:* Transient maintenance only; *C-82 Assignments:* 44-23050 (51), 45-57811 (48–49), 48-573 (50).

Alaskan Air Command (AAC)

Major command established 18 December 1945 to oversee the air defense systems in Alaska. Also supported SAC operations. Previously a numbered air force as the 11th Air Force.

1st Rescue Squadron: *Operating Base:* Fort Richardson, Alaska; *Notes:* Assigned as SC-82A conversions; *C-82 Assignments:* 45-57830 (48), 45-57831 (48).

10th Rescue Squadron: *Operating Base:* Elmendorf AFB, Alaska; *Notes:* Assigned as SC-82A conversions; *C-82 Assignments:* 45-57830 (48), 45-57831 (48–49).

39th Air Depot Wing: *Operating Base:* Elmendorf AFB, Alaska; *Notes:* Founded as 39th Air Depot GP 5 Jan 42. Renamed as a wing 28 Nov 50. De-activated 13 Apr 53; *C-82 Assignments:* 45-57763 (52–53), 45-57830 (50; 52), 48-574 (53), 48-581 (51–53).

54th Troop Carrier Squadron: *Operating Base:* Elmendorf AFB, Alaska; *Notes:* Attached to the 57th Fighter WG 1949–1951. Attached to the 5039th Air Transport GP 1951–1956; *C-82 Assignments:* 45-57763 (51–52), 45-57830 (48–49; 50–52), 48-574 (51–53), 48-577 (50), 48-580 (50), 48-581 (51–52).

57th Air Base Group: *Operating Base:* Elmendorf AFB, Alaska; *Notes:* Associated to the 57th Fighter WG; *C-82 Assignments:* 45-57830 (49–50), 45-57831 (49–50).

57th Fighter Wing: *Operating Base:* Elmendorf AFB, Alaska; *Notes:* Renamed 57th Fighter-Interceptor WG Sep 50. 4th; 7th; 8th; 37th and 54th TCSq Attached; *C-82 Assignments:* 45-57739 (50), 45-57830 (50), 45-57831 (50).

57th Maintenance & Supply Group: *Operating Base:* Elmendorf AFB, Alaska; *Notes:* Associated to the 57th Fighter WG; *C-82 Assignments:* 45-57765 (49), 45-57770 (48), 45-57772 (49), 45-57779 (48–49), 45-57813 (48–49), 45-57830 (49), 48-580 (49).

5020th Air Base Group: *Operating Base:* Davis AFB, Alaska; *C-82 Assignment:* 45-57767 (49).

5025th Maintenance Group: *Operating Base:* Elmendorf AFB, Alaska; *Notes:* Renamed from 5039th MNT GP 1 Jul 53. Deactivated 1 Jan 55; *C-82 Assignments:* 45-57763 (53–54), 48-574 (53–54), 48-581 (53).

5039th Maintenance Group: *Operating Base:* Elmendorf AFB, Alaska; *Notes:* Activated 13 Apr 53. Renamed 5025th MNT GP 1 Jul 53; *C-82 Assignments:* 45-57763 (53), 48-574 (53, ret 55), 48-581 (53).

5039th Air Base Wing: *Operating Base:* Elmendorf AFB, Alaska; *Notes:* Activated 13 Apr 53. Deactivated 1 Jun 57; *C-82 Assignments:* 48-574 (53–55), 48-581 (53–55).

5039th Aircraft Repair Squadron: *Operating Base:* Elmendorf AFB, Alaska; *Notes:* Activated 13 Apr 53. Renamed 5025th Aircraft Repair SQ 1 Jul 53, then back to 5039th 1 Jan 55. Renamed 5039th Field MNT SQ 1 Apr 56. Last USAF unit to operate the C-82; *C-82 Assignments:* 48-574 (ret 55), 48-581 (ret 55).

5039th Air Depot Wing: *Operating Base:* Elmendorf AFB, Alaska; *C-82 Assignment:* 48-580 (49–50).

5039th Air Transport Wing: *Operating Base:* Elmendorf AFB, Alaska; *Notes:* 54th TCSq attached; *C-82 Assignment:* 48-581 (53).

5064th Cold Weather Materiel Testing Unit: *Operating Base:* Ladd AFB, Alaska; *Notes:* Testing of tracked u/c in snow conditions; *C-82 Assignment:* 45-57757 (EC-82A 50).

Aircraft Maintenance: *Operating Base:* Ladd AFB, Alaska; *Notes:* Damaged beyond repair; *C-82 Assignment:* 45-57813 (48).

Alaska Air Lines Air Depot: *Operating Base:* Elmendorf AFB, Alaska; *Notes:* In for depot maintenance and repairs; *C-82 Assignments:* 45-57765 (49), 45-57772 (49), 48-580 (49).

Continental Air Command (CNC)

Established as a major command 1 December 1948 assuming control of the TAC and ADC up to 1 December 1950. Also administered the Air National Guard and Air Force Reserve. The units listed below are ones assigned C-82 aircraft after its establishment.

33rd Fighter-Interceptor Wing: *Operating Base:* Otis AFB, Massachusetts; *Notes:* Activated 1 Sep 49 flying F-84 Thunderjets and F-86 Sabres. One C-82 assigned as support aircraft. Wing later assigned to Tactical Air Command (TAC); *C-82 Assignment:* 48-586 (50).

2270th Air Base Squadron: *Operating Base:* New Castle Airport, Delaware; *C-82 Assignment:* 44-230340 (50).

2500th Air Base Wing: *Operating Base:* Mitchel AFB, New York; *C-82 Assignment:* 45-57811 (54–55).

4652th Air Base Squadron: *Operating Base:* New Castle Airport, Delaware; *C-82 Assignment:* 44-230340 (50–51).

Continental Air Forces (CAF)

Activated 12 December 1944 as a World War II major command consisting of the 1st, 2nd, 3rd and 4th Air Forces. Deactivated 21 March 1946 with components then reorganized into the Air Defense Command (ADC) and Strategic Air Command (SAC).

1st Air Force: *Operating Base:* Bolling Field, District of Columbia; *Notes:* Numbered air force assigned under CAF in 1944. Reorganized into the Air Defense Command (ADC) in 1946; *C-82 Assignment:* 45-25437 (C-82N 45-46).

9th TCSq (374th TCG): *Operating Base:* Greenville Field, South Carolina; *C-82 Assignment:* 44-22965 (46).

804th AAF Base Unit: *Operating Base:* Greenville Field, South Carolina; *C-82 Assignments:* 44-22965 (46), 44-22969 (46), 44-22970 (46).

HQ Support Squadron: *Operating Base:* Stout Field, Indiana; *C-82 Assignment:* 44-22965 (46).

Headquarters Command (HQC)

Established 15 December 1946 as Bolling Field Command for support of operations in the Washington, D.C., area. Redesignated as such 17 March 1948 and not deactivated until 1 July 1976.

1050th Maintenance & Supply Group: *Operating Base:* Andrews AFB, Maryland; *Notes:* Associated to the 1050th Air Base Wing; *C-82 Assignment:* 45-57774 (49).

1100th Air Base Wing: *Operating Base:* Bolling AFB, District of Columbia; *Notes:* Activated 16 Mar 49; *C-82 Assignment:* 44-23030 (52).

1100th Maintenance & Supply Group: *Operating Base:* Bolling AFB, District of Columbia; *Notes:* Associated to the 1100th AB WG; *C-82 Assignment:* 44-22991 (49).

Military Air Transport Service (MATS)

Previously known as Air Transport Command (ATC). Established 1 June 1948, also incorporating the Air Rescue Service (ARS) and Air Resupply & Communications Service (ARCS). MATS was further organized into the Military Air Transport Service, Continental Division (MTC) and Military Air Transport Service, Overseas Division (MTO). Apart from freight logistics, MATS also provided other services such as weather, photographic and aeromedical duties. Unless otherwise noted, all Air Rescue Service assignments are SC-82A conversions.

3rd Air Materiel (Overseas) Squadron: *Operating Base:* Tinker AFB, Oklahoma; *C-82 Assignments:* 44-23057 (53–54), 45-57832 (53).

80th Air Base Group: *Operating Base:* Dover AFB, Mississippi; *C-82 Assignment:* 45-57741 (53).

517th Air Base Group: *Operating Base:* Fort Nelson, Canada; *Notes:* Associated to the 517th Air Transport WG. Redesignated 1701st Air Transport WG 1 Oct 48. Home base is Great Falls AFB, Montana. Used in training pilots for the Berlin Airlift; *C-82 Assignment:* 45-57810 (48).

517th Maintenance & Supply Group: *Operating Base:* Great Falls AFB, Montana; *Notes:* Associated to the 517th Air Transport WG; *C-82 Assignment:* 45-57818 (48).

611th Aircraft Maintenance Squadron: *Operating Base:* McGuire AFB, New Jersey; *C-82 Assignment:* 44-23009 (54).

1225th Air Base Group: *Operating Base:* Pepperell AFB, Newfoundland, Canada; *C-82 Assignment:* 45-57798 (49–50).

1226th Air Base Group: *Operating Base:* Ernest Harmon AFB, Newfoundland, Canada; *Notes:* Reassigned to Northeast Air Command (NEAC) Oct 50; *C-82 Assignments:* 45-57735 (50), 45-57776 (50), 45-57798 (50), 45-57814 (49–50), 45-57819 (50), 45-57824 (50).

1227th Air Base Group: *Operating Base:* Goose Bay AB, Labrador, Canada; *C-82 Assignments:* 44-23031 (50), 45-57735 (49–50), 45-57798 (49), 45-57805 (49–50), 45-57822 (50), 48-572 (49).

1300th Air Base Wing: *Operating Base:* Mountain Home AFB, Idaho; *C-82 Assignment:* 44-23057 (52).

1400th Air Base Squadron: *Operating Base:* Keflavik Airport, Iceland; *Notes:* W/o, scrapped in Iceland; *C-82 Assignment:* 45-57818 (53–54).

1600th Air Transport Wing: *Operating Base:* Westover AFB, Massachusetts; *C-82 Assignments:* 44-23031 (50), 44-23036 (50).

1600th Maintenance & Supply Group: *Operating Base:* Westover AFB, Massachusetts; *C-82 Assignments:* 44-22963 (49), 45-57735 (49), 45-57824 (50).

1603rd Air Base Group: *Operating Base:* Wheelus AFB, Libya; *C-82 Assignments:* 45-57809 (51), 45-57810 (50), 45-57811 (51).

1603rd Maintenance & Supply Group: *Operating Base:* Wheelus AFB, Libya; *C-82 Assignment:* 45-57811 (51).

1631st Air Base Squadron: *Operating Base:* RAF Prestwick, England; *C-82 Assignments:* 44-23029 (53), 45-57768 (53–54).

1700th Air Transport Group: *Operating Base:* Kelly AFB, Texas; *C-82 Assignments:* 44-22967 (49–50), 44-22971 (49–50), 44-22978 (49), 45-57819 (49).

1701st Air Base Group: *Operating Base:* Great Falls AFB, Montana; *Notes:* Associated to the 1701st Air Transport GP/WG; *C-82 Assignments:* 45-57793 (49–50), 45-57819 (49–50).

1701st Air Transport Group/Wing: *Operating Base:* Great Falls AFB, Montana; *Notes:* Redesignated 1 Oct 48. Previously 517th Air Transport WG; *C-82 Assignments:* 44-23045 (50), 45-57793 (49–51), 45-57819 (49–50), 48-568 (49–50).

1701st Maintenance & Supply Group: *Operating Base:* Great Falls AFB, Montana; *Notes:* Associated to the 1701st Air Transport GP/WG; *C-82 Assignment:* 45-57812 (48–49).

1707th Training Squadron: *Operating Base:* Palm Beach Intl. Airport, Florida; *C-82 Assignments:* 45-57734 (53), 45-57736 (52), 45-57827 (52).

1739th Ferrying Squadron: *Operating Base:* Amarillo AFB, Texas; *C-82 Assignment:* 45-57744 (53–54).

2156th Technical Training Unit: *Operating Base:* MacDill AFB, Florida; *C-82 Assignment:* 45-57827 (50–51).

6501st Support Squadron: *Operating Base:* Wichita AFB, Kansas; *C-82 Assignment:* 45-57832 (51).

Air Rescue Service (ARS)

1st Air Rescue Squadron—*Operating Bases:* MacDill AFB, Florida, Albrook AFB, Panama Canal Zone, Ramey AFB, Puerto Rico: *C-82 Assignments:* 44-22966 (49), 44-22982 (49–50), 44-23041 (50–53), 44-23058 (50–52), 45-57734 (50–51), 45-57827 (52–53).

4th Air Rescue Squadron—*Operating Bases:* Hamilton AFB, California, March AFB, California, Lowry AFB, Colorado, McChord AFB, Washington; *Notes:* Ten SC-82A conversions assigned to B Flight; *C-82 Assignments:* 44-22972 (49–50), 44-22979 (49–50), 44-22983 (49–50), 44-22990 (49–50), 44-23019 (49–51), 44-23033 (50–53), 44-23057 (51–52), 45-57736 (50–51; 52), 45-57799 (unk-52), 45-57828 (50–52).

5TH AIR RESCUE SQUADRON—*Operating Bases:* MacDill AFB, Florida, Biggs AFB, Texas, Ellington AFB, Texas, Westover AFB, Massachusetts, Maxwell AFB, Alabama, Selfridge AFB, Michigan; *Notes:* Thirteen SC-82A conversions assigned to D Flight; *C-82 Assignments:* 44-22963 (48–49), 44-22966 (48–49), 44-22973 (49–50), 44-22976 (49–50), 44-22982 (49), 44-22984 (49–50), 44-22986 (49–50), 44-23015 (50; 52), 44-23021 (50), 44-23030 (50–52), 44-23036 (51–52), 45-57733 (50–52), 45-57737 (50–52).

6TH AIR RESCUE SQUADRON—*Operating Bases:* Westover AFB, Massachusetts, Goose Bay AB, Labrador, Canada, Ernest Harmon AFB, Newfoundland, Canada; *C-82 Assignments:* 44-22963 (49), 44-23011 (49–53), 44-23036 (50–51), 44-23057 (50–51), 48-574 (49–52).

7TH AIR RESCUE SQUADRON—*Operating Bases:* Wiesbaden AB, West Germany, Wheelus AFB, Libya; *Notes:* Three SC-82A conversions, s/n: 45-57762 assigned but not cvtd; *C-82 Assignments:* 44-23027 (50–52), 45-57762 (50), 45-57829 (50–51), 48-568 (50–51).

9TH AIR RESCUE SQUADRON—*Operating Bases:* Wiesbaden AB, West Germany, RAF Manston, England, RAF Sculthorpe, England; *Notes:* Three SC-82A conversions assigned to D Flight; *C-82 Assignments:* 44-23029 (51–52), 45-57829 (51–52), 48-568 (51–52).

27TH AIR RESCUE SQUADRON—*Operating Base:* Albrook AFB, Panama Canal Zone; *C-82 Assignment:* 44-23058 (52–53).

28TH AIR RESCUE SQUADRON—*Operating Base:* Ramey AFB, Puerto Rico; *C-82 Assignments:* 44-23041 (53), 45-57827 (53).

41ST AIR RESCUE SQUADRON—*Operating Base:* Hamilton AFB, California; *C-82 Assignment:* 44-23033 (52–53).

42ND AIR RESCUE SQUADRON—*Operating Base:* March AFB, California; *C-82 Assignment:* 45-57828 (52–53).

43RD AIR RESCUE SQUADRON—*Operating Base:* McChord AFB, Washington; *C-82 Assignment:* 44-23057 (52–53).

44TH AIR RESCUE SQUADRON—*Operating Base:* Lowry AFB, Colorado; *C-82 Assignment:* 45-57736 (52–53).

46TH AIR RESCUE SQUADRON—*Operating Base:* Westover AFB, Massachusetts; *C-82 Assignments:* 44-23036 (52–53), 45-57734 (53).

47TH AIR RESCUE SQUADRON—*Operating Base:* Ellington AFB, Texas; *C-82 Assignments:* 44-23015 (52–53), 45-57733 (53).

48TH AIR RESCUE SQUADRON—*Operating Base:* Maxwell AFB, Alabama; *C-82 Assignment:* 44-23030 (52–53).

49TH AIR RESCUE SQUADRON—*Operating Base:* Selfridge AFB, Michigan; *C-82 Assignment:* 45-57737 (52–53).

52ND AIR RESCUE SQUADRON—*Operating Base:* Ernest Harmon AFB, Newfoundland, Canada; *C-82 Assignment:* 48-574 (52–53).

58TH AIR RESCUE SQUADRON—*Operating Base:* Wheelus AFB, Libya; *C-82 Assignment:* 44-23027 (52–53).

66TH AIR RESCUE SQUADRON—*Operating Base:* RAF Manston, England; *C-82 Assignment:* 44-23029 (52–53).

67TH AIR RESCUE SQUADRON—*Operating Base:* RAF Sculthorpe, England; *C-82 Assignments:* 44-23029 (52), 48-568 (52–53).

69th Air Rescue Squadron—*Operating Bases:* Wiesbaden AB, West Germany; Furstenfeldbruck AB, West Germany; *C-82 Assignment:* 45-57829 (52–53).

84th Air Rescue Squadron—*Operating Bases:* Hamilton AFB, California; Furstenfeldbruck AB, West Germany; *C-82 Assignments:* 44-23033 (51), 45-57829 (53).

2150th Air Rescue Unit—*Operating Bases:* Hamilton AFB, California; McChord AFB, Washington; *C-82 Assignments:* 44-22972 (49), 44-22978 (48–49), 44-22979 (49), 44-22983 (49), 44-22990 (49), 44-23019 (48–49).

2151st Air Rescue Unit—*Operating Bases:* Lowry AFB, Colorado; Biggs AFB, Texas; Selfridge AFB, Michigan; *C-82 Assignments:* 44-22971 (48–49), 44-22976 (49), 44-22984 (49), 44-22986 (49).

2152nd Air Rescue Unit—*Operating Base:* Ernest Harmon AFB, Newfoundland, Canada; *C-82 Assignments:* 44-23011 (48–49), 48-574 (49).

2156th Air Rescue Unit—*Operating Bases:* MacDill AFB, Florida; Palm Beach Intl. Airport, Florida; *Notes:* Renamed 2156th Air Rescue SQ 1951; *C-82 Assignments:* 44-23015 (50–51), 45-57734 (51–52), 45-57736 (51–52), 45-57827 (51–52).

Air Resupply & Communications Service (ARCS)

1st AACS Installation & Maintenance Squadron—*Operating Base:* Tinker AFB, Oklahoma; *C-82 Assignments:* 44-23026 (50–53), 44-23031 (50–54), 44-23033 (54), 45-57734 (54), 45-57828 (53–54).

4th AACS Installation & Maintenance Squadron—*Operating Base:* Freising AB, West Germany; *C-82 Assignment:* 44-23029 (50–51).

1800th Airways & Air Communication Service (AACS) Wing—*Operating Base:* Tinker AFB, Oklahoma; *C-82 Assignments:* 44-22978 (49), 44-23029 (50), 45-57734 (54), 45-57832 (49).

1850th Airways & Air Communication Service (AACS) Squadron—*Operating Base:* Tinker AFB, Oklahoma; *C-82 Assignment:* 45-57832 (49–53).

1857th Airways & Air Communication Service (AACS) Squadron—*Operating Base:* Tinker AFB, Oklahoma; *C-82 Assignments:* 44-22978 (49–50), 44-23026 (50), 44-23031 (50).

Northeast Air Command (NEAC)

Major command established 1 October 1950 to oversee U.S. airpower in Greenland, Labrador, and the Newfoundland regions of Canada. Discontinued in 1957 with components going to the Air Defense Command (ADC) and Strategic Air Command (SAC).

6602nd Air Base Group/Wing: *Operating Base:* Ernest Harmon AFB, Newfoundland, Canada; *C-82 Assignments:* 45-57735 (50–52), 45-57776 (50–52), 45-57793 (51–53), 45-57805 (51), 45-57814 (50–52), 45-57819 (50–52), 45-57824 (50–52).

6603rd Air Base Group/Wing: *Operating Bases:* Ernest Harmon AFB, Newfoundland, Canada; Goose Bay, Labrador, Canada; *Notes:* Most aircraft in for maintenance; *C-82 Assignments:* 44-23011 (51), 45-57735 (52), 45-57771 (53), 45-57776 (51–52), 45-57807 (53), 45-57814 (53), 45-57824 (52; 53).

6622nd Air Transport Squadron: *Operating Base:* Ernest Harmon AFB, Newfoundland, Canada; *C-82 Assignments:* 45-57735 (52), 45-57776 (52), 45-57814 (52–53), 45-57824 (52–53).

Special Weapons Command (SWP)

Major command established 1 December 1949 for the responsibility of atomic weapons development. Lost major command status 1 April 1952 and reassigned to the Air Research and Development Command (ARD).

4901st Support Wing (Atomic): *Operating Base:* Kirtland AFB, New Mexico; *Notes:* Transient maintenance only; *C-82 Assignment:* 44-22981 (51).

Strategic Air Command (SAC)

Major command established 21 March 1946 to oversee the strategic bomber fleet with the ability to deploy to war globally at short notice. SAC also oversaw the aerial refueling fleet, atomic arsenal and strategic reconnaissance missions. The largest major command in the USAF and the most well-known, as it was the frontline command against any nuclear strike during the Cold War Era.

1st Maintenance & Supply Group: *Operating Base:* March AFB, California; *Notes:* One SC-82A assigned from the 2150th RES SQ during 1949; *C-82 Assignment:* 44-22972 (49).

7th Geodetic Squadron: *Home Base:* Topeka AFB, Kansas (Renamed Forbes AFB 10 Jun 49); *Notes:* Associated to the 55th SRC GP. Ten C-82s assigned in 1949 for aerial mapping duties; *C-82 Assignments:* 44-22969 (49), 44-22991 (48–49), 44-22993 (49), 44-22996 (49), 44-22997 (49), 44-22998 (49), 44-23000 (49), 44-23001 (49), 44-23005 (49), 44-23006 (49).

22nd Air Base Group: *Operating Base:* March AFB, California; *C-82 Assignments:* 45-57736 (52), 45-57737 (51).

22nd Bombardment Wing: *Operating Base:* March AFB, California; *C-82 Assignment:* 45-57828 (50–51).

55th Strategic Reconnaissance Group & 55th Maintenance & Supply Group: *Home Bases:* Topeka AFB, Kansas (from 30 Jun 48) (Renamed Forbes AFB 10 Jun 49); Ramey AFB, Puerto Rico (from 1 Nov 50); *Notes:* Designated as such 29 Jun 48. Undertook reconnaissance missions including mapping and aerial photographic duties. Aircraft were the RB-17 Flying Fortress, plus the RB-29 and RB-50 Superfortress. C-82s as base support aircraft. The 55th MSU GP is an associated component, as was the 7th Geodetic SQ, to which 10 of the 16 C-82s in the 55th were directly assigned.; *C-82 Service:* Sixteen aircraft 1949–1953; *C-82 Assignments:* 44-22969 (49), 44-22981 (52–53), 44-22991 (49), 44-22992 (49), 44-22993 (49), 44-22996 (49), 44-22997 (49), 44-22998 (49), 44-23000 (49), 44-23001 (49; 50–52), 44-23005 (49; 51–52), 44-23006 (49–52), 44-23009 (49; 50–52), 44-23018 (52–53), 44-23023 (52–53), 44-23047 (52–53).

56th Maintenance & Supply Group: *Operating Base:* Selfridge AFB, Michigan; *C-82 Assignment:* 44-22971 (48).

91st Air Base Group: *Home Base:* Barksdale AFB, Louisiana; *Notes:* Associated to the 91st SR GP; *C-82 Assignment:* 44-23052 (51).

91st Strategic Reconnaissance Group & 91st Maintenance & Supply Group: *Home Base:* Barksdale AFB, Louisiana; *Notes:* Activated 10 Nov 48 under the 311th Air Division assigned to SAC. The primary mission was worldwide reconnaissance including electronic and photographic missions. Aircraft were the RB-17 Flying Fortress, RB-29 and RB-50 Superfortress, and RB-45 Tornado. C-82s as base support aircraft. The 91st MSU GP is an associated component; *C-82 Service:* Twelve aircraft 1949–1950 assigned to Base Flight; *C-82 Assignments:* 44-22969 (49–50), 44-22991 (49–50), 44-22992 (49–50), 44-22993 (49–50), 44-22996 (49), 44-22997 (49–50), 44-22998 (49–50), 44-23000 (49–50), 44-23001 (49–50), 44-23005 (49–51), 44-23006 (49–50), 44-23009 (49–50).

93rd Air Base Group: *Operating Base:* Castle AFB, California; *C-82 Assignment:* 44-23013 (52).

97th Maintenance & Supply Group: *Operating Base:* Biggs AFB, Texas; *C-82 Assignment:* 44-22976 (49).

301st Air Base Group: *Operating Base:* Barksdale AFB, Louisiana; *C-82 Assignment:* 45-57794 (52).

306th Air Base Group: *Operating Base:* MacDill AFB, Florida; *C-82 Assignment:* 45-57734 (52).

307th Maintenance & Supply Group: *Operating Base:* MacDill AFB, Florida; *C-82 Assignments:* 44-22966 (49), 44-22982 (49).

803rd AF Base Unit: *Operating Base:* Davis-Monthan AFB, Arizona; *C-82 Assignment:* 44-23009 (54).

807th Air Base Group: *Operating Base:* March AFB, California; *C-82 Assignment:* 45-57832 (53).

809th Air Base Group: *Operating Base:* MacDill AFB, Florida; *C-82 Assignment:* 45-57734 (52–53).

Tactical Air Command (TAC)

Major command established 21 March 1946 to oversee tactical air power planning and utilization on a global scale. Became a sub-command of Continental Air Command (CNC) from 1 December 1948 to 1 December 1950, then re-established as a major command. By far the most prolific command for the C-82 Packet, as it incorporates the troop carrier groups.

10th Air Base Group: *Operating Base:* Pope AFB, North Carolina; *Notes:* Training duties; *C-82 Assignment:* 45-57824 (48).

10th Maintenance & Supply Group: *Operating Base:* Pope AFB, North Carolina; *Notes:* Associated to the 10th AB GP. Training and maintenance duties; *C-82 Assignments:* 43-13202 (48), 44-22981 (48), 44-22998 (48–49), 44-23002 (47–48), 44-23015 (48–49), 44-23017 (48), 44-23023 (48), 44-23026 (48), 45-57824 (48).

20th Fighter-Bomber Wing: *Operating Base:* Shaw AFB, South Carolina; *Notes:* Redesignated as such 20 Jan 50. Flew F-84 Thunderjets; *C-82 Assignment:* 44-23043 (50).

47th Maintenance & Supply Group: *Operating Base:* Biggs Field, Texas; *C-82 Assignments:* 44-23055 (47).

62nd Air Base Group: *Operating Base:* McChord Field, Washington; *Notes:* Associated to the 62nd TCG, training; *C-82 Assignments:* 44-23027 (48).

62nd Air Depot: *Operating Base:* McChord Field, Washington; *Notes:* Associated to the 62nd TCG; *C-82 Assignments:* 44-22965 (47), 44-22979 (47).

62th Maintenance & Supply Group: *Home Base:* McChord Field/AFB, Washington; *Notes:* Associated to the 62nd TCG; *C-82 Service:* Eighty-four aircraft 1947–1950; *C-82 Assignments:* 44-22961 (47–48), 44-22965 (47–48), 44-22970 (47–48), 44-22972 (47–48), 44-22975 (47–48), 44-22979 (47–48), 44-22980 (47–48), 44-23000 (48), 44-23009 (48), 44-23012 (47–48), 44-23013 (47), 44-23021 (47), 44-23023 (47), 44-23026 (47–48), 44-23026 (48–50), 44-23029 (47–48), 44-23031 (47–50), 44-23032 (47), 44-23033 (47–50), 44-23035 (47–48), 44-23036 (49–50), 44-23041 (48–50), 44-23057 (48–50), 44-23058 (48–50), 45-57733 (48–50), 45-57734 (48–50), 45-57735 (48–49), 45-57736 (48–49), 45-57737 (48–50), 45-57739 (48–49), 45-57741 (48–49), 45-57743 (48–49), 45-57744 (49–50), 45-57745 (47–50), 45-57747 (48), 45-57748 (48), 45-57749 (48–49), 45-57750 (48), 45-57751 (48), 45-57752 (48), 45-57753 (48–49), 45-57754 (47–48), 45-57755 (48–49), 45-57756 (48–49), 45-57757 (48), 45-57758 (48), 45-57759 (48–49), 45-57760 (48), 45-57761 (48–49), 45-57762 (49), 45-57764 (49), 45-57765 (49), 45-57766 (48–49), 45-57767 (49), 45-57768 (49), 45-57770 (48; 49–50), 45-57771 (49), 45-57772 (49–50), 45-57773 (49–50), 45-57774 (48; 49), 45-57775 (49), 45-57776 (48; 50), 45-57777 (49–50), 45-57778 (49), 45-57780 (49), 45-57781 (49–50), 45-57782 (49), 45-57800 (49), 45-57812 (48–49), 45-57820 (48; 49), 45-57826 (48; 49), 45-57827 (48–50), 45-57828 (48; 49–50), 45-57829 (48; 49–50), 45-57832 (48; 49), 48-577 (48–49), 48-579 (48; 49), 48-581 (48; 49–50), 48-582 (49), 48-583 (49), 48-584 (49–50), 48-585 (49–50), 48-586 (49), 48-587 (48–49).

62nd Troop Carrier Group: *Squadrons (Colors):* 4th TCSq (Red); 7th TCSq (Yellow); 8th TCSq (Blue); *Home Bases:* Bergstrom Field/AFB, Texas (from 7 Sep 46); McChord Field/AFB, Washington (from 7 Aug 47); *Notes:* Designated: 62nd TCG (Medium) 22 Aug 48; 62nd TCG (Heavy) 12 Oct 49. Deployments to Fort Defiance Virginia 1948; Elmendorf AFB Alaska 1948 and 1949; Pope AFB North Carolina 1948. Later re-equipped with the C-54 Skymaster and C-124 Globemaster II; *C-82 Service:* One hundred and five aircraft 1946–1950; *C-82 Assignments:* 44-22961 (47), 44-22963 (47), 44-22965 (47), 44-22968 (47), 44-22970 (47–48), 44-22972 (47), 44-22975 (47), 44-22978 (47), 44-22979 (46–47), 44-22980 (46–47), 44-23000 (46–48), 44-23001 (47), 44-23005 (47), 44-23009 (47–48), 44-23010 (depl 47), 44-23011 (46–47), 44-23012 (46–47), 44-23013 (46–47), 44-23016 (46–47), 44-23017 (46–47), 44-23018 (46–47), 44-23019 (46–47), 44-23020 (46), 44-23021 (46–47), 44-23023 (46–47), 44-23024 (46–47), 44-23025 (46–48), 44-23026 (46–47), 44-23027 (46–50), 44-23028 (46–47), 44-23029 (46–47), 44-23030 (46–48), 44-23031 (46–50), 44-23032 (46–47), 44-23033 (46–50), 44-23035 (46–47), 44-23036 (46–50), 44-23041 (47–50), 44-23057 (47–50), 44-23058 (47–50), 45-57733 (47–50), 45-57734 (47–50), 45-57735 (47–49), 45-57736 (47–49), 45-57737 (47–50), 45-57739 (47–49), 45-57741 (47–49), 45-47742 (47), 45-57743 (47–49), 45-57744 (47–49), 45-57745 (47–50), 45-57746 (47), 45-57747 (47–48), 45-57748 (47–48), 45-57749 (47–48), 45-57750 (47–48), 45-57751 (47–48), 45-57752 (47–48), 45-57753 (47–48), 45-57754 (47–48), 45-57755 (47–48), 45-57756 (47–48), 45-57757 (47–48), 45-57758 (47–48), 45-57759 (47–48), 45-57760 (47–48), 45-57761 (47–48), 45-57762 (47–49), 45-57763 (47–48), 45-57764 (47–49), 45-57765 (47–49), 45-57766 (47–49), 45-57767 (47–49), 45-57768 (47–49), 45-57770

C-82A s/n: 48-585 (msn: 10220) during an army exercise in December 1948. Note the 4th TCSq emblem on the nose. '585 would later go to the Brazilian Air Force and after retirement to museum display in Rio de Janeiro (Elton Schlimmer via Marvin Schlimmer).

(47–49), 45-57771 (47–49), 45-57772 (47–49), 45-57773 (47–49), 45-57774 (47–49), 45-57775 (47–49), 45-57776 (47–50), 45-57777 (47–49), 45-57778 (47–49), 45-57779 (47–48), 45-57780 (47–49), 45-57781 (47–49), 45-57782 (47–48), 45-57800 (48–49), 45-57812 (48–49), 45-57820 (48–49), 45-57826 (48–49), 45-57827 (48–50), 45-57828 (48–50), 45-57829 (48–50), 45-57832 (48–49), 48-577 (48–49), 48-579 (48–49), 48-580 (48–50), 48-581 (48–49), 48-582 (48–49), 48-583 (48–49), 48-584 (48–49), 48-585 (48–49), 48-586 (48–49), 48-587 (48–49).

64th Troop Carrier Group/Wing: *Squadrons:* 17th TCSq; 18th TCSq; 35th TCSq; *Home Base:* Donaldson AFB, South Carolina; *Notes:* Designated: 64th TCWG (Medium) 3 Jul 52. Training unit; *C-82 Service:* Forty-four aircraft 1952–1953; *C-82 Assignments:* 44-23007 (52–53), 44-23008 (52–53), 44-23012 (52–53), 44-23013 (52–53), 44-23017 (52–53), 44-23025 (52–53), 44-23032 (52–53), 44-23034 (52–53), 44-23037 (52–53), 44-23038 (52–53), 44-23039 (52–53), 44-23040 (52–53), 44-23043 (52–53), 44-23045 (52–53), 44-23046 (52–53), 44-23048 (52–53), 44-23049 (52–53), 44-23050 (52–53), 44-23051 (52–53), 44-23052 (52–53), 44-23053 (52–53), 44-23054 (52–53), 45-57735 (52–53), 45-57738 (52), 45-57749 (52), 45-57776 (52–53), 45-57788 (52–53), 45-57794 (52–53), 45-57795 (52–53), 45-57815 (52–53), 45-57822 (52–53), 45-57825 (52–53), 48-569 (52–53), 48-571 (52–53), 48-573 (52–53), 48-576 (52–53), 48-577 (52–53), 48-578 (52–53), 48-580 (52–53), 48-583 (52–53), 48-584 (52–53), 48-585 (52–53), 48-586 (52–53), 48-587 (52–53).

117th Reconnaissance (Tactical) Wing: *Operating Base:* Lawson Field, Georgia; *Notes:* Training duties; *C-82 Assignments:* 45-57738 (50–51), 48-584 (51), 48-587 (51).

302nd Troop Carrier Group: *Squadrons:* 355th TCSq; 356th TCSq; *Notes:* Reserve Group attached to the 62nd TCG 27 Jun 49–5 May 50 and 325th Fighter (All-Weather) WG 6 May 50–8 Jun 51. No direct C-82 assignments.

303rd AAF Base Unit: *Operating Base:* Greenville Field, South Carolina; *Notes:* Transport duties; *C-82 Assignments:* 44-22965 (46), 44-22970 (46), 44-23001 (46).

304th AAF Base Unit: *Operating Base:* Langley Field, Virginia; *C-82 Assignments:* 44-23024 (47).

309th AAF Base Unit: *Operating Bases:* Biggs Field, Texas; Greenville Field, South Carolina; *Notes:* Transport duties; *C-82 Assignments:* 44-22965 (46–47), 44-23001 (46–47).

310th AAF Base Unit: *Operating Base:* Pope Field, North Carolina; *Notes:* Twenty-four assignments. XC-82 for ground instructional duties; *C-82 Assignments:* 43-13202 (XC-82 46–48), 44-22969 (47), 44-22974 (46; 47), 44-22976 (46; 47), 44-22977 (47), 44-22982 (47), 44-22984 (47), 44-22985 (47), 44-22986 (47), 44-22988 (47), 44-22990 (47), 44-22992 (47), 44-22993 (47), 44-22994 (46–47), 44-22996 (47), 44-22999 (46), 44-23002 (47), 44-23005 (47), 44-23011 (47), 44-23021 (47), 44-23022 (46–47), 44-23037 (46–47), 44-23038 (46–47), 45-57738 (47).

311th AAF Base Unit: *Operating Base:* Bergstrom Field, Texas; *C-82 Assignments:* 44-22963 (47), 44-22978 (47), 44-23010 (depl 47), 44-23020 (47 for salvage), 44-23024 (depl 47), 44-23028 (47 for salvage), 44-23033 (46 for mods at Hagerstown).

313th AAF Base Unit: *Operating Base:* Greenville Field, South Carolina; *Notes:* Associated to the 313th TCG; *C-82 Assignments:* 44-22984 (depl 47), 44-23001 (47), 44-23046 (depl 47), 44-23048 (depl 47), 44-23055 (depl 47), 45-57738 (47).

313th Maintenance & Supply Group: *Home Base:* Bergstrom AFB, Texas; *Notes:* Associated to the 313th TCG; *C-82 Service:* Twenty-three aircraft 1947; 1948–1949; *C-82 Assignments:* 44-22967 (48–49), 44-22969 (48), 44-22975 (48), 44-22979 (48), 44-22980 (48), 44-22988 (48), 44-22989 (48), 44-22990 (48), 44-22991 (48), 44-23009 (48), 44-23010 (depl 47), 44-23012 (48), 44-23013 (48), 44-23023 (48), 44-23026 (48), 44-23029 (48), 44-23035 (48), 45-57786 (48), 45-57787 (48), 45-57790 (48), 45-57804 (48), 45-57807 (48), 45-57809 (48).

313th Troop Carrier Group: *Squadrons (Colors):* 29th TCSq (Red); 47th TCSq (Green); *Home Bases:* Langley Field, Virginia (from 25 Jun 47); Bergstrom Field, Texas (from 15 Jul 47); *Notes:* Designated: 313th TCG (Heavy) Jul 48; 313th TCG (Special) Feb 49; Deployment to Pope AFB North Carolina Apr 48.; *C-82 Service:* Forty-three aircraft 1947–1948; *C-82 Assignments:* 44-22961 (48), 44-22965 (48), 44-22969 (48), 44-22970 (48), 44-22972 (48), 44-22975 (48), 44-22976 (48), 44-22979 (48), 44-22980 (48), 44-22984 (48), 44-22988 (47–48), 44-22989 (48), 44-22990 (48), 44-22991 (48), 44-23003 (48), 44-23005 (47–48), 44-23009 (48), 44-23012 (48), 44-23013 (47–48), 44-23015 (48), 44-23016 (47–48), 44-23017 (47–48), 44-23023 (47–48), 44-23025 (48), 44-23026 (48), 44-23029 (48), 44-23035 (47–48), 45-57783 (47–48), 45-57784 (47–48), 45-57786 (47–48), 45-57787 (47–48), 45-57788 (47–48), 45-57789 (47–48), 45-57790 (47–48), 45-57792 (47–48), 45-57797 (48), 45-57803 (48), 45-57804 (48), 45-57806 (48), 45-57807 (48), 45-57808 (48), 45-57809 (48), 45-57811 (48).

314th AAF/AF Base Unit: *Operating Base:* Smyrna AFB, Tennessee; *Notes:* Associated to the 314th TCG; *C-82 Assignments:* 44-22965 (depl 47/to McChord Field), 44-22969 (48–49), 44-22979 (depl 47/to McChord Field), 44-23012 (depl 47/to McChord Field).

314th Air Base Group: *Operating Base:* Smyrna AFB, Tennessee; *Notes:* Associated to the 314th TCG; *C-82 Assignments:* 45-57783 (49).

314th Maintenance & Supply Group: *Home Base:* Smyrna AFB, Tennessee (Renamed Sewart AFB 25 Mar 50); *Notes:* Associated to the 314th TCG; *C-82 Service:* Twenty-six aircraft 1949–1950; *C-82 Assignments:* 44-22970 (50), 44-22980 (49), 44-22981 (50), 44-22985 (depl 50), 44-22989 (50), 44-23009 (49), 44-23012 (50), 44-23015 (49), 44-23025 (50), 44-23029 (49–50), 44-23037 (depl 50), 44-23048 (depl 50), 44-23051 (depl 49–50), 45-57749 (depl 49–50), 45-57750 (49–50), 45-57751 (depl 50), 45-57758 (50), 45-57760 (depl 50), 45-57761 (49–50), 45-57763 (49; 50), 45-57783 (49), 45-57784 (49), 45-57788 (49–50), 45-57789 (49), 45-57790 (49), 45-57808 (49).

314th Troop Carrier Group/Wing: *Squadrons (Colors):* 20th TCSq (Detached) (Yellow); 50th TCSq (Red); 61st TCSq (Green); 62nd TCSq (Blue); 334th TCSq; 2601st LTLSq (Attached); *Home Base:* Smyrna AFB, Tennessee (from 21 Oct 48) (Renamed Sewart AFB 25 Mar 50); *Notes:* Designated: 314th TCG (Heavy) 26 Jul 48; 314th TCG (Medium) 19 Nov 48; 314th Troop Carrier Wing Feb 50. Deployment to Laurinburg-Maxton Airport, North Carolina Apr 50. Re-equipped with the C-119 Flying Boxcar from 1950; *C-82 Service:* Ninety-nine aircraft 1948–1951; 1 1954; *C-82 Assignments:* 44-22970 (49–50), 44-22975 (49–50), 44-22976 (depl 48), 44-22980 (48–50), 44-22981 (50), 44-22984 (depl 48), 44-22988 (49–50), 44-22989 (49–50), 44-23007 (depl 49–50; 50), 44-23008 (depl 50; 50), 44-23009 (49), 44-23012 (49–51), 44-23013 (48–51), 44-23015 (49–50), 44-23016 (49–50), 44-23017 (49–50), 44-23018 (depl 49–50), 44-23023 (49–50), 44-23024 (depl 50), 44-23025 (49–50), 44-23026 (49–50), 44-23029 (49–50), 44-23030 (49–50), 44-23032 (50), 44-23035 (49), 44-23037 (depl 50; 50–51), 44-23038 (depl 50), 44-23039 (depl 49–50; 50), 44-23040 (50), 44-23043 (depl 49–50), 44-23045 (depl 49–50), 44-23046 (depl 50; 50), 44-23047 (depl 49–50; 51), 44-23048 (depl 49–50), 44-23049 (depl 49–50), 44-23050 (50), 44-23051 (depl 50; 50–51), 44-23052 (depl 49–50; 50), 44-23053 (depl 49–50), 44-23054 (depl 49–50), 44-23055 (depl 50), 45-57736 (49–50), 45-57738 (depl 50; 50), 45-57739 (49–50), 45-57742 (49–50), 45-57747 (49–50), 45-57749 (depl 50), 45-57750 (49–50), 45-57751 (49–50), 45-57752 (49–50), 45-57753 (49–50), 45-57754 (49), 45-57755 (49), 45-57756 (49), 45-57757 (50), 45-57758 (49–50), 45-57759 (49–50), 45-57760 (49–50), 45-57761 (49–51), 45-57762 (49), 45-57763 (49–50), 45-57764 (49), 45-57766 (53), 45-57777 (depl 54), 45-57783 (48–49), 45-57784 (49–50), 45-57786 (49), 45-57787 (49), 45-57788 (49–50), 45-57789 (49), 45-57790 (49), 45-57792 (49), 45-57794 (depl 50; 50–51), 45-57795 (50), 45-57803 (49), 45-57804 (49), 45-57806 (49–50), 45-57807 (49), 45-57808 (49), 45-57809 (49), 45-57811 (49), 45-57815 (depl 50), 45-57817 (49–50), 45-57822 (50), 45-57824 (depl 50), 45-57825 (depl 50), 48-569 (depl 50), 48-571 (depl 50), 48-573 (depl 50), 48-574 (depl 49–50), 48-576 (depl 50), 48-577 (49–50; depl 50), 48-578 (49–51), 48-581 (depl 50), 48-583 (49–50; 50–51), 48-584 (50–51), 48-585 (50), 48-586 (49–50), 48-587 (49–50).

316th AAF Base Unit: *Operating Bases:* Pope Field, North Carolina; Greenville AFB, South Carolina; *Notes:* Associated to the 316th TCG; *C-82 Assignments:* 44-22993 (46), 44-23033 (46, for mods at Hagerstown).

316th Maintenance & Supply Group: *Home Base:* Greenville AFB, South Carolina; *Notes:* Associated to the 316th TCG; *C-82 Service:* Seventy-one aircraft 1947–1949; *C-82 Assignments:* 44-22968 (47–49), 44-22969 (48), 44-22973 (47–49), 44-22974 (48–49), 44-22976 (48), 44-22977 (48–49), 44-22981 (48), 44-22982 (48–49), 44-22983 (48–49), 44-22984 (47–48), 44-22985 (48–49), 44-22986 (48–49), 44-22987 (48–49), 44-22988

(47), 44-22990 (47–48), 44-22991 (48), 44-22992 (48–49), 44-22993 (47–49), 44-22996 (48–49), 44-22997 (48–49), 44-22998 (48), 44-23002 (48–49), 44-23003 (48), 44-23006 (48–49), 44-23007 (48–49), 44-23008 (48), 44-23010 (47), 44-23021 (48), 44-23024 (48–49), 44-23032 (47), 44-23037 (49), 44-23038 (47–49), 44-23039 (48–49), 44-23040 (47), 44-23042 (48), 44-23043 (49), 44-23045 (49), 44-23046 (47–49), 44-23047 (47–48), 44-23048 (47–48), 44-23049 (48), 44-23050 (48), 44-23051 (48), 44-23052 (48), 44-23053 (48; 49), 44-23054 (48), 44-23055 (48), 45-57738 (47–49), 45-57740 (48), 45-57742 (48), 45-57783 (47), 45-57785 (48), 45-57791 (48), 45-57793 (49), 45-57794 (48), 45-57795 (48), 45-57796 (48), 45-57798 (49), 45-57802 (49), 45-57805 (49), 45-57814 (49), 45-57815 (48), 45-57818 (48), 45-57819 (49), 45-57821 (49), 45-57824 (48–49), 48-568 (49), 48-572 (49), 48-574 (48), 48-575 (49), 48-578 (49).

316th Troop Carrier Group/Wing: *Squadrons (Colors):* 36th TCSq (Red/White); 37th TCSq (Blue/White); 75th TCSq (Green/White); 77th TCSq; *Home Bases:* Pope Field/AFB, North Carolina (from 25 May 45); Greenville Field/AFB, South Carolina (from 25 Aug 47) (Renamed Donaldson AFB Mar 51); Smyrna AFB, Tennessee (from 4 Nov 49) (Renamed Sewart AFB 25 Mar 50); *Notes:* Designated: 316th TCG (Medium) Jun 48; 316th TCG (Heavy) Oct 49; 316th TCG (Medium) Jan 50. Detachments to Lawson Field 1946 and 1947. Deployments to Elmendorf AFB Alaska 1948; Guantanamo Bay, Cuba Feb-Mar 50. Re-equipped with the C-119 Flying Boxcar from 1949; *C-82 Service:* One hundred nineteen aircraft 1946–1951; *C-82 Assignments:* 44-22963 (46–47), 44-22965 (depl 46), 44-22968 (47–50), 44-22969 (47–48), 44-22970 (46–47), 44-22971 (46–47), 44-22972 (46–47), 44-22973 (46–48), 44-22974 (46–50), 44-22976 (46–48), 44-22977 (46–50), 44-22978 (46), 44-22979 (46), 44-22980 (46), 44-22981 (46–50), 44-22982 (46–48), 44-22983 (46–48), 44-22984 (46–48), 44-22985 (46–50), 44-22986 (46–48), 44-22987 (46–50), 44-22988 (46–47), 44-22989 (48), 44-22990 (46–47), 44-22991 (46–48), 44-22992 (46–48), 44-22993 (46–49), 44-22994 (46–47), 44-22995 (46), 44-22996 (46–48), 44-22997 (46–48), 44-22998 (46–48), 44-22999 (46), 44-23001 (46; depl 47), 44-23002 (46–50), 44-23003 (46–48), 44-23005 (46–47; depl 47), 44-23006 (46–48), 44-23007 (46–50), 44-23008 (47–50), 44-23009 (46–47), 44-23010 (46–49), 44-23011 (depl 47), 44-23013 (depl 47), 44-23016 (depl 47), 44-23018 (depl 47; 49–50), 44-23021 (47–50), 44-23022 (46), 44-23023 (depl 47), 44-23024 (47–50), 44-23025 (49–50), 44-23026 (depl 47), 44-23030 (depl 47), 44-23031 (depl 47), 44-23032 (47–50), 44-23033 (depl 47), 44-23035 (depl 47), 44-23037 (47–50), 44-23038 (47–50), 44-23039 (47–50), 44-23040 (47–50), 44-23041 (depl 47), 44-23042 (47–48), 44-23043 (47–50), 44-23044 (47), 44-23045 (47–51), 44-23046 (47–50), 44-23047 (47–50), 44-23048 (47–51), 44-23049 (47–50), 44-23050 (47–50), 44-23051 (47–50), 44-23052 (47–50), 44-23053 (47–51), 44-23054 (47–51), 44-23055 (47–50), 45-57738 (47–50), 45-57740 (48), 45-57742 (48–49), 45-57749 (49–50), 45-57751 (49), 45-57761 (depl 50), 45-57785 (47–48), 45-57788 (50), 45-57791 (47–48), 45-57793 (47–49), 45-57794 (47–50), 45-57795 (47–48; 50–51), 45-57796 (47–48), 45-57798 (48–49), 45-57802 (48–49), 45-57805 (48–49), 45-57810 (48–49), 45-57813 (48), 45-57814 (48–49), 45-57815 (48–51), 45-57816 (48–50), 45-57818 (48), 45-57819 (48–49), 45-57821 (48–49), 45-57822 (48–50), 45-57823 (48–49), 45-57824 (49–50), 45-57825 (48–51), 48-568 (48–49), 48-569 (48–51), 48-570 (48), 48-571 (48–51), 48-572 (48–49), 48-573 (48–51), 48-574 (48–51), 48-575 (48–49), 48-576 (48–51), 48-577 (50–51), 48-578 (48–49; depl 50), 48-581 (50–51), 48-583 (50), 48-584 (50), 48-585 (50).

318th AAF Base Unit: *Operating Base:* Lockbourne Field, Ohio; *C-82 Assignments:* 44-23011 (46–47).

319th AAF/AF Base Unit: *Operating Base:* Lawson Field, Georgia (Renamed Lawson AFB 1947); *Notes:* Twenty-one assignments. C-82N as ground instructional airframe; *C-82 Assignments:* 44-22961 (48), 44-22965 (48), 44-22971 (47), 44-22974 (47), 44-22994 (47), 44-23000 (48), 44-23001 (47–48), 44-23006 (47), 44-23007 (47), 44-23009 (47), 44-23019 (47), 44-23030 (48), 44-23043 (47), 44-23045 (47), 44-23046 (47), 44-23047 (47), 44-23048 (47), 44-23049 (49), 44-23054 (47), 45-25436 (46–47; C-82N), 45-57817 (48).

332nd Maintenance & Supply Group: *Operating Base:* Lockbourne AFB, Ohio; *Notes:* Assigned to salvage after crash; *C-82 Assignment:* 48-570 (48–49).

356th AF Base Unit: *Operating Base:* Marshall AFB, Kansas; *C-82 Assignment:* 44-23039 (47–48).

363rd Maintenance & Supply Group: *Operating Base:* Langley Field, Virginia; *Notes:* Associated to the 363rd Reconnaissance (Tactical) WG; *C-82 Assignment:* 44-23024 (47).

363rd Reconnaissance (Tactical) Wing: *Operating Bases:* Langley AFB, Virginia Shaw AFB, South Carolina (from 2 Apr 51); *Notes:* Re-activated 1 Sep 50 for photo recon missions with the RB-26 Invader. Later redesignated 363rd Tactical Reconnaissance WG. Assigned two C-82s as support aircraft; *C-82 Assignments:* 44-23031 (51–52), 48-587 (50).

375th Troop Carrier Group/Wing: *Squadrons:* 55th TCSq; 56th TCSq; 57th TCSq; *Home Base:* Greenville AFB, South Carolina (Renamed Donaldson AFB Mar 51); *Notes:* Designated: 375th TCG (Medium) 10 May 49. Deployments to Brownwood Field, Texas Mar 52; Grenier AFB, New Hampshire 1952; *C-82 Service:* Fifty-one aircraft 1950–1952; *C-82 Assignments:* 44-22981 (50–52), 44-23007 (50–52), 44-23008 (50–52), 44-23012 (51–52), 44-23013 (51–52), 44-23017 (50–52), 44-23018 (50–52), 44-23023 (50–52), 44-23024 (50), 44-23025 (50–52), 44-23032 (50–52), 44-23034 (51–52), 44-23037 (51–52), 44-23038 (51–52), 44-23039 (50–52), 44-23040 (50–52), 44-23043 (50–52), 44-23045 (51–52), 44-23046 (50–52), 44-23047 (51–52), 44-23048 (51–52), 44-23049 (50–52), 44-23050 (50–52), 44-23051 (51–52), 44-23052 (50–52), 44-23053 (51–52), 44-23054 (51–52), 45-57738 (50–52), 45-57739 (50), 45-57749 (50–52), 45-57761 (51), 45-57788 (50–52), 45-57794 (51–52), 45-57795 (51–52), 45-57815 (51–52), 45-57822 (50–52), 45-57825 (51–52), 48-569 (51–52), 48-571 (51–52), 48-573 (51–52), 48-574 (51), 48-576 (51–52), 48-577 (51–52), 48-578 (51–52), 48-580 (50–52), 48-581 (51), 48-583 (51–52), 48-584 (51–52), 48-585 (50–52), 48-586 (50–52), 48-587 (50–52).

433rd Troop Carrier Wing: *Home Base:* Greenville AFB, South Carolina (Renamed Donaldson AFB Mar 51); *Notes:* Three C-82s on deployment, equipped with the C-119 Flying Boxcar; *C-82 Assignments:* 44-22981 (depl 51), 44-23037 (depl 51), 48-586 (depl 51).

434th Troop Carrier Group: *Home Base:* Greenville Field, South Carolina; *Notes:* Eight C-82s assigned 1946, equipped with the C-46 Commando; *C-82 Assignments:* 44-22965 (depl 46), 44-22970 (46), 44-22990 (46), 44-22991 (46), 44-22994 (46), 44-22995 (46), 44-22996 (46), 44-22997 (46).

435th Troop Carrier Wing: *Operating Base:* Miami Intl. Airport, Florida; *Notes:* Equipped with the C-119 Flying Boxcar; *C-82 Assignment:* 44-23054 (depl 52).

4408th Air Base Squadron: *Operating Base:* Lawson AFB, Georgia; *C-82 Service:* Sixteen aircraft 1948–1950; *C-82 Assignments:* 44-22961 (48–49), 44-22975 (48), 44-23000 (48–49), 44-23001 (48–49), 44-23012 (49), 44-23017 (49), 44-23023 (49), 44-23025 (48–49), 44-23030 (48), 44-23053 (50), 45-57738 (50), 45-57786 (48–49), 45-57792 (48–49), 45-57803 (48–49), 45-57806 (48–49), 45-57817 (48–49).

4414th Air Base Squadron: *Operating Base:* Bergstrom AFB, Texas; *Notes:* All were held in storage. Some assigned to 20th & 334th TCSq of the 314th TCG before being reassigned; *C-82 Service:* Thirty-nine aircraft 1948–1949; *C-82 Assignments:* 44-22967 (49), 44-22969 (48), 44-22970 (48–49), 44-22972 (48–49), 44-22975 (48–49), 44-22976 (48–49), 44-22979 (48–49), 44-22980 (48), 44-22984 (48), 44-22988 (48–49), 44-22989 (48–49), 44-22990 (48–49), 44-22991 (48), 44-23005 (48), 44-23009 (48–49), 44-23012 (48–49), 44-23013 (48), 44-23016 (48–49), 44-23017 (48–49), 44-23023 (48–49), 44-23025 (48), 44-23026 (48–49), 44-23029 (48–49), 44-23035 (48–49), 45-57783 (48), 45-57784 (48–49), 45-57786 (48), 45-57787 (48–49), 45-57788 (48–49), 45-57789 (48–49), 45-57790 (48–49), 45-57792 (48), 45-57797 (48), 45-57803 (48), 45-57804 (48), 45-57806 (48), 45-57807 (48–49), 45-57808 (48–49), 45-57811 (48).

4418th Base Complement Squadron: *Operating Base:* Greenville AFB, South Carolina; *Notes:* Activated 16 Sep 50. De-activated 14 Jan 51; *C-82 Service:* Thirteen aircraft 1950–1951; *C-82 Assignments:* 44-22981 (50), 44-23018 (50–51), 44-23023 (50–51), 44-23024 (50–51), 44-23025 (50), 44-23046 (50–51), 44-23049 (50), 44-23050 (50–51), 44-23052 (50–51), 45-57739 (50), 45-57822 (50–51), 48-585 (50–51), 48-586 (51).

United States Air Forces in Europe (AFE/USAFE)

Major command established 7 August 1945 to oversee U.S. air power in post-war Europe.

10th Air Base Group: *Operating Base:* Erding AB, West Germany; *C-82 Assignment:* 44-23027 (50).

59th Air Depot Wing: *Operating Base:* Burtonwood Air Depot, England; *C-82 Assignments:* 44-23029 (51), 45-57792 (53), 45-57816 (52).

60th Air Base Group: *Operating Base:* Wiesbaden AB, West Germany; *Notes:* Associated to the 60th TCG. Five C-82s were assigned for Berlin Airlift duties during 1949. All were later assigned to the 513th TC(S)G. S/n: 45-57829 was assigned in 1950 for transient maintenance only; *C-82 Assignments:* 45-57740 (49), 45-57791 (49), 45-57796 (49), 45-57810 (49), 45-57818 (49), 45-57829 (50).

60th Troop Carrier Group/Wing: *Squadrons (Colors):* 10th TCSq (Red); 11th TCSq (Green); 12th TCSq (Blue); *Homes Bases:* Wiesbaden AB, Germany (from 15 Dec 48) (Designated Erbenheim by USAF prior to mid–1949) Rhein-Main AB, West Germany (from 1 Jul 50); *Notes:* Designated: 60th TCG (Medium) 1 Jul 48; 60th TCG (Heavy) 5 Nov 48; 60th TCG (Medium) 16 Nov 49. Most aircraft were processed through Kelly AFB Texas for depot maintenance on return to the U.S. The Wing re-equipped with the C-119 Flying Boxcar from 1953; *C-82 Service:* Fifty-three aircraft 1948–1953; *C-82 Assign-

A lineup of C-82A Packets ready for a mission (Giorgio Salerno Collection via A. Romano).

ments: 45-57740 (48–52), 45-57741 (49–53), 45-57742 (50), 45-57743 (49–50), 45-57744 (50–53), 45-57745 (50–53), 45-57747 (52–53), 45-57755 (49–53), 45-57756 (49–53), 45-57758 (52–53), 45-57762 (49–53), 45-57764 (49–53), 45-57765 (49–53), 45-57766 (49–53), 45-57767 (49–53), 45-57768 (49–53), 45-57770 (50–53), 45-57771 (49–53), 45-57772 (50–53), 45-57773 (50–53), 45-57774 (49–53), 45-57775 (49–53), 45-57777 (50–53), 45-57778 (49–53), 45-57780 (49–53), 45-57781 (50–51), 45-57782 (49–53), 45-57783 (49–53), 45-57784 (50–53), 45-57785 (48), 45-57786 (49–53), 45-57787 (49–53), 45-57789 (49–53), 45-57790 (49–53), 45-57791 (48–51), 45-57792 (49–53), 45-57796 (48–52), 45-57800 (49–53), 45-57801 (unk-51), 45-57803 (49–53), 45-57804 (50–53), 45-57806 (50–53), 45-57807 (49–53), 45-57808 (49–53), 45-57809 (49–51), 45-57810 (49–53), 45-57811 (49–53), 45-57812 (49–53), 45-57816 (50–52), 45-57817 (50–53), 45-57818 (48–53), 45-57820 (49–50), 45-57822 (50).

61st Maintenance & Supply Group: 60th TCG (Attached); *Home Base:* Rhein-Main AB, West Germany; *Notes:* Associated to the 61st TCG; *C-82 Service:* Twenty-seven aircraft (some deployed) 1949–1950; s*C-82 Assignments:* 45-57741 (49), 45-57743 (49), 45-57744 (50), 45-57745 (50), 45-57755 (49), 45-57762 (49), 45-57764 (49), 45-57765 (49), 45-57766 (49), 45-57767 (49), 45-57768 (49), 45-57770 (50), 45-57771 (49), 45-57772 (50), 45-57774 (depl 49), 45-57775 (49), 45-57777 (50), 45-57778 (49), 45-57780 (49), 45-57781 (50), 45-

A group of 60th TCG C-82A Packets in Italy during 1950. *From left to right:* s/n: 45-57744 (msn: 10114), s/n: 45-57770 (msn: 10140), s/n: 45-57773 (msn: 10143) and 45-57755 (msn: 10125) (Giorgio Salerno Collection via A. Romano).

57782 (depl 49), 45-57783 (depl 50), 45-57796 (depl 50), 45-57800 (49), 45-57809 (49), 45-57812 (depl 49), 45-57820 (depl 49).

61st Troop Carrier Group/Wing: 60th TCG (Attached); *Home Base:* Rhein-Main AB, West Germany; *Notes:* Designated: 61st TCG (Medium) 1 Jul 48; 61st TCG (Heavy) 15 Aug 48. The main 61st TCG aircraft at this time was the C-54 Skymaster; *C-82 Service:* Seventeen aircraft on deployment 1950–1951; *C-82 Assignments:* 45-57740 (depl 51), 45-57743 (depl 50), 45-57745 (depl 51), 45-57764 (depl 51), 45-57765 (depl 51), 45-57767 (depl 51), 45-57770 (depl 51), 45-57772 (depl 50), 45-57773 (depl 51), 45-57789 (depl 51), 45-57796 (depl 51), 45-57803 (depl 51), 45-57806 (depl 51), 45-57810 (depl 51), 45-57811 (depl 51), 45-57812 (depl 51), 45-57818 (depl 51).

73rd Air Depot Wing: *Operating Base:* Chateauroux-Deols AB, France; *C-82 Assignment:* 45-57780 (53).

80th Air Depot Wing: *Operating Base:* Nouasseur AB, French Morocco; *C-82 Assignments:* 45-57762 (52), 45-57782 (52).

85th Aircraft Maintenance Group: *Operating Base:* Erding AB, West Germany; *Notes:* Renamed as 85th Air Depot WG in 1950; *C-82 Assignments:* 44-23027 (51–52), 44-23029 (51), 45-57740 (52–53), 45-57756 (51), 45-57767 (52), 45-57777 (51), 45-57784 (51), 45-57789 (50), 45-57791 (51), 45-57807 (52), 48-568 (52).

513th Troop Carrier (Special) Group: *Operating Base:* Rhein-Main AB, West Germany; *Notes:* Activated 19 Nov 48 for services on the Berlin Airlift. Deactivated 16 Oct 49. Also serving indirectly, but not actually assigned, was JC-82A s/n: 45-57796; *C-82*

Assignments: 45-57740 (JC-82A 49), 45-57791 (JC-82A 49), 45-57810 (not cvtd. 49), 45-57818 (JC-82A 49).

7150th Air Base Group: *Operating Base:* Wiesbaden AB, West Germany; *Notes:* Depot maintenance and transport operations; *C-82 Assignments:* 44-23027 (52), 45-57786 (51), 45-57810 (51).

7160th Air Base Group: *Operating Base:* Erbenheim (Wiesbaden AB), Germany; *Notes:* Five C-82s performing transport operations with MATS 1948; *C-82 Assignments:* 45-57740 (48), 45-57785 (48), 45-57791 (48), 45-57796 (48), 45-57818 (48).

7165th Composite Group: *Operating Base:* Erbenheim (Wiesbaden AB), Germany; *Notes:* The five C-82s assigned to The Berlin Airlift performing transport operations with MATS 1948–1949. All later to the 60th AB GP and 513th TC(S)G; *C-82 Assignments:* 45-57740 (48–49), 45-57791 (48–49), 45-57796 (48–49), 45-57810 (49), 45-57818 (48–49).

7210th Aircraft Maintenance Group: *Operating Base:* Erding AB, Germany; *C-82 Assignment:* 45-57818 (48; 49).

7350th Air Base Group: *Operating Base:* Tempelhof AB, West Germany; *Notes:* Renamed 7350th Base Complement SQ 1950; *C-82 Assignments:* 45-57785 (48–49), 45-57789 (50).

7540th Depot Maintenance Squadron: *Operating Base:* Burtonwood Air Depot, England; *C-82 Assignment:* 44-23029 (51).

7559th Maintenance Depot Group: *Operating Base:* Burtonwood Air Depot, England; *C-82 Assignment:* 45-57768 (54).

Museums

USAF Museum/WPAFB Dayton, Ohio: The official United States Air Force Museum acquired two C-82 Packets for preservation in 1988. Ironically, these two were the very last C-82s to be retired from Air Force service in 1955. Ex-civil owned N4752C (10216/48–581) is displayed in USAF markings and red Arctic trim at the USAF Museum in Dayton, Ohio, and has had a complete restoration performed on it. Ex-civil N4753C (10209/48–574) is similarly marked and displayed at McChord AFB Museum in Washington State.

Non-USAF Organizations

Aircraft Engineering & Maintenance Co. (AEMCO): *Operating Location:* Oakland Intl. Airport, California; *Notes:* A subsidiary company of Transocean Air Lines, itself established as a commercial airline from 1946 to 1960. AEMCO looked after overhaul, upgrades and maintenance of Transocean's fleet plus any other aircraft contracts the company could get. During 1953–1954 AEMCO began the task of modernizing 14 C-82 Packets with upgraded communications and electronic equipment designated as Group A upgrades by the USAF. AEMCO are also known to have serviced USAF C-54, C-74, F-100 and T-33 aircraft at its Oakland facilities; *C-82 Assignments:* 44-23015 (53–54), 44-23027 (53–54), 44-23033 (53–54), 44-23046 (53–54), 44-23057 (53), 45-57734 (53–54), 45-57744 (53), 45-57767 (53), 45-57777 (53–54), 45-57806 (53–54), 45-57811 (53–54), 45-57812 (53), 45-57828 (53), 48-569 (53–54).

Royal Aircraft Establishment (RAE): *Operating Base:* Farnborough, England; *Notes:* British research and test establishment founded in 1904 and named as such in 1918. Assigned two C-82 Packets on loan from the USAF from Aug 51 to Nov 52 for various test duties; *C-82 Assignments:* 45-57740 (51–52), 45-57784 (51).

C-82A s/n: 48-581 (msn: 10216) under restoration at the USAF Museum at Dayton, Ohio (National Museum of the United States Air Force).

Brazil

Twelve C-82A Packet aircraft were acquired by the *Forca Aerea Brasileira* (FAB/Brazilian Air Force) through the U.S. Government's Military Assistance Program (MAP), which was set up after World War II to provide military hardware to foreign nations. The Packets were all signed over to Brazil from storage at Kelly AFB, Texas, on September 20, 1955, and departed for South America in January 1956. Initially the first C-82A was assigned Brazilian AF s/n: 2065, but this was soon changed to 2200, with sequencing for the rest following from 2201 through 2211.

The fleet were stationed at their home base of *Base Aerea dos Afonsos* (Afonsos AFB) in Rio de Janeiro, Brazil, being assigned to *no 2 Grupo de Transporte* (2nd Transport Group). This group was redesignated as *no 1/1 Grupo de Transporte de Tropa* (1st Troop Carrier Group) on January 22, 1958, for operations with the army's airborne units and parachute brigade.

The C-82 performed well with Brazil from 1956 up to 1968, transporting cargo and troops without a single aircraft being lost to accidents. They also took part in search and rescue missions and humanitarian causes. The fleet was retired on April 19, 1968, with all placed into storage for disposal; they were all replaced in service with the DeHavilland-Canada CC-115 Buffalo.

Nine were eventually scrapped, two were sold to civil operators in Brazil, and one (s/n: 2202) was assigned gate guardian duties at *Escola de Aeronautica* (EAer/Air Force

Section Two—Military Operators

School) nicknamed as "Sapao" (soap suds). It was transferred to the Museu Aeroespacial (MUSAL) at Campos dos Afonos AB, Rio de Janeiro, in 1986 for display and preservation.

FAB s/n	msn/USAF s/n	BOC	SOC	Disposition
2200	10219/48–584	Jan 56	27 Jul 70	Sold to civil operator.
2201	10221/48–586	Jan 56	2 Aug 68	Sold for scrap.
2202	10220/48–585	Jan 56	25 Nov 70	Preserved at MUSAL.
2203	10218/48–583	Jan 56	3 Sep 73	Sold for scrap.
2204	10215/48–580	Jan 56	25 Nov 70	Sold for scrap.
2205	10222/48–587	Jan 56	2 Aug 68	Sold for scrap.
2206	10212/48–577	Jan 56	3 Jul 73	Sold for scrap.
2207	10213/48–578	Jan 56	25 Sep 70	Sold to civil operator.
2208	10192/45–57822	Jan 56	25 Nov 70	Sold for scrap.
2209	10208/48–573	Jan 56	3 Sep 73	Sold for scrap.
2210	10206/48–571	Jan 56	3 Sep 73	Sold for scrap.
2211	10211/48–576	Jan 56	3 Sep 73	Sold for scrap.

Brazilian C-82A s/n: 2200 (msn: 10219) at Fort Worth, Texas, August 19, 1959 (Gary Kuhn Collection). *Bottom:* C-82A Packet with Brazilian AF s/n: 2210 (msn: 10206) (via José de Alvarenga).

Honduras

One C-82A Packet was acquired in 1957 by the *Fuerza Aerea Hondurena* (FAH /Honduran Air Force), based at Tegucigalpa Air Base in Honduras. It was purchased from a U.S. civil owner, Aircraft Equipment Co. of Miami, Florida. The aircraft was placed into service but according to several sources only saw limited service due to a lack of spare parts. It was sold back into the U.S. in 1963 but never saw any further regular use and became a derelict at Long Beach Airport in California until scrapped in 1972—still adorned in its Honduran Air Force livery.

FAH s/n	msn/USAF s/n	BOC	SOC	Disposition
793	10025/44-22981	27 Jun 57	25 Sep 63	Sold to U.S. civil operator.

Above: C-82A in Honduran AF livery with s/n: 793 (msn: 10025). Note the now classic cars and a B-25 Mitchell in the background (Gary Kuhn Collection). *Left:* Underwing detail on Honduran Air Force C-82A s/n: 793 (msn: 10025) (G. Pat Macha).

Section Three

Civil Operators/Owners

When C-82 retirement began in mid–1953, a total of 128 aircraft were eventually retired into storage at Kelly AFB, Texas; Hill AFB, Utah; and the aircraft storage yard at Davis-Monthan AFB, Arizona, with three more USAF retirements elsewhere. From here the aircraft were readied for purchase by civil operators with sales taking place from August 1955 through March 1956.

Of the 224 C-82 Packets delivered to the USAF, the service suffered the loss of as many as 53 airframes in service. Since the single XC-82, three C-82N and up to 36 C-82As (2 C-82As, 1 XC-119A, 1 to NACA, and 32 NACA crash tests), had already been disposed of in one way or another, this left a total of 131 Packets the Air Force placed into storage during the 1953 to 1955 period.

The following table lists the subsequent civil sale distribution from these three bases including the additional civil sale of Packets from other locations and the NACA disposals that had previously taken place in 1950:

Base	*Retired In*	*Civil Sales*
Kelly AFB, Texas:	75	**60**
Hill AFB, Utah:	39	**30**
Davis-Monthan AFB, Arizona:	14	**12**
Elmendorf AFB, Alaska:	2	**2**
Fairchild Aircraft, Maryland:	1	**1**
NACA Assignments:		**32**
Other Civil Disposals:		**3**
		Total: 140

The two aircraft at Elmendorf were retired in August 1955 and were the last two C-82 aircraft in service with the USAF.

The C-82 sold out of Fairchild Aircraft was s/n: 44-23036, on bailment from the USAF for Jet-Pak tests with Fairchild until 1957.

The "Other Civil Disposals" were two ex-Brazilian AF and the C-82 assigned to the NACA/NASA; it was retired to Davis-Monthan in 1961 and scrapped.

Twelve from Kelly AFB went to the Brazilian AF in 1955.

The remaining 14 unsold C-82 Packets were scrapped by the USAF.

See Appendix II for a full rundown of C-82 retirement bases and NACA assignments

The following pages record known registered civil operators and owners, which are presented under their appropriate country of business and are listed in strict alphabetical order either by company name or by first name for individuals. For U.S.–based operators, company and individual names are presented as they were at the time of purchase on the

FAA Bill of Sale document. The city and country listed are the company or person's main place of occupation or business. Other locations of operation are listed in the text where possible. Foreign companies are spelled, where possible, in the language of their country of origin. For many Latin American countries this is, in many cases, Spanish or Portuguese. Aircraft are listed first by their registration at the time of purchase; then aircraft msn & military s/n; period of ownership; and lastly any relevant remarks.

ARGENTINA

SEICA S.R.L./Buenos Aires

Three C-82 Packet aircraft rsved 1960 but sale canx. Reg rsved but ntu were: LV-PRU (10052/44-23008); LV-PRV (10051/44-23007) and LV-PRW (10056/44-23012).

TRANSCARGA S.A./Buenos Aires

One C-82 with delivery reg: LV-PNY (10106/45-57736) in service from 1960 to 1966; Re-reg: LV-GIS 1959. The only C-82 to have actually been registered and operated in Argentina.

Argentinean serving C-82A LV-GIS (msn: 10106) of Transcarga at Ezeiza Airport, Argentina, on July 24, 1964 (Marcelo Miranda).

Transportes Aereos Costa Atlantica (TACA) S.A.

No details. One C-82 (10045/44-23001) reg: LV-PRP rsved 1960 but sale canx.

BOLIVIA

Aero Inca Ltda.

One C-82 CP-983 (10147/45-57777) purchased out of Brazil in 1972. Stored until 1973, then put into service. Aero Inca was owned by the Inti Raymi Mining Co., which was owned by ex–Bolivian President Gonzalo Sanchez de Losada. Leased for a period to Sociedad Agropecuaria Tohomonoco, a large agricultural colonization project being undertaken near La Paz. Aircraft was sold in 1976 to Lineas Aereas Canedo (LAC).

Aerovias Condor Ltda./La Paz

Founded in 1958 by Hugo Mirabal. Two C-82 Packets were acquired from 1959 to support oil and gold mining operations going on in Bolivia at that time. The company closed in 1963 with CP-677 then going to TABSA. CP-678 had crashed in 1960.

CP-677	10117/45-57747	1960–1963
CP-678	10128/45-57758	1959

Direccion De Aeronautica Civil (DAC)

Bolivia's civil aviation authority acquired one C-82 CP-665 (10198/45-57828) to help promote civil aviation, but the aircraft crashed near Puerto Heath, Bolivia, during its delivery flight on 24 Aug 60. As delivery had not taken place, reg CP-665 was not yet applied, and the aircraft crashed likely still marked with its previous operator's reg.

Lineas Aereas Canedo (LAC)

One C-82 CP-983 (10147/45-57777) acquired in 1976, named *Mobby-Dick* [sic] by company owner Rolando Canedo Lopez, who also repainted the aircraft with red side-stripes.

Lloyd Aereo Boliviano (LAB)/Cochabamba

One of the main domestic and international airlines of Bolivia, founded in 1925 and operating up to 2010. Leased one C-82 CP-614 (10198/45-57828) from LEBCA INTERNATIONAL INC. of Florida for a one-month period in 1955 in order to gain a contract to supply an oil drilling exploration project north of Coroico.

Transportes Aereos Benianos S.A. (TABSA)/La Paz

Nonscheduled cargo carrier founded in 1963. A C-82 CP-677 (10117/45-57747) was acquired in 1963. Crashed while in service 15 Mar 70.

Ex-Mexicana C-82A XA-LOL (msn: 10136) had dorsal fins and was earmarked for export to Bolivia as CP-693. Although the aircraft was marked as such, the sale was canceled and it ended up derelict, as seen here at Long Beach Airport, California (Bruce Orriss).

Transportes Aereos Itenez

Owned and operated by Captain Jose Villaroel. One C-82 CP-983 (10147/45-57777) acquired in 1976, only briefly flown before crashing on 27 Jan 77, killing Captain Villaroel and five others.

Registrations Not Taken Up

CP-634	10137/45-57767	1959	Canx export.
CP-693	10136/45-57766	1960	Canx., but reg on aircraft.
CP-694	10126/45-57756	1960	Canx., but reg on aircraft.
CP-697	10177/45-57807	1960	Canx export.
CP-772	unk	ntu	Rsvd for Luis Torres Pascoe.
CP-1036	unk	ntu	Rsvd for Sociedad Agropecuaria Tohomonoco Ltda.

BRAZIL

Amazonia Transporte, Industria e Comercio/Belem

No details. An unfortunate and short association with the C-82, as both aircraft were lost to accidents within a year of each other.

PT-DLP	10219/48-584	1970-1971	Crashed 1971.
PT-DNZ	10213/48-578	1970	Crashed 1970.

Aristek Ltda./San Paulo

Brazilian company specializing in various aviation products and services. Purchased one C-82 PP-CEL (10153/45-57783) in 1979 but never put it into service. The aircraft was abandoned at Manaus Airport around 1983. Scrapped in 2010.

Avimotor Suprimentos Ltda./Rio de Janeiro

Importers and exporters of aircraft engines and parts. One C-82A PP-CEL (10153/45-57783) in service from 1973 to 1974.

Frigosul/Manaus

A Brazilian company founded in 1947 dealing in refrigerated meat products. Had one C-82 PP-CEL (10153/45-57783) on a limited basis from 1974, but it was seized by Shell Oil in 1976 for fuel payments not being met. Shell sold the aircraft in 1979 but it never left storage at Manaus Intl. Airport.

Servicos Aereos Cruzeiro Do Sul/Rio de Janeiro

Originally founded in 1927 in association with German interests. Renamed as Servicos Aereos Cruzeiro do Sul S.A. (SACI) during 1942 when German control was removed. The largest South American operator of the C-82 with a total of ten aircraft purchased from the late 1950s and flown until the early 1970s. Although a large fleet, not more than a few were in service at any one time. PP-CEF, -CEH and -CEM crashed in service, and PP-CEI, -CEJ and -CFF were spares acquisitions only.

This leaves PP-CEE, -CEG, -CEK and -CEL the only Packets to have had any sort of a lengthy career with Cruzeiro, servicing various cargo routes throughout Brazil and its neighboring countries. The company also owned up to 34 DC-3s at one point and operated 19 Convairs concurrently with their C-82 Packets.

PP-CEE	10144/45-57774	1957–1965	Named *Hercules*.
PP-CEF	10200/45-57830	1957–1958	Named *Centauro*, crashed 1958.
PP-CEG	10141/45-57771	1957–1965	Scrapped.
PP-CEH	10115/45-57745	1957–1958	Crashed 1958.
PP-CEI	10185/45-57815	1957–1960	Spares only.
PP-CEJ	10156/45-57786	1958–1960	Spares only.
PP-CEK	10147/45-57777	1957–1972	Named *Atlas*, Jet-Packet 1600.
PP-CEL	10153/45-57783	1958–1973	Named *Coronel*.
PP-CEM	10180/45-57810	1957–1960	W/o ground accident 1960.
PP-CFF	10182/45-57812	1959	Spares only.

Top: An excellent flying shot of C-82A PP-CEG (msn: 10141) in Servicos Aereos Cruzeiro do Sul livery (Sergio Luis dos Santos Collection). *Bottom:* Brazilian C-82A PP-CEE's (msn: 10144) post-flying life in Rio de Janeiro. Sadly, this fantastic novelty bar only lasted a year or so before closing down with the C-82 scrapped soon after (Martin Bernsmuller [AeroMuseum]).

CHILE

Aerolineas Flecha Austral Ltda. (ALFA)/Santiago

International and domestic cargo charter company operated one C-82 in the mid- to late 1960s, identity unknown.

Linea Aerea De Publicidad Ltda. (TAXPA)/Santiago

Formed in 1958 performing a variety of roles including fish spotting, air taxi services, crop spraying, aerial photography and surveying using light aircraft such as Cessnas, Pipers and Stinsons. One C-82 CC-CAE (10045/44-23001) was used for outsized cargo work from 1966.

Ricardo de Varennes/Arica

Owner of the RIVAERO CO. who operated two C-82 Jet-Packets from 1958 to 1966. Reg: CC-CRA-0507 was originally assigned to C-82 N6989C (10059/44-23015).

CC-CRA-0507	10071/44-23027	1958–1959	Jet-Packet 3200.
CC-CRB-0508	10045/44-23001	1958–1966	Jet-Packet 1600.

Rivaereo Co./Arica

See under: Ricardo de Varennes

COLOMBIA

Aerovias Helices Ltda./Bogota

One C-82 Packet HK-906 (10063/44-23019) purchased from LACE. Transported cars and trucks between Bogota and Soledad in Barranquilla. W/o in 1960.

Capt. Gustavo Torres/Bogota

Company name: Gustavo Torres Buena Ventura. Two C-82 Packets from 1956 to 1958.

HK-906	10063/44-23019	1956–1958	—
HK-930	10099/44-23055	1956–1958	W/o 1958.

Lineas Aereas Del Caribe Ltda. (LIDCA)/Barranquilla

Founded in 1953. Operated two C-46 Commandos and two C-82 Packets acquired from 1956.

HK-914	10107/45-57737	1956	W/o 1956.
HK-915	10203/48-568	1956–unk	W/o pre-1965.

Lineas Aereas Del Colombianas Expresas Ltda. (LACE)/Bogota

Few details, but known to have operated flights along all major Colombian routes and international flights to Panama City and Miami, Florida. Three C-82 Packets from 1956 to 1959. Also operated a number of C-46 Commandos.

HK-426	10199/45-57829	1956–1959	Named *Arauca*.
HK-468	10198/45-57828	1957–1959	Named *Leticia*.
HK-906	10063/44-23019	1958–?	—

C-82A HK-468 (msn: 10198) at Miami, Florida, in June 1957 as operated by Lineas Aereas del Colombianas Expresas (LACE) of Colombia (Gary Kuhn).

Lloyd Aereo de Colombiano S.A. (LAC)/Bogota

One C-82 HK-918 (10091/44-23047) was in service from 1959 until it crashed prior to 1964. Three additional registrations (HK-919X, HK-920X and HK-921X) were not taken up.

Mercantil Colombiana Ltda./Bogota

One C-82 HK-924 (10119/45-57749) from 1956 to 1969. Company president was Julio C. Cuadros. The C-82 was w/o in an accident, during 1958.

Robert I. Dever/Barranquilla

No details. One C-82 reg unk (10063/44-23019) acquired in 1955. Sold to Capt. Gustavo Torres in 1956.

Servicios Especiales Aereos (SEA) Ltda./Bogota

Three Packets, with some purchased under the company president's name, (Luis) Carlos Herrera. The most successful operator of C-82s in Colombia with service from 1959 to 1973. Herrera also appears to have had another company named Servicios Integrales Aeronauticos (SIA) Ltda. Some aircraft also purchased under the name Lilia Lizcano de Herrera. SEA also operated a C-46 Commando on its cargo routes. Apparently some of SEA's C-82s were used in a film starring American actress Jane Russell.

HK-426	10199/45-57829	1959–1973	Named *Arauca*.
HK-583	10158/45-57788	1960–1971	W/o 1971.
HK-777	10159/45-57789	1959–1961	W/o 1961.

Vagon Volante de Colombia Ltda./Barranquilla

One C-82 HK-913X (10210/48-575) acquired in 1956 but w/o later that year.

GREECE

Delta Technical & Business School/Athens

One ex-Mecom Oil C-82 N127E (10150/45-57780) was donated in 1972 for ground studies and technical instruction at this aviation school at Athens Intl. Airport. It was delivered in 1974 and remained with the school until scrapped in 1986.

GUATEMALA

Aviateca Guatemalteca/Guatemala City

Full name is Empresa Guatemalteca de Aviacion. Began operations with C-82s from 1957 through 1960 when oil operations ceased. TG-AYA was retained until 1961 for the purpose of removing oil drilling equipment. They appear to have leased the C-82s from the U.S.

TG-ATA	10006/44-22962	1957–1958	W/o 1958.
TG-AVA	10202/45-57832	1958	W/o 1958 before reg applied.
TG-AXA	10078/44-23034	1958–1960	—
TG-AYA	10150/45-57780	1959–1961	—
TG-AZA	10069/44-23025	1959–1960	—

Aviateca Guatemalteca registered C-82A TG-AVA (msn: 10202) at Miami International Airport, Florida. The aircraft appears airworthy but there seems to be quite a lot of skin damage along the lower fuselage, indicating perhaps a recent mishap (Gary Kuhn Collection).

Feliamas Robert Press

No details. One C-82 TG-DAC-79 (10094/44-23050) in 1959.

Luis Marcutia de Leon

No details. One C-82 TG-DAC-79 (10094/44-23050) from 1958 to 1959.

The Ohio Oil Co. of Guatemala/Puerto Barrios

A U.S. oil company founded in 1887 with headquarters established in Findlay, Ohio, in 1905. Became one of the major American oil companies, with international drilling sites in Canada and South America. Prospecting in Guatemala began in 1943. Operated four C-82s in support of drilling operations from the late 1950s to the early 1960s. The aircraft were operated by their Supply and Transportation Dept. based at Findlay Airport, Ohio. Renamed as the Marathon Oil Co. in 1962.

TG-OOC-2	10172/45-57802	1959–1961
TG-OOC-3	10104/45-57734	1959–1960
TG-OOC-4	10165/45-57795	1960–1963
TG-OOC-5	10163/45-57793	1960–1963

Transportes Aereos Guatemalecos (TAG)/Guatemala City

No details, but not the same company as the TAG airline formed in 1969. One C-82 TG-DAC-79 (10094/44-23050) in 1958.

Guatemalan-registered C-82A TG-DAC-79 (msn: 10094) at Miami International Airport, Florida, in the late 1960s. The background aircraft are rare Northrop YC-125 Raiders (Gary Kuhn Collection).

HONDURAS

Compania Maderera S.A./Tegucigalpa

No details. Two C-82s operated briefly from 1957 to 1958.

XH-139	10048/44-23004	1957
XH-143-P	10094/44-23050	1958

Servicio Aereos De Honduras S.A. (SAHSA)/Tegucigalpa

Founded in 1944 by local interests and Pan American Airways. Services began in 1945 with routes throughout Honduras and flights to El Salvador and Guatemala. Operated

DC-3 and C-46 aircraft as well as C-82s for cargo. XH-163 was leased from U.S. owner George B. Alder.

XH-139	10048/44-23004	1957	Crashed.
HR-SAM	10103/45-57733	1962–1963	Leased; was XH-163, HR-163, HR-163P.

Honduran C-82A XH-139 (msn: 10048) after crashing at Trujillo Airport in Honduras (Captain Paul J. Holsen II Collection).

Mexico

Compania Mexicana de Aviacion S.A. (CMA)/Mexico City

Translates as Mexican Aircraft Co. but often referred to by its initials C.M.A., which were also featured on their aircraft. It was founded on August 20, 1924, for the purpose of flying gold cross-country to avoid bandits. In 1929, Pan American Airways purchased a major share in the company and it eventually became Mexico's main airline service. It was rebranded as MEXICANA AIRLINES at some point in the late 1950s with routes throughout Mexico plus regular services to Havana and Los Angeles flying the DC-3, DC-4, DC-6 and DC-7. The "CARGA CMA" division operated four C-82 Packets from 1957, these aircraft featuring the unique "Mexicana Dorsal Fillets" on the vertical stabilizers to improve yaw characteristics. The Packets were withdrawn and stored around 1960, all being subsequently purchased by Steward-Davis Inc. and ferried to Long Beach, California. Mexicana acquired two additional C-82s (XA-LIY, XA-LIZ) from TAMSA when they ceased operations in 1960. XB-PEJ appears not to have entered service with Mexicana and may have been a spare parts source.

XA-LIY	10092/44-23048	1960–?	—
XA-LIZ	10095/44-23051	1960–?	—
XA-LOJ	10110/45-57740	1957–1962	Dorsal Fillets.
XA-LOK	10126/45-57756	1957–1962	Dorsal Fillets.
XA-LOL	10136/45-57766	1957–1962	Dorsal Fillets.
XA-MAW	10177/45-57807	1957–1961	Dorsal Fillets.
XB-PEJ	10160/45-57790	?	—

XA-LOJ was one of four C-82As (msn: 10110) owned by Mexican operator Compania Mexicana de Aviacion featuring dorsal fin extensions. It's seen here in flight over Mexico City in 1957 (Steward-Davis).

Distribudora Mexicana S.A.

No details. Appear to have obtained two C-82 Packets during 1956 which were subsequently purchased or leased by CMA. XB-PEK did enter service as XA-MAW but XB-PEJ appears to have remained in storage.

XB-PEK	10177/45-57807	1956	To XA-MAW.
XB-PEJ	10160/45-57790	1956	—

Guest Aerovias Mexico S.A./Mexico City

Founded in 1946 by Winston Guest as Aerovias Guest S.A., a Mexican passenger airline with destinations including Western Europe, New York, Panama and Miami. Renamed as such in 1954. With an increase in freight demand in the mid–1950s, Guest acquired two C-82 Packets, both marked with "AEROCARGA" (Aero Cargo) on the outer undercarriage doors. XA-LIL has the distinction of being the first ex–USAF C-82 to enter civil service in 1955. Guest was taken over by Aeronaves de Mexico in 1962.

XA-LIK	10128/45-57758	?–1960
XA-LIL	10117/45-57747	1955–1960

C-82A XA-LIK (msn: 10128) of Guest Aerovias Mexico S.A. in Mexico in the mid– to late 1950s. Note the distinctive bird logo on the fuselage side (José Villela G.).

La Consolidada, S.A./Mexico City

The transport division of Altos Hornos de Mexico S.A. (AHMSA), a Mexican steel works company. One C-82 (10154/ 45-57784) with reg: XB-KOI was used for carrying heavy loads of steel and supplies from 1955. Featured panoramic windows on rear clamshell doors and fuselage. Final disposition is unknown, but it is known to have still been in Mexico during 1959.

An interesting view of a "panoramic window" modified C-82A in Mexico during August 1959. XB-KOI (msn: 10154) was operated by Mexican company La Consolidada S.A. (George E. Goodhead, Jr., via Author Collection).

Roberto M. Tribolet/Culiacan

Businessman who ran an air-seafood/cargo transportation operation from Culiacan and Mazatlan to destinations across Mexico. Operated one C-82 (10106/45-57736) with reg: XB-ZUZ, from 1956 to 1962 for this purpose.

Section Three—Civil Operators/Owners   123

Transportes Aereos Mexicanos S.A. (TAMSA)/Merida

Obtained three C-82 Packets from L.B. Smith Aircraft Corp. in Miami, Florida, in 1955 with service entry in 1956. XA-LIW crashed in 1957. XA-LIY and XA-LIZ were taken over by CMA when they acquired TAMSA's routes in 1960.

XA-LIW	10093/44-23049	1955–1957
XA-LIY	10092/44-23048	1955–1960
XA-LIZ	10095/44-23051	1955–1960

City of Hermosillo

Not an owner/operator, but C-82 N6887C (10059/44-23015) was disposed of to Hermosillo City in 1983, having been abandoned at the local airport by U.S. owners Steward-Davis since 1970. It was used as a display item at a local children's park until removed and scrapped in late 2005.

Unknown Operators

XB-YOA   10128/45-57758

PANAMA

Expreso Aereo Panama S.A./Panama City

No details. Registrations not taken up, but registered in Peru with Expreso Aereo Peruano S.A., an affiliated company.

HP-219	10150/45-57780	1956
HP-220	10202/45-57832	1956

A C-82A with Panamanian registration HP-219 (msn: 10150), apparently at Miami International, Florida, in 1956 before being exported to Peru as OB-WAE-438 (Gary Kuhn Collection).

International Aviation Investment Corp./Panama City

No details. One C-82 N2057A (10091/44-23047) acquired in 1957 for resale into Latin America.

Peru

Compania Aerea Mercantil S.A. (CAMSA)

No details. One C-82 OB-TAI-438 (10150/45-57780) in 1956.

Expreso Aereo Peruano S.A. (EAPSA)/Lima

Parent company was Expreso Aereo Panama S.A., operated four C-82 Packets from 1956 to 1962. Also leased C-82 OB-UAD-508 (10137/45-57767) in 1959. It's more than likely OB-RAB-458 was never delivered and never entered service.

OB-RAA-439	10202/45-57832	1956–1958	Re-reg: OB-WAF-439; OB-UAB-439.
OB-RAB-458	10198/45-57828	1957	Re-reg: OB-WAG-458.
OB-TAI-438	10150/45-57780	1956–1959	Re-reg: OB-WAE-438; OB-UAA-438.
OB-UAF-531	10051/44-23007	?–1962	W/o 1962.

Peru registered C-82A OB-WAE-438 (msn: 10150) sometime during 1957. Note the nose art and flags by the crew entry door (Gary Kuhn).

Minerales y Metales S.A./Lima

Also has offices in New York, N.Y. One C-82 OB-LHF-508 (10137/45-57767) in 1957, re-reg: OB-UAD-508 1959. Aircraft left abandoned in 1963.

Rutas Aereas del Peru S.A. (RAPSA) /

One C-82 OB-RAA-439 (10202/45-57832) ordered but canx in 1956.

Trans-Peruana de Aviacion S.A./Lima

Air-taxi company formed in 1961. One C-82 OB-T-749 (10133/45-57763) serving on freight services from 1964 to 1967. The company went bankrupt in 1970.

Unknown Operators

OB-UAE-528	10069/44-23025	1960–?	—
OB-WAC-479	10028/44-22984	?	Re-reg: OB-T-479.

One of these aircraft each to these operators:
Compania Aereo Mercantil S.A. (CAMSA)
Rutas Aereas Del Peru S.A. (RAPSA)

SURINAM

Lawa Goudvelden N.V./Paramaribo

A Dutch gold mining company (Lawa Goldfields) that set up mining operations along the Lawa River in 1956. They acquired one C-82 N7852B (10057/44-23013) in 1958, but for reasons unknown it was never exported to Surinam or registered in that country; they onsold it in 1960. A dredging operation was conducted from 1963 to 1969 with dredge parts flown in by a leased Steward-Davis C-82 N6887C (10059/44-23015). Named the *Jungle Queen*, this dredge remains rusting and disused in the Eau Claire Valley in Surinam to this day. They were also investors in the C-82 Jet-Packet program run by Steward-Davis with N6887C painted in Lawa colors.

UNITED STATES OF AMERICA

A.C. Mosley or Jean Mosley/Fairbanks, Alaska

See under: Far North Flying Service

Advance Co. Inc./Miami, Florida

No details. Four C-82s from 1955 to 1960. All sold to local dealers.

N5113B	10094/44-23050	1955–1958	To Thuel Schuhart.
N5116B	10089/44-23045	1955–1960	To Frank Ambrose Aviation.
N5118B	10078/44-23034	1955–1958	To Aviation Facilities Inc.
N5119B	10069/44-23025	1955–1958	To Aviation Facilities Inc.

Aerodex Inc./Miami, Florida

A CAA-approved repair station that converted surplus military aircraft for civil service. Apparently run by the same owner as L.B. Smith Aircraft Corp. Two C-82s briefly registered in 1955.

N2047A	10184/45-57814	1955
N2048A	10154/45-57784	1955

Aero Enterprises Inc./Elkhart and Dunlap, Indiana

Aircraft dealer of various makes and models including Cessna and Piper. Six C-82 Packets acquired in 1962, all then sold and registered to Peter Bercut.

N56582	10176/45-57806	1962	Hull only.
N6243C	10074/44-23030	1962	—
N6245C	10055/44-23011	1962	—
N6246C	10062/44-23018	1962	—
N7850B	10098/44-23054	1962	—
N7851B	10082/44-23038	1962	—

Aeronautical Cargo Co.

See under: Ben Epstein, Trustee for Ben, Leonard and Stanley W. Epstein

Air Agency Inc./Miami, Florida

One C-82 N74810 (10150/45-57780) from 1961 to 1962.

Air Cargo Equipment Inc./Miami, Florida

President was Ralph A. Smith and one THUEL V. SCHUHART, according to some files, was the company's secretary-treasurer. N75399 was converted as an aerial sprayer and both were later exported to Honduras.

N5113B	10094/44-23050	1958
N75399	10048/44-23004	1956–1957

Aircraft Equipment Co./Miami, Florida

No details. One C-82 N6244C (10025/44-22981) owned in 1957.

Aircraft Leasing Corp. of Florida Inc./Miami Intl. Airport, Florida

No details. One C-82 N75398 (10006/44-22962) owned in 1957. Exported to Guatemala.

Airnews Inc./San Antonio, Texas

Few details. General manager was pilot and aircraft mechanic Solomon Cohen. Three C-82 Packets from 1960 to 1961; operations with Airnews are unknown.

N74046	10052/44-23008	1960–1961
N74047	10056/44-23012	1960–1961
N74048	10096/44-23052	1960–1961

Airparts Inc./Miami, Florida

No details. One C-82 N5121B (10164/45-57794) owned in 1962.

Alaska Aircraft Leasing Inc./Anchorage, Alaska

An Alaska-based aircraft leasing company, which also owned three C-119 Flying Boxcars. Owned one C-82 Jet-Packet 3400 N9701F (10184/45-57814) from 1987 until 1992.

Albert J. Leeward d/b/a Leeward Aeronautical Service/ Fort Wayne, Indiana

See under: Leeward Aeronautical Sales Inc.

Allied Aircraft Sales/Tucson, Arizona

One of several scrap yard dealers located around the giant AMARC facility in Tucson. One ex-Steward-Davis C-82 N6999C (10077/44-23009) was acquired in a derelict state from 1975 through to 1981.

American Airmotive Corp./Miami, Florida

Founded in the 1950s for the conversion of Stearman Model 75 biplanes into agricultural aircraft. Although not confirmed, they appear to have had at least one C-82 Packet, N75887 (10160/45-57790), at some point in 1955–56. They may also have had four others in the same registration batch: N75884 (10110/45-57740); N75885 (10126/45-

57756); N75886 (10136/45-57766) and N75888 (10177/45-57807), but this is also not confirmed. All were exported to Mexico.

Arthur R. Hunter/San Francisco, California

Acting on behalf of North Shore Goldfields Ltd. of Toronto, Canada. One C-82 N7852B (10057/44-23013) was acquired during 1960 but was never exported. North Shore Goldfields Ltd. were investors in New Frontier Airlift Corp., which had been set up by Steward-Davis Inc. The aircraft was subsequently sold to New Frontier.

Aviation Enterprises/Scottsdale, Arizona

No details. One C-82 N4833V (10075/44-23031) in 1960.

Aviation Facilities Inc./Miami, Florida

Few details. A partnership between Thomas R. Green (who ran Dispatch Services Inc.), F.D. Jordan and R.H. Hubsch. Four C-82s from 1957 to 1960 for export. It seems this company may actually be derived from Dispatch Services, as the P.O. Box address at Miami Intl. Airport is the same for both companies.

N5118B	10078/44-23034	1958	Exported Guatemala.
N5119B	10069/44-23025	1958–1959	Exported Guatemala.
N5120B	10163/45-57793	1960	Exported Guatemala.
N75398	10006/44-22962	1957	To Aircraft Leasing Corp.

Ball Bros. Inc./Anchorage, Alaska

Founded by pilot brothers Newt, Burt and Jerry Ball in order to transport fresh fish for processing, the company used a variety of cargo aircraft. They operated C-82 Jet-Packet 3400 N9701F (10184/45-57814) from 1978 to 1982 in support of the business. Their father was Alaskan aviation legend Albert Ball Sr., who had founded Western Alaska Airlines in 1953. Ball Bros. Inc. was renamed Northern Pacific Transport Inc. in 1982, the C-82 remaining in service until 1987.

Bankers Life & Casualty Co./Chicago, Illinois

A U.S. insurance company specializing in health and medical care insurance. Their investment department, in 1955, purchased 29 C-82 Packets from the USAF. The aircraft were stored at Miami Intl. Airport with Miami-based wholesale supplier of aircraft and equipment Florida Aviation Corp. looking after the furnishing and care of the airframes. Many went to Miami aircraft dealers such as Advance Co. Inc. and L.B. Smith Aircraft Corp. before being exported. This was the single largest purchase of C-82s by a civilian entity directly from the USAF.

N5100B	10159/45-57789	1955–1959	Exported Colombia HK-777.
N5101B	10158/45-57788	1955–1960	Exported Colombia HK-583.
N5102B	10152/45-57782	1955–1960	Possible export lease, then sold.
N5103B	10148/45-57778	1955–?	Possibly exported/scrapped.
N5104B	10146/45-57776	1955–1959	Sold for scrap.
N5105B	10145/45-57775	1955–1959	Sold for scrap.
N5106B	10143/45-57773	1955–?	Possibly exported/scrapped.
N5107B	10140/45-57770	1955–1959	Sold for scrap.
N5108B	10135/45-57765	1955–1959	Sold for scrap.
N5109B	10125/45-57755	1955	Disposition unk.

N5110B	10111/45-57741	1955–?	Possibly exported/scrapped.
N5111B	10097/44-23053	1955–?	Possibly exported/scrapped.
N5112B	10095/44-23051	1955	To L.B. Smith Aircraft Corp.
N5113B	10094/44-23050	1955	To Advance Co. Inc.
N5114B	10093/44-23049	1955	To L.B. Smith Aircraft Corp.
N5115B	10092/44-23048	1955	To L.B. Smith Aircraft Corp.
N5116B	10089/44-23045	1955	To Advance Co. Inc.
N5117B	10083/44-23039	1955–1956	To L.B. Smith Aircraft Corp.
N5118B	10078/44-23034	1955	To Advance Co. Inc.
N5119B	10069/44-23025	1955	To Advance Co. Inc.
N5120B	10163/45-57793	1955–1960	To Aviation Facilities Inc.
N5121B	10164/45-57794	1955–1962	To Airparts Inc.
N5122B	10165/45-57795	1955–?	To Lewis Consultants Inc.
N5123B	10178/45-57808	1955–?	Possibly exported/scrapped.
N5124B	10187/45-57817	1955–?	Possibly exported/scrapped.
N5125B	10195/45-57825	1955–?	Possibly exported/scrapped.
N5126B	10170/45-57800	1955–?	Possibly exported/scrapped.
N5127B	10173/45-57803	1955–1959	Sold for scrap.
N5128B	10174/45-57804	1955–1959	Sold for scrap.

B.C. Swensen (Swensair Parts)/Pensacola, Florida

Aircraft and parts dealer in Florida. Owned one C-82 N5116B (10089/44-23045) from 1961 to 1962.

Ben Epstein, Trustee for Ben, Leonard and Stanley Epstein/Miami Beach, Florida

A co-partnership later known as the Aeronautical Cargo Co. located near Miami Intl. Airport, Florida. Up to nine C-82s registered from 1955 to 1961. It's not known if these aircraft actually flew in service or were merely stored at this time. All were later acquired by New Frontier Airlift Corp. S/n: 44-23007 does not seem to have an N-number allocation but was cited by an Argentinean purchaser to have belonged to Ben Epstein.

—	10051/44-23007	1960
N74038	10061/44-23017	1955–1961
N74039	10134/45-57764	1955–1961
N74041	10076/44-23032	1955–1961
N74042	10081/44-23037	1955–1961
N74043	10087/44-23043	1955–1961
N74044	10162/45-57792	1955–1961
N74046	10052/44-23008	1955–1960
N74047	10056/44-23012	1955–1960
N74048	10096/44-23052	1955–1960

Ben W. Widtfeldt/San Francisco, California–Phoenix, Arizona

See under: M&W Aircraft Leasing

N4829V	10073/44-23029	1956
N4833V	10075/44-23031	1959–1960
N4834V	10103/45-57733	1959

Ben W. Widtfeldt & Harry S. McCandless/Council Bluffs, Iowa

See under: M&W Aircraft Leasing

N4832V	10070/44-23026	1955
N4833V	10075/44-23031	1955
N4834V	10103/45-57733	1955

N4835V	10106/45-57736	1955
N6233C	10197/45-57827	1955
N6234C	10198/45-57828	1955
N6235C	10199/45-57829	1955

Biegert Bros. Inc./Phoenix, Arizona

Started in 1946 as a spraying and dusting company by Max and Thelma Biegert. Also operated Lockheed Twins, B-17 and DC-4 aircraft as sprayers. The company closed in 1983. Briefly owned a C-82 N4833V (10075/44-23031) from 1960 to 1961.

Big Piney Aviation Inc./Big Piney, Wyoming

Founded in 1950 by Truman E. Miley and wife Flora Miley, their first aircraft being a Douglas B-18. One C-82 N4830V (10133/45-57763) registered under Miley's name from 1955 to 1961, then registered directly to Big Piney Aviation from 1961 to 1964 for aerial spraying duties. It was converted to an aerial tanker in 1960 for forest fire trials but was never used operationally. Miley is also known for purchasing a number of P-51 Mustangs.

Bob's Airpark/Tucson, Arizona

Owned by Robert A. Hoover, who was vice-president of Allied Aircraft Sales in Tucson. He obtained the sole C-82 N6999C (10077/44-23033) at Allied in 1981 for display purposes. The park closed in 2000 and the collection was broken up, with the C-82 being reduced to scrap and spares.

See also: Allied Aircraft Sales.

C-82A N6999C (msn: 10077) stored at Tucson International Airport, Arizona, during December 1971. It would later go to Bob's Airpark as a display item (Steve Kraus/John Wegg Collection).

Boothe Leasing Corp./San Francisco, California

Formed in 1956 by D. P. Boothe for general equipment leasing. Acquired in 1962 by the Greyhound Corp. as the Greyhound Leasing & Financial Corp. Two C-82s were owned and leased back to United Heckathorn Inc. and their subsidiary SkySpray Inc.

N4829V   10073/44-23029   1956–1959   —
N4832V   10070/44-23026   1956   W/o 1956

Briles Wing & Helicopter Inc./Medford, Oregon

Helicopter business formed in 1957 by Paul R. Briles. Owned one C-82 Jet-Packet 3400 N9701F (10184/45-57814) from 1973 to 1978 for the purpose of transporting helicopters and spare parts to any part of the world. The C-82 could fit two Bell 206B Jet Rangers or one Bell 205 or 212 helicopter into its cargo hold. By 1975 the C-82 had clocked 100,000 air miles hauling helicopters to locations like Alaska, South America, Singapore, and as far away as Australia—that epic journey, made in 1974, was to deliver a Bell 205 to Airfast Helicopters of Sydney. The aircraft retained its previous owner's TWA side stripes with "Briles Wing & Helicopter ph: 390-3554" the only signage added to the fuselage. The C-82 was based out of Santa Monica Airport in California during its time with Briles.

C-82A Jet-Packet 3400 N9701F (msn: 10184) now owned in this photograph by Briles Wing & Helicopter, but still carrying previous owner TWA Airlines red fuselage trim (G. Pat Macha).

D&G Inc./Greybull, Wyoming

Created as a kind of aircraft leasing company by Hawkins & Powers Aviation Inc. founders Dan Hawkins and Gene Powers and run in conjunction with their H&P operations. Registered their C-82 Jet-Packet 3400 N9701F (10184/45-57814) to this company in 1993.

See Also: Hawkins & Powers Aviation Inc.

Darryl G. Greenamyer Inc./Rancho Santa Fe, California

Famous American aviator best known as having been an SR-71 test pilot for Lockheed and for his participation in the Reno Air Races. Briefly owned three ex–NAC Inc. C-82s in 1988. N4752C and N4753C were soon sold to the USAF Museum for display. N5102B became derelict and was sold to H&P INC. in parts.

N4752C	10216/48-581	1988	—
N4753C	10209/48-574	1988	—
N5102B	10152/45-57782	1988-1995	Jet-Packet 1600

Dispatch Services Inc./Miami, Florida

Few details. Company president during 1955 was Thomas R. Green, who appears to have leased N54210 to Fairchild Aircraft for a period of 12 months for experimental and research duties. Both C-82s were later exported to Peru via Panama. See also: Aviation Facilities Inc.

N54210	10150/45-57780	1955-1956
N54211	10202/45-57832	1956

Donald B. Sittman & Alfred E. Merhige/Miami, Florida

No details. One C-82 N2054A (10202/45-57832) from 1955 to 1956.

E.M. Edwards/Sacramento, California

Evan Markum Edwards. One C-82 N5102B (10152/45-57782) from 1960 to 1961.

Esso Standard (Guatemala) Inc./Wilmington, Delaware

U.S. oil company. Their aviation division operated two C-82 Packets in Guatemala to support oil exploration in the region.

N5121B	10164/45-57794	1962-1963	Re-reg: N128E.
N74810	10150/45-57780	1962-1963	Re-reg: N127E.

Ewell K. Nold Jr./South Houston, Texas

Renowned pilot who flew for the MECOM OIL CO. in the Middle East during the 1960s. He was also well known for buying and selling vintage aircraft. Briefly brought and sold two C-82 Packets in the 1960s, N136E being onsold to Mecom Oil Co. but never exported, becoming a derelict at Long Beach Airport.

N136E	10025/44-22981	1963
N4829V	10073/44-23029	1962

Fairchild-Hiller Corp./Hagerstown, Maryland

Reserved eight New Frontier Airlift Corp. C-82 aircraft 14 Jan 1967 with new FAA registrations but never took delivery or ownership of any. Reasons for these reservations are unclear, as all aircraft were, for the most part, derelict. Some sources quote Fairchild's "Missile Division" as the purchaser.

N6769A	10087/44-23043	N6850A	10075/44-23031
N6781A	10134/45-57764	N6856A	10056/44-23012
N6782A	10052/44-23008	N6857A	10076/44-23032
N6845A	10162/45-57792	N6862A	10061/44-23017

Far North Flying Service Inc./Fairbanks, Alaska

Alaskan aircraft company run by Alton C. Mosley and Jean Mosley. Both C-82s were transferred to M&F INC. in 1963, a company Al Mosley was also a partner in. See also: M&F Inc.

N4829V	10073/44-23029	1962–1963	—
N8009E	10071/44-23027	1961–1963	Jet-Packet 3200.

The First National Bank of Anchorage/Anchorage, Alaska

Repossessed C-82 N9701F (10184) in 1992 from Alaska Aircraft Leasing Inc.

Florida Aircraft Leasing Corp./Fort Lauderdale, Florida

One C-82 Jet-Packet 3200 N8009E (10071/44-23027) operated as a lease aircraft from 1968 to 1980. Leases included operators Americana, Ecuador, in 1971 and Pacific Alaska Airways in 1977.

Flying B. Inc./Anchorage, Alaska

No details. One C-82 Jet-Packet 3200 N8009E (10071/44-23027) from 1980 to 1995. Became derelict after retirement, sold to H&P INC. in parts.

Francis L. Duncan/Rockville, Maryland, and New York, N.Y.

Appears to be a U.S. sales agent for Brazilian operator Servicos Aereos Cruzeiro do Sul, as all aircraft were exported to this operator from Leeward Aeronauctical Sales Inc. via this individual.

N6247C	10200/45-57830	1957	Exported Brazil PP-CEF.
N7853B	10141/45-57771	1957–1958	Exported Brazil PP-CEG.
N7854B	10185/45-57815	1957	Exported Brazil PP-CEI.
N7855B	10153/45-57783	1957	Exported Brazil PP-CEL.
N7856B	10147/45-57777	1957–1958	Exported Brazil PP-CEK.
N7857B	10182/45-57812	1957–1959	Exported Brazil PP-CFF.
unk	10115/45-57745	1957	Exported Brazil PP-CEH.
unk	10144/45-57774	1957	Exported Brazil PP-CEE.
unk	10156/45-57786	1957	Exported Brazil PP-CEJ.
unk	10180/45-57810	1957	Exported Brazil PP-CEM.

Frank Ambrose Aviation Co. Inc./Miami, Florida

Florida-based aviation company who are well known for having purchased examples of the rare Northrop C-125 Raider. Acquired, likely in a derelict state, one C-82 N5116B (10089/44-23045) in 1960, reselling it in 1961.

Fuzzy Furlong/Miami, Florida

A Florida resident well known for speedboat racing, appears to have operated some sort of scrap yard in Miami. Six unsold C-82s from Bankers Life & Casualty Co. went to Furlong for scrap around 1959.

N5104B	10146/45-57776	N5108B	10135/45-57765
N5105B	10145/45-57775	N5127B	10173/45-57803
N5107B	10140/45-57770	N5128B	10174/45-57804

George B. Alder/Chattanooga, Tennessee

U.S. businessman with aviation interests in Honduras. He owned a fleet of PT-17 Stearman biplanes converted as sprayers that worked the banana plantations of the United Fruit Co. in Honduras and Guatemala and the cotton fields of southern Honduras. Purchased one C-82 N4834V (10103/45-57733) in 1959 as a cargo and support aircraft for his business. It crashed on July 29, 1965, off the coast of Campeche, Mexico; the crew all survived, but the aircraft was lost.

George T. Baker Aviation School/Miami Intl. Airport, Florida

Started in 1939 as an aviation industry training program. It was named as such in 1961 when the school's current site was donated to the program by the then National Airlines president George T. Baker. They acquired one non-airworthy C-82 airframe (10132/45-57762) for ground and technical instruction duties from 1971 to 1974.

Hagerstown Aviation Museum/Hagerstown, Maryland

A nonprofit volunteer organization for the preservation of Hagerstown's aviation heritage, namely aircraft produced at the Fairchild plant located at Hagerstown's airport. Founded in 2005, the museum has acquired three C-82 Packets for preservation. N9701F is complete, but N5102B and N8009E are derelict and will be restored for various themed displays.

N5102B	10152/45-57782	2006–present	Jet-Packet 1600.
N8009E	10071/44-23027	2006–present	Jet-Packet 3200.
N9701F	10184/45-57814	2006–present	Jet-Packet 3400.

Harry R. Playford/St. Petersburg, Florida

Partner in Madden & Playford Aircraft Inc., an aircraft sales, finance and leasing company. Playford ran several companies offering nonscheduled cargo services using L-18 and DC-3 aircraft. Acquired five C-82s that were stored at Pinellas Airport in Florida for resale into Latin America. M.A. Madden was the president for Madden & Playford Aircraft Inc. at the time of these purchases.

N2057A	10091/44-23047	1955–1957	Ferried as N6238C.
N2058A	10099/44-23055	1955–1956	Ferried as N6239C.
N2060A	10104/45-57734	1955–1957	Ferried as N6240C.
N2064A	10119/45-57749	1955–1956	Ferried as N6242C.
N2065A	10172/45-57802	1955–1957	Ferried as N6241C.

Hawkins & Powers Aviation Inc./Greybull, Wyoming

Often abbreviated as H&P Inc. Established in 1969 by Dan Hawkins and Gene Powers, this company has become a legend among the aviation community for their wide use of piston-engined aircraft in freight, agricultural, fisheries and fire-bombing roles. Aircraft on their registers included the A-26, C-47, C-54, C-97, C-119, C-130, P-2 and PB4Y-2. H&P have the distinction of being the last company in the world to operate a C-82 commercially. N9701F was acquired in 1992 and served on a limited basis until grounded and stored in 2000. H&P closed in 2005 and the C-82 was sold at auction in 2006, along with the hulls of N5102B and N8009E, to the Hagerstown Aviation Museum. See also: D&G Inc.

N5102B	10152/45-57782	1995–2005	Jet-Packet 1600.
N8009E	10071/44-23027	1995–2005	Jet-Packet 3200.
N9701F	10184/45-57814	1992–1993	Jet-Packet 3400.

Henry A. Smith/Richmond, California

President for New Frontier Airlift Corp. Seven C-82 aircraft were registered under his name before being transferred to New Frontier. See also: New Frontier Airlift Corp.

N4833V	10075/44-23031	1961
N74038	10061/44-23017	1961–1963
N74039	10134/45-57764	1961–1963
N74041	10076/44-23032	1961–1963
N74042	10081/44-23037	1961–1963
N74043	10087/44-23043	1961–1963
N74044	10162/45-57792	1961–1963

Interior Airways Inc./Fairbanks, Alaska

Founded by Jim Magoffin in 1946 as an air-taxi and charter company. Incorporated in 1954 when the company won the contract to support the construction of the DEW Line using C-46s and C-47s. Acquired two C-82s in 1963 to support oil exploration in Alaska. N208M crashed in 1965, so Jet-Packet N5102B was purchased to replace it. Became Alaska International Air in 1972 with the C-82s retired or sold in favor of Lockheed L-100 transports.

N208M	10163/45-57793	1963–1965	Crashed 1965.
N209M	10165/45-57795	1963–1979	Derelict from 1973.
N5102B	10152/45-57782	1965–1973	Jet-Packet 1600.

John W. Mecom/Houston, Texas

American businessman, independent oilman and founder of the Mecom Oil Co. Two C-82 Packets were operated in the Middle East from 1963 in support of Mecom's oil operations. Both aircraft were based at Aden in Yemen. N128E was shot down by Egyptian MiG fighters in late 1964. N127E served until wfu in late 1967 and donated to an aviation school in Athens, Greece. N136E was purchased but never put into service. Other Mecom Oil aircraft included a Curtiss C-46 N9588Z, Douglas B-23 N86E and Lockheed Lodestar N5231N.

N127E	10150/45-57780	1963–1974
N128E	10164/45-57794	1963–1964
N136E	10025/44-22981	1963–1972

Mecom Oil Company–owned C-82A N127E (msn: 10150) at RAF Khormaksar (Aden International Airport), Yemen, during 1964. As compared with many other C-82s, Mecom's Packets were kept tidy with little or no signs of wear or outdated markings (Ray Deacon).

L.B. Smith Aircraft Corp./Miami, Florida

Founded in 1947 at Miami Intl. Airport, L.B. Smith quickly became one of the foremost aircraft conversion, overhaul and modification centers in the U.S. They completed many executive aircraft interiors for many types from the Douglas DC-3 to the Lockheed Jetstar. Their most famous conversions were the Douglas A-26 mods such as the *Smith Tempo I* and *Tempo II* and the Curtiss C-46 as the *Smith Super 46*. Up to 18 C-82 Packets were acquired in 1955, demilitarized and exported to Latin American buyers. Three (N2055A, N2059A, N5117B) remained unsold and stored with L.B. Smith for up to nine years before being destroyed in a hurricane.

N2047A	10184/45-57814	1955	To Selk Co.
N2948A	10154/45-47784	1955	Exported Mexico XB-KOI.
N2054A	10202/45-57832	1955	To a Miami dealer.
N2055A	10067/44-23023	1955–1964	Destroyed by Hurricane Cleo.
N2056A	10063/44-23019	1955	Exported Colombia HK-906.
N2057A	10091/44-23047	1955	To a U.S. dealer.
N2058A	10099/44-23055	1955	To a U.S. dealer.
N2059A	10102/44-23058	1955–1964	Destroyed by Hurricane Cleo.
N2060A	10104/45-57734	1955	To a U.S. dealer.
N2061A	10107/45-57737	1955–1956	Exported Colombia HK-914.
N2062A	10203/48–568	1955–1956	Exported Colombia HK-915.
N2063A	10210/48–575	1955–1956	Exported Colombia HK-913.
N2064A	10119/45-57749	1955	To a U.S. dealer.
N2065A	10172/45-57802	1955	To a U.S. dealer.
N5112B	10095/44-23051	1955	Exported Mexico XA-LIZ.
N5114B	10093/44-23049	1955	Exported Mexico XA-LIW.
N5115B	10092/44-23048	1955	Exported Mexico XA-LIY.
N5117B	10083/44-23039	1956–1964	Destroyed by Hurricane Cleo.

LEBCA International Inc./Miami, Florida

A U.S. based subsidiary company of the Venezuelan corporation Linea Expresa Bolivar Compania Anonima (LEBCA) founded in 1949 operating domestic and international cargo services. They also flew DC-3, DC-4, DC-4M and C-46 aircraft but ceased operations on 31 Jan 68. The president of LEBCA at this time was H.R. Perez, who also had an interest in Colombian operator Linea Aereas Del Colombianas Expresas (LACE) Ltda., which brought C-82s HK-426 and HK-468.

N6233C	10197/45-57827	1955–?	Disposition unk.
N6234C	10198/45-57828	1955–1957	Exported Colombia HK-468.
N6235C	10199/45-57829	1955–1956	Exported Colombia HK-426.
N75398	10006/44-22962	1955–1956	To a U.S. dealer.

Leeward Aeronautical Sales Inc./Fort Wayne, Indiana

Has also been known as Leeward Aeronautical Inc. and Leeward Aeronauctical Service. Company president and founder was American Albert J. Leeward, a former ferry pilot for the RCAF during World War II. After the war he began purchasing, restoring and reselling Cessna aircraft, among other types, his business growing from there. Up to 21 C-82s were acquired for resale to Latin American operators from 1955. Leeward was also involved with Trans-International Airlines Inc. and a small charter service called Trans-Gaspesian Airlines Ltd., flying a C-82, several DC-3s and a DC-6. Leeward relocated to Miami, Florida, in late 1955 or early 1956.

N56582	10176/45-57806	1956–1962	To Aero Enterprises Inc.
N6243C	10074/44-23030	1955–1962	To Aero Enterprises Inc.

N6244C	10025/44-22981	1955-1957	To Aircraft Equipment Co.
N6245C	10055/44-23011	1955-1962	To Aero Enterprises Inc.
N6246C	10062/44-23018	1955-1962	To Aero Enterprises Inc.
N6247C	10200/45-57830	1955-1957	To F.L. Duncan.
N75398	10006/44-22962	1955	To a U.S. dealer.
N75399	10048/44-23004	1955	To a U.S. dealer.
N7849B	10084/44-23040	1955-1959	To U.S. operator Alaska.
N7850B	10098/44-23054	1955-1962	To Aero Enterprises Inc.
N7851B	10082/44-23038	1955-1962	To Aero Enterprises Inc.
N7852B	10057/44-23013	1955-1958	To Dutch gold mining co.
N7853B	10141/45-57771	1955-1957	To F.L. Duncan.
N7854B	10185/45-57815	1955-1957	To F.L. Duncan.
N7855B	10153/45-57783	1955-1957	To F.L. Duncan.
N7856B	10147/45-57777	1955-1957	To F.L. Duncan.
N7857B	10182/45-57812	1956-1957	To F.L. Duncan.
unk	10115/45-57745	?-1957	To F.L. Duncan.
unk	10144/45-57774	?-1956	Uruguay/To F.L. Duncan.
unk	10156/45-57786	?-1957	To F.L. Duncan.
unk	10180/45-57810	?-1957	To F.L. Duncan.

Lewis Consultants Inc.

No details. One C-82 N5122B (10165/45-57795). Purchase date unknown, but exported to Guatemala in 1960.

M&F Inc./Fairbanks, Alaska

Originally named Mosley & Freericks, a company founded by Alton C. Mosley and Charles Freericks. Mosley transferred his two C-82s, N4829V and N8009E, from Far North Flying Service to M&F Inc. in 1963. They went out of business in 1967, their two remaining Packets being repossessed and sold to Robert G. Sholton. See also: Mosley & Freericks.

N4829V	10073/44-23029	1963-1964	Jet-Packet 3400. W/o 1965.
N7849B	10084/44-23040	1960-1967	-
N8009E	10071/44-23027	1963-1967	Jet-Packet 3200.

M&W Aircraft Leasing/Council Bluffs, Iowa

Leasing company founded by Harry S. McCandless and Ben W. Widtfeldt (M&W) at Council Bluffs Municipal Airport, where McCandless Flying Service was based. McCandless is also well known for his acquisitions of P-51 Mustangs. Eight C-82s were initially registered to the company's owners in 1955. N6233C, N6234C and N6235C were soon sold off and the remaining "N48xxV"-registered Packets were leased or sold to United Heckathorn Corp. and its aerial subsidiary SkySpray Inc. Three C-82s were at one point earmarked for lease to Switzerland but were not exported. M&W sold off the last of its C-82 fleet in 1959. See also: Ben W. Widtfeldt; Ben W. Widtfeldt & Harry S. Mccandless; United Heckathorn Corp.

N4832V	10070/44-23026	1955-1956
N4833V	10075/44-23031	1955-1959
N4834V	10103/45-57733	1955-1959
N4835V	10106/45-57736	1955-1956

Madden & Playford Aircraft Inc./St. Petersburg, Florida

See under: Harry R. Playford

Master Equipment Co./Cheyenne, Wyoming

Founded in 1945 by Ralph S. Johnson, specializing in aircraft sprayer conversions. Johnson became particularly well known for his agricultural conversions of ex-U.S. Navy PV-1 and PV-2 aircraft. He converted two C-82s into sprayers that served until 1961, when they were both purchased by New Frontier Airlift Corp.

```
N4828V    10085/44-23041    1955-1961
N53228    10080/44-23036    1957-1961
```

Maurice L. Carlson/Anchorage, Alaska

See under: Northern Air Cargo Inc.

Mecom Oil Co./Houston, Texas

See under: John W. Mecom.

Miami Aircraft Maintenance Inc./Miami, Florida

No details. One C-82 N5121B (10164/45-57794) in 1962.

Montgomery Construction Co./Grove City, Pennsylvania

No details. Operated one C-82 N4962V (10137/45-57767) from 1955 to 1957.

Mosley & Freericks/Fairbanks, Alaska

Alaskan aircraft company founded by Alton C. Mosley and Charles Freericks. The company was renamed as M&F INC. in 1960. One C-82 N7849B (10084/44-23040) was registered from 1959 to 1960 before going to M&F Inc. See also: M&F INC.

National Advisory Committee for Aeronautics (NACA)

Founded in 1915 as a U.S. federal agency for the purpose of promoting and researching aeronautical technology. The NACA continued through to 1958, when its assets and personnel were transferred to the newly formed NASA. One C-82 was acquired by the NACA in 1947 for use in research activities and the carriage of outsized cargoes. It was assigned NACA/NASA fleet no. 107 in a bare metal finish with white upper fuselage, red tails and trim, and the NASA logo below the flight-deck.

```
107       10100/44-23056    1947-1961
```

Thirty-two service-weary C-82 aircraft were assigned to the NACA's Lewis Flight Propulsion Laboratory at Cleveland Intl. Airport, Ohio, for research into aircraft crash fires, how they spread, and any solutions that might be developed for crash fire suppression. The aircraft arrived from February to August 1950, when they were prepared for duty. Known test identities were: M-I, T-1, X2, Y2, Y3 (44-22976), Y5, 6, Y6, 7, Y7, Y8 and 10 (44-22979). The actual testing took place six miles east of Ravenna, Ohio, at the Ravenna Arsenal Crash Test Runway (N41 10 21.07/W081 07 39.03). A rough airstrip was built nearby with the arriving C-82 (for high-wing tests) and around twenty C-46 (for low-wing tests) aircraft taxied along roads to reach the test area. Testing was conducted from 1950 to 1953. Each aircraft was propelled along the runway by remote control, the wings slicing through poles, causing the fuel to ignite. Each test was recorded on high-speed cameras for later analysis. The burnt-out remains of thirty C-82s were later buried on site. Two C-82s (s/n: 44-22984 and 44-22991) not used were subsequently sold to civil buyers.

10007/44-22963	10020/44-22976	10032/44-22988
10010/44-22966	10021/44-22977	10033/44-22989
10011/44-22967	10022/44-22978	10034/44-22990
10012/44-22968	10023/44-22979	10035/44-22991
10013/44-22969	10024/44-22980	10036/44-22992
10014/44-22970	10026/44-22982	10037/44-22993
10015/44-22971	10027/44-22983	10041/44-22997
10016/44-22972	10028/44-22984	10042/44-22998
10017/44-22973	10029/44-22985	10044/44-23000
10018/44-22974	10030/44-22986	10046/44-23002
10019/44-22975	10031/44-22987	

Top: Around 30 C-82A Packets were destroyed for crash tests conducted by the NACA from 1950 to 1953. *Bottom:* Various fuel spill tests were also conducted to see how fire spreads during an aircraft crash (both photographs courtesy NASA Glenn Research Center, Cleveland, Ohio).

National Aeronautics & Space Administration (NASA)
See under: National Advisory Committee For Aeronautics (NACA)

National Air & Space Museum (NASM)/Washington, D.C.
Acquired one ex–Steward-Davis C-82 N6997C (10050/44-23006) in 1973 from a batch being scrapped by Steward-Davis. Remained stored until sold to the Pima Air & Space Museum in Tucson, Arizona in 1985.

New Frontier Airlift Corp./Phoenix, Arizona
See under: Steward-Davis Inc.

North Shore Goldfields Ltd./Toronto, Canada
See under: Arthur R. Hunter

Northern Air Cargo (NAC) Inc./Anchorage, Alaska
Founded in 1956 by Robert G. Sholton and Maurice L. Carlson as a charter air freight service throughout Alaska. Owning up to five C-82 Packets, among other types, they pioneered air freight transportation in the Alaskan State. N4752C and N4753C were the flagship C-82s, giving 29 years and 29,000 hours of service without any major incidents. N5102B was registered to company co-founder M.L. Carlson from 1973, then registered to NAC from 1981; all C-82s were retired by 1984–85. NAC continues freight services today in Alaska. See also: Robert G. Sholton

N4752C	10216/48-581	1970–1988	—
N4753C	10209/48-574	1970–1988	—
N5102B	10152/45-57782	1981–1988	Jet-Packet 1600.

C-82A N4752C (msn: 10216) of Northern Air Cargo Inc. at Anchorage, Alaska, September 16, 1969 (Norm Taylor).

Northern Pacific Transport Inc./Anchorage, Alaska
See under: Ball Bros. Inc.

The Ohio Oil Company/Findlay, Ohio

See under country: GUATEMALA

Outsized Cargo Inc./Kenai, Alaska

No details. One C-82 Jet-Packet 3200 N8009E (10071/44-23027) operated during 1980.

Peter Bercut/San Francisco, California

San Francisco businessman and Commissioner for Parks and Recreation. Appears to have owned several C-82 aircraft for business reasons. The two derelicts, #23018 and #23054 listed below, can be seen in a documentary on actor James Garner's racing interests titled *The Racing Scene* (1969).

N56582	10176/45-57806	1962–?	Hull only.
N6243C	10074/44-23030	1962–1971	—
N6245C	10055/44-23011	1962–1971	—
N6246C	10062/44-23018	1962–1971	Derelict 1969.
N7850B	10098/44-23054	1962–1971	Derelict 1969.
N7851B	10082/44-23038	1962–1971	—

Derelict and forgotten at Sebring, Florida, in the late 1960s is C-82A N7850B (msn: 10098), at the time registered to Peter Bercut of San Francisco. The United States Air Force s/n "423054" can just partly be made out on the tail (National Museum of the United States Air Force).

Pima Air & Space Museum/Tucson, Arizona

Located near Davis-Monthan AFB and the giant USAF AMARC center. Acquired one ex-Steward-Davis C-82 N6997C (10050/44-23006) for preservation and display in 1985.

The Pride Capital Group LLC/Deerfield, Illinois

Purchased C-82 Packets N5102B (10152), N8009E (10071) and N9701F (10184) from Hawkins & Powers Aviation Inc. in 2005 for auction.

Richard S. Lowe/Miami, Florida–Bigelow, Minnesota

No details. Purchased four C-82s all for resale and export.

N6233C	10197/45-57827	1955
N6234C	10198/45-57828	1955
N6235C	10199/45-57829	1955
N75398	10006/44-22962	1956–1957

Robert G. Sholton/Anchorage, Alaska

Co-founder of Northern Air Cargo (NAC) Inc. in 1956 as an air charter freight service. N4752C and N4753C became NAC's leading C-82 aircraft from 1955 right through to their withdrawal in 1984. N7849B was acquired in 1967, eventually becoming derelict after 1971. N8009E was only briefly owned before being sold to a lease operator in Florida. See also: Northern Air Cargo (NAC) Inc.

N4752C	10216/48–581	1955–1970	Re-reg to NAC Inc.
N4753C	10209/48–574	1955–1970	Re-reg to NAC Inc.
N7849B	10084/44-23040	1967–1971	Became derelict after 1971.
N8009E	10071/44-23027	1967–1968	Jet-Packet 3200.

Rodest & Company/New York, New York

Legal company for resale of aircraft into Latin America. Employed Miami based Aero Supply Associates Inc. to service and ready aircraft for export.

N2058A	10099/44-23055	1956	Exported Colombia HK-930.
N2063A	10210/48–575	1956	Exported Colombia HK-913X.
N2064A	10119/45-57749	1956	Exported Colombia HK-924.

Royal International Corp./Miami, Florida

No details. Two C-82s registered from 1957 to 1959, both exported to Guatemala in 1959.

N2060A	10104/45-57734	1957–1959
N2065A	10172/45-57802	1957–1959

Samuel C. Rudolph/Los Angeles, California

Known only as a Los Angeles businessman who, it appears, started out as Samuel C. Rudolph & Associates Inc. in 1946. Purchased eight C-82 Packets on 9 Jan 56 from Davis-Monthan AFB. Appears to have had close ties with Steward-Davis Inc., as many aircraft were onsold to them. Six of the remaining eight were registered to Rudolph's company S.C. Rudolph Lumber Corp. from 1958, with all then going to New Frontier Airlift Corp. (Steward-Davis Inc.) by 1962. See also: S.C. Rudolph Lumber Corp.

N5095V	10071/44-23027	1956
N6985C	10090/44-23046	1956–1958
N6989C	10059/44-23015	1956–1958
N6990C	10045/44-23001	1956–1958
N6996C	10049/44-23005	1956–1958
N6997C	10050/44-23006	1956–1958
N6998C	10053/44-23009	1956–1958
N6999C	10077/44-23033	1956–1958

Samuel C. Rudolph, Nathan Sidell, Charles E. Katz (Joint Venturers)/Los Angeles, California

Appears to be a separate business venture by Samuel C. Rudolph to buy and sell C-82s into Latin America. Eleven aircraft were purchased in 1955. All were soon sold to Leeward Aeronauctical Sales Inc.

N6243C	10074/44-23030	1955
N6244C	10025/44-22981	1955
N6245C	10055/44-23011	1955
N6246C	10062/44-23018	1955
N6247C	10200/45-57830	1955
N75398	10006/44-22962	1955
N75399	10048/44-23004	1955
N7849B	10084/44-23040	1955
N7850B	10098/44-23054	1955
N7851B	10082/44-23038	1955
N7852B	10057/44-23013	1955

S.C. Rudolph Lumber Corp./Los Angeles, California

See under: Samuel C. Rudolph

N5095V	10071/44-23027	1959–1961	Jet-Packet 3200, re-reg: N8009E.
N6985C	10090/44-23046	1958–1962	
N6996C	10049/44-23005	1958–1962	
N6997C	10050/44-23006	1958–1962	
N6998C	10053/44-23009	1958–1962	
N6999C	10077/44-23033	1958–1962	

Selk Co./North Hollywood, California

One C-82 N2047A (10184/45-57814) from 1955 to 1956. Leased to Israeli company Bedek Aviation out of Tel Aviv.

Skyspray Inc.

See under: United Heckathorn Corp.

Small Bussiness Administration/Washington D.C.

A U.S. government agency. Repossessed C-82s N7849B (10084) and N8009E (10071) from M&F INC. in 1967 on behalf of the First National Bank of Fairbanks, Alaska.

Smock & Jenner Inc./Cincinnati, Ohio

No details. All sold to Ben Epstein, aka: Aeronautical Cargo Co.

N74038	10061/44-23017	1955
N74039	10134/45-57764	1955
N74041	10076/44-23032	1955
N74042	10081/44-23037	1955
N74043	10087/44-23043	1955
N74044	10162/45-57792	1955
N74046	10052/44-23008	1955
N74047	10056/44-23012	1955
N74048	10096/44-23052	1955

Steward-Davis Inc./Gardena and Long Beach, California, and New Frontier Airlift Corp./Phoenix, Arizona

The most significant operator of the C-82 was first founded in 1946 by Herb Steward and Stanley Davis as an engine overhaul and repair company. They soon moved into the aircraft modification business selling surplus PBY Catalinas as the improved Super Catalina. They became the leading C-82 affiliate through the following developments: (1) Became the sole C-82 Type Certificate (AR-15) holder in July, 1955. (2) Developed the C-82 for greater performance as the Jet-Packet and Skytruck with an auxiliary Jet-Pak utilizing the Westinghouse J30 and J34 engine. (3) The sole C-82 parts supplier with a massive spares inventory. (4) C-82 service provider to operators in the U.S. and Latin America. Up to thirty-two Packets were at one point at their Long Beach S-D facility in the late 1950s, their main office shifting there in 1962. Steward-Davis also developed a J34 Jet-Pak for the Fairchild C-119.

New Frontier Airlift Corp. was a holding company created by Steward-Davis in 1961, also in partnership with North Shore Goldfields Ltd. and Lawa Goudvelden for marketing of the new C-82 Jet-Packet. A board was set up in the locally famous Luhrs Building in Phoenix, Arizona, with Henry A. Smith as president, aircraft then being acquired from various sources. Although the venture was initially promising, with various lease options for customers, only nine conversions are ever known to have been made. The remaining airframes had to be scrapped when New Frontier went bankrupt in 1970. The last C-82s at Long Beach were scrapped in 1972. S-D continued on in the aerospace industry until Herb Steward retired in 1990.

The table below lists Steward-Davis Inc. and New Frontier's officially registered C-82 inventory. N6887C, N6985C and N74127 were S-D workhorses. Most other aircraft remained unconverted and stored—"N69xxC" reg mainly in Arizona, "N740xx" reg mainly in Florida, with the rest at Long Beach, California. N6887C, N4833V, N53228 and one other airframe (likely N7852B or N5116B) were used for the Hollywood motion picture *The Flight of the Phoenix* (1965). N9701F was briefly owned in 1973, but only for overhaul and resale. One C-82 N136E was not owned by S-D but was stored at their facility. Two C-82s not owned by S-D but Jet-Pak converted were N4829V and PP-CEK.

N4828V	10085/44-23041	1961–1971	Skypallet prototype.
N4833V	10075/44-23031	1961–1971	Stored.
N5095V	10071/44-23027	1956–1958	Jet-Packet 3200.
N5102B	10152/45-57782	1961–1963	Jet-Packet 1600.
N5116B	10089/44-23045	1962–1971	Derelict airframe.
N53228	10080/44-23036	1961–1971	Stored.
N6985C	10090/44-23046	1962–1972	Jet-Packet 3400.
N6989C	10059/44-23015	1958–1971	Jet-Packet 1600, re-reg: N6887C.
N6990C	10045/44-23001	1958	Jet-Packet 1600.
N6996C	10049/44-23005	1962–1971	Stored.
N6997C	10050/44-23006	1962–1971	Stored, to Pima Museum.
N6998C	10053/44-23009	1962–1971	Stored.
N6999C	10077/44-23033	1962–1975	Stored, to Allied Aircraft Sales.
N74038	10061/44-23017	1963–1971	Stored.
N74039	10134/45-57764	1963–1971	Stored.
N74041	10076/44-23032	1963–1971	Stored.
N74042	10081/44-23037	1963–1971	Stored.
N74043	10087/44-23043	1963–1971	Stored.
N74044	10162/45-57792	1963–1971	Stored.
N74046	10052/44-23008	1961–1971	Stored.
N74047	10056/44-23012	1961–1971	Stored.

N74048	10096/44-23052	1961–1971	Stored.
N74127	10177/45-57807	1961–1964	Skytruck Mk. I.
N7852B	10057/44-23013	1960–1971	re-reg: N7884C.
N9701F	10184/45-57814	1973	Jet-Packet 3400.
—	10110/45-57740	1962–1972	ex–Mexicana XA-LOJ.
—	10126/45-57756	1962–1971	ex–Mexicana XA-LOK.
—	10136/45-57766	1962–1972	ex–Mexicana XA-LOL.

See Section One for the complete Steward-Davis story.

Top: C-82A Jet-Packet 1600 N6887C (msn: 10059) in the late 1960s after being cleaned to a bare-metal finish in a new role as a Flying Repair Station (Andre Van Loon Collection). *Bottom:* C-82A N6985C (msn: 10090) seen here with the J3400 Jet-Pak installed (Andre Van Loon Collection).

Swensair Parts/Pensacola, Florida

See under: B.C. Swensen.

Tanana Investment Corp./Fairbanks, Alaska

One C-82 Jet-Packet 1600 N5102B (10152/45-57782) from 1963 to 1965. Various leases including one to Wien Alaska Airlines Inc. with "Wien" actually marked on the aircraft.

Thuel V. Schuhart/Miami, Florida

Partner with Daniel E. Murray in legal firm Schuhart & Murray, based at Miami Intl. Airport. Three C-82s were briefly registered in Schuhart's name and he appears to have also been an agent for Leeward Aeronautical Sales Inc., and in 1958, the secretary-treasurer for Air Cargo Equipment Inc.

N5113B	10094/44-23050	1958
N75398	10006/44-22962	1955
N75399	10048/44-23004	1955–1956

Trans World Airlines (TWA) Inc./Kansas City, Kansas

A major American airline from 1925 until 2001, under the control of famed aviator Howard Hughes from 1939 to the 1960s. Acquired one C-82 N2047A (10184/45-57814) in 1956, which was rebuilt as a Flying Repair Station for service in Europe based out of Orly Field, Paris. Registered as N9701F in 1960, it valiantly served TWA's airliner fleet throughout the 1960s, the TWA C-82 becoming a well-recognized aircraft at various European airports. Sold in 1973.

Classic shot of C-82A Jet-Packet 3400 N9701F (msn: 10184) at Orly, Paris (John Wegg).

Truman E. Miley/Roy, Utah

See under: Big Piney Aviation Inc.

United Airlines Inc./Chicago, Illinois

A major American airline founded in 1926 and named as such in 1934. Aside from being a carrier of passengers throughout the U.S., they were also a major mover of air mail during this time and into the 1940s. Entered into a lease with the USAAF for one C-82 Packet NC8855 (10060/44-23016) in October 1946 for a test flight involving the en route sorting of mail for a faster delivery. However, the widely publicized United Flying Mail Car experiment ultimately proved impractical, and the C-82 was returned to the USAAF by mid–October 1946.

An envelope that was part of the United Flying Mail Car's experimental flight in 1946, introducing the five-cent air mail stamp (author collection).

United Heckathorn Corp./Richmond, California

Founded in 1947, this company had built a reputation, at the time, as a first-class agricultural chemical supplier. Their subsidiary company, SkySpray Inc., had a fleet of up to 25 aircraft for aerial spraying, including five C-82 Packets converted with chemical tanks in the cargo holds. Two C-82s (N4829V, N4832V) were directly registered to United Heckathorn, with three others, N4833V (10075), N4834V (10103) and N4835V (10106), leased from M&W Aircraft Leasing. All became known as the Hayward Packets, since spraying operations were conducted from Hayward Airport in California. Both United-owned Packets were reregistered to the Boothe Leasing Corp. from 1956 and leased back to United Heckathorn during this period. N4829V was converted to an aerial tanker in 1957 for forest fire trials and flew one fire season, but apparently without much success.

N4829V	10073/44-23029	1956–1962	—
N4832V	10070/44-23026	1956	W/o 1956.

Walter Soplata/Newbury, Ohio

Private individual who amassed a large warbird collection on his rural property. Acquired one C-82 (10035/44-22991) from the NACA at Cleveland Intl. Airport, Ohio, sometime in the mid- to late 1950s.

Detail view of the SkySpray logo on C-82A N4829V (msn: 10073) during August 1958 (Earl Holmquist via Author Collection).

Whitney-Ben Trading Co./Calexico, California

No details. Company president was Mobley M. Milam. Two C-82s purchased from the USAF, then sold to other operators.

N4829V	10073/44-23029	1955–1956
N4830V	10133/45-57763	1955

URUGUAY

Aerovias Monder/Montevideo

Freight services ran from Ezeiza, Argentina, to Caracas, Venezuela, through to Miami, Florida. The company is named after its owners, Jose Marti Montal and Alberto Luis De Ridder. C-82 services began 18 Apr 56 and continued through to 4 Jun 57, when CX-AQA was sold to Brazil as PP-CEE. CX-AQB appears to have gone back to the U.S. only to be scrapped around 1959 in Florida.

CX-AQA	10144/45-57774	1956–1957
CX-AQB	10145/45-57775	1956–1957

C-82A Packet CX-AQA (msn: 10144) in unique Monder livery (Dick Phillips Collection).

Lorenzo Castelluci

No details. One C-82 CX-AQA (10144/45-57774) during 1956.

Jose Balbi/Montevideo

No details. One C-82 CX-AQA (10144/45-57774) during 1956.

Venezuela

Linea Aeropostal Venezolana (LAV)/Caracas

Venezuelan airline founded in 1933. Possibly leased one C-82 YV-C-LBA (10198/45-57828) for a short period from Colombian operator Linea Aereas del Colombianas Expresas (LACE) Ltda. LAV flew routes from Venezuela to the U.S., Colombia and Peru.

C-82A Packet marked as YV-C-LBA and seemingly under lease to Linea Aeropostal Venezolana in Venezuela. The LACE company markings, however, indicate it belongs to that Colombian operator (Peter J. Marson Collection).

Yemen

A. Besse & Co. (Aden) Ltd./Aden

Aden-based company founded by French businessman Antonin Besse (1877–1951), who were agents for several insurance, airline and shipping companies. They appear to have reserved a Yemeni reg: VR-ABD for a Mecom Oil Co.–owned C-82 (10028/44-22981), and the aircraft was marked as such, but it was never exported.

Section Four

Production Histories

Aircraft are presented in order of manufacturer's serial number with military serial number, buzz number and type designation placed adjacent. To help break up the text and to assist with swifter acquisition of any desired piece of data, unit assignments and changes of civil ownership are separated by way of a double "//" slash.

Notes on Military Histories: Assignment dates given are those as presented on the IARC cards. Actual unit acquisition or change of unit assignment, however, was often prior to these dates by up to two weeks, it has been found.

Although all 224 C-82 IARCs were able to be obtained, several, over the years, were either incorrectly recorded to microfilm or simply unable to be located at the time of writing, these being:

msn/s/n / IARC File Status

10108/45-57738 / Some parts indecipherable.
10142/45-57772 / Some parts indecipherable.
10169/45-57799 / Missing.
10171/45-57801 / Incomplete.
10186/45-57816 / Some parts indecipherable.

Notes on Civil Registrations: During the course of research, N-number files were obtained from the FAA in Oklahoma City. Dates given are taken from the Bill of Sale documents in the files, which is the primary indicator of a change of civil ownership. Physical change of ownership, however, was often prior or post the dates given. In some cases these dates are "paper changes" only, with many aircraft never actually entering service with their new owners.

Although all known C-82 N-number records were attempted to be located, not all could be acquired. It's therefore noted here which U.S. based registrations were missing, not able to be located, or incomplete at the time of writing:

N-number / msn/s/n / File Status

N1799 / 0126/45-57756 / Records missing.
N2779 / 10110/45-57740 / Records missing.
N5109B / 10125/45-57755 / Records missing.
N7856B / 10147/45-57777 / Records missing.
N54211 / 10202/45-57832 / Records not located.
N75884 / 10110/45-57740 / Records not located.
N75885 / 10126/45-57756 / Records not located.

N-number / msn/s/n / File Status

N75886 & N93067 / 10136/45-57766 / Records not located.
N75888 / 10177/45-57807 / Records not located.
N5122B & N209M / 10165/45-57795 / Records incomplete.
N6236C & N54210 / 10150/45-57780 / Records incomplete, existing records under N127E.

Many official foreign civil registration files were also unable to be obtained. This is largely due to South American countries' not retaining records, or records simply being lost or destroyed during the previous decades.

10001 / 43-13202 / XC-82-FA

Prototype aircraft. ff: 10 Sep 1944 at the Fairchild Aircraft Maryland plant. Made nationwide public and promotional appearances, nicknamed the Flying Boxcar // Engaged in flight-testing first at Hagerstown, then to Wright Field Ohio 27-May 45 for further tests // 310th AAF BAS (TAC) Pope Field North Carolina 30 Nov 46 as ground instructional airframe for paratroop training // Avble to USAF: 2 Mar 48; Acc: 30 Apr 48; Del: 30 Apr 48 to USAF // 10th MSU GP (TAC) Pope AFB North Carolina 22 Jul 48. Assigned to reclamation and salvage and dropped from inventory 21 Oct 48. Final Disposition: Scrapped.

XC-82 s/n: 43-13202 (msn: 10001) (National Museum of the United States Air Force).

10002

Canceled XC-82-FA prototype.

10003 / 44-22959/CQ-959 / C-82A-1-FA

First production C-82A. ff: 30 May 45 // Acc: 5 Jun 45; Avble: unk; Del: 11 Jun 45 to USAAF // Assigned ATSC Dallas Texas 14 Jun 45 for ferrying duties // 4806th AAF BAS(ATSC) Fairchild Aircraft Maryland 21 Aug 45 // 4862nd AAF BAS (ATSC) Fairchild

Aircraft Maryland 3 Oct 45 // 4000th AAF BAS (ATSC) Wright Field Ohio 17 Jan 46. Relegated to ground instructional duties and technical school 31 Jul 46; stored 12 Dec 46. Final Disposition: Scrapped.

10004 / 44-22960/CQ-960 / C-82A-1-FA

Avble: unk; Acc & Del: 30 Jun 45 to USAAF // 4000th AAF BAS (ATSC) Wright Field Ohio 18 Aug 45; assigned test duties at Wright Field & Patterson Field, Ohio and Fairchild Aircraft Maryland; assignments to 4020th & 4120th AAF BAS (AMC). Crash-landed due to engine failure 1.5 miles NW of Cormey Ohio 14 Aug 47. Pilot: Thomas T. Clarke, no fatalities but aircraft "damaged beyond repair." Assigned to reclamation and salvage 4 Sep 47. Dropped from inventory 16 Mar 48. Final Disposition: Accident.

10005 / 44-22961/CQ-961 / C-82A-1-FA

Avble: 2 Oct 45; Acc & Del: 10 Oct 45 to USAAF // Aircraft Production Division (ATSC) Dayton Field Ohio 14 Oct 45 // 4000th AAF BAS (ATSC) Patterson Field Ohio 17 Jan 46; multiple assignments to Fairchild Aircraft Maryland (AMC) for tests // 62nd TCG (TAC) Bergstrom Field Texas 17 Jul 47; 62nd to McChord Field Washington 7 Aug 47; 62nd MSU GP (TAC) McChord AFB, Washington 30 Sep 47 // 313th TCG (TAC) Bergstrom AFB Texas 10 Feb 48 // 319th AF BAS (TAC) Lawson AFB Georgia 31 Mar 48 // 4408th AB SQ (TAC) Lawson AFB Georgia 3 Aug 48. Assigned to reclamation and salvage 4 Oct 49 due to "abnormal deterioration in use." Dropped from inventory 14 Oct 49. One source quotes the fuselage was sent to Bikini Atoll for use in nuclear tests, but this has not been confirmed. Final Disposition: Scrapped.

C-82A s/n: 44-22961 (msn: 10005) on display at the General Electric Air Research Lab at Schenectady, New York, on June 22, 1946. Note the buzz number, CQ-961, on the boom. This was the last of three production C-82As built with the slightly blunter Duramold nose and army olive drab livery (Richard Lockett via Air-and-Space.com).

10006 / 44-22962/CQ-962 / C-82A-1-FA

Acc: 31 Oct 45; Avble: 3 Dec 45; Del: 15 Dec 45 to USAAF. First C-82A delivered with all-metal nose extension and in a polished bare metal finish // 4000th AAF BAS (AMC) Patterson Field Ohio 31 Mar 46 for experimental and test work; to Fairchild Aircraft Maryland (AMC) for mods 19 Jun 46; transferred to Wright Field Ohio 10 Sep 46; to Fairchild Aircraft Maryland (AMC) for mods 21 Apr 47 // 2750th AB GP (AMC) WPAFB Ohio 25 Oct 48; cvtd to EC-82A for experimental and research duties // Air Research and Development HQ (ARD) WPAFB Ohio 17 Apr 51; renamed Wright Air Development Center (ARD) 22 Jun 51; to 6502nd Parachute Development Test GP (ARD) El Centro Naval Air Station California 17 Feb 52 // Fairchild Aircraft Maryland (AMC) 12 Jun 52 on bailment; likely for conversion as the Group A prototype with upgraded flight-deck communications and electronic equipment // Wfu to Ogden Air Materiel Area (AMC) Hill AFB Utah 2 Apr 54 and stored. Dropped from inventory 8 Jul 54 // Samuel C. Rudolph, Nathan Sidell, Charles J. Katz (Joint Venturers) Los Angeles California 29 Sep 55 reg: N75398 // Albert J. Leeward d/b/a Leeward Aeronautical Service Fort Wayne Indiana 17 Aug 55 (paper sale made prior to acquisition from the Air Force); ownership transferred to Leeward Aeronautical Sales Inc. Fort Wayne Indiana same day // Thuel V. Schuhart (Agent) Miami Florida 12 Sep 55 (paper sale made prior to acquisition from the Air Force) // LEBCA International Inc. Miami Florida 13 Sep 55 (paper sale made prior to acquisition from the Air Force) // Richard S. Lowe Bigelow Minnesota 5 Jun 56 // Aviation Facilities Inc. Miami Florida 14 Oct 57 // Aircraft Leasing Corp. of Florida Inc. Miami Intl. Airport Florida 17 Oct 57 // Empresa Guatemalteca de Aviacion (Aviateca Guatemalteca) Guatemala Nov 57 reg: TG-ATA. Had an engine failure after take-off from La Aurora Intl. Airport, Guatemala 6 Feb 58 and made a forced landing in Guatemala City, fatalities unk, nfd. Another source states the aircraft had an u/c failure and made a forced landing at La Aurora after dumping the cargo. Final Disposition: Accident.

C-82A s/n: 44-22962 (msn: 10006) was extensively used as a test aircraft (National Museum of the United States Air Force).

10007 / 44-22963/CQ-963 / C-82A-1-FA

Acc: 23 Nov 45; Avble: unk; Del: 19 Dec 45 to USAAF Ladd Field Alaska // 4000th AAF BAS (ATSC) Patterson Field Ohio 27 Mar 46; multiple assignments to Fairchild Aircraft Maryland (AMC) for mods // 316th TCG (TAC) Lawson Field Georgia (detached) 26 Aug 46; assigned 75th TCSq // 62nd TCG (TAC) Bergstrom Field, Texas 11 Mar 47 // 311th AAF BAS (TAC) Bergstrom Field, Texas 8 Jul 47 // To Fairchild Aircraft Maryland (AMC) for mods 23 Jul 47 // 5th RES SQ (ATC) Westover Field Massachusetts 28 Aug 47; cvtd to SC-82A; to 4000th AF BAS (AMC) Patterson Field Ohio 10 Dec 47 // 6th RES SQ (MATS) Westover AFB Massachusetts 5 Oct 49; to 1600th MSU GP (MATS) Westover AFB Massachusetts 13 Oct 49; to Mobile Air Materiel Area (AMC) Brookley AFB, Alabama 15 Nov 49 for mnt // Warner-Robins Air Materiel Area (AMC) Robins AFB Georgia 6 Dec 49; cvtd back to C-82A // Wfu and assigned to National Advisory Committee for Aeronautics (NACA) 22 Jun 50 for experimental air-crash tests. Dropped from inventory 29 Jun 50. Final Disposition: Tested to Destruction.

10008 / 44-22964/CQ-964 / C-82A-1-FA

Acc: 30 Nov 45; Avble: unk; Del: 20 Dec 45 to USAAF Ladd Field Alaska // 4112nd AAF BAS (AMC) Olmsted Field Pennsylvania 26 May 46 // Fairchild Aircraft Maryland (AMC) for mods 14 Jul 46. Suffered a landing accident at Offutt Field Nebraska 18 Jul 46. Pilot: Usto F. Schulz, no fatalities but aircraft extensively damaged // 130th AAF BAS (ADC) Offutt Field Nebraska 13 Aug 46; assessed as "damaged beyond repair" // 4131st AAF BAS (ADC) Offutt Field Nebraska 29 Sep 46; grounded and awaiting disposition orders // 131st AAF BAS (ADC) Offutt Field Nebraska 15 Jan 47. 131st to PGC 31 Mar 47. Assigned to reclamation and salvage and dropped from inventory 29 Aug 47. Final Disposition: Accident.

10009 / 44-22965/CQ-965 / C-82A-1-FA

Acc: 21 Dec 45; Avble: 3 Jan 46; Del: 10 Jan 46 to USAAF; Cincinnati Ferrying Division (ATC) for ferrying; also ferried by the 555th AAF BAS (ATC) // Assigned to CAF HQ Support Squadron Stout Field Indiana 16 Jan 46 // 9th TCSq (374th TCG/CAF) Greenville Field South Carolina 19 Feb 46. Minor damage from in-flight bird strike at Barksdale Field 25 Feb 46 // 804th AAF BAS (CAF) Greenville Field South Carolina 4 Mar 46 // 303rd AAF BAS (TAC) Greenville Field South Carolina 2 May 46; deployment to 434th TCG (TAC) Greenville Field South Carolina 25 Jun 46; to Fairchild Aircraft Maryland (AMC) for mods 25 Jul 46; assigned 37th TCSq (316th TCG) 11 Aug 46. Minor taxiing accident at Greenville Field South Carolina 24 Sep 46; no fatalities // 309th AAF BAS (TAC) Biggs Field Texas 20 Nov 46; to Fairchild Aircraft Maryland (AMC) for mods 19 Mar 47 // 62nd TCG (TAC) Bergstrom Field Texas 21 Jun 47; deployment to 314th AAF BAS (TAC) McChord Field Washington 13 Aug 47; 62nd Air Depot (TAC) McChord Field Washington for repairs 20 Aug 47; 62nd MSU GP (TAC) McChord Field Washington 31 Aug 47 // 313th TCG (TAC) Bergstrom AFB Texas 14 Feb 48 // 319th AF BAS (TAC) Lawson AFB Georgia 31 Mar 48. Suffered engine failure 13 Aug 48 and crew forced to bail out. Pilot: Philip R. Hewmiller, no fatalities but aircraft destroyed on impact 40 miles NE Gadsden Alabama. Assigned to reclamation and dropped from inventory 15 Oct 48. Final Disposition: Accident.

10010 / 44-22966/CQ-966 / C-82A-1-FA

Acc: 31 Dec 45; Avble: 24 Jan 46; Del: 4 Feb 46 to USAAF; Cincinnati Ferrying Division (ATC) for ferrying // 1103rd AAF BAS (ATC) Morrison Field Florida 12 Feb 46 for test duties; to Fairchild Aircraft Maryland (ATSC/AMC) 10 Jul 46 for mods // 62nd AAF BAS (ATC) Westover Field Massachusetts 16 Apr 47 // 5th RES SQ (ATC) Westover Field Massachusetts 7 Jul 47; cvtd as SC-82A; dep overseas 24 Jul 47 to 11 Aug 47; to Fairchild Aircraft Maryland (AMC) 18 Sep 47 for mods; to 5th at MacDill AFB Florida 31 Oct 47; deployment to 307th MSU GP (SAC) MacDill AFB Florida 18 Jan 49 // 1st RES SQ (MATS) MacDill AFB Florida 5 Oct 49 // Warner-Robins Air Materiel Area (AMC) Robins AFB Georgia 19 Dec 49; cvtd back to C-82A // Wfu and assigned to National Advisory Committee for Aeronautics (NACA) 22 Jun 50 for experimental air-crash tests. Dropped from inventory 26 Aug 50. Final Disposition: Tested to Destruction.

10011 / 44-22967/CQ-967 / C-82A-1-FA

Acc: 31 Dec 45; Avble: 4 Feb 46; Del: 11 Feb 46 to USAAF; Cincinnati Ferrying Division (ATC) for ferrying // 3704th AAF BAS (TC) Keesler Field Mississippi 20 Feb 46 for technical training; multiple assignments to Fairchild Aircraft Maryland (ATSC/AMC) for mods starting 8 Aug 46. Suffered a landing accident at Kessler Field Mississippi 26 Sep 47 due to mechanical failure, no fatalities and aircraft repaired // 313th MSU GP (TAC) Bergstrom AFB Texas 2 Sep 48 // 4414th AB SQ (CNC) Bergstrom AFB Texas 9 Feb 49 for storage // 1700th Air Transport Group (MATS) Kelly AFB Texas 28 Mar 49; to San Antonio Air Materiel Area (AMC) Kelly AFB Texas 4 May 49 for depmnt; to San Bernardino Air Depot (AMC) Norton AFB California 20 Dec 49 // Wfu and assigned to National Advisory Committee for Aeronautics (NACA) 22 Mar 50 for experimental air-crash tests. Dropped from inventory 29 Mar 50. Final Disposition: Tested to Destruction.

10012 / 44-22968/CQ-968 / C-82A-1-FA

Acc: 31 Jan 46; Avble: 8 Feb 46; Del: 4 Mar 46 to USAAF // 4152nd AAF BAS (ATSC) Lockbourne Field Ohio 7 Mar 46 for tests; 4152nd to Clinton County Field Ohio 5 May 46; multiple assignments to Fairchild Aircraft Maryland (AMC) for mods starting 10 Jul 46. Minor damage in ground collision at Clinton County Field Ohio 24 Oct 46, no fatalities // 62nd TCG (TAC) Bergstrom Field Texas 18 Jun 47 // to Fairchild Aircraft Maryland (AMC) for mods 21 Jul 47 // 316th TCG (TAC) Greenville AFB South Carolina 17 Oct 47; multiple assignments to 316th MSU GP (TAC) Greenville AFB South Carolina; to Middletown Air Materiel Area (AMC) Olmsted AFB Pennsylvania 29 Apr 49 for mnt; 316th to Smyrna AFB Tennessee 4 Nov 49; depl to Guantanamo Bay Cuba 28 Feb 50 // Wfu and assigned to National Advisory Committee for Aeronautics (NACA) 20 Mar 50 for experimental air-crash tests. Dropped from inventory 30 Mar 50. Final Disposition: Tested to Destruction.

10013 / 44-22969/CQ-969 / C-82A-5-FA

Acc: 25 Feb 46; Avble: 26 Feb 46; Del: 5 Mar 46 to USAAF; Cincinnati Ferrying Division (ATC) for ferrying; also ferried by the 554th AAF BAS (ATC) // 804th AAF

BAS (CAF) Greenville Field South Carolina 13 Mar 46 // Fairchild Aircraft Maryland (AMC) for mods 2 Apr 46; served as a test aircraft // 310th AAF BAS (TAC) Pope Field North Carolina 4 Feb 47; to Fairchild Aircraft Maryland (AMC) for mods 18 Jun 47 // 316th TCG (TAC) Greenville AFB South Carolina 7 Oct 47; multiple assignments to 316th MSU GP (TAC) Greenville AFB South Carolina starting 19 Feb 48 // 313th MSU GP (TAC) Bergstrom AFB Texas 26 May 48; multiple assignments to 313th TCG (TAC) Bergstrom AFB Texas starting 14 Jun 48 // 4414th AB SQ (TAC) Bergstrom AFB Texas 13 Oct 48 for storage // 314th AF BAS (TAC) Smyrna AFB Tennessee 22 Nov 48 // 7th Geodetic SQ (55th SRC/SAC) Topeka AFB Kansas 3 Jan 49 with depl to Mt Home AFB Idaho // 55th MSU GP (55th SRC/SAC) Topeka AFB Kansas 16 Mar 49; renamed Forbes AFB 10 Jun 49 // Oklahoma Air Materiel Area (AMC) Tinker AFB Oklahoma 3 Oct 49 // 91st Strategic Reconn Group (SAC) Barksdale AFB Louisiana 3 Nov 49 // Wfu and assigned to National Advisory Committee for Aeronautics (NACA) 15 Feb 50 for experimental air-crash tests. Dropped from inventory 24 Feb 50. Final Disposition: Tested to Destruction.

C-82A s/n: 44-22969 (msn: 10013) being readied for crash tests with the NACA (courtesy NASA Glenn Research Center, Cleveland, Ohio).

10014 / 44-22970/CQ-970 / C-82A-5-FA

Acc & Avble: 26 Feb 46; Del: 8 Mar 46 to USAAF; Cincinnati Ferrying Division (ATC) for ferrying; also ferried by the 554th AAF BAS (ATC) // 804th AAF BAS (CAF) Greenville Field South Carolina 13 Mar 46 // 303rd AAF BAS (TAC) Greenville Field South Carolina 2 May 46 // 434th TCG (TAC) Greenville Field South Carolina 23 Jun 46; to Fairchild Aircraft Maryland (AMC) for mods 10 Jul 46 // 4112th AAF BAS (AMC) Olmsted Field Pennsylvania 29 Jul 46 // 316th TCG (TAC) Greenville Field South Carolina (detached) 14 Sep 46; assigned 37th TCSq; depl to Lawson Field Georgia 17 Oct 46 assigned 75th TCSq // 62nd TCG (TAC) Bergstrom Field Texas 6 Feb 47; assigned 4th TCSq; to Fairchild Aircraft Maryland (AMC) for mods 21 Apr 47. Damaged in minor taxiing accident at Myrtle Beach Field South Carolina 13 Jun 47, no fatalities. 62nd to McChord Field 7 Aug 47; multiple assignments to 62nd MSU GP (TAC) McChord Field Washington starting 16 Sep 47 // 313th TCG (TAC) Bergstrom AFB Texas 8 Mar 48; assigned 47th TCSq; depl to Pope AFB North Carolina 14 Apr 48 // 4414th AB SQ (TAC)

Bergstrom AFB Texas 13 Oct 48 for storage // 314th TCG (TAC) Smyrna AFB Tennessee 23 Mar 49; to Warner-Robins Air Materiel Area (AMC) Robins AFB Georgia 7 Apr 49; 314th MSU GP (TAC) Smyrna AFB Tennessee 13 Jan 50 // Wfu and assigned to National Advisory Committee for Aeronautics (NACA) 6 Apr 50 for experimental air-crash tests. Dropped from inventory 11 Apr 50. Final Disposition: Tested to Destruction.

10015 / 44-22971/CQ-971 / C-82A-5-FA

Acc & Avble: 27 Feb 46; Del: 14 Mar 46 to USAAF; Cincinnati Ferrying Division (ATC) for ferrying // 316th TCG (TAC) Lawson Field Georgia (detached) 15 May 46; assigned 75th TCSq; to Fairchild Aircraft Maryland (AMC) for mods 7 Aug 46; depl to Greenville Field South Carolina 20 Aug 46; assigned 37th TCSq // 319th AAF BAS (TAC) Lawson Field Georgia 25 May 47 // 5th RES SQ (ATC) Westover Field Massachusetts 17 Jul 47; cvtd to SC-82A; to Fairchild Aircraft Maryland (AMC) for mods 31 Aug 47. Damaged in a landing accident at Selfridge AFB Michigan 19 Apr 48, likely while on delivery flight to the 9th RES SQ, no fatalities // 56th MSU GP (SAC) Selfridge AFB Michigan 19 Apr 48 for repairs // 9th RES SQ (ATC) Selfridge AFB Michigan 11 May 48 // 2151st RES UT (MATS) Lowry AFB Colorado 9 Sep 48 // 1700th Air Transport Group (MATS) Kelly AFB Texas 3 May 49; cvtd back to C-82A // Wfu and assigned to National Advisory Committee for Aeronautics (NACA) 29 Mar 50. Dropped from inventory 5 Apr 50. Served for a period as an engine test-bed for research into jet engine thrust reverse development. Final Disposition: Tested to Destruction.

C-82A s/n: 44-22971 (msn: 10015) was used as a test-bed airframe by the NACA after USAF service. Note the prominent MATS logo from the aircraft's service with the 1700th Air Transport Group at Kelly Air Force Base, Texas (courtesy NASA Glenn Research Center, Cleveland, Ohio).

10016 / 44-22972/CQ-972 / C-82A-5-FA

Acc: 28 Feb 46; Avble: 5 Mar 46; Del: 13 Mar 46 to USAAF; Cincinnati Ferrying Division (ATC) for ferrying; also ferried by the 554th AAF BAS (ATC) // 316th TCG (TAC) Lawson Field Georgia (detached) 20 Mar 46; assigned 75th TCSq. Damaged in a landing accident at Lawson Field Georgia 22 Mar 46, no fatalities and aircraft repaired. To Fairchild Aircraft Maryland (AMC) for mods 7 Aug 46 // 62nd TCG (TAC) Bergstrom Field Texas 10 Feb 47; to Fairchild Aircraft Maryland (AMC) for mods 23 Mar 47; 62nd to McChord Field 7 Aug 47; 62nd MSU GP (TAC) McChord AFB Washington 30 Sep 47 // 313th TCG (TAC) Bergstrom AFB Texas 5 Feb 48; assigned 47th TCSq; depl to Pope AFB North Carolina 14 Apr 48 // 4414th AB SQ (TAC) Bergstrom AFB Texas 13 Oct 48 for storage // 2150th RES UT (MATS) Hamilton AFB California 13 Jan 49; cvtd to SC-82A; depl to March AFB California 7 Apr 49; to 1st MSU GP (SAC) March AFB California 15 Jun 49 // 4th RES SQ (MATS) March AFB California 5 Oct 49 // Wfu and assigned to National Advisory Committee for Aeronautics (NACA) 13 Mar 50 for experimental air-crash tests. Dropped from inventory 29 Mar 50. Final Disposition: Tested to Destruction.

10017 / 44-22973/CQ-973 / C-82A-5-FA

Avble: 11 Mar 46; Acc: 12 Mar 46; Del: 20 Mar 46 to USAAF; ferried by the 554th & 555th AAF BAS (ATC) // 316th TCG (TAC) Pope Field North Carolina 25 Mar 46. Minor mechanical failure at Myrtle Beach Field South Carolina 10 Jun 46. To Fairchild Aircraft Maryland (AMC) for mods 30 Jul 46; to 4000th AAF BAS (AMC) Patterson Field Ohio 12 Aug 46, later to Wright Field; to 4117th AAF BAS (AMC) Robins Field Georgia 27 Mar 47; to Fairchild Aircraft Maryland (AMC) for mods 19 May 47; 316th to Greenville Field South Carolina 25 Aug 47; multiple assignments to 316th MSU GP (TAC) Greenville AFB South Carolina starting 17 Nov 47; to 4127th AF BAS (AMC) McClellan AFB California 16 Dec 47. Taxiing accident at McClellan AFB California 13 Dec 48, no fatalities. Experienced an engine failure at McClellan AFB California 23 Dec 48, no fatalities and aircraft landed safely // 5th RES SQ (MATS) Westover AFB Massachusetts 31 Jan 49; cvtd to SC-82A; to San Antonio Air Materiel Area (AMC) Kelly AFB Texas 22 Jul 49 for mnt; deployment to Maxwell AFB Alabama 22 Aug 49 // Wfu and assigned to National Advisory Committee for Aeronautics (NACA) 11 Apr 50 for experimental air-crash tests. Dropped from inventory 16 May 50. Final Disposition: Tested to Destruction.

10018 / 44-22974/CQ-974 / C-82A-5-FA

Avble: 11 Mar 46; Acc: 13 Mar 46; Del: 15 Mar 46; Cincinnati Ferrying Division (ATC) for ferrying; also ferried by the 554th AAF BAS (ATC) // 316th TCG (TAC) Lawson Field Georgia (detached) 24 Mar 46; aircraft reassigned to Pope Field North Carolina 7 Jul 46; assigned 36th TCSq; multiple assignments to 310th AAF BAS (TAC) Pope Field North Carolina starting 7 Jul 46; to Fairchild Aircraft Maryland (AMC) for mods 8 Aug 46; multiple assignments to 319th AAF BAS (TAC) Lawson Field Georgia starting 27 Mar 47; to Fairchild Aircraft Maryland (AMC) for mods 19 May 47; 316th to Greenville Field South Carolina 25 Aug 47; 316th MSU GP (TAC) Greenville AFB South Carolina 29 Jan 48; to Middletown Air Materiel Area (AMC) Olmsted AFB Pennsylvania 4 Jun 49 for mnt; 316th to Smyrna AFB Tennessee 4 Nov 49; depl to Guantanamo Bay Cuba 28 Feb 50 // Wfu and assigned to National Advisory Committee for Aeronautics (NACA) 20 Mar 50 for experimental air-crash tests. Dropped from inventory 30 Mar 50. Final Disposition: Tested to Destruction.

10019 / 44-22975/CQ-975 / C-82A-5-FA

Acc: 20 Mar 46; Avble & Del: 27 Mar 46 to USAAF; retained at Fairchild Aircraft Maryland (AMC) as a test aircraft // 62nd TCG (TAC) Bergstrom Field Texas 6 Apr 47; 62nd to McChord Field Washington 7 Aug 47; 62nd MSU GP (TAC) McChord AFB Washington 30 Sep 47 // 313th TCG (TAC) Bergstrom AFB Texas 14 Feb 48; 313th MSU GP (TAC) Bergstrom AFB Texas 8 May 48 // 4414th AB SQ (TAC) Bergstrom AFB Texas 11 Oct 48 for storage; to 4408th AB SQ (TAC) Lawson AFB Georgia 12 Nov 48 // 314th TCG (CNC) Smyrna AFB Tennessee 23 Mar 49; 314th MSU GP (CNC) Smyrna AFB Tennessee 25 Apr 49; to Warner-Robins Air Materiel Area (AMC) Robins AFB Georgia 20 May 49 // Wfu and assigned to National Advisory Committee for Aeronautics (NACA) 6 Apr 50 for experimental air-crash tests. Dropped from inventory 11 Apr 50. Final Disposition: Tested to Destruction.

10020 / 44-22976/CQ-976 / C-82A-5-FA

Acc: 26 Mar 46; Avble: 5 Apr 46; Del: 16 Apr 46 to USAAF; Cincinnati Ferrying Division (ATC) for ferrying; also ferried by the 554th AAF BAS (ATC). Minor landing accident due to mechanical failure 12 Apr 46 at the Hagerstown plant, likely during the delivery flight // 316th TCG (TAC) Pope Field North Carolina 14 Apr 46; assigned 36th TCSq. Landing accident at Pope Field North Carolina 15 Apr 46, no fatalities and aircraft repaired; to Fairchild Aircraft Maryland (AMC) for mods 28 May 47; multiple assignments to 310th AAF BAS (TAC) Pope Field North Carolina starting 16 Jun 46; 316th to Greenville Field 25 Aug 47; assigned 37th TCSq; multiple assignments to 316th MSU GP (TAC) Greenville AFB South Carolina starting 14 Jan 48 // 313th TCG (TAC) Bergstrom AFB Texas 13 Apr 48 // 4414th AB SQ (TAC) Bergstrom AFB Texas 13 Oct 48 for storage;

C-82A s/n: 44-22976 (msn: 10020), marked as Y3 after a "successful crash" at the Ravenna Arsenal, Ohio (courtesy NASA Glenn Research Center, Cleveland, Ohio).

depl to 20th TCSq (314th TCG) 22 Nov 48 // 2151st RES UT (MATS) Biggs AFB Texas 27 Jan 49; cvtd to SC-82A; to 97th MSU GP (SAC) Biggs AFB Texas 22 Apr 49 // 5th RES SQ (MATS) Biggs AFB Texas 5 Oct 49 // Wfu and assigned to National Advisory Committee for Aeronautics (NACA) 31 Mar 50 for experimental air-crash tests. Dropped from inventory 7 Apr 50. Final Disposition: Tested to Destruction.

10021 / 44-22977/CQ-977 / C-82A-5-FA

Acc: 26 Mar 46; Avble: 3 Apr 46; Del: 8 Apr 46 to USAAF; Cincinnati Ferrying Division (ATC) for ferrying; also ferried by the 550th AAF BAS (ATC) // 316th TCG (TAC) Lawson Field Georgia (detached) 12 Apr 46. Ground looped at Gravelly Point Field Washington, D.C. 18 May 46, no fatalities and aircraft repaired. To 503rd AAF BAS (ATC) Gravelly Point Field Washington, D.C. 29 May 46; to 4112th AAF BAS (AMC) Olmsted Field Pennsylvania 15 Sep 46; to Fairchild Aircraft Maryland (AMC) for mods 16 Dec 46; aircraft to Pope Field North Carolina 18 Feb 47; assigned 36th TCSq; to Fairchild Aircraft Maryland (AMC) for mods 15 Apr 47; 316th to Greenville Field 25 Aug 47; to 310th AF BAS (TAC) Pope AFB North Carolina 13 Oct 47; to 1100th AF BAS (ATC) McClellan AFB California 22 Dec 47; 316th MSU GP (TAC) Greenville AFB South Carolina 8 Jan 48; to Middletown Air Materiel Area (AMC) Olmsted AFB Pennsylvania 24 Apr 49 for mnt; to Sacramento Air Materiel Area (AMC) McClellan AFB California 5 Sep 49; 316th to Smyrna AFB 4 Nov 49; depl to Guantanamo Bay Cuba 28 Feb 50 // Wfu and assigned to National Advisory Committee for Aeronautics (NACA) 20 Mar 50 for experimental air-crash tests. Dropped from inventory 30 Mar 50. Final Disposition: Tested to Destruction.

10022 / 44-22978/CQ-978 / C-82A-5-FA

Acc: 31 Mar 46; Avble: 2 Apr 46; Del: 15 Apr 46 to USAAF; Cincinnati Ferrying Division (ATC) for ferrying; also ferried by the 554th AAF BAS (ATC) // 316th TCG (TAC) Pope Field North Carolina 14 Apr 46; assigned 36th TCSq. Suffered minor damage in a crash landing at Hamilton Field California 11 May 46, no fatalities and aircraft repaired // 401st AAF BAS (ADC) Hamilton Field California 16 May 46 // To Fairchild Aircraft Maryland (AMC) for mods 1 Jan 47 // 62nd TCG (TAC) Bergstrom Field Texas 11 Feb 47 // 311th AAF BAS (TAC) Bergstrom Field Texas 10 Jul 47 // To Fairchild Aircraft Maryland (AMC) for mods 23 Jul 47 // 62nd AAF BAS (ATC) McChord Field Washington 16 Sep 47 // 8th RES SQ (ATC) Hamilton AFB California 7 Mar 48; cvtd to SC-82A // 2150th RES UT (MATS) Hamilton AFB California 7 Sep 48 // 1700th Air Transport Group (MATS) Kelly AFB Texas 6 Apr 49; cvtd back to C-82A // 1800th AACS WG (MATS) Tinker AFB Oklahoma 8 Sep 49 // 1857th AACS SQ (MATS) Tinker AFB Oklahoma 21 Sep 49 // Wfu and assigned to National Advisory Committee for Aeronautics (NACA) 4 Apr 50 for experimental air-crash tests. Dropped from inventory 19 Apr 50. Final Disposition: Tested to Destruction.

10023 / 44-22979/CQ-979 / C-82A-5-FA

Acc: 31 Mar 46; Avble: 5 Apr 46; Del: 12 Apr 46 to USAAF; Cincinnati Ferrying Division (ATC) for ferrying; also ferried by the 554th AAF BAS (ATC) // 316th TCG

(TAC) Pope Field North Carolina 2 May 46; to Fairchild Aircraft Maryland (AMC) for mods 30 Jul 46 // 62nd TCG (TAC) Bergstrom Field Texas 17 Sep 46; assigned 8th TCSq; to Fairchild Aircraft Maryland (AMC) for mods 4 Mar 47; 62nd to McChord Field 7 Aug 47; to 314th AAF BAS (TAC) McChord Field Washington 14 Aug 47; 62nd Air Depot (TAC) McChord Field Washington 20 Aug 47; 62nd MSU GP (TAC) McChord Field Washington 31 Aug 47 // 313th TCG (TAC) Bergstrom AFB Texas 19 Mar 48; assigned 47th TCSq; depl to Pope AFB Texas 14 Apr 48; 313th MSU GP (TAC) Bergstrom AFB Texas 18 Aug 48 // 4414th AB SQ (TAC) Bergstrom AFB Texas 13 Oct 48 for storage // 2150th RES UT (MATS) Hamilton AFB California 17 Jan 49; cvtd to SC-82A; assignments to 78th MSU GP (CNC) Hamilton AFB California starting 26 Apr 49 // 4th RES SQ (MATS) Hamilton AFB California 5 Oct 49; aircraft to March AFB California 7 Oct 49 // Wfu and assigned to National Advisory Committee for Aeronautics (NACA) 23 Mar 50 for experimental air-crash tests. Dropped from inventory 25 May 50. Final Disposition: Tested to Destruction.

C-82A s/n: 44-22979 (msn: 10023), marked as 10, prior to being catapulted down the crash test runway at Ravenna, Ohio. Note the nose wheel brace used to keep the aircraft on track (courtesy NASA Glenn Research Center, Cleveland, Ohio).

10024 / 44-22980/CQ-980 / C-82A-5-FA

Avble: 17 Apr 46; Acc: 26 Apr 46; Del: 29 May 46 to USAAF // 2002nd AFF Base Unit (TC) Stewart Field New York 5 Jun 46 for pilot training // ferried by the 554th AAF BAS (ATC) // 316th TCG (TAC) Pope Field North Carolina 7 Jul 46; to Fairchild Aircraft Maryland (AMC) for mods 30 Jul 46 // 62nd TCG (TAC) Bergstrom Field Texas 17 Sep 46; assigned to 8th TCSq; to Fairchild Aircraft Maryland (AMC) for mods 23 Mar 47; 62nd to McChord Field 7 Aug 47; 62nd MSU GP (TAC) Bergstrom Field Texas 16 Sep 47 // 313th TCG (TAC) Bergstrom AFB Texas 8 Mar 48; assigned 47th TCSq; depl to Pope AFB North Carolina 14 Apr 48; 313th MSU GP (TAC) Bergstrom AFB Texas 18 Aug 48 // 4414th AB SQ (TAC) Bergstrom AFB Texas 13 Oct 48 for storage // 314th TCG

(TAC) Smyrna AFB Tennessee 22 Nov 48; 314th MSU GP (CNC) Smyrna AFB Tennessee 3 Mar 49; to Warner-Robins Air Materiel Area (AMC) Robins AFB Georgia 6 Apr 49 for special projects // Wfu and assigned to National Advisory Committee for Aeronautics (NACA) 29 Mar 50 for experimental air-crash tests. Dropped from inventory 7 Apr 50. Final Disposition: Tested to Destruction.

10025 / 44-22981/CQ-981 / C-82A-5-FA

Acc: 17 Apr 46; Avble & Del: unk, to USAAF; ferried by the 554th AAF BAS (ATC) // 316th TCG (TAC) Pope Field North Carolina 12 May 46; assigned 36th TCSq; to Fairchild Aircraft Maryland (AMC) for mods 1 Aug 46 & 24 Nov 46; aircraft transferred to Greenville AFB South Carolina 15 Oct 47; to 1100th AF BAS (ATC) McClellan AFB California 14 Dec 47; to 10th MSU GP (TAC) Pope AFB North Carolina 7 Apr 48; 316th MSU GP (TAC) Pope AFB North Carolina 29 Jun 48; to Warner-Robins Air Materiel Area (AMC) Robins AFB Georgia 14 Mar 49 for depmnt; to 2750th AB GP (AMC) WPAFB Ohio 28 Jul 49; 316th to Smyrna AFB Tennessee 4 Nov 49; depl to Guantanamo Bay Cuba 28 Feb 50 // 314th TCG (CNC) Smyrna AFB Tennessee 28 Mar 50; assigned 2601st Light Assault SQ; Smyrna renamed Sewart AFB 25 Mar 50; depl to Laurinburg-Maxton Airport North Carolina 24 Apr 50 // 375th TCG (CNC) Greenville AFB South Carolina 24 Oct 50; deployment to 4418th Base Complement SQ (CNC) Greenville AFB South Carolina 30 Nov 50; to 433rd TCWG (TAC) Greenville AFB South Carolina 1 Feb 51; to 4901st Support WG (Atomic) (SPW) Kirtland AFB New Mexico 18 Jun 51; depl to Brownwood Field Texas 6 Mar 52 // 55th Strategic Reconn WG (SAC) Ramey AFB Puerto Rico 15 Jul 52; to Davis-Monthan AFB Arizona 13 Oct 52; 55th to Forbes AFB Kansas 26 Oct 52 // Wfu to Ogden Air Materiel Area (AMC) Hill AFB Utah 12 May 53 and stored. Dropped from inventory 8 Jul 54 // Samuel C. Rudolph, Nathan Sidell, Charles J. Katz (Joint Venturers) Los Angeles California 28 Sep 55 reg: N6244C // Albert J. Leeward

This C-82A (msn: 10025) was acquired by a United States operator after service in the Honduran Air Force. It was stored at Long Beach Airport, California, until eventually scrapped in 1972. It's seen here in early 1965 while still in a stored but flyable condition (Ed Coates Collection).

d/b/a Leeward Aeronautical Service Fort Wayne Indiana 17 Aug 55 (paper sale made prior to acquisition from the Air Force); ownership transferred to Leeward Aeronautical Sales Inc. Fort Wayne Indiana same day; cert of reg not issued until 7 May 57 by which time Leeward was relocated to Miami Florida // Aircraft Equipment Co. Miami Florida 27 Jun 57 for export to Honduran Air Force the same day; reg: N6244C canx 5 Nov 57 // Fuerza Aerea Hondurena (FAH) Tegucigalpa Honduras s/n: 793. In service with the Honduran Air Force from 1957 to 1963 but only saw limited service due to a lack of spares // Ewell K. Nold Jr. Houston Texas 25 Sep 63 reg: N136E // John W. Mecom (Mecom Oil Co.) Houston Texas 5 Nov 63; stored at Long Beach Airport with Steward-Davis Inc.; listed as wfu 18 May 65. Steward-Davis made repairs to inner left wing 7 Apr 66. Yemeni reg: VR-ABD rsvd but ntu, apparently for a potential sale to A. Besse & Co. (Aden) Ltd. of Yemen; photographic evidence shows reg: VR-ABD was applied before that of N136E. However, the aircraft remained at Long Beach Airport, becoming a derelict minus engines. Listed as scrapped 18 Apr 72. Final Disposition: Scrapped.

10026 / 44-22982/CQ-982 / C-82A-5-FA

Acc: 15 Apr 46; Avble: 19 Apr 46; Del: 22 Apr 46 to USAAF; ferried by the 554th AAF BAS (ATC) // 316th TCG (TAC) Pope Field North Carolina 12 May 46; assigned 36th TCSq; to Fairchild Aircraft Maryland (AMC) for mods 30 Jul 46 & 3 Dec 46; multiple assignments to 310th AAF BAS (TAC) Pope Field North Carolina starting 20 Jul 47; 316th to Greenville Field 25 Aug 47; 316th MSU GP (TAC) Greenville AFB South Carolina 1

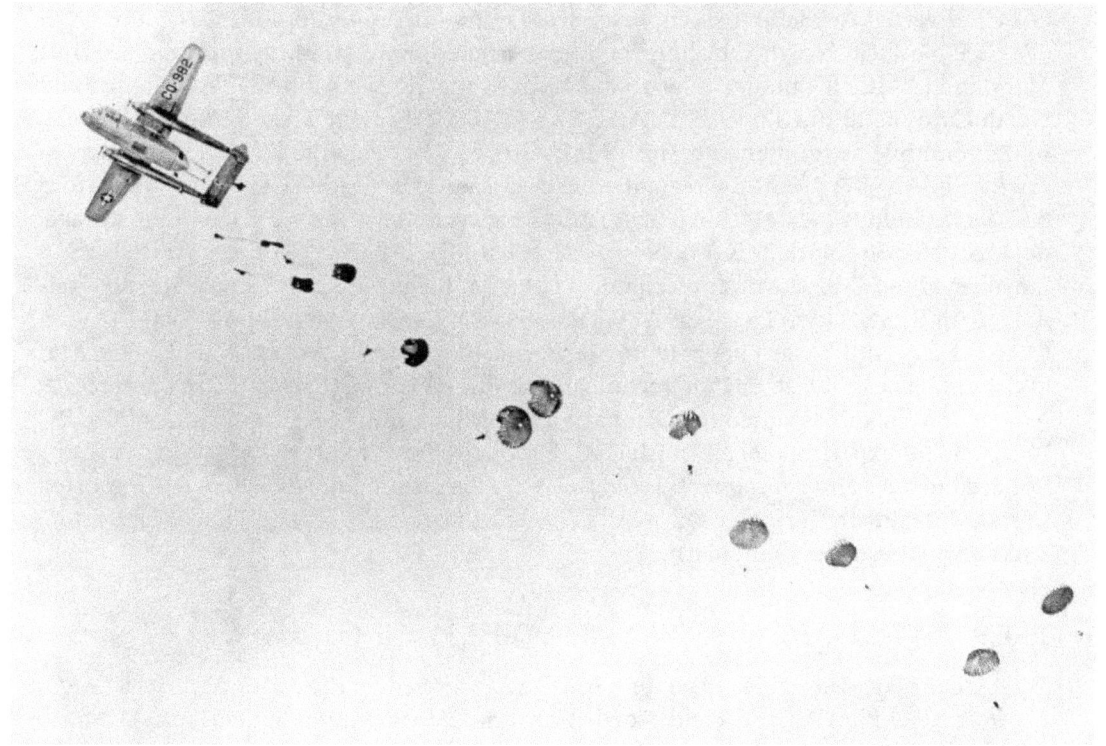

Paratroops jumping from C-82A Packet s/n: 44-22982 (msn: 10026) (Unites States Air Force).

Mar 48; 5th RES SQ (MATS) MacDill AFB Florida 6 Jan 49; cvtd to SC-82A // 307th MSU GP (SAC) MacDill AFB Florida 29 Sep 49 // 1st RES SQ (MATS) MacDill AFB Florida 1 Nov 49 // Wfu and assigned to National Advisory Committee for Aeronautics (NACA) 31 Mar 50 for experimental air-crash tests. Dropped from inventory 3 Apr 50. Final Disposition: Tested to Destruction.

10027 / 44-22983/CQ-983 / C-82A-5-FA

Acc: 17 Apr 46; Avble & Del: unk to USAAF; ferried by the 554th AAF BAS (ATC) // 316th TCG (TAC) Pope Field North Carolina 12 May 46; assigned 36th TCSq. Landing accident at Tinker Field Oklahoma 24 May 46, no fatalities. To 4136th AAF BAS (AMC) Tinker Field Oklahoma 5 Jun 46; to Fairchild Aircraft Maryland (AMC) for mods 4 Aug 47; 316th to Greenville Field 25 Aug 47; 316th MSU GP (TAC) Greenville AFB South Carolina 11 May 48 // 2150th RES UT (MATS) Hamilton AFB California 1 Feb 49; cvtd to SC-82A; to 316th MSU GP (TAC) Greenville AFB South Carolina 28 Apr 49; to 78th MSU GP (CNC) Hamilton AFB California 3 Aug 49 // 4th RES SQ (MATS) Hamilton AFB California 5 Oct 49 // Wfu and assigned to National Advisory Committee for Aeronautics (NACA) 4 Apr 50 for experimental air-crash tests. Dropped from inventory 12 Apr 50. Final Disposition: Tested to Destruction.

10028 / 44-22984/CQ-984 / C-82A-5-FA

Acc & Avble: 18 Apr 46; Del: 10 May 46 to USAAF; ferried by the 554th AAF BAS (ATC); diverted to Memphis Tennessee 15 May 46 for domestic project // 316th TCG (TAC) Pope Field North Carolina 7 Jul 46; assigned 37th TCSq; to Fairchild Aircraft Maryland (AMC) for mods 30 Jul 46 & 22 Apr 47; to 310th AAF BAS (TAC) Pope Field North Carolina 10 Jun 47; to 313th AAF BAS (TAC) Greenville Field South Carolina 30 Jul 47; multiple assignments to 316th MSU GP (TAC) Greenville Field North Carolina starting 18 Aug 47; 316th to Greenville Field 25 Aug 47 // 313th TCG (TAC) Bergstrom AFB Texas 10 Jul 48 // 4414th AB SQ (TAC) Bergstrom AFB Texas 13 Oct 48 for storage; depl to 20 TCSq (314th TCG) 19 Nov 48 // 2151st RES UT (MATS) Biggs AFB Texas 10 Jan 49; cvtd to SC-82A. Minor mechanical failure at Biggs AFB Texas 23 Apr 49, no fatalities // 5th RES SQ (MATS) Biggs AFB Texas 5 Oct 49; to San Antonio Air Materiel Area (AMC) Kelly AFB Texas 14 Sep 49; to Oklahoma Air Materiel Area (AMC) Tinker AFB Oklahoma 31 Oct 49; to 3415th Technical Training WG (TC) Lowry AFB Colorado 19 Nov 49 // Wfu and assigned to National Advisory Committee for Aeronautics (NACA) 10 May 50 for experimental air-crash tests. Dropped from inventory 10 May 50. Airframe not used in tests and subsequently sold to civil interests, no known U.S. reg. // Exported to unk operator in Peru reg: OB-WAC-479; later re-reg: OB-T-479. Final Disposition: Unknown (Presumed Scrapped).

10029 / 44-22985/CQ-985 / C-82A-5-FA

Acc: 23 Apr 46; Avble & Del: unk to USAAF; ferried by the 554th AAF BAS (ATC) // 316th TCG (TAC) Pope Field North Carolina 28 May 46; assigned 36th TCSq; to Fairchild Aircraft Maryland (AMC) for mods 30 Jul 46 & 13 Mar 47; to 310th AAF BAS (TAC) Pope Field North Carolina 4 Aug 47; 316th to Greenville Field 25 Aug 47; multiple assignments to 316th MSU GP (TAC) Greenville AFB North Carolina starting 26 Apr 48; to Middletown Air Materiel Area (AMC) Olmsted AFB Pennsylvania 28 Apr 49 for mnt; 316th to Smyrna AFB 4 Nov 49; depl to 314th MSU GP (TAC) Smyrna AFB Tennessee 26 Jan 50; depl to Guantanamo Bay Cuba 28 Feb 50 // Wfu and assigned to National Advisory Committee for Aeronautics (NACA) 20 Mar 50 for experimental air-crash tests. Dropped from inventory 30 Mar 50. Final Disposition: Tested to Destruction.

10030 / 44-22986/CQ-986 / C-82A-5-FA

Avble: 19 Apr 46; Acc: 26 Apr 46; Del: 29 May 46 to USAAF; ferried by the 554th AAF BAS (ATC) // 316th TCG (TAC) Pope Field North Carolina 7 Jul 46; assigned 36th TCSq; to Fairchild Aircraft Maryland (AMC) for mods 1 Aug 46 & 22 Apr 47. Minor mid-air collision over Pope Field North Carolina 10 May 47, no fatalities and aircraft repaired. Multiple assignments to 310th AAF BAS (TAC) Pope Field North Carolina starting 12 May 47; 316th to Greenville Field 25 Aug 47; 316th MSU GP (TAC) Greenville AFB North Carolina 6 May 48 // 2151st RES UT (MATS) Selfridge AFB Michigan 3 Mar 49; cvtd SC-82A // 5th RES SQ (MATS) Selfridge AFB Michigan 5 Oct 49. Made a forced landing at Selfridge AFB Michigan 1 Feb 50 due to mechanical failure, no fatalities and aircraft repaired; deployment to 56th MSU GP (CNC) Selfridge AFB Michigan 2 Feb 50; to 56th Fighter-Interceptor WG (CNC) Selfridge AFB Michigan 21 Feb 50 // Wfu and assigned to National Advisory Committee for Aeronautics (NACA) 9 May 50 for experimental air-crash tests. Dropped from inventory 25 May 50. Final Disposition: Tested to Destruction.

10031 / 44-22987/CQ-987 / C-82A-5-FA

Avble: 24 Apr 46; Acc: 30 Apr 46; Del: 29 May 46 to USAAF; ferried by the 554th AAF BAS (ATC) // 316th TCG (TAC) Pope Field North Carolina 7 Jul 46; assigned to 36th TCSq; to Fairchild Aircraft Maryland (AMC) for mods 1 Aug 46 & 7 Apr 47; 316th to Greenville Field 25 Aug 47; 316th MSU GP (TAC) Greenville AFB North Carolina 1 May 48; to Warner-Robins Air Materiel Area (AMC) Robins AFB Georgia 22 Mar 49 for depmnt; 316th to Smyrna AFB 4 Nov 49; depl to Guantanamo Bay Cuba 28 Feb 50 // Wfu and assigned to National Advisory Committee for Aeronautics (NACA) 20 Mar 50 for experimental air-crash tests. Dropped from inventory 30 Mar 50. Final Disposition: Tested to Destruction.

10032 / 44-22988/CQ-988 / C-82A-5-FA

Avble: 29 Apr 46; Acc: 3 May 46; Del: 31 May 46 to USAAF; ferried by the 554th AAF BAS (ATC) // 316th TCG (TAC) Pope Field North Carolina 7 Jul 46; assigned 37th TCSq; to Fairchild Aircraft Maryland (AMC) for mods 1 Aug 46 & 13 Apr 47; multiple assignments to 310th AAF BAS (TAC) Pope Field North Carolina starting 1 Jul 47; 316th to Greenville Field 25 Aug 47; multiple assignments to 316th MSU GP (TAC) Greenville Field North Carolina 9 Sep 47 // 313th TCG (TAC) Bergstrom AFB Texas 21 Dec 47; 313th MSU GP (TAC) Bergstrom AFB Texas 12 Feb 48 // 4414th AB SQ (TAC) Bergstrom AFB Texas 13 Oct 48 for storage // 314th TCG (CNC) Smyrna AFB Tennessee 5 Apr 49; assigned 2601st Light Assault SQ // Wfu and assigned to National Advisory Committee for Aeronautics (NACA) 3 Apr 50 for experimental air-crash tests. Dropped from inventory 11 Apr 50. Final Disposition: Tested to Destruction.

10033 / 44-22989/CQ-989 / C-82A-10-FA

Avble: 8 May 46; Acc: 28 May 46; Del: 15 Jul 46 to USAAF // Retained as a test and experimental aircraft, several tests saw the aircraft fitted with reverse pitch propellers featuring larger hubs. Assignments to: Caldwell Field (AMC) New Jersey 21 Jul 46; Fairchild Aircraft Maryland (AMC) 17 Sep 46; Hartford Field Connecticut (AMC) 11 Dec 46; 4000th AAF BAS (AMC) Patterson Field Ohio 28 Jan 47; Fairchild Aircraft Maryland (AMC) 11 May 47; 4152nd AAF BAS (AMC) Clinton County Field Ohio 30 Jun 47 // 316th TCG (TAC) Greenville AFB South Carolina 1 Jan 48 // 313th TCG (TAC) Bergstrom AFB Texas 9 Jan 48; 313th MSU GP (TAC) Bergstrom AFB Texas 18 Aug 48 // 4414th AB SQ (TAC) Bergstrom AFB Texas 13 Oct 48 for storage // 314th TCG (CNC) Smyrna AFB Tennessee 23 Mar 49; assigned 2601st Light Assault SQ; to Warner-Robins Air Materiel Area (AMC) Robins AFB Georgia 20 May 49; to 314th MSU GP (CNC) Smyrna AFB Tennessee 13 Jan 50 // Wfu and assigned to National Advisory Committee for Aeronautics (NACA) 29 Mar 50 for experimental air-crash tests. Dropped from inventory 7 Apr 50. Final Disposition: Tested to Destruction.

C-82A s/n: 44-22989 (msn: 10033). Note the positioning of the buzz number, CQ-989, on the boom. These were later displayed on the forward fuselage (National Museum of the United States Air Force).

10034 / 44-22990/CQ-990 / C-82A-10-FA

Avble: 9 May 46; Acc: 28 May 46; Del: 26 Jul 46 to USAAF; ferried by the 554th AAF BAS (ATC); to 434th TCG (TAC) Greenville Field South Carolina; diverted to Memphis Tennessee 4 Aug 46 for domestic project // 316th TCG (TAC) Pope Field North Carolina 30 Sep 46; assigned 36th TCSq; to Fairchild Aircraft Maryland (AMC) for mods 1 Apr 47; to 310th AAF BAS (TAC) Pope Field North Carolina 26 Aug 47; aircraft to Greenville AFB South Carolina 15 Oct 47; multiple assignments to 316th MSU GP (TAC) Greenville AFB South Carolina starting 17 Dec 47 // 313th MSU GP (TAC) Bergstrom AFB Texas 29 Mar 48; 313th TCG (TAC) Bergstrom AFB Texas 1 Apr 48; assigned 47th

TCSq; depl to Pope AFB North Carolina 14 Apr 48 // 4414th AB SQ (TAC) Bergstrom AFB Texas 13 Oct 48 for storage // 2150th RES UT (MATS) Hamilton AFB California 24 Jan 49; cvtd to SC-82A; to 78th MSU GP (CNC) Hamilton AFB California 23 May 49 & 20 Jul 49 // 4th RES SQ (MATS) Hamilton AFB California 5 Oct 49 // Warner-Robins Air Materiel Area (AMC) Robins AFB Georgia 9 Jan 50 // Wfu and assigned to National Advisory Committee for Aeronautics (NACA) 22 Jun 50 for experimental air-crash tests. Dropped from inventory 29 Jul 50. Final Disposition: Tested to Destruction.

10035 / 44-22991/CQ-991 / C-82A-10-FA

Avble: 17 May 46; Acc: 29 May 46; Del: 26 Jul 46 to USAAF; ferried by the 554th AAF BAS (ATC); to 434th TCG (TAC) Greenville Field South Carolina; diverted to Memphis Tennessee 4 Aug 46 for domestic project // 316th TCG (TAC) Pope Field North Carolina 30 Sep 46; assigned 36th TCSq; to Fairchild Aircraft Maryland (AMC) for mods 1 Apr 47; aircraft to Greenville AFB South Carolina 15 Oct 47; multiple assignments to 316th MSU GP (TAC) Greenville AFB South Carolina starting 7 Jan 48 // 313th TCG (TAC) Bergstrom AFB Texas 2 Jul 48; 313th MSU GP (TAC) Bergstrom AFB Texas 18 Aug 48 // 4414th AB SQ (TAC) Bergstrom AFB Texas 13 Oct 48 for storage // 7th Geodetic SQ (55th SRC/SAC) Topeka AFB Kansas 29 Dec 48; depl to Mt Home AFB Idaho 3 Jan 49 // 55th Strategic Reconn GP (SAC) Forbes AFB Kansas 27 Jun 49; to 1100th MSU GP (HQC) Bolling AFB District of Columbia 22 Aug 49 // 91st Strategic Reconn GP (SAC) Barksdale AFB Louisiana 13 Oct 49; depl to Mt Home AFB Idaho 8 Nov 49 // Wfu and assigned to National Advisory Committee for Aeronautics (NACA) 15 Feb 50 for experimental air-crash tests. Dropped from inventory 6 Mar 50. Aircraft not used for testing and subsequently sold to a private collector, Walter Soplata of Newbury Ohio. Photographic evidence shows the Packet was painted and readied for crash tests but appears not to have been used before testing was concluded. Although Walter kept the fuselage section, he later sold the wings and booms for scrap. One of the u/c struts was used to build a boom-truck that was used on the farm into the 1990s. Walter Soplata died on 5 Nov 2010. His son Wally, a 757 captain, has confirmed at the time of this writing that the C-82, and the rest of Walter's unique aircraft collection, remains on the family property with no current plans for any restoration or sale of the aircraft. The oldest existing C-82 airframe. Final Disposition: Preserved.

10036 / 44-22992/CQ-992 / C-82A-10-FA

Avble: 22 May 46; Acc: 31 May 46; Del: 8 Aug 46 to USAAF; ferried by the 554th AAF BAS (ATC); diverted to Memphis Tennessee 11 Aug 46 for domestic project // 316th TCG (TAC) Pope Field North Carolina 30 Sep 46; assigned 36th TCSq; to Fairchild Aircraft Maryland (AMC) for mods 1 Apr 47; to 310th AAF BAS (TAC) Pope Field North Carolina 9 Jun 47; aircraft to Greenville AFB South Carolina 15 Oct 47; 316th MSU GP (TAC) Greenville AFB South Carolina 12 May 48; to Warner-Robins Air Materiel Area (AMC) Robins AFB Georgia 14 Mar 49 for depmnt // 55th Strategic Reconn GP (SAC) Forbes AFB Kansas 8 Aug 49 // 91st Strategic Reconn GP (SAC) Barksdale AFB Louisiana 13 Oct 49; to Ogden Air Materiel Area (AMC) Hill AFB Utah 11 Oct 49. Suffered moderate damage in a forced landing due to mechanical failure 21 Oct 49 at Hill AFB Utah, no fatalities. To San Antonio Air Materiel Area (AMC) Kelly AFB Texas 3 Nov 49 for depot maintenance // Wfu and assigned to National Advisory Committee for Aeronautics (NACA) 15 Feb 50 for experimental air-crash tests. Dropped from inventory 23 Mar 50. Final Disposition: Tested to Destruction.

10037 / 44-22993/CQ-993 / C-82A-10-FA

Avble: 22 May 46; Acc: 31 May 46; Del: 11 Jul 46 to USAAF; to 300th AAF BAS (TAC) // 316th AAF BAS (TAC) Pope Field North Carolina 19 Jul 46; 316th TCG (TAC) Pope Field North Carolina 16 Dec 46; assigned 36th TCSq; to Fairchild Aircraft Maryland (AMC) for mods 13 Apr 47; multiple assignments to 310th AAF BAS (TAC) Pope Field North Carolina starting 8 May 47; aircraft to Greenville AFB South Carolina 15 Oct 47. Experienced a mid-air bird strike over Greenville AFB South Carolina 20 Nov 47, no fatalities and aircraft repaired; multiple assignments to 316th MSU GP (TAC) Greenville AFB South Carolina starting 9 Dec 47; to Warner-Robins Air Materiel Area (AMC) Robins AFB Georgia 14 Mar 49 for depmnt // 55th Strategic Reconn GP (SAC) Forbes AFB Kansas 1 Sep 49; assigned 7th Geodetic SQ // 91st Strategic Reconn GP (SAC) Barksdale AFB Louisiana 13 Oct 49 // Wfu and assigned to National Advisory Committee for Aeronautics (NACA) 15 Feb 50 for experimental air-crash tests. Dropped from inventory 6 Mar 50. Final Disposition: Tested to Destruction.

10038 / 44-22994/CQ-994 / C-82A-10-FA

Avble: 27 May 46; Acc: 31 May 46; Del: 29 Jul 46 to USAAF; ferried by the 554th AAF BAS (ATC); to 434th TCG (TAC) Greenville Field South Carolina; diverted to Memphis Tennessee 4 Aug 46 for domestic project // 316th TCG (TAC) Pope Field North Carolina 14 Aug 46; assigned 37th then 36th TCSq. Landing accident at Pope Field North Carolina 21 Nov 46, no fatalities and minor damage. Deployment to 310th AAF BAS (TAC) Pope Field North Carolina 3 Dec 46; to Fairchild Aircraft Maryland (AMC) for mods 19 May 47; to 319th AAF BAS (TAC) Lawson Field Georgia 3 Jul 47. Suffered engine failure 9 Dec 47 and crew forced to bail out. Pilot: Richard D. Stevens, no fatalities but aircraft destroyed on impact 11 miles NNE of Eglin AFB Florida. Assigned to reclamation 22 Dec 47. Dropped from inventory 2 Feb 48. Final Disposition: Accident.

10039 / 44-22995/CQ-995 / C-82A-10-FA

Avble: 31 May 46; Acc: 12 Jun 46; Del: 29 Jul 46 to USAAF; ferried by the 554th AAF BAS (ATC); to 434th TCG (TAC) Greenville Field South Carolina // 316th TCG (TAC) Pope Field North Carolina 11 Aug 46; assigned 37th TCSq; to Memphis Tennessee 4 Sep 46 for domestic project. Experienced a landing accident due to mechanical failure 17 Sep 46 at Miami Airport Florida. Pilot: Clarence G. Weishar, no fatalities but aircraft badly damaged. Assigned to 4006th AAF BAS (AMC) Miami Airport Florida 19 Sep 46; assessed as "damaged beyond repair." Assigned to salvage 21 Nov 46; to reclamation 25 Aug 47. Dropped from inventory 14 Apr 48. Final Disposition: Accident.

10040 / 44-22996/CQ-996 / C-82A-10-FA

Avble: 4 Jun 46; Acc: 13 Jun 46; Del: 29 Jul 46 to USAAF; ferried by the 554th AAF BAS (ATC); to 434th TCG (TAC) Greenville Field South Carolina // 316th TCG (TAC)

Pope Field North Carolina 11 Aug 46; assigned 37th then 36th TCSq; to Memphis Tennessee 4 Sep 46 for domestic project. Suffered a taxiing accident due to mechanical failure at Pope Field North Carolina 6 Jan 47; no fatalities. To 310th AAF BAS (TAC) Pope Field North Carolina 7 Jan 47 for repairs; aircraft to Greenville AFB South Carolina 15 Oct 47; to 1100th AF BAS (ATC) McClellan AFB California 14 Dec 47; to Fairchild Aircraft Maryland (AMC) for mods 22 Jan 48. Landing accident due to mechanical failure at Greenville Field 20 May 48, no fatalities. 316th MSU GP (TAC) Greenville AFB South Carolina 21 May 48; depl to Shaw AFB South Carolina 11 Oct 48; to Warner-Robins Air Materiel Area (AMC) Robins AFB Georgia 12 Oct 48 // 7th Geodetic SQ (55th SRC/SAC) Topeka AFB Kansas 12 May 49 with depl to Mt Home AFB Idaho // 55th Strategic Reconn GP (SAC) Forbes AFB Kansas 27 Jun 49 // 91st Strategic Reconn GP (SAC) Barksdale AFB Louisiana 13 Oct 49. Crashed on take-off 4 Nov 49 7 miles south of Bossier City Louisiana. Pilot: Richard W. McKinzie and crew killed, aircraft w/o. Assigned reclamation 6 Dec 49. Dropped from inventory 5 Jan 50. Final Disposition: Accident.

10041 / 44-22997/CQ-997 / C-82A-10-FA

Avble: 7 Jun 46; Acc: 24 Jun 46; Del: 29 Jul 46 to USAAF; ferried by the 554th AAF BAS (ATC); to 434th TCG (TAC) Greenville Field South Carolina // 316th TCG (TAC) Pope Field North Carolina 14 Aug 46; assigned 37th then 36th TCSq; to Memphis Tennessee 4 Sep 46 for domestic project. Minor structural failure at Pope Field North Carolina 5 Dec 46, no fatalities. To Fairchild Aircraft Maryland (AMC) for mods 27 Apr 47; aircraft to Greenville AFB South Carolina 15 Oct 47; to 1100th AF BAS (ATC) McClellan AFB California 14 Dec 47; multiple assignments to 316th MSU GP (TAC) Greenville AFB South Carolina starting 26 Feb 48; 7th Geodetic SQ (55th SRC/SAC) Topeka AFB Kansas 1 Jun 49 with depl to Mt Home AFB Idaho // 55th Strategic Reconn GP (SAC) Forbes AFB Kansas 27 Jun 49 // 91st Strategic Reconn GP (SAC) Barksdale AFB Louisiana 13 Oct 49; depl to Mt Home AFB Idaho 8 Nov 49 // Wfu and assigned to National Advisory Committee for Aeronautics (NACA) 15 Feb 50 for experimental air-crash tests. Dropped from inventory 24 Feb 50. Final Disposition: Tested to Destruction.

10042 / 44-22998/CQ-998 / C-82A-10-FA

Avble: 11 Jun 46; Acc: 20 Jun 46; Del: 5 Sep 46 to USAAF // 316th TCG (TAC) Lawson Field Georgia (detached) 12 Sep 46; assigned 75th TCSq; to Fairchild Aircraft Maryland (AMC) for mods 21 Nov 46 & 5 Jun 47; to Greenville Field South Carolina 20 Jul 47; multiple assignments to 316th MSU GP (TAC) Greenville AFB South Carolina starting 29 Jan 48 // 10th MSU GP (TAC) Pope AFB North Carolina 20 Apr 48 // 7th Geodetic SQ (55th SRC/SAC) Topeka AFB Kansas 2 Mar 49 with depl to Mt Home AFB Idaho // 55th Strategic Reconn GP (SAC) Forbes AFB Kansas 27 Jun 49 // 91st Strategic Reconn GP (SAC) Barksdale AFB Louisiana 13 Oct 49 // Wfu and assigned to National Advisory Committee for Aeronautics (NACA) 16 Feb 50 for experimental air-crash tests. Dropped from inventory 24 Feb 50. Final Disposition: Tested to Destruction.

10043 / 44-22999/CQ-999 / C-82A-10-FA

Avble: 14 Jun 46; Acc: 25 Jun 46; Del: 9 Aug 46 to USAAF; ferried by the 554th AAF BAS (ATC); 316th TCG (TAC) Pope Field North Carolina 20 Aug 46; assigned 36th TCSq.

Damaged in a landing accident at Pope Field North Carolina 30 Sep 46, no fatalities // 310th AAF BAS (TAC) Pope Field North Carolina 2 Oct 46, assessed as "damaged beyond repair" and grounded awaiting reclamation. Briefly assigned Class 32 museum status but assigned to scrap 16 Mar 47. Dropped from inventory 18 Aug 47. Final Disposition: Accident.

10044 / 44-23000/CQ-000 / C-82A-10-FA

Avble: 19 Jun 46; Acc: 27 Jun 46; Del: 19 Aug 46 to USAAF // 4140th & 4000th AAF BAS (AMC) Patterson Field Ohio 19 Aug 46. Minor take-off accident due to mechanical failure at Patterson Field Ohio 4 Sep 46, no fatalities and aircraft repaired // 62nd TCG (TAC) Bergstrom Field Texas 24 Oct 46; to Fairchild Aircraft Maryland (AMC) for mods 22 Apr 47; 62nd to McChord Field Washington 7 Aug 47; assigned 8th TCSq; to 4127th AF BAS (AMC) McClellan AFB California 8 Dec 47; 62nd MSU GP (TAC) McChord AFB Washington 3 Nov 48 // 319th AF BAS (TAC) Lawson AFB Georgia 12 Mar 48 // 4408th AB SQ (TAC) Lawson AFB Georgia 23 Aug 48 // to Ogden Air Materiel Area (AMC) Hill AFB Utah 31 Jan 49 // 7th Geodetic SQ (55th SRC/SAC) Topeka AFB Kansas 15 Jun 49 with depl to Mt Home AFB Idaho // 55th Strategic Reconn GP (SAC) Forbes AFB Kansas 27 Jun 49 // 91st Strategic Reconn GP (SAC) Barksdale AFB Louisiana 13 Oct 49 // Wfu and assigned to National Advisory Committee for Aeronautics (NACA) 15 Feb 50 for experimental air-crash tests. Dropped from inventory 24 Feb 50. Final Disposition: Tested to Destruction.

10045 / 44-23001/CQ-001 / C-82A-10-FA

Avble: 21 Jun 46; Acc: 30 Jun 46; Del: 23 Aug 46 to USAAF; ferried by the 554th AAF BAS (ATC) // 316th TCG (TAC) Pope Field North Carolina 31 Aug 46 // 303rd AAF BAS (TAC) Greenville Field South Carolina 9 Sep 46 // 309th AAF BAS (TAC) Greenville Field South Carolina 4 Nov 46; to Fairchild Aircraft Maryland (AMC) for mods 30 Apr 47 // 313th AAF BAS (TAC) Greenville Field South Carolina 16 Jun 47 // 62nd TCG (TAC) Bergstrom Field Texas 24 Jun 47 // 319th AAF BAS (TAC) Lawson Field Georgia 24 Jul 47; depl to 316th TCG (TAC) Greenville AFB South Carolina 22 Sep 47; assigned 37th TCSq. Suffered an engine failure at Lawson AFB Georgia 31 Oct 47 no fatalities and aircraft landed safely // 4408th AB SQ (TAC) Lawson AFB Georgia 23 Aug 48, held in reserve // 7th Geodetic SQ (55th SRC/SAC) Topeka AFB Kansas 3 Feb 49 with depl to Mt Home AFB Idaho // 55th Strategic Reconn GP (SAC) Forbes AFB Kansas 27 Jun 49; depl to Ladd AFB Alaska 22 Jul 49. Engine failure over Gould Arkansas 5 Oct 49, aircraft landed safely // 91st MSU GP (SAC) Barksdale AFB Louisiana 10 Oct 49 // 91st Strategic Reconn WG (SAC) Barksdale AFB Louisiana 1 Mar 50; depl to Elmendorf AFB Alaska 26 Apr 50 // 55th Strategic Reconn WG (SAC) Ramey AFB Puerto Rico 15 Nov 50; depl to Ladd AFB Alaska 1 Jun 51; depl to Castle AFB California 6 Jan 52; to 2750th AB WG (AMC) WPAFB Ohio 3 Jul 52 // Warner-Robins Air Materiel Area (AMC) Robins AFB Georgia 25 Jul 52, likely modernized to Group A standard // 501st Air Defense GP (ADC) O'Hare Int. Airport Illinois 15 Sep 53; to Oklahoma Air Materiel Area (AMC) Tinker AFB Oklahoma 23 Jul 54; to 4750th Training GP (ADC) Yuma AFB Arizona 27 Jul 54; to 2845th Air Force Depot WG (AMC) Griffiss AFB New York 3 Dec 54 // Wfu to 3040th Aircraft Storage SQ (AMC) Davis-Monthan AFB Arizona 16 Feb 55 and stored. Dropped from inventory 1 Aug 55 // Samuel C. Rudolph Los Angeles California 9 Jan 56 reg: N6990C; cert of reg issued 18 Apr 58 // Steward-Davis Inc. Gardena California 15 Jul 58; cvtd to sprayer aircraft with 1,000 U.S. gallon cargo hold tank and associated plumbing equipment by Acme Aircraft Torrance California 15 Jul 58; cvtd to Steward-Davis Jet-Packet 1600 1958 with J30-W Jet-Pak // Ricardo de Varennes (Rivaereo Co.) Arica Chile 12 Sep 58 reg: CC-CRB-0508. N6990C reg canx 30 Sep 58. Earmarked for sale or lease to Transportes Aereos Costa Atlantica (TACA) S.A. Argentina, reg: LV-PRP rsved 2 Feb 60 but ntu and aircraft not delivered // Linea Aerea de Publicidad Ltda. (Taxpa) Santiago Chile 11 Apr 66 reg: CC-CAE. Wfu and stored at Los Cerrillos Airport Santiago 1971–75; reg canx 28 Aug 72; noted as bku with wings and booms stored separately; scrapped by 1977. Final Disposition: Scrapped.

10046 / 44-23002/CQ-002 / C-82A-10-FA

Avble: 27 Jun 46; Acc: 8 Jul 46; Del: 7 Aug 46 to USAAF; ferried by the 554th AAF BAS (ATC); diverted to Memphis Tennessee 8 Aug 46 for domestic project // 316th TCG (TAC) Pope Field North Carolina 11 Aug 46; assigned 36th TCSq; to Fairchild Aircraft Maryland (AMC) for mods 22 Apr 47. Landing accident at Pope Field North Carolina 25 Jul 47, no fatalities. To 310th AAF BAS (TAC) Pope Field North Carolina 30 Jul 47 for repairs; 316th to Greenville Field South Carolina 25 Aug 47; to 10th MSU GP (TAC) Pope AFB North Carolina 3 Dec 47; multiple assignments to 316th MSU GP (TAC) Pope AFB North Carolina starting 20 Jul 48; 316th to Smyrna AFB Tennessee 4 Nov 49; depl to Guantanamo Bay Cuba 28 Feb 50 // Wfu and assigned to National Advisory Committee for Aeronautics (NACA) 20 Mar 50 for experimental air-crash tests. Dropped from inventory 30 Mar 50. Final Disposition: Tested to Destruction.

10047 / 44-23003/CQ-003 / C-82A-10-FA

Avble: 2 Jul 46; Acc: 15 Jul 46; Del: 26 Aug 46 to USAAF; ferried by the 554th AAF BAS (ATC); diverted to Memphis Tennessee 29 Aug 46 for domestic project // 316th TCG (TAC) Lawson Field Georgia (detached) 31 Aug 46; assigned 75th TCSq; to Fairchild Aircraft Maryland (AMC) for mods 7 May 47; to Greenville Field South Carolina 20 Jul 47; 316th MSU GP (TAC) Pope AFB North Carolina 1 Feb 48 // 313th TCG (TAC) Bergstrom AFB Texas 9 Feb 48; assigned 21st TCSq. Experienced an in-flight mechanical failure over Mobile Alabama 1 Mar 48, crew bailed out. Pilot: Joseph L. Baldwin, no fatalities but aircraft destroyed on impact. Assigned reclamation 19 Mar 48. Dropped from inventory 15 Oct 48. Final Disposition: Accident.

10048 / 44-23004/CQ-004 / C-82A-15-FA

Avble: 24 Apr 46; Acc: 31 May 46; Del: 29 Jul 46 to USAAF as a flight-test aircraft. To Fairchild Aircraft Maryland (AMC) for test duties; bailment to Federal Aircraft Works Minneapolis St. Paul Airport Minnesota 31 Oct 46 for u/c snow ski installation but tests not immediately conducted // 4000th AAF BAS (AMC) Wright Field Ohio 26 Jan 47 for experimental and test work; bailment to Minneapolis St. Paul Airport Minnesota 5 Mar 47 for test duties; to Fairchild Aircraft Maryland (AMC) 13 Oct 47. Snow ski experiments conducted at Ladd AFB Alaska Apr 48 but without much success. Snow skis later modified and further tests conducted in Canada but results remained unsatisfactory. Minor landing accident at Baer Field Indiana 19 Jun 48, no fatalities // 2750th AB GP (AMC) WPAFB Ohio 7 Feb 49, cvtd to EC-82A for test work. AMC bailment to Stanley Aviation Corp. Buffalo New York 22 Sep 49 // Air Research and Development HQ (ARD) WPAFB Ohio 17 Apr 51; renamed Wright Air Development Center (ARD) 22 Jun 51. Snow ski tests abandoned // Armament Test HQ (ARD) Eglin AFB Florida 25 Feb 52 for test support duties; renamed Air Force Armament Test Center 1 Feb 53; to 3525th Pilot Training WG (TC) Williams AFB Arizona 9 Dec 52; to Ogden Air Materiel Area (AMC) Hill AFB Utah 13 Feb 53; modernized to Group A standard. Minor take-off accident at Eglin AFB Florida 15 May 53; no fatalities // 6520th Test Support WG (ARD) (Laurence G.) Hanscom AFB Massachusetts 25 Sep 53 // Wfu to Ogden Air Materiel Area (AMC) Hill AFB Utah 2 Aug 54 and stored. Dropped from inventory 9 May 55 // Samuel C. Rudolph, Nathan Sidell, Charles J. Katz (Joint Venturers) Los Angeles California 29 Sep 55 reg: N75399 // Albert J. Leeward d/b/a Leeward Aeronautical Service Fort Wayne Indiana 17 Aug 55 (paper sale made prior to acquisition from the Air Force); ownership transferred to Leeward Aeronautical Sales Inc. Fort Wayne Indiana same day // Thuel V. Schuhart (Agent) Miami Florida 12 Sep 55 (paper sale made prior to acquisition from the Air Force) // Air Cargo Equipment Inc. Miami Florida 14 Dec 56. Sold to Caribbean Construction Corp. Coral Gables Florida 4 Jan 57 but sale didn't go through. Control surfaces re-skinned, flap and u/c actuator motors overhauled with addition of hydraulic assist on main u/c, work completed 11 Feb 57 by Lopez-Grace Aviation Inc. at Fort Lauderdale Florida. Cvtd to sprayer aircraft 27 Apr 57 for use in gypsy moth pesticide spraying, 785 U.S. gal tank installed with under-wing spray booms plus Vickers hydraulic pump equipment. Exported to Honduras, reg: N75399 canx 23 Sep 57 // Compania Maderera S.A. Tegucigalpa Honduras Sep 1957 reg: XH-139 // Servicio Aereos de Honduras S.A. (SAHSA) Tegucigalpa Honduras 1957. Crashed on take-off at Trujillo Airport Honduras, date and fatalities unk, aircraft w/o. Final Disposition: Accident.

EC-82A s/n: 44-23004 (msn: 10048) (National Museum of the United States Air Force).

C-82A N75399 (msn: 10048) probably during late 1955, just after its sale to civil owner Samuel C. Rudolph. It was later exported to Honduras in 1957 (Dick Phillips Collection).

10049 / 44-23005/CQ-005 / C-82A-15-FA

Avble: 22 Jul 46; Acc: 31 Jul 46; Del: 21 Aug 46 to USAAF; ferried by the 554th AAF BAS (ATC); diverted to Memphis Tennessee 27 Aug 46 // 316th TCG (TAC) Lawson Field Georgia (detached) 14 Sep 46; assigned 75th TCSq // 62nd TCG (TAC) Bergstrom Field Texas 10 Feb 47; assigned 8th TCSq; to 310th AF BAS (TAC) Pope Field North Carolina 15 Apr 47; to Fairchild Aircraft Maryland (AMC) for mods 7 May 47; 62nd to McChord Field Washington 7 Aug 47; depl to 316th TCG (TAC) Greenville AFB South Carolina 15 Nov 47 // 313th TCG (TAC) Bergstrom AFB Texas 23 Dec 47; assigned 47th TCSq; depl to Pope AFB North Carolina 14 Apr 48 // 4414th AB SQ (TAC) Bergstrom AFB Texas 13 Oct 48 for storage // 7th Geodetic SQ (55th SRC/SAC) Topeka AFB Kansas 12 Jan 49 with depl to Mt Home AFB Idaho // 55th Strategic Reconn GP (SAC) Forbes AFB Kansas 27 Jun 49 // 91st Strategic Reconn GP (SAC) Barksdale AFB Louisiana 13 Oct 49; to San Antonio Air Materiel Area (AMC) Kelly AFB Texas 8 Dec 49; depl to Ladd AFB Alaska 27 Jun 50 & 29 Aug 50. Landing accident resulting in a ground loop at Tulsa MAP Oklahoma 28 Sep 50, no fatalities—aircraft at the time assigned to 322nd Strategic Reconn SQ. To Oklahoma Air Materiel Area (AMC) Tinker AFB Oklahoma 30 Sep 50 for depmnt // 55th Strategic Reconn WG (SAC) Ramey AFB Puerto Rico 26 Jun 51 // Warner-Robins Air Materiel Area (AMC) Robins AFB Georgia 29 Jul 52 for storage; removed from storage 14 May 53; modernized to Group A standard // 501st Air Defense GP (ADC) O'Hare Int. Airport Illinois 21 Oct 53; to Oklahoma Air Materiel Area (AMC) Tinker AFB Oklahoma 3 Mar 54 & 16 Apr 54; to 2750th AB WG (AMC) WPAFB Ohio 19 Oct 54 // Wfu to 3040th Aircraft Storage SQ (AMC) Davis-Monthan AFB Arizona 17 Feb 55 and stored. Dropped from inventory 1 Aug 55 // Samuel C. Rudolph Los Angeles California 9 Jan 56 reg: N6996C // S.C. Rudolph Lumber Corp. Los Angeles California 30 Jun 58 // New Frontier Airlift Corp. Phoenix Arizona & Steward-Davis Inc. Gardena California 5 Feb 62—purchased for Steward-Davis Jet-Packet program; stored along with N6997C, N6998C and N6999C at Tucson Airport Arizona, but no buyers or conversion work carried out. Reg revoked 1 Feb 71. Final Disposition: Scrapped.

C-82A N6996C (msn: 10049) stored at Tucson International Airport, Arizona, during December 1971 (Steve Kraus/John Wegg Collection).

10050 / 44-23006/CQ-006 / C-82A-15-FA

Avble: 23 Jul 46; Acc: 31 Jul 46; Del: 19 Aug 46 to USAAF; ferried by the 554th AAF BAS (ATC); diverted to Memphis Tennessee 25 Aug 46 // 316th TCG (TAC) Lawson Field Georgia (detached) 25 Aug 46; assigned 75th TCSq; to Fairchild Aircraft Maryland (AMC) for mods 2 Dec 46 & 7 May 47; to Greenville Field South Carolina 20 Jul 47; to 319th AF BAS (TAC) Lawson AFB Georgia 12 Oct 47 // 316th MSU GP (TAC) Greenville Field North Carolina 15 Jun 48; placed in storage 29 Jul 48; removed from storage 2 May

Above and top of next page: Two photographs of C-82A s/n: 44-23006 (msn: 10050) on display at the Pima Air & Space Museum in Tucson, Arizona. As can be seen, the outside of the aircraft has been restored for display, but the interior remains as yet unrestored. Although registered with a civil operator as N6997C, it never actually entered civil service and remained stored until acquired by Pima in 1985 (Pima Air & Space Museum).

49 // 7th Geodetic SQ (55th SRC/SAC) Topeka AFB Kansas 15 Jun 49 with depl to Mt Home AFB Idaho // 55th Strategic Reconn GP (SAC) Forbes AFB Kansas 27 Jun 49; to 91st Strategic Reconn GP (SAC) Barksdale AFB Louisiana 13 Oct 49; to Ramey AFB Puerto Rico 22 Oct 51 // Warner-Robins Air Materiel Area (AMC) Robins AFB Georgia 25 Jul 52 for storage; removed from storage 1 Oct 53; modernized to Group A standard // 501st Air Defense GP (ADC) O'Hare Int. Airport Illinois 21 Oct 53 // Wfu to 3040th Aircraft Storage SQ (AMC) Davis-Monthan AFB Arizona 21 Feb 55 and stored. Dropped from inventory 1 Aug 55 // Samuel C. Rudolph Los Angeles California 9 Jan 56 reg: N6997C // S.C. Rudolph Lumber Corp. Los Angeles California 30 Jun 58 // New Frontier Airlift Corp. Phoenix Arizona & Steward-Davis Inc. Gardena California 5 Feb 62—purchased for Steward-Davis Jet-Packet program; stored along with N6996C, N6998C and N6999C at Tucson Airport Arizona, but no buyers or conversion work carried out. Reg revoked 1 Feb 71 // National Air & Space Museum Washington, D.C., 1973; acquired in a derelict condition and stored at the Pima Air & Space Museum in Tucson Arizona. Acquired by Pima in 1985 and restored for display where it remains to this day. Final Disposition: Preserved.

10051 / 44-23007/CQ-007 / C-82A-15-FA

Avble: 29 Jul 46; Acc: 31 Jul 46; Del: 5 Sep 46 to USAAF // 316th TCG (TAC) Lawson Field Georgia (detached) 12 Sep 46; assigned 75th TCSq.; to Fairchild Aircraft Maryland (AMC) for mods 7 May 47; to 319th AAF BAS (TAC) Lawson Field Georgia 20 Jul 47; multiple assignments to 316th MSU GP (TAC) Greenville AFB South Carolina starting 2 Apr 48; to 3203rd MSU GP & 3200th Proof Test GP (APG) Eglin AFB Florida 3 Nov

48 for experimental duties; 316th to Smyrna AFB Tennessee 4 Nov 49; multiple depls to 314th TCG (CNC) Smyrna AFB Tennessee starting 25 Nov 49; assigned 2601st Light Assault SQ; depl to Guantanamo Bay Cuba 28 Feb 50; Smyrna AFB renamed Sewart AFB 25 Mar 50; depl to 314th TCG (CNC) depl to Laurinburg-Maxton Airport North Carolina 20 Apr 50 // 314th TCWG (TAC) Stewart AFB Tennessee 21 Jul 50 // 375th TCWG (CNC) Greenville AFB South Carolina 8 Nov 50; to Warner-Robins Air Materiel Area (AMC) Robins AFB Georgia 15 Sep 51 for depmnt; depl to Brownwood Field Texas 5 Mar 52 // 64th TCWG (TAC) Donaldson AFB South Carolina 14 Jul 52; to Oklahoma Air Materiel Area (AMC) Tinker AFB Oklahoma 14 Jun 53 // Wfu to San Antonio Air Materiel Area (AMC) Kelly AFB Texas 26 Jun 53 and stored. Dropped from inventory 1 Jul 54 // No known U.S. owner or reg. but apparently owned by Ben Epstein & Associates. Earmarked for sale to SEICA S.R.L. Buenos Aires Argentina, reg: LV-PRV rsved 8 Feb 60 but ntu and aircraft not delivered // Expreso Aereo Peruano S.A. (EAPSA) Lima Peru, date unk, reg: OB-UAF-531. W/o 11 Mar 62, cause and fatalities unk, nfd. Final Disposition: Accident.

10052 / 44-23008/CQ-008 / C-82A-15-FA

Avble: 31 Jul 46; Acc: 23 Aug 46; Del: 9 Sep 46 to USAAF // To Fairchild Aircraft Maryland (AMC) 10 Sep 46 // 4000th AAF BAS (AMC) Patterson & Wright Fields Ohio 19 Feb 47 for experimental duties; to 4152nd AAF BAS (AMC) Clinton County Field Ohio 19 Mar 47. Minor landing accident at Hagerstown Airport (Fairchild Aircraft) Maryland 14 Apr 47, no fatalities and aircraft repaired. To Fairchild Aircraft Maryland (AMC) 17 Apr 47 // 316th TCG (TAC) Greenville AFB South Carolina 15 Sep 47; assigned 37th TCSq; 316th MSU GP (TAC) Greenville AFB South Carolina 2 Apr 48 & 1 Jul 48; to Warner-Robins Air Materiel Area (AMC) Robins AFB Georgia 14 Mar 49; 316th to Smyrna AFB Tennessee 4 Nov 49; multiple depls to 314th TCG (CNC) Smyrna AFB Tennessee starting 28 Feb 50, Smyrna AFB renamed Sewart AFB 25 Mar 50; depl to 314th TCG (CNC) Laurinburg-Maxton Airport North Carolina 20 Apr 50; depl to Guantanamo Bay Cuba 6 Mar 50 // 314th TCWG (CNC) Sewart AFB Tennessee 21 Jul 50 // 375th TCWG (CNC) Greenville AFB South Carolina 31 Oct 50; assigned 57th TCSq; to Warner-Robins Air Materiel Area (AMC) Robins AFB Georgia 6 Apr 51 & 7 Nov 51 for depmnt; depl to Brownwood Field Texas 5 Mar 52. Suffered minor in-flight fire over Lometa Texas 12 Mar 52, aircraft landed safely with no fatalities // 64th TCWG (TAC) Donaldson AFB South Carolina 14 Jul 52; assigned 35th TCSq. Minor ground accident at Pope AFB North Carolina 18 Nov 52, no fatalities // Wfu to San Antonio Air Materiel Area (AMC) Kelly AFB Texas 26 Jun 53 and stored. Dropped from inventory 1 Jul 54 // Smock & Jenner Inc. Cincinnati Ohio 16 Aug 55 reg: N74046 // Ben Epstein, Trustee for Ben, Leonard and Stanley W. Epstein (Aeronautical Cargo Co.) Miami Beach Florida 29 Dec 55. Earmarked for sale to Seica S.R.L. Buenos Aires Argentina, reg: LV-PRU rsved 8 Feb 60 but ntu and aircraft not delivered // Airnews Inc. San Antonio Texas 1 Mar 60 // New Frontier Airlift Corp. Phoenix Arizona 24 Apr 61—purchased for Steward-Davis Jet-Packet program, but no buyers or conversion work carried out. One of eight C-82A derelicts for Fairchild-Hiller Corp. Maryland; reg: N6782A rsved 1967 but ntu. Photographic evidence shows N74046 derelict with other Packets at Miami Intl. Airport Florida in the late 1960s. N74046 reg revoked 18 Jan 71. Final Disposition: Scrapped.

10053 / 44-23009/CQ-009 / C-82A-15-FA

Avble: 6 Aug 46; Acc: 20 Aug 46; Del: 5 Sep 46 to USAAF // 316th TCG (TAC) Lawson Field Georgia (detached) 12 Sep 46; assigned 75th TCSq // 62nd TCG (TAC) Bergstrom Field Texas 11 Mar 47; to 319th AAF BAS (TAC) Lawson Field Georgia 23 Apr 47; to Fairchild Aircraft Maryland (AMC) 20 May 47; 62nd to McChord Field Washington 7 Aug 47; to 4127th AF BAS (AMC) McClellan AFB California 8 Dec 47; 62nd MSU GP (TAC) McChord AFB Washington 16 Mar 48 // 313th TCG (TAC) Bergstrom AFB Texas 7 Apr 48; 313th MSU GP (TAC) Bergstrom AFB Texas 15 Sep 48 // 4414th AB SQ (TAC) Bergstrom AFB Texas 13 Oct 48 for short-term storage // 314th TCG (CNC) Smyrna AFB Tennessee 5 Apr 49; 314th MSU GP (CNC) Smyrna AFB Tennessee 2 May 49 // 55th Strategic Reconn GP (SAC) Forbes AFB Kansas 29 Aug 49 // 91st Strategic Reconn GP (SAC) Barksdale AFB Louisiana 13 Oct 49; depl to Ladd AFB Alaska 8 Jun 50 // 55th Strategic Reconn WG (SAC) Barksdale AFB Louisiana 21 Nov 50; to Ramey AFB Puerto Rico 22 Oct 52 // Warner-Robins Air Materiel Area (AMC) Robins AFB Georgia 29 Jul 52 for storage; removed from storage 14 May 53; modernized to Group A standard // 501st Air Defense GP (ADC) O'Hare Int. Airport Illinois 10 Jan 54 // 568th Air Defense GP (ADC) McGuire AFB New Jersey 17 Jan 54; to Middletown Air Materiel Area (AMC) Olmsted AFB Pennsylvania 19 Mar 54; to 519th Air Defense GP (ADC) Suffolk AFB Virginia 8 Jun 54 // 611th Aircraft Maintenance SQ (MATS) McGuire AFB New Jersey 8 Jul 54 // 521st Air Defense GP (ADC) Sioux City MAP Iowa 19 Aug 54; to 803rd AF BAS (SAC) Davis-Monthan AFB Arizona 9 Sep 54 // Wfu to 3040th Aircraft Storage SQ (AMC) Davis-Monthan AFB Arizona 7 Mar 55 and stored. Dropped from inventory 1 Aug 55 // Samuel C. Rudolph Los Angeles California 9 Jan 56 reg: N6998C // S.C. Rudolph Lumber Corp. Los Angeles California 30 Jun 58 // New Frontier Airlift Corp. Phoenix Arizona & Steward-Davis Inc. Gardena California 5 Feb 62—purchased for Steward-Davis Jet-Packet program; stored along with N6996C, N6997C and N6999C at Tucson Airport Arizona, but no buyers or conversion work carried out. Reg revoked 1 Feb 71. Final Disposition: Scrapped.

10054 / 44-23010/CQ-010 / C-82A-15-FA

Avble: 12 Aug 46; Acc: 26 Aug 46; Del: 5 Sep 46 to USAAF // 316th TCG (TAC) Lawson Field Georgia (detached) 12 Sep 46; assigned 75th TCSq; depl to 62nd TCG (TAC) Bergstrom Field Texas 6 Feb 47; to 311th AAF BAS (TAC) Bergstrom Field Texas 6 Apr 47; to 313th MSU GP (TAC) Bergstrom Field Texas 18 Aug 47; 316th to Greenville Field South Carolina 25 Aug 47; briefly assigned 316th MSU GP (TAC) Greenville AFB South Carolina 8 Oct 47; to Fairchild Aircraft Maryland (AMC) for mods 1 Jan 48; depl to Elmendorf AFB Alaska 2 Jul 48; assigned 37th TCSq. Suffered a mechanical failure 30 miles NE Nenana Alaska 9 Aug 48, no fatalities. Crashed due to in-flight mechanical failure 14 Jan 49 1 mile N Haineth North Carolina. Pilot: Lake W. Stroup, plus two other crew killed, paratroops onboard at the time bailed out prior to crash. Assigned to reclamation 19 Jan 49. Dropped from inventory 8 Mar 49. Final Disposition: Accident.

10055 / 44-23011/CQ-011 / C-82A-15-FA

Avble: 21 Aug 46; Acc: 27 Aug 46; Del: 5 Sep 46 to USAAF // 62nd TCG (TAC) Bergstrom Field Texas 14 Sep 46; to 318th AAF BAS (TAC) Lockbourne Field Ohio 30

Nov 46; depl to 316th TCG (TAC) Pope Field North Carolina 21 May 47; to 310th AAF BAS (TAC) Pope Field North Carolina 25 May 47; 62nd to McChord Field Washington 7 Aug 47; 62nd AF BAS (ATC) McChord AFB Washington 2 Oct 47 // 5th RES SQ (ATC) MacDill AFB Florida 7 Oct 47; cvtd to SC-82A; to Fairchild Aircraft Maryland (AMC) for mods 29 Oct 47 & 1 Jan 48 // 62nd AF BAS (ATC) McChord AFB Washington 12 Feb 48 // 8th RES SQ (ATC) McChord AFB Washington 7 Mar 48 // 5th RES SQ (MATS) Westover AFB Massachusetts 7 Jul 48 // 141st AF BAS (ADC) McChord AFB Washington 20 Jul 48 // 2152nd RES UT (MATS) Ernest Harmon AFB Newfoundland Canada 6 Dec 48; depl to Goose Bay AB Labrador Canada 7 Dec 48 // 6th RES SQ (MATS) Ernest Harmon AFB Newfoundland Canada 25 Apr 49; depl to Goose Bay AB Labrador Canada 10 Aug 49; Warner-Robins Air Materiel Area (AMC) Robins AFB Georgia 23 Dec 49 for depmnt; to 6603rd AB GP (NEAC) Goose Bay Labrador Canada 1 Oct 51; to Ogden Air Materiel Area (AMC) Hill AFB Utah 2 Oct 51 for special assignment. Suffered mechanical failure while taxiing at Goose AB Labrador Canada 7 Mar 52, no fatalities // Wfu to Ogden Air Materiel Area (AMC) Hill AFB Utah 27 May 53 and stored. Dropped from inventory 8 Jul 54 // Samuel C. Rudolph, Nathan Sidell, Charles J. Katz (Joint Venturers) Los Angeles California 29 Sep 55 reg: N6245C // Albert J. Leeward d/b/a Leeward Aeronautical Service Fort Wayne Indiana 17 Aug 55 (paper sale made prior to acquisition from the Air Force); ownership transferred to Leeward Aeronautical Sales Inc. Fort Wayne Indiana same day; cert of reg not issued until 7 May 57 by which time Leeward was relocated to Miami Florida // Aero Enterprises Inc. Elkhart Indiana 28 Feb 62 // Peter Bercut San Francisco California 14 Feb 62; cert of reg issued 17 Sep 62. Listed as "destroyed" and reg canx 22 Nov 71. Final Disposition: Unknown (Presumed Scrapped).

10056 / 44-23012/CQ-012 / C-82A-15-FA

Avble: 26 Aug 46; Acc: 29 Aug 46; Del: 5 Sep 46 to USAAF // 62nd TCG (TAC) Bergstrom Field Texas 14 Sep 46; assigned 8th TCSq; to Fairchild Aircraft Maryland (AMC) 29 Apr 47; 62nd to McChord Field Washington 7 Aug 47; depl to 314th AAF BAS (TAC) McChord Field Washington 13 Aug 47; 62nd MSU GP (TAC) McChord Field Washington 31 Aug 47 & 12 Nov 47 // 313th TCG (TAC) Bergstrom AFB Texas 14 Feb 48; briefly to 313th MSU GP (TAC) Bergstrom AFB Texas 28 Sep 48 // 4414th AB SQ (TAC) Bergstrom AFB Texas 13 Oct 48 for short-term storage // 4408th AB SQ (CNC) Lawson AFB Georgia 23 Mar 49 // 314th TCG (CNC) Smyrna AFB Tennessee 13 May 49; assigned 2601st Light Assault SQ; briefly to 314th MSU GP (CNC) Smyrna AFB Tennessee 26 Jan 50; Smyrna AFB renamed Sewart AFB 25 Mar 50; Warner-Robins Air Materiel Area (AMC) Robins AFB Georgia 6 Feb 51 for depmnt // 375th TCWG (TAC) Donaldson AFB South Carolina 9 Aug 51; Warner-Robins Air Materiel Area (AMC) Robins AFB Georgia 9 Oct 51 for depmnt; depl to Brownwood Field Texas 10 Mar 52 // 64th TCWG (TAC) Donaldson AFB South Carolina 14 Jul 52 // Wfu to San Antonio Air Materiel Area (AMC) Kelly AFB Texas 7 Jul 53 and stored. Dropped from inventory as 1 Jul 54 // Smock & Jenner Inc. Cincinnati Ohio 16 Aug 55 reg: N74047 // Ben Epstein, Trustee for Ben, Leonard and Stanley W. Epstein (Aeronautical Cargo Co.) Miami Beach Florida 29 Dec 55. Earmarked for sale to SEICA S.R.L. Buenos Aires Argentina, reg: LV-PRW rsved 8 Feb 60 but ntu and aircraft not delivered // Airnews Inc. San Antonio Texas 1 Mar 60 // New Frontier Airlift Corp. Phoenix Arizona 24 Apr 61—purchased for Steward-Davis Jet-Packet program but no buyers or conversion work carried out. One of eight C-82A derelicts for Fairchild-Hiller Corp. Maryland; reg: N6856A rsved 1967 but ntu. Photographic evidence shows one C-82A (10132/45-57762), derelict at Miami Intl. Airport in the late 1960s, crudely marked as "N74047," but there's no record to show this registration was ever transferred to this airframe. Who applied this reg and why remains a mystery. N74047 reg revoked 18 Jan 71. Final Disposition: Scrapped.

10057 / 44-23013/CQ-013 / C-82A-15-FA

Avble: 29 Aug 46; Acc: 11 Sep 46; Del: 1 Nov 46 to USAAF // 62nd TCG (TAC) Bergstrom Field Texas 11 Nov 46; assigned 8th TCSq; to Fairchild Aircraft Maryland (AMC) 4 May 47; depl to 316th TCG (TAC) Pope Field North Carolina 20 May 47; 62nd to McChord Field Washington 7 Aug 47; 62nd MSU GP (TAC) McChord Field Washington 16 Sep 47 // 313th TCG (TAC) Bergstrom AFB Texas 30 Dec 47; assigned 47th TCSq; 313th MSU GP (TAC) Bergstrom AFB Texas 12 Feb 48 & 8 Sep 48; depl to Pope AFB North Carolina 14 Apr 48 // 4414th AB SQ (TAC) Bergstrom AFB Texas 13 Oct 48 for short-term storage // 314th TCG (CNC) Smyrna AFB Tennessee 31 Dec 48; assigned 2601st Light Assault SQ; to Warner-Robins Air Materiel Area (AMC) Robins AFB Georgia 4 Apr 49 & 25 Feb 51; to Mobile Air Materiel Area (AMC) Brookley AFB, Alabama 12 Apr 50; Smyrna AFB renamed Sewart AFB 25 Mar 50 // 375th TCWG (TAC) Donaldson

Striking view of C-82A s/n: 44-23013 (msn: 10057) (National Museum of the United States Air Force).

AFB South Carolina 18 Jul 51; Warner-Robins Air Materiel Area (AMC) Robins AFB Georgia 28 Sep 51 for depmnt; to 93rd AB GP (SAC) Castle AFB California 7 Jan 52; depl to Brownwood Field Texas 2 Mar 52 // 64th TCWG (TAC) Donaldson AFB South Carolina 14 Jul 52 // Wfu to San Antonio Air Materiel Area (AMC) Kelly AFB Texas 7 Jul 53 and stored. Dropped from inventory 1 Jul 54 // Samuel C. Rudolph, Nathan Sidell, Charles J. Katz (Joint Venturers) Los Angeles California 10 Aug 55 reg: N7852B // Albert J. Leeward d/b/a Leeward Aeronautical Service Fort Wayne Indiana 17 Aug 55; ownership transferred to Leeward Aeronautical Sales Inc. Fort Wayne Indiana same day; cert of reg not issued until 2 May 57 by which time Leeward was relocated to Miami Florida // Lawa Goudvelden N.V. Paramaribo Surinam 29 Oct 58; a license to export was applied for 12 Nov 58 with reg: N7852B canx 12 May 59 but the aircraft was never exported // Arthur R. Hunter (on behalf of North Shore Goldfields Ltd. Toronto Canada) San Francisco California 24 Mar 60; reg: N7852B rsved but ntu, aircraft never registered in Canada // Steward-Davis Inc. Gardena California 1 Aug 60 reg: N7884C // New Frontier Airlift Corp. Phoenix Arizona 13 Jul 61; cert of reg applied for 7 May 63 but according to records never issued. This is a somewhat elusive C-82 as its general whereabouts and civil operations have never been known, neither has it apparently ever been photographed. There's a slim possibility N7884C was cut up by Steward-Davis for the 20th Century–Fox film *The Flight of the Phoenix* (1965), being used for interior filming at Fox Studios; however, this is merely a theory based on a series of deductions. That airframe might just as easily have been N5116B (10089/44-23045). N7884C reg revoked 17 Dec 70. Final Disposition: Unknown (Presumed Scrapped).

10058 / 44-23014/CQ-014 / C-82A-15-FA

Avble: 4 Sep 46; Acc: 11 Sep 46; Del: 17 Oct 46 to USAAF // 4000th AAF BAS (AMC) Patterson Field Ohio 19 Oct 46 for service as a test aircraft; to Wright Field Ohio 28 Nov 46. Minor landing accident at NAF Mustin Pennsylvania 16 Aug 47, no fatalities. To Fairchild Aircraft Maryland (AMC) for mods 14 Oct 47 // 2750th AB GP (AMC) WPAFB Ohio 27 Oct 48; cvtd to EC-82A for further experimental and test duties. Crash-landed due to engine failure 14 Jul 49 at WPAFB Ohio. Pilot: Robert L. Northrup plus crew killed in crash, aircraft w/o. Assigned to reclamation 18 Sep 49. Dropped from inventory 27 Sep 49. Final Disposition: Accident.

10059 / 44-23015/CQ-015 / C-82A-15-FA

Avble: 9 Sep 46; Acc: 16 Sep 46; Del: 23 Sep 46 to USAAF Ladd Field Alaska // 609th AAF BAS (PGC) Eglin Field Florida 23 Mar 47 // 611th AAF BAS (PGC) Eglin Field Florida 14 Apr 47 // 605th AF BAS (PGC) Eglin AFB Florida 1 Oct 47 // To Fairchild Aircraft Maryland (AMC) for mods 30 Dec 47 // 313th TCG (TAC) Bergstrom AFB Texas 10 Mar 48 // 10th MSU GP (TAC) Pope AFB North Carolina 8 May 48 // 314th TCG (CNC) Smyrna AFB Tennessee 17 Feb 49; briefly to 314th MSU GP (CNC) Smyrna AFB Tennessee 22 Mar 49; to Warner-Robins Air Materiel Area (AMC) Robins AFB Georgia 6 Apr 49; assigned 2601st Light Assault SQ (314th) 5 Oct 49 // 5th RES SQ (MATS) Biggs AFB Texas 7 Apr 50; cvtd to SC-82A; to 5th at Ellington AFB Texas 19 Jul 50 // 2156th RES UT (MATS) MacDill AFB Florida 30 Oct 50; to 3525th Pilot Training WG (TC) Williams AFB Arizona 11 Jan 51; to Middletown Air Materiel Area (AMC) Olmsted AFB

Pennsylvania 17 Sep 51 // 5th RES SQ (MATS) Ellington AFB Texas 18 Mar 52; to 3605th Navigator Training Wing (TC) Ellington AFB Texas 17 Apr 52; to San Antonio Air Materiel Area (AMC) Kelly AFB Texas 26 May 52 // 47th RES SQ (MATS) Ellington AFB Texas 22 Dec 52; to San Antonio Air Materiel Area (AMC) Kelly AFB Texas 27 Feb 53 // Aircraft Engineering & Maintenance Co. (AMC) Oakland California 12 Jul 53 on bailment; cvtd back to C-82A standard and modernized to Group A standard // 501st Air Defense GP (ADC) O'Hare Int. Airport Illinois 28 Apr 54 // 2nd Fighter-Interceptor SQ (ADC) McGuire AFB New Jersey 12 May 54 // 521st Air Defense GP (ADC) Sioux City MAP Iowa 3 Aug 54 // 35th Air Division (ADC) Dobbins AFB Georgia 4 Oct 54 // Wfu to 3040th Aircraft Storage SQ (AMC) Davis-Monthan AFB Arizona 16 Mar 55 and stored. Dropped from inventory 1 Aug 55 // Samuel C. Rudolph Los Angeles California 9 Jan 56 reg: N6989C // Steward-Davis Inc. Gardena California 29 May 58. Cvtd to Steward-Davis Jet-Packet 1600 Jun 58 with J30-W Jet-Pak. Earmarked for export to Rivaereo Co. Arica Chile 30 Jun 58 reg: CC-CRA-0507, photographic evidence shows aircraft marked as such, export canx in favor of C-82A N5095V (10071). Re-reg: N6887C 1958. Fabric control surfaces upgraded to metal 10 Jan 61. Leased to Dutch mining company Lawa Goudvelden N.V. 10 Jan 61 flying dredging and gold mining equipment into Surinam; repainted in a Lawa Goudvelden livery. The cargoes included a Bucyrus-Erie Co. 4.5 cubic foot bucket-line dredger along with tools, jigs and other specialized equipment for assembly in Surinam. A series of flights were made throughout 1961, the first around January 10, a second around May 10 and a third around September 6. Steward-Davis employee Bob Thayer recalls flying on the Surinam flights in N6887C: "Sometime during the '60s one of their large gold dredges was transported from Long Beach Airport to Paramaribo, Surinam, then transported by land into the jungle for assembly and operation. Steward-Davis employees Cecil Johns was pilot and Ted Whaley flew right seat and I accompanied it as loadmaster." Whaley's logbook shows N6887C to have been based in Surinam from Dec 62 through Mar 63 with flights being made between Zandery Airport and Maripasoela Airstrip // New Frontier Airlift Corp. Phoenix Arizona 13 Mar 61—ownership change only, aircraft still operated by Steward-Davis Inc. Cvtd to Steward-Davis Jet-Packet 1600A 18 Aug 61 with R-2800AM2H engines and hydraulic nose wheel steering. Leased to USAF for flight-tests at Edwards AFB 28 Aug 61 to evaluate Jet-Packet performance. Leased to *Las Vegas Sun* newspaper 6 Jan 64 along with Steward-Davis C-82 N74127. Leased to Eureka Merchants Assoc. 6 Jan 65 to assist with supplies to flood-damaged Humboldt County. Major radio & nav upgrade 8 Jan 65. Leased to 20th Century–Fox film *The Flight of the Phoenix* (1965) 29 Jun 65 for flying scenes filmed over Imperial Valley sand dunes during Jul 65; Jet-Pak removed for film scenes; crew was Earl Bellotte, Ted Whaley or Don Dinoff, and Bob Thayer. Cvtd to Steward-Davis "Flying Repair Station" 21 Sep 65. Leased to 20th Century Fox in carriage of film props for *Doctor Dolittle* (1967) 8 Aug 66, in this case flying a fake snail prop to Saint Lucia. N6887C was loaded up at Long Beach on 4 Oct 66 with the fake snail, arriving at the filming location on the island-country of Saint Lucia in the eastern Caribbean on 7 Oct 66; one of the pilots was Steward-Davis employee Ted Whaley. N6887C left Saint Lucia on 9 Oct 66, returning to Long Beach on 12 Oct 66 after a stop in Yuma, Arizona. A total of almost 53 hours was flown by N6887C in order to deliver the snail movie prop. Film lease to Fouad Said Productions 12 Dec 66 for transporting film equipment. Impounded at Hermosillo Airport Mexico 11 May 70 after making a forced landing due to engine trouble; it was found the C-82 had not filed a flight plan to enter Mexican airspace. Flight crew Ted Whaley, Don Dinoff and Tim

Mulligan returned to the U.S., but the aircraft remained impounded at Hermosillo Airport and was eventually abandoned by Steward-Davis. FAA reg revoked 3 Sep 71 // Gifted to the city of Hermosillo in 1983, where it was displayed at the *Parque Popular Infantil*, a children's' science theme park. Painted in a bright yellow and blue livery, the C-82 became known as the *avion de la ciencia*—"plane of science," enthralling and educating many children over the next 22 years. Removed Nov 2005 during a park upgrade. Final Disposition: Scrapped.

Top: **Flying in Rivaereo markings is Steward-Davis's C-82A N6989C (msn: 10059) with Chilean reg. CC-CRA-0507. This export was later canceled, with the reg then going to N5095V (msn: 10071) (Steward-Davis).** *Bottom*: **Jet-Packet 1600 N6887C (msn: 10059) at Edwards Air Force Base in 1961 (United States Air Force).**

Top: Jet-Packet 1600 N6887C (msn: 10059) probably in late 1965 at Long Beach (Andre Van Loon Collection). *Bottom*: C-82A N6887C (msn: 10059) being loaded with the movie prop snail for *Doctor Dolittle* (1967) during October 1966 and destined for delivery to the Caribbean (Rebecca Wiant Collection).

10060 / 44-23016/CQ-016 / C-82A-15-FA

Avble: 11 Sep 46; Acc: 16 Sep 46; Del: 24 Sep 46 to USAAF // AAF lease to United Airlines Inc. Chicago Illinois 27 Sep 46 to evaluate in-flight mail sorting. The concept was to introduce a coast-to-coast 5-cent airmail stamp with mail being sorted en route, reducing delivery times and hence postage costs. Temp certificate reg: NC8855; named as the United Flying Mail Car. Fairchild Aircraft fitted out the cargo hold with sorting tables, mailbag hooks and storage, extra lighting and other equipment. The first flight was on 1 Oct 46 from New York (East Coast) to Seattle (West Coast) with stops at Cleveland, Chicago, Omaha, Denver, Cheyenne, Salt Lake City, San Francisco (terminating U.S. Air Mail Route 1), then continuing to Sacramento, Medford, Eugene, then to Boeing Field at Seattle. The return flight was back to Fairchild at Hagerstown. There was much publicity at the time, the trip taking twelve hours from coast to coast complete with thirteen onboard staff sorting the mail bags in the air. The concept, however, was found to be largely impractical, with little time actually saved by sorting the mail en route. The future projected use of faster aircraft and more frequent schedules soon resulted in the project's cancellation. The aircraft was returned to the USAAF 8 Oct 46; NC8855 reg canx 13 Dec 46 // 62nd TCG (TAC) Bergstrom Field Texas 18 Dec 46; assigned 8th TCSq; to 8th AF Reserve Flying Training SQ (AMC) Fairchild Aircraft Maryland 22 Apr 47; depl to 316th TCG (TAC) Pope Field North Carolina 15 May 47; 62nd to McChord Field Washington 7 Aug 47 // 313th TCG (TAC) Bergstrom AFB Texas 23 Dec 47; to Warner-Robins Air Materiel Area (AMC) Robins AFB Georgia 3 Sep 48 for depmnt // 4414th AB SQ (TAC) Bergstrom AFB Texas 13 Oct 48 for short-term storage // 314th TCG (CNC) Smyrna AFB Tennessee 24 Feb 49; assigned 20th TCSq; to Warner-Robins Air Materiel Area (AMC) Robins AFB Georgia 20 May 49; assigned 2601st Light Assault SQ (314th) Smyrna AFB Tennessee 3 Nov 49; Smyrna AFB renamed Sewart AFB 25 Mar 50 // 81st Fighter-Interceptor WG (CNC) Larson AFB Washington 29 Jun 50. Made a forced landing due to engine failure at Cheyenne Municipal Airport (MAP) Wyoming 3 Aug 50. Pilot:

C-82A s/n: 44-23016 (msn: 10060) as the United Flying Mail Car NC8855 at Hagerstown, Maryland, in October 1946 (Lyle S. Mitchell via Hagerstown Aviation Museum).

Peter J. Brylinski Jr., no fatalities but aircraft was assessed as "damaged beyond repair." Assigned to reclamation and salvage 7 Aug 50. Dropped from inventory 21 Nov 50. Final disposition: Accident.

10061 / 44-23017/CQ-017 / C-82A-15-FA

Avble: 16 Sep 46; Acc: 18 Sep 46; Del: 3 Oct 46 to USAAF // 62nd TCG (TAC) Bergstrom Field Texas 6 Oct 46; assigned 8th TCSq; to Fairchild Aircraft Maryland (AMC) 19 May 47; 62nd to McChord Field Washington 7 Aug 47 // 313th TCG (TAC) Bergstrom AFB Texas 18 Nov 47; to 10th MSU GP (TAC) Pope AFB North Carolina 20 Jul 48 // 4414th AB SQ (TAC) Bergstrom AFB Texas 13 Oct 48 for short-term storage // 4408th AB SQ (CNC) Lawson AFB Georgia 5 Apr 49 // 314th TCG (CNC) Smyrna AFB Tennessee 13 May 49; assigned 2601st Light Assault SQ 13 Oct 49; Smyrna AFB renamed Sewart AFB 25 Mar 50 // 81st Fighter-Interceptor Wing (CNC) Larson AFB Washington 13 Jul 50 // 375th TCWG (TAC) Greenville AFB South Carolina 8 Dec 50; assigned 55th TCSq; depl to Grenier AFB New Hampshire 3 Mar 51. Moderately damaged while parked at Wheeler-Sack AAF New York 10 Feb 52 when a C-46D Commando (s/n: 44-77508) crashed after take-off. The C-46D was the ninth of seventeen taking off for an exercise when it made a sharp 60-degree turn soon after leaving the runway and smashed into a row of parked aircraft. The four crew on the C-46D were killed and five of the 32 paratroopers onboard were injured. Another parked C-82A (45-57795) and an L-17B Navion (48–1064) were also damaged. Depl to Brownwood Field Texas 10 Mar 52 // 64th TCWG (TAC) Donaldson AFB South Carolina 14 Jul 52 // Wfu to San Antonio Air Materiel Area (AMC) Kelly AFB Texas 26 Jun 53 and stored. Dropped from inventory 1 Jul 54 // Smock & Jenner Inc. Cincinnati Ohio 16 Aug 55 reg: N74038 // Ben Epstein, Trustee for Ben, Leonard and Stanley W. Epstein (Aeronautical Cargo Co.) Miami Beach Florida 29 Dec 55 // Henry A. Smith Richmond California 24 May 61 // New Frontier Airlift Corp. Berkeley California 1 May 63—purchased for Steward-Davis Jet-Packet program, but no buyers or conversion work carried out. One of eight C-82A derelicts for Fairchild-Hiller Corp. Maryland; reg: N6862A rsved 1967 but ntu. N74038 reg revoked 5 Feb 71. Final Disposition: Scrapped.

10062 / 44-23018/CQ-018 / C-82A-15-FA

Avble: 18 Sep 46; Acc: 20 Sep 46; Del: 8 Oct 46 to USAAF // 62nd TCG (TAC) Bergstrom Field Texas 9 Oct 46; assigned 8th TCSq; to 4103rd AAF BAS (ADC) Jackson Field Mississippi 22 Dec 46; to Fairchild Aircraft Maryland (AMC) 4 May 47; depl to 316th TCG (TAC) Pope Field North Carolina 20 May 47. Suffered a minor take-off accident at Kirtland Field New Mexico 12 Jul 47, no fatalities // 428th AAF BAS (AMC) Kirtland Field New Mexico 21 Jul 47 // 4121st AF BAS (AMC) Kelly AFB Texas 14 Dec 47; also assigned to San Antonio Air Materiel Center at Kelly AFB // 316th TCG (CNC) Smyrna AFB Tennessee 13 Jul 49; multiple depls to 314th TCG (CNC) Smyrna AFB Tennessee starting 25 Nov 49; assigned 2601st Light Assault SQ; depl to Guantanamo Bay Cuba 28 Feb 50; Smyrna AFB renamed Sewart AFB 25 Mar 50; depl to 314th TCG (CNC) Laurinburg-Maxton Airport North Carolina 21 Apr 50 // 375th TCWG (CNC) Greenville AB South Carolina 2 Nov 50; to 4418th Base Complement SQ (CNC) Greenville AFB South Carolina 8 Nov 50 & 27 Dec 50; to Warner-Robins Air Materiel Area (AMC)

Robins AFB Georgia 29 Sep 51 for depmnt; depl to Brownwood Field Texas 6 Mar 52 // 55th Strategic Reconn WG (SAC) Ramey AFB Puerto Rico 28 May 52; to 55th at Forbes AFB Kansas 2 Jan 53 // Wfu to Ogden Air Materiel Area (AMC) Hill AFB Utah 7 May 53 and stored. Dropped from inventory 8 Jul 54 // Samuel C. Rudolph, Nathan Sidell, Charles J. Katz (Joint Venturers) Los Angeles California 29 Sep 55 reg: N6246C // Albert J. Leeward d/b/a Leeward Aeronautical Service Fort Wayne Indiana 17 Aug 55 (paper sale made prior to acquisition from the Air Force); ownership transferred to Leeward Aeronautical Sales Inc. Fort Wayne Indiana same day; cert of reg not issued until 7 May 57 by which time Leeward was relocated to Miami Florida // Aero Enterprises Inc. Elkhart Indiana 28 Feb 62 // Peter Bercut San Francisco California 14 Feb 62; cert of reg issued 17 Sep 62. Photographed at Sebring, Florida, in late 1969 appearing extremely derelict as though it had been damaged in a storm. It was covered in mud and debris, and the fabric control surfaces were punctured. Also parked nearby was s/n: 44-23054 (N7850B). Both aircraft were still in their USAF liveries with no visible civil markings applied. Listed as "destroyed" and reg canx 22 Nov 71. Final Disposition: Unknown (Presumed Scrapped).

10063 / 44-23019/CQ-019 / C-82A-20-FA

Avble: 23 Sep 46; Acc: 26 Sep 46; Del: 8 Oct 46 to USAAF // 62nd TCG (TAC) Bergstrom Field Texas 9 Oct 46; multiple assignments to 62nd AAF BAS (ATC) Bergstrom Field Texas starting Oct 46; to 319th AAF BAS (TAC) Lawson Field Georgia 13 May 47; 62nd to McChord Field Washington 7 Aug 47; to Fairchild Aircraft Maryland (AMC) for mods 1 Jan 48 // 8th RES SQ (ATC) McChord AFB Washington 19 May 48; cvtd to SC-82A // 2150th RES UT (MATS) McChord AFB Washington 7 Sep 48 // 4th RES SQ (MATS) McChord AFB Washington 5 Oct 49; to Ogden Air Materiel Area (AMC) Hill AFB Utah for mnt 11 Mar 50 // Ogden Air Materiel Area (AMC) Hill AFB Utah 6 Nov 51 for depmnt; cvtd back to C-82A. Placed in storage at Ogden 21 Jan 53; removed from storage 25 Mar 53. Wfu at Ogden 18 Jan 54. Dropped from inventory 8 Jul 54 // L.B. Smith Aircraft Corp. Miami Florida 19 Sep 55 reg: N2056A // Robert I. Dever Barranquilla Colombia 1 Dec 55 reg: unk; aircraft mortgaged to Dever through the Isthmanian Aviation Corp., a Panama corporation; mortgage discharged 21 Feb 56. N2056A reg canx 23 Feb 56 // Capt. Gustavo Torres Bogota Colombia 1956 reg: HK-906 // Lineas Aereas del Colombianas Expresas (LACE) Ltda. Bogota Colombia 6 Jun 58 // Aerovias Helices Ltda. Bogota Colombia date unk. W/o at Barranquilla, Colombia 3 Jun 60, cause and fatalities unk, nfd. Final Disposition: Accident.

10064 / 44-23020/CQ-020 / C-82A-20-FA

Avble: 24 Sep 46; Acc: 2 Oct 46; Del: 8 Oct 46 to USAAF // 62nd TCG (TAC) Bergstrom Field Texas 14 Oct 46; assigned 4th TCSq. Experienced a taxiing accident at Bergstrom Field 4 Nov 46. Pilot: Vivan J. Harvey, no fatalities but aircraft "damaged beyond repair" // 311th AAF BAS (TAC) Bergstrom Field Texas 5 Jan 47 awaiting disposal; bku for salvage 17 Mar 47. Dropped from inventory 19 Jun 47. The C-82A credited with the shortest service history, less than one month! Final Disposition: Accident.

10065 / 44-23021/CQ-021 / C-82A-20-FA

Avble: 30 Sep 46; Acc: 7 Oct 46; Del: 1 Nov 46 to USAAF // 62nd TCG (TAC) Bergstrom Field Texas 9 Dec 46; to 310th AAF BAS (TAC) Pope Field North Carolina 15 Apr 47; to Fairchild Aircraft Maryland (AMC) for mods 8 Jun 47; 62nd to McChord Field Washington 7 Aug 47; briefly to 62nd MSU GP (TAC) McChord AFB Washington 18 Sep 47 // 316th TCG (TAC) Greenville AFB South Carolina 30 Oct 47; assigned 37th TCSq; briefly to 316th MSU GP (TAC) Greenville AFB South Carolina 18 Mar 48; depl to Elmendorf AFB Alaska 2 Jul 48; to Middletown Air Materiel Area (AMC) Olmsted AFB Pennsylvania 7 May 49; 316th to Smyrna AFB Tennessee 4 Nov 49; depl to Guantanamo Bay Cuba 28 Feb 50; Smyrna AFB renamed Sewart AFB 25 Mar 50 // 5th RES SQ (MATS) Maxwell AFB Alabama 10 May 50; cvtd to SC-82A. Made a belly crash-landing due to engine failure 31 Jul 50 2 miles W Tallahassee Florida. Pilot: Laurence F. Tapper, no fatalities but aircraft w/o. Assigned to reclamation 21 Aug 50. Dropped from inventory 12 Oct 50. Final Disposition: Accident.

10066 / 44-23022/CQ-022 / C-82A-20-FA

Avble: 3 Oct 46; Acc: 14 Oct 46; Del: 23 Oct 46 to USAAF // 316th TCG (TAC) Pope Field North Carolina 23 Oct 46; assigned 36th TCSq. Suffered a take-off accident at Pope Field North Carolina 13 Dec 46. Pilot: William P. Carlyon, no fatalities // 310th AAF BAS (TAC) Pope Field North Carolina 16 Dec 46; repairs undertaken but later deemed as "damaged beyond repair." Bku for salvage 9 Jan 47. Dropped from inventory 24 Jul 47. Final Disposition: Accident.

10067 / 44-23023/CQ-023 / C-82A-20-FA

Avble: 8 Oct 46; Acc: 15 Oct 46; Del: 1 Nov 46 to USAAF // 62nd TCG (TAC) Bergstrom Field Texas 11 Nov 46; assigned 8th TCSq; to Fairchild Aircraft Maryland (AMC) 1 Apr 47; depl to 316th TCG (TAC) Pope Field North Carolina 15 May 47; 62nd to McChord Field Washington 7 Aug 47; several assignments to 62nd MSU GP (TAC) McChord AFB Washington starting 23 Sep 47 // 313th TCG (TAC) Bergstrom AFB Texas 23 Dec 47; 313th MSU GP (TAC) Bergstrom AFB Texas 12 Feb 48; to 10th MSU GP (TAC) Pope AFB North Carolina 20 Jul 48 // 4414th AF BAS (TAC) Bergstrom AFB Texas 13 Oct 48 for short-term storage // 4408th AB SQ (CNC) Lawson AFB Georgia 31 Jan 49 // 314th TCG (CNC) Smyrna AFB Tennessee 7 Jun 49; assigned 2601st Light Assault SQ 5 Oct 49; Smyrna AFB renamed Sewart AFB 25 Mar 50 // 375th TCWG (TAC) Greenville AFB South Carolina 12 Dec 50; to 4418th Base Complement SQ (TAC) Greenville AFB South Carolina 12 Dec 50; to Warner-Robins Air Materiel Area (AMC) Robins AFB Georgia 5 Jul 51 for depmnt; depl to Grenier AFB New Hampshire 9 Jan 52; to 4681st AB SQ (ADC) Grenier AFB New Hampshire 4 Mar 52; depl to Brownwood Field Texas 20 Mar 52 // 55th Strategic Reconn WG (SAC) Ramey AFB Puerto Rico 28 May 52; to 55th at Forbes AFB Kansas 23 Feb 53 // Wfu to Ogden Air Materiel Area (AMC) Hill AFB Utah 15 Jun 53 and stored. Dropped from inventory 8 Jul 54 // L.B. Smith Aircraft Corp. Miami Florida 19 Sep 55 reg: N2055A. Destroyed by Hurricane Cleo while stored at Miami Intl. Airport Florida 27 Aug 64. Also destroyed were C-82s N2059A (10102) and N5117B (10083). Reg canx 5 Feb 71. Final Disposition: Accident.

C-82A Packet s/n: 44-23023 (msn: 10067) of L.B. Smith Aircraft Corp., with civil reg N2055A, was damaged beyond repair during Hurricane Cleo in 1964 (Peter J. Marson Collection).

10068 / 44-23024/CQ-024 / C-82A-20-FA

Avble: 10 Oct 46; Acc: 18 Oct 46; Del: 1 Nov 46 to USAAF // 62nd TCG (TAC) Bergstrom Field Texas 4 Nov 46; assigned 4th TCSq. Minor damage in a weather-related incident 60 miles E San Antonio Texas 11 Dec 46. Landing accident at Bergstrom Field Texas 21 Dec 46, no fatalities and aircraft repaired. To 311th AAF BAS (TAC) Bergstrom Field Texas 9 Jan 47. Damaged in an engine failure at take-off accident at Langley Field Virginia 9 Jun 47, no fatalities. To 304th AAF BAS (TAC) Langley Field Virginia 12 Jun 47 for repairs // 363rd MSU GP (TAC) Langley Field Virginia 18 Aug 47 // 316th TCG (TAC) Greenville AFB South Carolina 6 Oct 47; assigned 37th TCSq; to Fairchild Aircraft Maryland (AMC) for mods 11 Nov 47; multiple assignments to 316th MSU GP (TAC) Greenville AFB South Carolina starting 28 Mar 48; depl to Elmendorf AFB Alaska 2 Jul 48; to Middletown Air Materiel Area (AMC) Olmsted AFB Pennsylvania 7 May 49; 316th to Smyrna AFB Tennessee 4 Nov 49; depl to Guantanamo Bay Cuba 28 Feb 50; Smyrna AFB renamed Sewart AFB 25 Mar 50; multiple depls to 314th TCG (CNC) Laurinburg-Maxton Airport North Carolina 24 Apr 50 & Sewart AFB Tennessee starting 20 Apr 50 // 375th TCWG (CNC) Greenville AFB South Carolina 14 Nov 50; assigned 55th TCSq. Brakes failed during a fast taxi run at Greenville AFB 17 Nov 50 and the aircraft went into a ditch. Pilot: unk, no fatalities // 4418th Base Complement SQ (CNC) Greenville AFB South Carolina 20 Nov 50; aircraft assessed as "damaged beyond repair" and scrapped. Dropped from inventory 9 Jan 51. Final Disposition: Accident.

10069 / 44-23025/CQ-025 / C-82A-20-FA

Avble: 14 Oct 46; Acc: 17 Oct 46; Del: 1 Nov 46 to USAAF // 62nd TCG (TAC) Bergstrom Field Texas 11 Nov 46; to Fairchild Aircraft Maryland (AMC) 7 Apr 47; 62nd to McChord Field Washington 7 Aug 47; to 4127th AF BAS (AMC) McClellan AFB California 8 Dec 47 // 313th TCG (TAC) Bergstrom AFB Texas 5 Feb 48; to 4127th AF BAS

(AMC) McClellan AFB California 10 Feb 48 // 4414th AF BAS (TAC) Bergstrom AFB Texas 13 Oct 48 for short-term storage // 4408th AB SQ (TAC) Lawson AFB Georgia 16 Nov 48 // Multiple assignments between 314th & 316th TCG (CNC) Smyrna AFB Tennessee starting 27 Jul 49; assignments to 2601st Light Assault SQ (314th) & 314th MSU GP (CNC); 316th depl to Guantanamo Bay Cuba 2 Feb 50; Smyrna AFB renamed Sewart AFB 25 Mar 50 // 78th Fighter-Interceptor WG (CNC) Hamilton AFB California 5 Jul 50 // 325th Fighter (All-Weather) WG (CNC) McChord AFB Washington 19 Aug 50 // 375th TCWG (TAC) Greenville AFB South Carolina 10 Dec 50; assigned 56th TCSq; to 4418th Base Complement SQ (TAC) Greenville AFB South Carolina 10 Dec 50; to Warner-Robins Air Materiel Area (AMC) Robins AFB Georgia 11 Oct 51 for depmnt; depl to Brownwood Field Texas 4 Mar 52. Minor taxiing accident at Brownwood Field Texas 2 Apr 52, possibly hit parked C-82A s/n: 44-23040, no fatalities // 64th TCWG (TAC) Donaldson AFB South Carolina 14 Jul 52 // Wfu to San Antonio Air Materiel Area (AMC) Kelly AFB Texas 8 Jul 53 and stored. Dropped from inventory 1 Jul 54 // Bankers Life & Casualty Co. Chicago Illinois 7 Sep 55 reg: N5119B // Advance Co. Inc. Miami Florida 21 Oct 55 // Aviation Facilities Inc. Miami Florida 8 Nov 58 // Empresa Guatemalteca de Aviacion (Aviateca Guatemalteca) Guatemala Jun 59 reg: TG-AZA; reg canx 28 Mar 60 // To Peru 27Apr 60 reg: OB-UAE-528, operator unk; subsequent history unk. N5119B reg revoked 17 Jun 71. Final Disposition: Unknown (Presumed Scrapped).

10070 / 44-23026/CQ-026 / C-82A-20-FA

Avble: 17 Oct 46; Acc: 31 Oct 46; Del: 1 Nov 46 to USAAF // 62nd TCG (TAC) Bergstrom Field Texas 6 Nov 46; assigned 8th TCSq; to Fairchild Aircraft Maryland (AMC) 21 Apr 47; depl to 316th TCG (TAC) Pope Field North Carolina 15 May 47; 62nd to McChord Field Washington 7 Aug 47; 62nd MSU GP (TAC) McChord AFB Washington 28 Oct 47; to 10th MSU GP (TAC) Pope AFB North Carolina 17 Apr 48 // 313th MSU GP (TAC) Bergstrom AFB Texas 8 Jun 48; 313th TCG (TAC) Bergstrom AFB Texas 22 Jun 48; to 10th MSU GP (TAC) Pope AFB North Carolina 20 Jul 48 // 4414th AB SQ (TAC) Bergstrom AFB Texas 13 Oct 48 for short-term storage // 314th TCG GP (CNC) Smyrna AFB Tennessee 24 Feb 49; assigned 20th & 50th TCSq. Landing accident due to mechanical failure at Bergstrom AFB Texas 4 Mar 49, no fatalities and aircraft repaired by 4414th AF BAS at Bergstrom. To Warner-Robins Air Materiel Area (AMC) Robins AFB Georgia 6 Apr 49 & 16 Dec 49. Mechanical failure at Robins AFB Georgia 9 Dec 49, no fatalities // 1857th AACS SQ (MATS) Tinker AFB, Oklahoma 7 Apr 50 // 1st AACS Installation & Maintenance SQ (MATS) Tinker AFB Oklahoma 5 Jul 50; to Oklahoma Air Materiel Area (AMC) Tinker AFB Oklahoma 31 Oct 51 & 4 Sep 53; to 3500th Pilot Training WG (TC) Reese AFB Texas 14 Apr 53. Aircraft suffered a landing accident when it landed short at Reese AFB Texas 14 Apr 53, on its delivery flight(?), no fatalities // Wfu to Ogden Air Materiel Area (AMC) Hill AFB Utah 22 Sep 53 and stored. Dropped from inventory 8 Jul 54 // Ben W. Widtfeldt & Harry S. McCandless Council Bluffs Iowa 23 Aug 55 reg: N4832V // M&W Aircraft Leasing Council Bluffs Iowa 7 Sep 55 // United Heckathorn Corp. Richmond California 6 Mar 56; cvtd to sprayer aircraft 1 Jun 56 with four internal tanks and associated spray equipment, work carried out by McCabe Aircraft Service at Hayward Airport, California. Noted to have SkySpray logo on fuselage // Boothe Leasing Corp. San Francisco California 9 Jul 56. Crashed 8 Aug 56 at Boca Raton Airport Florida when the aircraft lost control due to engine failure on a go-around. The worst U.S.–based civilian C-82 crash with five fatalities: pilot Charles W. Day (34 yrs), copilot Rae F. Howry (32 yrs), and passengers Allen Johnson (18 yrs), Warren Rogers (23 yrs), and John Tichenor (44 yrs). The aircraft departed Masters Field, Florida, for Boca Raton Airport, Florida, at 0448 hrs along with United Heckathorn's other C-82 N4829V to load up a spray solution of DDT. They were carrying out spray operations in order to eradicate an infestation of Mediterranean fruit fly within the state of Florida. En route the crew of N4829V noted intermittent wisps of blue smoke coming from the port engine on N4832V. As the aircraft came in to land at Boca Raton the smoke trail became more pronounced with witnesses on the ground stating one engine sounded very rough and uneven. N4832V then began a go-around and started to climb out in a left-hand turn. The turn continued into a stall followed by an "over the top" spin, the C-82 then crashing into the ground and bursting into flames about 1,500 ft from the airport just after 0500 hrs. The subsequent investigation revealed the following factors and chain of events:

1. Both pilots were properly qualified and fit for operations.
2. Aircraft weights were well within limits (take-off weight 35 to 36,000 lb) with control cables and control surfaces found to be functional with no signs of any malfunction.
3. The weather was not a factor in the accident.
4. The intended runway for landing was clear of obstructions and persons.
5. It was found the port engine lost power due to a complete failure of the rear master rod bearing. This was a progressive failure over time and something not easily picked up on during general visual inspections of the engine. Hard sludge was found to be clogging the lubricating oil ports, which is probably what began the deterioration of the bearing. Over time, piston damage had occurred, with complete master rod failure occurring only in the last few minutes of the flight. This accounts for the smoke puffs from the exhaust and rough, backfiring sounds that were heard on the ground.
6. It appears N4832V was badly aligned for a landing along Runway 4 (were the crew distracted by early signs of engine trouble? If a rough-sounding engine could be heard on the ground, the crew certainly would have heard it). The C-82 was already one-third of the way along Runway 4 when a go-around was initiated.
7. The crew might actually have been aware of the rough-running engine but, it seems, unaware of the engine's total loss of power until too late, as a climbing left-hand turn was undertaken with u/c and flaps then retracted. The unfeathered, drag-inducing port propeller, plus a low airspeed from the aborted landing, resulted in a stall and loss of directional control for the aircraft. The now uncontrollable turn and climb continued into an "over the top" spin into the ground.
8. Examination of the engines and propellers revealed the port engine to be delivering low rotational speeds and the starboard engine to be delivering high rotational speeds at the time of impact. The port engine propeller was unfeathered, which would have been causing high induced drag on the airplane at a time when full power was needed. These factors indicate the crew were unaware of the port engine power loss. The crew's unawareness lies in the fact that it was a power failure *from the engine* as opposed to a *failure of the engine*—the engine was still running, so the pilots likely thought they had full power available until it was too late.

Cause: N4832V lost power in the port engine just after the pilot initiated a go-around. The port engine propeller, however, remained unfeathered as the plane was climbing into a left-hand turn with an already low airspeed. The lack of adequate power, and an unfeathered, drag-inducing left propeller, together pulled the aircraft into the left turn more acutely until a stall condition set in, resulting in a loss of directional control. The pilot, likely using full top rudder to kick out of the turn, inadvertently put the aircraft into an "over the top" spin with fatal results. Reg canx 1968 by Greyhound Leasing & Financial Corp. Chicago Illinois who at that time were the registration holders. Final Disposition: Accident.

Skyspray C-82A N4832V (msn: 10070) at Hayward Airport, California, during May 1956, just a few months before it crashed in Florida, killing all five onboard (William T. Larkins).

10071 / 44-23027/CQ-027 / C-82A-20-FA

Avble: 21 Oct 46; Acc: 25 Oct 46; Del: 1 Nov 46 to USAAF // 62nd TCG (TAC) Bergstrom Field Texas 11 Nov 46; assigned 8th TCSq; to Fairchild Aircraft Maryland (AMC) 27 Apr 47; 62nd to McChord Field Washington 7 Aug 47; to 1455th AAF BAS (ATC) East Base Field Montana 28 Aug 47; multiple assignments to 62nd MSU GP (TAC) McChord AFB Washington starting 20 Apr 48; briefly to 62nd AB GP (TAC) McChord AFB Washington 1 Sep 48 for flight training; to Middletown Air Materiel Area (AMC) Olmsted AFB Pennsylvania 26 Mar 49 // 7th RES SQ (MATS) Wheelus AFB Libya 6 Apr 50; cvtd to SC-82A; depls to Wiesbaden AB West Germany 28 Apr 50, 10th AB GP (AFE) Erding AB West Germany 8 Dec 50 & 85th Air Depot WG (AFE) Erding AB West Germany 16 Nov 51. Structural failure occurred 5 miles SSE of Wiesbaden AB West Germany 27 Apr 52, no fatalities and aircraft landed safely. To 7150th AB GP (AFE) Wiesbaden AB West Germany 1 May 52 for repairs // 58th RES SQ (MATS) Wheelus AFB Libya 4 Nov 52 // Aircraft Engineering & Maintenance Co. (AMC) Oakland California 3 Jul 53 on bailment; cvtd back to C-82A standard and modernized to Group A standard // 567th Air Defense GP (ADC) McChord AFB Washington 5 Jan 54; to 3415th Technical Training WG (TC) Lowry AFB Colorado 26 Jan 54; to Oklahoma Air Materiel Area (AMC) Tinker

AFB Oklahoma 4 Nov 54 // Wfu to 3040th Aircraft Storage SQ (AMC) Davis-Monthan AFB Arizona 21 Feb 55 and stored. Dropped from inventory 1 Aug 55 // Samuel C. Rudolph Los Angeles California 9 Jan 56 reg: N5095V // Steward-Davis Inc. Gardena California 18 Sep 56; cvtd to Steward-Davis Jet-Packet 3200 with twin J30-W Jet-Pak, used for Jet-Packet demos and flight-testing during 1957 // Ricardo de Varennes (Rivaereo Co.) Arica Chile 14 Jul 58 reg: CC-CRA-0507 // S.C. Rudolph Lumber Corp. Los Angeles California 25 Apr 59 reg: N5095V; re-reg: N8009E 19 Jun 61 // Far North Flying Service Fairbanks Alaska 17 Jun 61; damaged right wing when the right u/c collapsed while stationary on the ground early 1963. Steward-Davis employee Bob Thayer spent a period of time on N8809E in Alaska and recounted his experiences to the author:

> Although I have flown in many types of flying machines in my 53 year career in aviation, none holds a greater place in my heart than the ugly, clumsy looking, noisy, always forgiving Fairchild C-82. Over the 31 years that was spent in the employ of S-D Inc., many hours were spent aloft in the C-82 during test flights or with the many customers involved. A very special airplane to fill some very special needs for our very special customers like Al Mosley, owner of Far North Flying Service in Fairbanks, Alaska, who was one of my favorites. On my first trip to oversee the service flights of a newly delivered "Skytruck," we left to deliver supplies to a Dew-Line station on Indian Mountain in the Brooks Range, most of which included 55 gallon drums of diesel fuel and gasoline for the equipment. With virtually no sound proofing and relatively short stacks on the R-2800s, plus the whine of the J30 turbojets operating at high idle, intercom was the only means of verbal communication. As we approached the south face of the mountain, knowing that we needed a few more thousand feet to clear the top, I was sure that Al had said 'there it is!', pointing to a clearing in the trees. As improbable as it seemed it was not a misunderstanding. He lined up for a straight in landing on what appeared to be about a 15% uphill pee [sic] gravel landing strip carved out of a forest. As quickly as we touched down he gave the engines take-off power for the up-hill climb. As we hit the top of the strip it flattened out for 200–300 feet before ending at a vertical cliff dead ahead, chopping all power and standing hard on the brakes, he made a complete u-turn and came to a stop in perfect position for the down-hill take-off. After unloading the cargo we received a new load of empty 55 gallon drums to be returned to Fairbanks. This had been the most unusual landing that I had ever experienced and I knew that the down-hill take-off could not be aborted. Inasmuch as our load had been considerably lightened, Al felt no need to use the jet-assist, consequently, we managed to top a pine tree with the elevator on our way out, which left a nasty gap in the linen covering. Upon returning to Fairbanks, with the assistance of an aerostand and a roll of silver duct tape, the elevator was as good as new. The aircraft was later used to deliver the U.S. Geophysical Survey boats to Point Barrow for the exploration of the North Sea; it delivered a D4 Caterpillar tractor to an antimony mine in the tundra; Alaskan king grabs in specially designed ice containers and many, many other unique loads that could not be handled by any other aircraft.

// M&F Inc. Fairbanks Alaska 23 Feb 63 // Small Business Administration 27 Nov 67, repossessed aircraft from M&F Inc. on behalf of First National Bank of Fairbanks Alaska // Robert G. Sholton Anchorage Alaska 30 Nov 67 // Florida Aircraft Leasing Corp. Fort Lauderdale Florida 27 Nov 68; radio & nav. upgrade 30 Oct 69; main spar, wing and corrosion repairs made late 1975; leases to Americana, Ecuador 1971 and Pacific Alaska Airways, Alaska 1977 // Outsized Cargo Inc. Kenai Alaska 25 Jun 80 // Flying B. Inc. Anchorage Alaska 15 Sep 1980; wfu and bku after 1987 // Hawkins & Powers Aviation Inc. Greybull Wyoming 16 Jun 95 in dismantled condition // The Pride Capital Group

Opposite, top: **C-82A s/n: 44-23027 (msn: 10071). Note the squadron markings on the nose and tails (National Museum of the United States Air Force).** *Middle:* **Steward-Davis C-82A Jet-Packet 3200 N5095V (msn: 10071) in Mexico during 1957 on a demonstration tour. The PBY-6A Catalina is XB-YUP (José Villela G.).** *Bottom:* **C-82A N5095V (msn: 10071) suffered a minor accident early on in its civilian career. It was repaired and returned to service, flying into the 1980s (Steward-Davis).**

C-82A Jet-Packet 3200 N8009E (msn: 10071) being refueled in the late 1960s at an airport in California while operating with the Florida Aircraft Leasing Corp (G. Pat Macha).

LLC. Deerfield Illinois 1 Sep 05 for auctioneering // Hagerstown Aviation Museum Hagerstown Maryland 30 Aug 06; fuselage and minor components stored for museum display. Final Disposition: Preserved.

10072 / 44-23028/CQ-028 / C-82A-20-FA

Avble: 23 Oct 46; Acc: 31 Oct 46; Del: 1 Nov 46 to USAAF // 62nd TCG (TAC) Bergstrom Field Texas 6 Nov 46; assigned 8th TCSq; to Fairchild Aircraft Maryland (AMC) for mods 9 Apr 47. Made a belly crash-landing due to engine failure 10 miles SE Austin Texas 11 May 47. Pilot: Ralph Bloemendaal, no fatalities but aircraft "damaged beyond repair" // 311th AAF BAS (TAC) Bergstrom Field Texas 13 May 47 awaiting disposal; bku for salvage 15 May 47. Dropped from inventory 4 Sep 47. Final Disposition: Accident.

10073 / 44-23029/CQ-029 / C-82A-20-FA

Avble: 25 Oct 46; Acc: 31 Oct 46; Del: 1 Nov 46 to USAAF // 62nd TCG (TAC) Bergstrom Field Texas 11 Nov 46; assigned 8th TCSq; to Fairchild Aircraft Maryland (AMC) 1 Apr 47; 62nd to McChord Field Washington 7 Aug 47; 62nd MSU GP (TAC) McChord AFB Washington 12 Nov 47 // 313th TCG & 313th MSU GP (TAC) Bergstrom AFB Texas 21 Mar 48 // 4414th AB SQ (TAC) Bergstrom AFB Texas 13 Oct 48 for short-term storage // 314th TCG GP (CNC) Smyrna AFB Tennessee 24 Feb 49; assigned 20th TCSq; multiple assignments to 314th MSU GP (CNC) Smyrna AFB Tennessee starting 13 Apr 49; to Mobile Air Materiel Area (AMC) Brookley AFB, Alabama 2 Nov 49; Smyrna AFB renamed Sewart AFB 25 Mar 50 // 1800th AACS WG (MATS) Tinker AFB, Oklahoma 20 Apr 50 // 4th AACS Installation & Maintenance SQ (MATS) Freising AB West Germany 30 Jun 50; to 85th Air Depot WG (AFE) Erding AB West Germany 5 Feb 51 //

9th RES SQ (MATS) RAF Manston England 12 Aug 51, cvtd to SC-82A; to 7540th Depot Maintenance GP (AFE) Burtonwood Air Depot England 19 Nov 51 & 59th Air Depot WG (AFE) Burtonwood Air Depot England 21 Dec 51; to RAF Sculthorpe England 22 Aug 52 // 66th RES SQ (MATS) RAF Manston England 4 Nov 52; to 67th RES SQ (MATS) RAF Sculthorpe England 5 Dec 52; to 1631st AB SQ (MATS) RAF Prestwick Scotland 15 Apr 53 // Wfu to Ogden Air Materiel Area (AMC) Hill AFB Utah 9 Aug 53 and stored. Dropped from inventory 8 Jul 54 // Whitney-Ben Trading Co. Calexico California 22 Aug 55 reg: N4829V // Ben W. Widtfeldt San Francisco California 23 Feb 56 // United Heckathorn Corp. Richmond California 6 Mar 56; cvtd to sprayer aircraft 1 Jun 56 with four internal tanks and associated spray equipment, work carried out by McCabe Aircraft Service at Hayward Airport, California. Noted to have SkySpray logo on fuselage // Boothe Leasing Corp. San Francisco California 9 Jul 56; engine servicing 12 Apr 57 by Aviation Power Supply Inc. Burbank, California. Cvtd to aerial tanker 20 Sep 57 with two 800 U.S. gal tanks and slipper tank for trials with the U.S. Forest Service, flew as a tanker in a Redding California fire on 25 Sep 57 making several runs, the slipper tank was not successful; cvtd back 5 Jun 58 // United Heckathorn Corp. Richmond California 21 Oct 59 // Ewell K. Nold Jr. South Houston Texas 5 Jan 62; repairs made to stabilizer trim tabs 16 Jul 62 // A.C. Mosley or Jean Mosley d/b/a Far North Flying Service Fairbanks Alaska 14 Jul 62 // M&F Inc. Fairbanks Alaska 23 Feb 63; nose wheel steering and braking system upgrade 26 Feb 63. Cvtd to Steward-Davis Jet-Packet 3400A with J34-WE Jet-Pak Mar 63. Engine servicing 11 Oct 63 by Eight Air Depot Inc. Sebring, Florida. Leases to Geophysical Service Inc. 2 Jul 64; F&W Construction Co. 16 Jul 64; Ghemm Co. Inc. 27 Jul 64 and B&A Co. 3 Aug 64. Landing accident 3 Aug 64 at Granite Mountain Airport Alaska, two crew and two passengers uninjured but aircraft w/o. Pilot misjudged his approach and undershot the runway causing the u/c to collapse, the airframe subsequently caught fire. Reg canx 6 Jan 65. Final Disposition: Accident.

C-82A N4829V (msn: 10073) newly marked with its civil registration but still in 67th RES Sq livery from its previous USAF service in England (Dick Phillips Collection).

10074 / 44-23030/CQ-030 / C-82A-20-FA

Avble: 30 Oct 46; Acc: 30 Oct 46; Del: 1 Nov 46 to USAAF // 62nd TCG (TAC) Bergstrom Field Texas 6 Nov 46; assigned 8th TCSq; to Fairchild Aircraft Maryland

(AMC) 24 Mar 47; depl to 316th TCG (TAC) Pope Field North Carolina 15 May 47; 62nd to McChord Field Washington 7 Aug 47 // 319th AF BAS (TAC) Lawson AFB Georgia 4 Mar 48; to 3010th AF BAS (TC) Williams AFB Arizona 4 Mar 48 // 4408th AB SQ (TAC) Lawson AFB Georgia 23 Aug 48. Had a take-off accident due to mechanical failure at Lawson AFB Georgia 25 Oct 48, no fatalities and aircraft repaired // Warner-Robins Air Materiel Area (AMC) Robins AFB Georgia 16 Dec 48 // 314th TCG GP (CNC) Smyrna AFB Tennessee 13 Sep 49; assigned 2601st Light Assault SQ; Smyrna AFB renamed Sewart AFB 25 Mar 50 // 5th RES SQ (MATS) Selfridge AFB Michigan 16 Jun 50; cvtd to SC-82A; to Sacramento Air Materiel Area (AMC) McClellan AFB California 7 Sep 50 for depmnt; depl to Maxwell AFB Alabama 15 Mar 51; to 1100th AB WG (HQC) Bolling AFB District of Columbia 18 May 52; to San Antonio Air Materiel Area (AMC) Kelly AFB Texas 23 Jul 52 & 11 Oct 52 // 48th RES SQ (MATS) Maxwell AFB Alabama 4 Nov 52 // Wfu to Ogden Air Materiel Area (AMC) Hill AFB Utah 9 Jun 53 and stored. Dropped from inventory 8 Jul 54 // Samuel C. Rudolph, Nathan Sidell, Charles J. Katz (Joint Venturers) Los Angeles California 29 Sep 55 reg: N6243C // Albert J. Leeward d/b/a Leeward Aeronautical Service Fort Wayne Indiana 17 Aug 55 (paper sale made prior to acquisition from the Air Force); ownership transferred to Leeward Aeronautical Sales Inc. Fort Wayne Indiana same day; cert of reg not issued until 7 May 57 by which time Leeward was relocated to Miami Florida // Aero Enterprises Inc. Elkhart Indiana 28 Feb 62 // Peter Bercut San Francisco California 14 Feb 62; cert of reg issued 17 Sep 62. FAA lists as "destroyed" and reg canx 22 Nov 71. Final Disposition: Unknown (Presumed Scrapped).

10075 / 44-23031/CQ-031 / C-82A-20-FA

Avble: 30 Oct 46; Acc: 5 Nov 46; Del: 2 Dec 46 to USAAF // 62nd TCG (TAC) Bergstrom Field Texas 18 Dec 46; to Fairchild Aircraft Maryland (AMC) for mods 24 Mar 47; depl to 316th TCG (TAC) Pope Field North Carolina 15 May 47; 62nd to McChord Field Washington 7 Aug 47; multiple assignments to 62nd MSU GP (TAC) McChord AFB Washington starting 15 Nov 47; to Middletown Air Materiel Area (AMC) Olmsted AFB Pennsylvania 6 Apr 49 // 1857th AACS SQ (MATS) Tinker AFB, Oklahoma 23 Mar 50; to 1600th Air Transport WG (MATS) Westover AFB Massachusetts 28 Apr 50; to 1227th AB GP (MATS) Goose AB Labrador 29 May 50 // 1st AACS Installation & Maintenance SQ (MATS) Tinker AFB Oklahoma 5 Jul 50; to Warner-Robins Air Materiel Area (AMC) Robins AFB Georgia 16 May 51; to 363rd Tactical Reconnaissance WG (TAC) Shaw AFB South Carolina 19 Dec 51; to Oklahoma Air Materiel Area (AMC) Tinker AFB Oklahoma 9 Jun 53 // Wfu to Ogden Air Materiel Area (AMC) Hill AFB Utah 14 Jan 54 and stored. Dropped from inventory 8 Jul 54 // Ben W. Widtfeldt & Harry S. McCandless Council Bluffs Iowa 23 Aug 55 reg: N4833V // M&W Aircraft Leasing Council Bluffs Iowa 7 Sep 55. Lease to SkySpray Inc. for aerial spray work 1956 but there's no evidence to suggest spray equipment was ever installed. Supposed lease to Switzerland reg: HB-AAB but ntu // Ben W. Widtfeldt Phoenix Arizona 23 Mar 59. Lease to Wiley Electronics Co. Arizona 9 Jul 59 for aerial photography contract // Aviation Enterprises Scottsdale Arizona 23 Mar 60 // Biegert Bros. Inc. Phoenix Arizona 29 Apr 60 // Henry A. Smith Richmond California 30 Mar 61 // New Frontier Airlift Corp. Phoenix Arizona 30 Mar 61—purchased for Steward-Davis Jet-Packet program. Fuselage leased to 20th Century–Fox film *The Flight of the Phoenix* (1965) for Imperial Valley outdoor location scenes. Placed back in open storage at Long Beach Airport late 1965. One of eight C-82A derelicts

for Fairchild-Hiller Corp. Maryland; reg: N6850A rsved 1967 but ntu. Likely scrapped 1970–71. FAA reg revoked 10 Dec 70. Final Disposition: Scrapped.

Top: C-82A N4833V (msn: 10075) during an aerial photographic lease with Wiley Electronics Co. in 1963 (Ed Coates Collection). *Bottom:* Derelict at Long Beach in the late 1960s is *Phoenix* movie star C-82A N4833V (msn: 10075) (Andre Van Loon Collection).

10076 / 44-23032/CQ-032 / C-82A-20-FA

Avble: 31 Oct 46; Acc: 12 Nov 46; Del: 18 Nov 46 to USAAF // 62nd TCG (TAC) Bergstrom Field Texas 24 Nov 46; assigned 8th TCSq; to Fairchild Aircraft Maryland (AMC) 17 Apr 47; depl to 316th TCG (TAC) Pope Field North Carolina 15 May 47; 62nd to McChord Field Washington 7 Aug 47; 62nd MSU GP (TAC) McChord Field Washington 16 Sep 47. Suffered a minor taxiing accident at McChord AFB Washington 25 Oct 47, no fatalities, aircraft already assigned 316th TCG—36th TCSq // 316th TCG (TAC) Greenville AFB South Carolina 6 Nov 47; assigned 37th TCSq; 316th MSU GP (TAC) Greenville AFB South Carolina 8 Dec 47; depl to Elmendorf AFB Alaska 2 Jul 48; to Warner-Robins Air Materiel Area (AMC) Robins AFB Georgia 20 Sep 49 for depmnt; 316th to Smyrna AFB Tennessee 4 Nov 49, Smyrna AFB renamed Sewart AFB 25 Mar 50; multiple assignments to 314th TCWG (CNC) Sewart AFB Tennessee starting 8 May 50 // 375th TCWG (CNC) Greenville AFB South Carolina 12 Nov 50; to Warner-Robins Air Materiel Area (AMC) Robins AFB Georgia 5 Jul 51 for depmnt; depls to Grenier AFB New Hampshire 3 Jan 52 & Brownwood Field Texas 20 Mar 52 // 64th TCWG (TAC) Donaldson AFB South Carolina 14 Jul 52; assigned 17th TCSq. Involved in a "personal injury" incident at Altus Oklahoma 25 Jan 53, nfd // Wfu to San Antonio Air Materiel Area (AMC) Kelly AFB Texas 2 Jul 53 and stored. Dropped from inventory 1 Jul 54 // Smock & Jenner Inc. Cincinnati Ohio 16 Aug 55 reg: N74041 // Ben Epstein, Trustee for Ben, Leonard and Stanley W. Epstein (Aeronautical Cargo Co.) Miami Beach Florida 29 Dec 55 // Henry A. Smith Richmond California 24 May 61 // New Frontier Airlift Corp. Berkeley California 1 May 63—purchased for Steward-Davis Jet-Packet program, but no buyers or conversion work carried out. One of eight C-82A derelicts for Fairchild-Hiller Corp. Maryland; reg: N6857A rsved 1967 but ntu. N74041 reg revoked 5 Feb 71. Final Disposition: Scrapped.

10077 / 44-23033/CQ-033 / C-82A-20-FA

Avble: 12 Nov 46; Acc: 22 Nov 46; Del: 2 Dec 46 to USAAF; assigned 311th then 316th AAF BAS (AMC) but retained at Fairchild Hagerstown for mods // 62nd TCG (TAC) Bergstrom Field Texas 18 Dec 46; assigned 8th TCSq; to Fairchild Aircraft Maryland (AMC) 9 Apr 47. Had a landing accident at NAS San Diego California 10 Apr 47, no fatalities and aircraft repaired. Depl to 316th TCG (TAC) Pope Field North Carolina 15 May 47; 62nd to McChord Field Washington 7 Aug 47; multiple assignments to 62nd MSU GP (TAC) McChord AFB Washington starting 31 Dec 47; to Middletown Air Materiel Area (AMC) Olmsted AFB Pennsylvania 6 Apr 49 // 4th RES SQ (MATS) McChord AFB Washington 7 Mar 50; cvtd to SC-82A; to Hamilton AFB California with 4th RES SQ 26 Apr 50; to 2750th AB WG (AMC) WPAFB Ohio 25 Jul 50; to 78th Fighter-Interceptor WG (CNC) Hamilton AFB California 28 Jul 50; to March AFB California with 4th RES SQ 31 Oct 50; to 84th RES SQ (MATS) Hamilton AFB California 27 Feb 51; to Sacramento Air Materiel Area (AMC) McClellan AFB California 5 Jun 51; to 78th Fighter-Interceptor WG (ADC) Hamilton AFB California 8 Jan 52 via Hamilton AFB Flight Service; to 4702nd Defense WG (ADC) Hamilton AFB California 6 Feb 52 // 41st RES SQ (MATS) Hamilton AFB California 4 Nov 52 // Aircraft Engineering & Maintenance Co. (AMC) Oakland California 1 Aug 53 on bailment; cvtd back to C-82A standard and modernized to Group A standard // 1st AACS Installation & Maintenance SQ (MATS) Tinker AFB Oklahoma 1 Feb 54 // 567th Air Defense GP (ADC) McChord AFB Washington 19 May 54; to Oklahoma Air Materiel Area (AMC) Tinker AFB Oklahoma 6 Nov 54 // Wfu to 3040th Aircraft Storage SQ (AMC) Davis-Monthan AFB Arizona 21 Feb 55 and stored. Dropped from inventory 1 Aug 55 // Samuel C. Rudolph Los Angeles California 9 Jan 56 reg: N6999C // S.C. Rudolph Lumber Corp. Los Angeles California 30 Jun 58 // New Frontier Airlift Corp. Phoenix Arizona & Steward-Davis Inc. Gardena

California 5 Feb 62—purchased for Steward-Davis Jet-Packet program; stored along with N6996C, N6997C and N6998C at Tucson Airport Arizona, but no buyers or conversion work carried out. Reg revoked 1 Feb 71 // Allied Aircraft Sales Tucson Arizona 6 Oct 75 // Bob's Airpark Tucson Arizona 30 Jan 81. Placed on display unrestored and in a very derelict condition with other similar aircraft at Bob's Airpark located near Tucson Airport; bku for scrap after 2000. Final Disposition: Scrapped.

10078 / 44-23034/CQ-034 / C-82A-25-FA

Avble: 8 Nov 46; Acc: 20 Nov 46; Del: 11 Dec 46 to USAAF // 4000th AAF BAS (AMC) Patterson & Wright Fields Ohio 12 Dec 46; to 1377th AAF BAS (ATC) Westover Field Massachusetts 19 May 47. Had an in-flight mechanical failure 5 miles west of Dayton Ohio 17 Jul 47, no fatalities and aircraft repaired. Listed as being with the 4020th AAF BAS at the time but the IARC does not reflect this. // 2750th AB WG (AMC) WPAFB Ohio 27 Oct 48, cvtd to EC-82A for experimental duties. Suffered minor damage due to a mechanical failure at WPAFB Ohio 18 Apr 50, no fatalities // 375th TCWG (TAC) Greenville AFB South Carolina 8 Jan 51, cvtd back to C-82A standard; to Warner-Robins Air Materiel Area (AMC) Robins AFB Georgia 7 Sep 51 for depmnt; depl to Brownwood Field Texas 8 Mar 52 // 64th TCWG (TAC) Donaldson AFB South Carolina 14 Jul 52; to Warner-Robins Air Materiel Area (AMC) Robins AFB Georgia 4 Apr 53 for depmnt // Wfu to San Antonio Air Materiel Area (AMC) Kelly AFB Texas 2 Jul 53 and stored. Dropped from inventory 1 Jul 54 // Bankers Life & Casualty Co. Chicago Illinois 7 Sep 55 reg: N5118B // Advance Co. Inc. Miami Florida 21 Oct 55 // Aviation Facilities Inc. Miami Florida 8 Nov 58 // Empresa Guatemalteca de Aviacion (Aviateca Guatemalteca) Guatemala 7 Dec 58 reg: TG-AXA; wfu 1960 and flown back to the U.S.; subsequent history unk. N5118B reg revoked 17 Jun 71. Final Disposition: Unknown (Presumed Scrapped).

10079 / 44-23035/CQ-035 / C-82A-25-FA

Avble: 15 Nov 46; Acc: 25 Nov 46; Del: 9 Dec 46 to USAAF // 62nd TCG (TAC) Bergstrom Field Texas 12 Dec 46; depl to 316th TCG (TAC) Pope Field North Carolina 19 May 47; 62nd to McChord Field Washington 7 Aug 47; 62nd MSU GP (TAC) McChord AFB Washington 31 Dec 47 // 313th TCG (TAC) Bergstrom AFB Texas 7 Apr 48; assigned 47th TCSq; depl to Pope AFB North Carolina 14 Apr 48. Had a ground collision at Greenville AFB South Carolina 21 Apr 48, no fatalities and aircraft repaired. 313th MSU GP (TAC) Bergstrom AFB Texas 14 Sep 48 // 4414th AB SQ (TAC) Bergstrom AFB Texas 13 Oct 48 for storage; depl to 20th TCSq (314th TCG) 22 Nov 48 // 314th TCG (CNC) Smyrna AFB Tennessee 24 Feb 49; assigned 334th TCSq. Encountered bad weather while flying over the northern state of Para Brazil 1 Mar 49; unable to land, the C-82A ran out of fuel, forcing the crew to bail out. Pilot: Paul W. Saffold, no fatalities but the aircraft was destroyed on impact. Assigned to reclamation 31 May 49. Dropped from inventory 16 Aug 49. Final Disposition: Accident.

10080 / 44-23036/CQ-036 / C-82A-25-FA

Avble: 20 Nov 46; Acc: 25 Nov 46; Del: 9 Dec 46 to USAAF // 62nd TCG (TAC) Bergstrom Field Texas 12 Dec 46; assigned to 4th TCSq; 62nd to McChord Field

Washington 7 Aug 47; to Fairchild Aircraft Maryland (AMC) for mods 25 Aug 47; depl to Elmendorf AFB Alaska 1 Apr 48; multiple assignments to 62nd MSU GP (CNC) McChord AFB Washington starting 10 Mar 49 // 6th RES SQ (MATS) Westover AFB Massachusetts 13 Mar 50; cvtd to SC-82A; to 1600th Air Transport Wing (MATS) Westover AFB Massachusetts 15 May 50. Minor landing accident at Blair Civil Air Patrol Pennsylvania 25 Oct 50, no fatalities // 5th RES SQ (MATS) Westover AFB Massachusetts 20 Feb 51 // 46th RES SQ (MATS) Westover AFB Massachusetts 18 Nov 52 // USAF bailment to Fairchild Aircraft Maryland 25 May 53; cvtd back to C-82A standard. Fitted with Fairchild J44-R Jet-Pak for flight-tests into use of jet augmentation on the C-82A. USAF lease and tests approved 15 Jun 54; USAF ownership retained but carried civil reg: N53228. Dropped from inventory by commercial sale in 1957, has the distinction of being the last C-82A retired by the USAF // Master Equipment Co. Cheyenne Wyoming 30 Jan 57; reg:

Top: C-82A s/n: 44-23036 (msn: 10080) was leased to Fairchild Aircraft as N53228 from 1954 to 1956 for the purpose of testing a Fairchild J44-R engine as a jet-pak (Fairchild). *Bottom:* Movie star C-82A N53228 (msn: 10080) languishing at Long Beach Airport, California, during 1970, still adorned in *The Flight of the Phoenix* (1965) Arabco Oil Co. livery (Bruce Orriss).

N53228 retd, reg: N5903V resved but ntu. Cvtd to a pesticide sprayer 19 Apr 57 with a 2,640 U.S. gal tank in the hold and associated spray equipment // New Frontier Airlift Corp. Phoenix Arizona 16 Jun 61—purchased for Steward-Davis Jet-Packet program. Fuselage leased to 20th Century-Fox film *The Flight of the Phoenix* (1965) for indoor studio-based scenes. Placed back in open storage Long Beach Airport late 1965. Likely scrapped 1970–71. FAA reg revoked 11 Jan 71. Final Disposition: Scrapped.

10081 / 44-23037/CQ-037 / C-82A-25-FA

Avble: 21 Nov 46; Acc: 30 Nov 46; Del: 11 Dec 46 to USAAF // 310th AAF BAS (TAC) Pope Field North Carolina 18 Dec 46; depl to 316th TCG (TAC) Pope Field North Carolina 7 Feb 47 // 316th TCG (TAC) Pope Field North Carolina 21 May 47; assigned 36th & 37th TCSq; 316th to Greenville Field South Carolina 25 Aug 47; to Middletown Air Materiel Area (AMC) Olmsted AFB Pennsylvania 4 Jun 49; 316th MSU GP (CNC) Greenville AFB South Carolina 14 Oct 49; 316th to Smyrna AFB Tennessee 4 Nov 49. Suffered a mechanical failure at McClellan AFB California 10 Dec 49, no fatalities. To Sacramento Air Materiel Area (AMC) McClellan AFB California 14 Dec 49 for depmnt; multiple depls to 314th TCG & MSU GP (CNC) Smyrna AFB Tennessee starting 23 Jan 50; 316th depl to Guantanamo Bay Cuba 28 Feb 50; Smyrna AFB renamed Sewart AFB 25 Mar 50; depl to 314th TCG (CNC) Laurinburg-Maxton Airport North Carolina 24 Apr 50 // 314th TCWG (CNC) Sewart AFB Tennessee 1 Nov 50 // 375th TCWG (TAC) Greenville AFB South Carolina 27 Jan 51; assigned 56th TCSq. Minor ground accident at Greenville AFB South Carolina 1 May 51, no fatalities. Depl to 433rd TCWG (TAC) Donaldson AFB South Carolina 3 May 51; to Warner-Robins Air Materiel Area (AMC) Robins AFB Georgia 28 Sep 51 for depmnt; depl to Brownwood Field Texas 4 Mar 52 // 64th TCWG (TAC) Donaldson AFB South Carolina 14 Jul 52 // Wfu to San Antonio Air Materiel Area (AMC) Kelly AFB Texas 7 Jul 53 and stored. Dropped from inventory 1 Jul 54 // Smock & Jenner Inc. Cincinnati Ohio 16 Aug 55 reg: N74042 // Ben Epstein, Trustee for Ben, Leonard and Stanley W. Epstein (Aeronautical Cargo Co.) Miami Beach Florida 29 Dec 55 // Henry A. Smith Richmond California 24 May 61 // New Frontier Airlift Corp. Berkeley California 1 May 63—purchased for Steward-Davis Jet-Packet program, but no buyers or conversion work carried out. N74042 reg revoked 5 Feb 71. Final Disposition: Scrapped.

10082 / 44-23038/CQ-038 / C-82A-25-FA

Avble: 25 Nov 46; Acc: 30 Nov 46; Del: 11 Dec 46 to USAAF // 310th AAF BAS (TAC) Pope Field North Carolina 18 Dec 46; depl to 316th TCG (TAC) Pope Field North Carolina 7 Feb 47 // 316th TCG (TAC) Pope Field North Carolina 7 Aug 47; assigned 36th TCSq; 316th to Greenville Field South Carolina 25 Aug 47; multiple depls to 316th MSU GP (TAC) Greenville AFB South Carolina starting 11 Dec 47; to Middletown Air Materiel Area (AMC) Olmsted AFB Pennsylvania 6 Apr 49; 316th to Smyrna AFB Tennessee 4 Nov 49. Developed an in-flight mechanical failure 10 miles SW of Waddsworth Nevada 16 Dec 49, some occupants bailed out and the aircraft then made an emergency landing, no fatalities. To Sacramento Air Materiel Area (AMC) McClellan AFB California 22 Dec 49 for depmnt; depl to 314th TCG (CNC) Smyrna AFB Tennessee 16 Jan 50; 316th depl to Guantanamo Bay Cuba 28 Feb 50; Smyrna AFB renamed Sewart AFB 25 Mar 50; depl to 314th TCG (CNC) Laurinburg-Maxton Airport North Carolina 20 Apr 50. Had a landing accident due to mechanical failure at McClellan AFB California 19 Jul 50, no fatalities—listed as assigned to 325th AB GP (HQ SQ) but IARC does not record this // 325th Fighter (All-Weather) WG (CNC) McChord AFB Washington 21 Jul 50 // Sacramento Air Materiel Area (AMC) McClellan AFB California 24 Jul 50 for depmnt // 375th TCWG (TAC) Greenville AFB South Carolina 5 Jan 51; depl to Brownwood Field Texas 6 Mar 52 // 64th TCWG (TAC) Donaldson AFB South Carolina 14 Jul 52 // Wfu to San Antonio Air Materiel Area (AMC) Kelly AFB Texas 26 Jun 53 and stored. Dropped from inventory 1 Jul 54 // Samuel C. Rudolph, Nathan Sidell, Charles J. Katz (Joint Venturers) Los Angeles California 10 Aug 55 reg: N7851B // Albert J. Leeward d/b/a Leeward Aeronautical Service Fort Wayne Indiana 17 Aug 55; ownership transferred to Leeward Aeronautical Sales Inc. Fort Wayne Indiana same day; cert of reg not issued until 2 May 57 by which time Leeward was relocated to Miami Florida // Aero Enterprises Inc. Dunlap Indiana 20 Feb 62 // Peter Bercut San Francisco California 14 Feb 62; subsequent history unk, might have been exported to Latin America. FAA lists as "destroyed-scrapped" 1972; reg canx 14 Sep 73. Final Disposition: Unknown (Presumed Scrapped).

10083 / 44-23039/CQ-039 / C-82A-25-FA

Avble: 30 Nov 46; Acc: 9 Dec 46; Del: 30 Dec 46 to USAAF // 316th TCG (TAC) Greenville Field South Carolina (detached) 7 Jan 47; assigned 37th TCSq; 316th to Greenville Field South Carolina 25 Aug 47. Landing accident at Marshall AFB Kansas 11 Oct 47, no fatalities and aircraft repaired. To 356th AF BAS (TAC) Marshall AFB Kansas 13 Oct 47; to 4136th AF BAS (AMC) Tinker AFB Oklahoma 16 Mar 48; 316th MSU GP (TAC) Greenville AFB South Carolina 1 Sep 48; 316th to Smyrna AFB Tennessee 4 Nov 49; multiple depls to 314th TCG (CNC) Smyrna AFB Tennessee starting 25 Nov 49; assigned 2601st Light Assault SQ; 316th depl to Guantanamo Bay Cuba 28 Feb 50; Smyrna

C-82A Packet s/n: 44-23039 (msn: 10083), registered as N5117B with L.B. Smith Aircraft Corp., was wrecked in Hurricane Cleo while parked at Miami International Airport, Florida, in 1964. The two vertical fins in the background belong to C-82A s/n: 44-23058 (msn: 10102) registered N2059A, also a write-off (Peter J. Marson Collection).

AFB renamed Sewart AFB 25 Mar 50; depl to 314th TCG (CNC) Laurinburg-Maxton Airport North Carolina 30 Apr 50 // 314th TCWG (CNC) Sewart AFB Tennessee 21 Jul 50 // 375th TCWG (TC) Greenville AFB South Carolina 8 Nov 50; to Warner-Robins Air Materiel Area (AMC) Robins AFB Georgia 9 Jul 51 for depmnt; depl to Grenier AFB New Hampshire 3 Jan 52; depl to Brownwood Field Texas 8 Mar 52 // 64th TCWG (TAC) Donaldson AFB South Carolina 14 Jul 52 // Wfu to San Antonio Air Materiel Area (AMC) Kelly AFB Texas 14 Jul 53 and stored. Dropped from inventory 1 Jul 54 // Bankers Life & Casualty Co. Chicago Illinois 7 Sep 55 reg: N5117B // L.B. Smith Aircraft Corp. Miami Florida 26 Mar 56. Destroyed by Hurricane Cleo while stored at Miami Intl. Airport Florida 27 Aug 64. Also destroyed were C-82s N2055A (10067) and N2059A (10102). Reg canx 18 Feb 71. Final Disposition: Accident.

10084 / 44-23040/CQ-040 / C-82A-25-FA

Avble: 4 Dec 46; Acc: 13 Dec 46; Del: 30 Dec 46 to USAAF // 316th TCG (TAC) Greenville Field South Carolina (detached) 7 Jan 47; assigned 37th TCSq; 316th to Greenville Field South Carolina 25 Aug 47; briefly to 316th MSU GP (TAC) Greenville AFB South Carolina 17 Nov 47; to Warner-Robins Air Materiel Area (AMC) Robins AFB Georgia 1 Apr 49; 316th to Smyrna AFB Tennessee 4 Nov 49; depl to Guantanamo Bay Cuba 28 Feb 50; Smyrna AFB renamed Sewart AFB 25 Mar 50; depl to 314th TCG (CNC) Laurinburg-Maxton Airport North Carolina 20 Apr 50 // 314th TCWG (CNC) Sewart AFB Tennessee 21 Jul 50; assigned 2601st Light Assault SQ // 375th TCWG (CNC) Greenville AFB South Carolina 1 Nov 50; assigned 56th TCSq; to 2270th AB SQ (CNC) New Castle Airport Delaware 7 Nov 50. Suffered a take-off accident at New Castle Airport Delaware 13 Nov 50, no fatalities and aircraft repaired. To 4652th AB SQ (CNC) New Castle Airport Delaware 1 Dec 50; to Middletown Air Materiel Area (AMC) Olmsted AFB Pennsylvania 8 Nov 51 for depmnt; depl to Brownwood Field Texas 8 Mar 52. Minor taxiing accident at Brownwood Field Texas 2 Apr 52. Parked at the time, it appears to have been hit by another taxiing aircraft, possibly C-82A s/n: 44-23025. Involved in an unidentified drop-accident over Brooks AFB Texas 12 Jun 52; damage, fatalities or injuries, if any, unk. To San Antonio Air Materiel Area (AMC) Kelly AFB Texas 12 Jun 52 // 64th TCWG (TAC) Donaldson AFB South Carolina 14 Jul 52; assigned 18th TCSq. Had a landing accident due to mechanical failure at Donaldson AFB South Carolina 1 Jul 53, no fatalities // Wfu to San Antonio Air Materiel Area (AMC) Kelly AF Texas 9 Sep 53 and stored. Dropped from inventory 1 Jul 54 // Samuel C. Rudolph, Nathan Sidell, Charles J. Katz (Joint Venturers) Los Angeles California 10 Aug 55 reg: N7849B // Albert J. Leeward d/b/a Leeward Aeronautical Service Fort Wayne Indiana 17 Aug 55; ownership transferred to Leeward Aeronautical Sales Inc. Fort Wayne Indiana same day; cert of reg not issued until 2 May 57 by which time Leeward was relocated to Miami Florida // Mosley & Freericks Fairbanks Alaska 10 Apr 59; aircraft weight and balance checked 11 Apr 59 by American Airmotive Corp. Miami Florida; engines, fluids, electrical, braking & hydraulic systems overhauled and control surfaces re-skinned 19 Apr 59 by Wien Alaska Airlines Fairbanks Alaska; repairs made 25 Apr 59 by Wien Alaska Airlines to lower right vertical fin; horizontal stabilizer damaged while aircraft being loaded, repairs made 30 Apr 59 by Wien Alaska Airlines // M&F Inc. Fairbanks Alaska 7 Sep 60 // Small Business Administration 27 Nov 67, repossessed aircraft from M&F Inc. on behalf of the First National Bank of Fairbanks Alaska // Robert G. Sholton Anchorage Alaska 30 Nov 67 // the Air

C-82A Packet N7849B (msn: 10084) of Northern Air Cargo Inc. in Alaska (Peter J. Marson Collection).

Museum Ontario California 1 Mar 71; derelict state and unflyable, aircraft not delivered and reg ntu; ownership returned to Robert Sholton in 1972. Last noted as being on a fire dump in Fairbanks Alaska from 1973 to 1979. Final Disposition: Scrapped.

10085 / 44-23041/CQ-041 / C-82A-25-FA

Avble: 9 Dec 46; Acc: 15 Dec 46; Del: 8 Jan 47 to USAAF // 62nd TCG (TAC) Bergstrom Field Texas 9 Jan 47; assigned 8th TCSq; depl to 316th TCG (TAC) Pope Field North Carolina 15 May 47. Landing accident at Hagerstown Airport Maryland 26 May 47, no fatalities and aircraft repaired. 62nd to McChord Field Washington 7 Aug 47; to Fairchild Aircraft (AMC) Maryland for mods 25 Aug 47; multiple assignments to 62nd MSU GP (TAC) McChord AFB Washington starting 10 Mar 48; depls to Pope AFB North Carolina 13 Apr 48 & Pasadena California 18 Aug 48 // 1st RES SQ (MATS) MacDill AFB Florida 28 Mar 50; cvtd to SC-82A; aircraft to Ramey AFB Puerto Rico 11 Sep 50; to San Antonio Air Materiel Area (AMC) Kelly AFB Texas 22 Sep 50; to Sacramento Air Materiel Area (AMC) McClellan AFB California 5 Oct 50; to Mobile Air Materiel Area (AMC) Brookley AFB, Alabama 20 Mar 51, 9 Feb 52 & 6 Jul 52 for depmnt // 28th RES SQ (MATS) Ramey AFB Puerto Rico 18 Jun 53 // Wfu to Ogden Air Materiel Area (AMC) Hill AFB Utah 22 Jun 53 and stored. Dropped from inventory 8 Jul 54 // Master Equipment Co. Cheyenne Wyoming 9 Aug 55 reg: N4828V. Cvtd to sprayer aircraft 26 Jun 56 equipped with four 675 U.S. gal tanks in the hold with wing-mounted spray booms // New Frontier Airlift Corp. Phoenix Arizona 16 Jun 61. Cvtd to Steward-Davis Skypallet by the removal of the fuselage decking and installation of a central internal hoist. Design work was begun in 1963 with a finished prototype ready by 1965. Photographic evidence shows a working conversion was completed, but there are no FAA files to show it actually flew or got beyond an experimental demonstrator. De-reg 10 Dec 70. Final Disposition: Scrapped.

10086 / 44-23042/CQ-042 / C-82A-25-FA

Avble: 9 Dec 46; Acc: 18 Dec 46; Del: 17 Jan 47 to USAAF // 316th TCG (TAC) Lawson Field Georgia (detached) 22 Jan 47; assigned 75th TCSq; 316th to Greenville Field South Carolina 20 Aug 47; multiple assignments to 316th MSU GP (TAC) Greenville AFB South Carolina starting 8 Jan 48. Crashed due to engine failure 10 miles S Greenville South Carolina 16 Dec 48. Pilot: Paul A. Tacsik and other crew killed. Assigned to reclamation 20 Dec 48. Dropped from inventory 25 Apr 49. Final Disposition: Accident.

10087 / 44-23043/CQ-043 / C-82A-25-FA

Avble: 11 Dec 46; Acc: 18 Dec 46; Del: 17 Jan 47 to USAAF // 316th TCG (TAC) Lawson Field Georgia (detached) 22 Jan 47; assigned 75th TCSq; to 319th AAF BAS (TAC) Lawson Field Georgia 20 Jul 47; 316th to Greenville Field South Carolina 25 Aug 47; to Middletown Air Materiel Area (AMC) Olmsted AFB Pennsylvania 4 Jun 49; 316th MSU GP (CNC) Greenville AFB South Carolina 30 Sep 49; 316th to Smyrna AFB Tennessee 4 Nov 49; depl to 314th TCG (CNC) Smyrna AFB Tennessee 25 Nov 49; assigned 2601st Light Assault SQ; to Warner-Robins Air Materiel Area (AMC) Robins AFB Georgia 49–50 for depmnt; 316th depl to Guantanamo Bay Cuba 28 Feb 50; Smyrna AFB renamed Sewart AFB 25 Mar 50; depl to 314th TCG (CNC) Laurinburg-Maxton Airport North Carolina 30 Apr 50 // 20th Fighter-Bomber WG (CNC) Shaw AFB South Carolina 14 Jul 50 // 375th TCWG (CNC) Greenville AFB South Carolina 7 Nov 50; to Warner-Robins Air Materiel Area (AMC) Robins AFB Georgia 30 Nov 51 for depmnt; depl to Brownwood Field Texas 11 Mar 52 // 64th TCWG (TAC) Donaldson AFB South Carolina 14 Jul 52; assigned 35th TCSq. Suffered a landing accident due to structural failure at High Point Airport North Carolina 1 Dec 52, no fatalities. To Warner-Robins Air Materiel Area (AMC) Robins AFB Georgia 24 Mar 53 for depmnt // Wfu to San Antonio Air Materiel Area (AMC) Kelly AFB Texas 14 Jul 53 and stored. Dropped from inventory 1 Jul 54 // Smock & Jenner Inc. Cincinnati Ohio 16 Aug 55 reg: N74043 // Ben Epstein, Trustee for Ben, Leonard and Stanley W. Epstein (Aeronautical Cargo Co.) Miami Beach Florida 29 Dec 55 // Henry A. Smith Richmond California 24 May 61 // New Frontier Airlift Corp. Berkeley California 1 May 63—purchased for Steward-Davis Jet-Packet program, but no buyers or conversion work carried out. One of eight C-82A derelicts for Fairchild-Hiller Corp. Maryland; reg: N6769A rsved 1967 but ntu. N74043 reg revoked 5 Feb 71. Final Disposition: Scrapped.

10088 / 44-23044/CQ-044 / C-82A-25-FA

Avble: 13 Dec 46; Acc: 19 Dec 46; Del: 17 Jan 47 to USAAF // 316th TCG (TAC) Lawson Field Georgia (detached) 22 Jan 47; assigned 75th TCSq. Suffered a taxiing accident at Keesler Field Mississippi 2 May 47. Pilot: Edwin T. McDonald, no fatalities // 3704th AAF BAS (TC) Keesler Field Mississippi 8 May 47 for repairs but later deemed as "damaged beyond repair." Airframe assigned to technical training duties 26 May 47 // 3380th Technical Training WG (TC) Keesler AFB Mississippi 28 Aug 48 for ground instructional duties. Assigned to reclamation and scrapped 21 Feb 49. Dropped from inventory 25 Apr 49. Final Disposition: Accident.

10089 / 44-23045/CQ-045 / C-82A-25-FA

Avble: 16 Dec 46; Acc: 20 Dec 46; Del: 17 Jan 47 to USAAF // 316th TCG (TAC) Lawson Field Georgia (detached) 22 Jan 47; assigned 75th TCSq; to 319th AAF BAS (TAC) Lawson Field Georgia 14 Oct 47; 316th to Greenville Field South Carolina 25 Aug 47; to Middletown Air Materiel Area (AMC) Olmsted AFB Pennsylvania 4 Jun 49; 316th MSU GP (CNC) Greenville AFB South Carolina 3 Oct 49; 316th to Smyrna AFB Tennessee 4 Nov 49; depl to 314th TCG (CNC) Smyrna AFB Tennessee 25 Nov 49; assigned 2601st Light Assault SQ; 316th depl to Guantanamo Bay Cuba 28 Feb 50; Smyrna AFB renamed Sewart AFB 25 Mar 50; depl to 314th TCG (CNC) Laurinburg-Maxton Airport North Carolina 20 Apr 50; to 1701st Air Transport WG (MATS) Great Falls AFB Montana 5 Nov 50 // 375th TCWG (TAC) Greenville AFB South Carolina 13 Mar 51; to Warner-Robins Air Materiel Area (AMC) Robins AFB Georgia 5 Jul 51 & 1 Sep 51 for depmnt; depl to Brownwood Field Texas 8 Mar 52 // 64th TCWG (TAC) Donaldson AFB South Carolina 14 Jul 52 // Wfu to San Antonio Air Materiel Area (AMC) Kelly AFB Texas 2 Jul 53 and stored. Dropped from inventory 1 Jul 54 // Bankers Life & Casualty Co. Chicago Illinois 7 Sep 55 reg: N5116B // Advance Co. Inc. Miami Florida 21 Oct 55 // Frank Ambrose Aviation Co. Inc. Miami Florida 9 Feb 60 // B.C. Swensen (Swensair Parts) Pensacola Florida 7 Nov 61; wfu Feb 62 // Steward-Davis Inc. Long Beach California 1962 as a derelict. There's a slim possibility N5116B was cut up by Steward-Davis for the 20th Century–Fox film *The Flight of the Phoenix* (1965), being used for interior filming at Fox Studios; however, this is merely a theory based on a series of deductions. The airframe might just as easily have been N7884C (10057/44-23013). Reg canx 25 Jan 71. Final Disposition: Scrapped.

10090 / 44-23046/CQ-046 / C-82A-25-FA

Avble: 18 Dec 46; Acc: 26 Dec 46; Del: 17 Jan 47 to USAAF // 319th AAF BAS (TAC) Lawson Field Georgia 21 Jan 47 // 316th TCG (TAC) Lawson Field Georgia (detached) 22 Jan 47; assigned 75th TCSq; to 313th AAF BAS (TAC) Greenville Field South Carolina 17 Feb 47; 316th to Greenville Field South Carolina 25 Aug 47; multiple assignments to 316th MSU GP (TAC) Greenville AFB South Carolina starting 22 Dec 47; to Middletown Air Materiel Area (AMC) Olmsted AFB Pennsylvania 9 Apr 49; 316th to Smyrna AFB Tennessee 4 Nov 49; depl to Guantanamo Bay Cuba 28 Feb 50; Smyrna AFB renamed Sewart AFB 25 Mar 50; depl to 314th TCG (CNC) Laurinburg-Maxton Airport North Carolina 20 Apr 50; multiple depls to 314th TCWG (CNC) Sewart AFB Tennessee starting 22 Jun 50 // 314th TCWG (CNC) Sewart AFB Tennessee 8 Nov 50 // 375th TCWG (TAC) Greenville AFB South Carolina 12 Dec 50; to 4418th Base Complement SQ (TAC) Greenville AFB South Carolina 12 Dec 50; to Warner-Robins Air Materiel Area (AMC) Robins AFB Georgia 18 Sep 51 for depmnt; depl to Grenier AFB New Hampshire 4 Dec 51; depl to Brownwood Field Texas 2 Apr 52 // 64th TCWG (TAC) Donaldson AFB South Carolina 14 Jul 52 // Aircraft Engineering & Maintenance Co. (AMC) Oakland California 21 Jul 53; modernized to Group A standard // 521st Air Defense GP (ADC) Sioux City MAP Iowa 19 Jan 54; to Oklahoma Air Materiel Area (AMC) Tinker AFB Oklahoma 20 Jan 54; to Ogden Air Materiel Area (AMC) Hill AFB Utah 2 Jul 54; to 3320th Technical Training WG (TC) Amarillo AFB Texas 21 Jul 54; to 4901st Support WG (ARD) Kirtland AFB New Mexico 1 Sep 54 // Wfu to 3040th Aircraft Storage SQ (AMC) Davis-Monthan

AFB Arizona 14 Mar 55 and stored. Dropped from inventory 1 Aug 55 // Samuel C. Rudolph Los Angeles California 9 Jan 56 reg: N6985C; cert of reg issued 1 Aug 57 // S. C. Rudolph Lumber Corp. Los Angeles California 30 Jun 58 // New Frontier Airlift Corp. Phoenix Arizona & Steward-Davis Inc. Gardena California 5 Feb 62. Cvtd to Steward-Davis Jet-Packet 3400 with J34-WE Jet-Pak; saw active freight service with Steward-Davis but FAA records show no lease work undertaken. Wfu late '60s and stored in open at Long Beach, California; reg revoked 1 Feb 71; moved to off-airport storage area and engines removed; scrapped by mid–1972. Final Disposition: Scrapped.

Top: C-82A N6985C (msn: 10090) prior to conversion to Jet-Packet standards at Long Beach in 1960 (Ed Coates Collection). *Bottom:* C-82A N6985C (msn: 10090) was a Jet-Packet 3400 and Steward-Davis lease aircraft with a sporty and colorful livery. It is seen here at Long Beach Airport, California, in 1970, with engines removed and sold off. Its days are now very numbered (Bruce Orriss).

10091 / 44-23047/CQ-047 / C-82A-25-FA

Avble: 19 Dec 46; Acc: 8 Jan 47; Del: 24 Jan 47 to USAAF // 316th TCG (TAC) Lawson Field Georgia (detached) 26 Jan 47; assigned 75th TCSq; to 319th AAF BAS (TAC) Lawson Field Georgia 20 Jul 47; 316th to Greenville Field South Carolina 25 Aug 47; multiple assignments to 316th MSU GP (TAC) Greenville AFB South Carolina starting 17 Nov 47; 316th to Smyrna AFB Tennessee 4 Nov 49; multiple depls to 314th TCG (CNC) Stewart AFB Tennessee starting 25 Nov 49; assigned 2601st Light Assault SQ; depl to Guantanamo Bay Cuba 28 Feb 50; Smyrna AFB renamed Sewart AFB 25 Mar 50; depl to 314th TCG (CNC) Laurinburg-Maxton Airport North Carolina 26 Apr 50 // 314th TCWG (TAC) Sewart AFB Tennessee 17 Feb 51 // 375th TCWG (TAC) Donaldson AFB South Carolina 21 Jul 51; assigned 55th TCSq; to Warner-Robins Air Materiel Area (AMC) Robins AFB Georgia 11 Aug 51 & 24 Oct 51 for depmnt; depl to Grenier AFB New Hampshire 3 Jan 52; depl to Brownwood Field Texas 4 Mar 52. Had a drop mishap (with C-82A s/n: 48–583) near Gatesville Texas 28 Mar 52, no fatalities // 55th Strategic Reconn WG (SAC) Ramey AFB Puerto Rico 1 Jul 52; to Forbes AFB Kansas 3 May 53 // Wfu to Ogden Air Materiel Area (AMC) Hill AFB Utah 28 May 53 and stored. Dropped from inventory 8 Jul 54 // L.B. Smith Aircraft Corp. Miami Florida 19 Sep 55 reg: N2057A // Harry R. Playford (Madden & Playford Aircraft Inc.) St. Petersburg Florida 21 Sep 55; ferried from Ogden, Utah, with reg: N6238C but later canx in favor of N2057A; one of five C-82As based at Pinellas Airport, Florida // International Aviation Investment Corp. Panama 1957 for resale into Latin America; N2057A reg canx 5 Nov 57 // Lloyd Aereo de Colombiano S.A. (LAC) Bogota Colombia 25 Apr 1959 reg: HK-918. W/o in accident prior to 1964, cause and fatalities unk, nfd. HK-918 reg canx 18 Jun 69. Final Disposition: Accident.

10092 / 44-23048/CQ-048 / C-82A-25-FA

Avble: 26 Dec 46; Acc: 8 Jan 47; Del: 17 Jan 47 to USAAF // 319th AAF BAS (TAC) Lawson Field Georgia 21 Jan 47 // 316th TCG (TAC) Lawson Field Georgia (detached) 22 Jan 47; assigned 75th TCSq; to 313th AAF BAS (TAC) Greenville Field South Carolina 31 Jul 47; multiple assignments to 316th MSU GP (TAC) Greenville AFB South Carolina starting 18 Aug 47; 316th to Greenville Field South Carolina 25 Aug 47; to Warner-Robins Air Materiel Area (AMC) Robins AFB Georgia 14 Mar 49 for depmnt; 316th to Smyrna AFB Tennessee 4 Nov 49; multiple depls to 314th TCG (CNC) Smyrna AFB Tennessee starting 25 Nov 49; assigned 2601st Light Assault SQ; to 314th MSU GP (CNC) Smyrna AFB Tennessee 26 Jan 50; depl to Guantanamo Bay Cuba 28 Feb 50; Smyrna AFB renamed Sewart AFB 25 Mar 50; depl to 314th TCG (CNC) Laurinburg-Maxton Airport North Carolina 24 Apr 50 // 375th TCWG (CNC) Greenville AFB South Carolina 10 Mar 51; to Warner-Robins Air Materiel Area (AMC) Robins AFB Georgia 15 Sep 51 for depmnt; depl to Brownwood Field Texas 8 Mar 52 // 64th TCWG (TAC) Donaldson AFB South Carolina 14 Jul 52; to Middletown Air Materiel Area (AMC) Olmsted AFB Pennsylvania 28 Apr 53 for depmnt // Wfu to San Antonio Air Materiel Area (AMC) Kelly AFB Texas 26 Jun 53 and stored. Dropped from inventory 1 Jul 54 // Bankers Life & Casualty Co. Chicago Illinois 7 Sep 55 reg: N5115B // L.B. Smith Aircraft Corp. Miami Florida 16 Nov 55 // Transportes Aereos Mexicanos S.A. (TAMSA) Merida Mexico 16 Nov 55 reg: XA-LIY; departed U.S. 26 Nov 55; U.S. reg canx 24 Feb 56 // Compania Mexicana de Aviacion

S.A. Mexico City Mexico, 1960; subsequent history unk. Final Disposition: Unknown (Presumed Scrapped).

C-82A XA-LIY (msn: 10092) of Transportes Aereos Mexicanos S.A. (TAMSA) in Mexico (José Villela G.).

10093 / 44-23049/CQ-049 / C-82A-30-FA

Avble: 30 Dec 46; Acc: 3 Feb 47; Del: 11 Feb 47 to USAAF // 319th AAF BAS (TAC) Lawson Field Georgia 11 Feb 47 // 316th TCG (TAC) Lawson Field Georgia (detached) 13 Feb 47; assigned 75th TCSq. Had a landing accident at Dekker Aux Strip Alabama 3 May 47, no fatalities and aircraft repaired. 316th to Greenville Field South Carolina 25 Aug 47; to 319th AF BAS (TAC) Lawson Field Georgia 6 Oct 47; 316th MSU GP (TAC) Greenville AFB South Carolina 29 Jul 48; 316th to Smyrna AFB Tennessee 4 Nov 49; multiple depls to 314th TCG (CNC) Smyrna AFB Tennessee starting 25 Nov 49; assigned

C-82A XA-LIW (msn: 10093) of Transportes Aereos Mexicanos S.A. (TAMSA) in Mexico (José Villela G.).

2601st Light Assault SQ; depl to Guantanamo Bay Cuba 28 Feb 50; Smyrna AFB renamed Sewart AFB 25 Mar 50; depl to 314th TCG (CNC) Laurinburg-Maxton Airport North Carolina 21 Apr 50 // 375th TCWG (CNC) Greenville AFB South Carolina 31 Oct 50; assigned 55th TCSq; to 4418th Base Complement SQ (CNC) Greenville AFB South Carolina 8 Nov 50. Made a forced landing due to an onboard fire at Donaldson AFB South Carolina 11 Sep 51, no fatalities and aircraft repaired // 64th TCWG (TAC) Donaldson AFB South Carolina 14 Jul 52 // Wfu to San Antonio Air Materiel Area (AMC) Kelly AFB Texas 7 Jul 53 and stored. Dropped from inventory 1 Jul 54 // Bankers Life & Casualty Co. Chicago Illinois 7 Sep 55 reg: N5114B // L.B. Smith Aircraft Corp. Miami Florida 16 Nov 55 // Transportes Aereos Mexicanos S.A. (TAMSA) Merida Mexico 16 Nov 55 reg: XA-LIW; departed U.S. 9 Dec 55; U.S. reg canx 23 Feb 56. Crashed soon after take-off 30 Oct 57 near Campeche Mexico, three crew killed. Final Disposition: Accident.

10094 / 44-23050/CQ-050 / C-82A-30-FA

Avble: 3 Jan 47; Acc: 16 Jan 47; Del: 28 Jan 47 to USAAF // 316th TCG (TAC) Lawson Field Georgia (detached) 29 Jan 47, assigned 75th TCSq; to Greenville Field South Carolina 20 Jul 47; 316th MSU GP (TAC) Greenville AFB South Carolina 25 Mar 48; depl to Elmendorf AFB Alaska 2 Jul 48, assigned 37th TCSq; 316th to Smyrna AFB Tennessee 4 Nov 49. Provided with USAF crew to Lippert Pictures for film production of *Operation Haylift* (1950) shot in Ely, Nevada. Depl to Guantanamo Bay Cuba 7 Mar 50; Smyrna renamed Sewart AFB 25 Mar 1950; depl to 314th TCG (CNC) Laurinburg-Maxton Airport North Carolina 20 Apr 50; to Warner-Robins Air Materiel Area (AMC) Robins AFB Georgia 2 May 50 for depmnt // 314th TCWG (CNC) Sewart AFB Tennessee 21 Jul 50 // 375th TCWG (TAC) Greenville AFB South Carolina 22 Dec 50, assigned 56th TCSq; to 4418th Base Complement SQ (TAC) Greenville AFB South Carolina 27 Dec 50; to 3800th Air University WG (AU) Maxwell AFB Alabama 17 Mar 51 for tranmnt. Minor landing accident at Donaldson AFB South Carolina 18 Oct 51, no fatalities. To Warner-Robins Air Materiel Area (AMC) Robins AFB Georgia 3 Jan 52 for depmnt; depl to Brownwood Field Texas 6 Apr 52 // 64th TCWG (TAC) Donaldson AFB South Carolina 14 Jul 52 // Wfu to San Antonio Air Materiel Area (AMC) Kelly AFB Texas 2 Jul 53 and stored. Dropped from inventory 1 Jul 54 // Bankers Life & Casualty Co. Chicago Illinois 7 Sep 55 reg: N5113B // Advance Co. Inc. Miami Florida 21 Oct 55 // Thuel V. Schuhart Miami Florida 29 Jan 58 // Air Cargo Equipment Inc. Miami Florida 20 Mar 58 // Compania Maderera S.A. Tegucigalpa Honduras 24 Jun 58 reg: XH-143-P; U.S. reg canx 21 Apr 58 // Transportes Aereos Guatemalecos (TAG) Guatemala 8 Oct 58 reg: TG-DAC-79; Honduran reg canx 15 Dec 58 // Luis Marcutia de Leon Guatemala 25 Nov 58 // Feliamas Robert Press 12 May 59. Named *Corronga* at some point with an attractive female motif on the nose. Noted late 1960s stored at Miami Intl. Airport Florida in a derelict condition. Final Disposition: Scrapped.

10095 / 44-23051/CQ-051 / C-82A-30-FA

Avble: 8 Jan 47; Acc: 22 Jan 47; Del: 3 Feb 47 to USAAF // 316th TCG (TAC) Lawson Field Georgia (detached) 3 Feb 47; assigned 75th TCSq; 316th to Greenville Field South Carolina 25 Aug 47; 316th MSU GP (TAC) Greenville AFB South Carolina 19 May 48; to 3203rd MSU GP (APG) Eglin AFB Florida 19 Jul 49; to Warner-Robins Air Materiel Area

(AMC) Robins AFB Georgia 23 Aug 49 for depmnt; 316th to Smyrna AFB Tennessee 4 Nov 49; multiple depls to 314th MSU GP & 314th TCG (CNC) Smyrna AFB Tennessee starting 25 Nov 49; depl to Guantanamo Bay Cuba 28 Feb 50; Smyrna AFB renamed Sewart AFB 25 Mar 50; depl to 314th TCG (CNC) Laurinburg-Maxton Airport North Carolina 24 Apr 50 // 314th TCWG (CNC) Sewart AFB Tennessee 26 Sep 50; to Mobile Air Materiel Area (AMC) Brookley AFB, Alabama 2 Oct 50 & 21 Mar 51 for depmnt // 375th TCWG (TAC) Greenville AFB South Carolina 29 Dec 51; to Warner-Robins Air Materiel Area (AMC) Robins AFB Georgia 4 Jan 52 for depmnt; depl to Brownwood Field Texas 25 Mar 52 // 64th TCWG (TAC) Donaldson AFB South Carolina 14 Jul 52 // Wfu to San Antonio Air Materiel Area (AMC) Kelly AFB Texas 5 Aug 53 and stored. Dropped from inventory 1 Jul 54 // Bankers Life & Casualty Co. Chicago Illinois 7 Sep 55 reg: N5112B // L.B. Smith Aircraft Corp. Miami Florida 16 Nov 55 // Transportes Aereos Mexicanos S.A. (TAMSA) Merida Mexico 16 Nov 55 reg: XA-LIZ; departed U.S. 17 Jan 1956; U.S. reg canx 23 Feb 56 // Compania Mexicana de Aviacion S.A. Mexico City Mexico, 1960; subsequent history unk. Final Disposition: Unknown (Presumed Scrapped).

C-82A XA-LIZ (msn: 10095) of Transportes Aereos Mexicanos S.A. (TAMSA) in Mexico (José Villela G.).

10096 / 44-23052/CQ-052 / C-82A-30-FA

Avble: 13 Jan 47; Acc: 24 Jan 47; Del: 17 Mar 47 to USAAF // 316th TCG (TAC) Lawson Field Georgia (detached) 17 Mar 47; assigned 75th TCSq; 316th to Greenville Field South Carolina 25 Aug 47; 316th MSU GP (TAC) Greenville AFB South Carolina 3 Aug 48; 316th to Smyrna AFB Tennessee 4 Nov 49; multiple depls to 314th TCG (CNC) Smyrna AFB Tennessee starting 25 Nov 49; assigned 2601st Light Assault SQ; depl to Guantanamo Bay Cuba 28 Feb 50; Smyrna AFB renamed Sewart AFB 25 Mar 50; depl to 314th TCG (CNC) Laurinburg-Maxton Airport North Carolina 26 Apr 50 // 314th TCG (CNC) Sewart AFB Tennessee 8 Nov 50 // 375th TCWG (CNC) Greenville AFB South Carolina 28 Dec 50; to 4418th Base Complement SQ (CNC) Greenville AFB South Carolina 28 Dec 50; to San Antonio Air Materiel Area (AMC) Kelly AFB Texas 5 Feb 51; to 91st AB GP (SAC) Barksdale AFB Louisiana 6 Jun 51; to Warner-Robins Air Materiel Area (AMC) Robins AFB Georgia 12 Oct 51 for depmnt; depl to Brownwood Field Texas 10 Mar 52 // 64th TCWG (TAC) Donaldson AFB South Carolina 14 Jul 52 // Wfu to San Antonio Air

Materiel Area (AMC) Kelly AFB Texas 7 Jul 53 and stored. Dropped from inventory 1 Jul 54 // Smock & Jenner Inc. Cincinnati Ohio 16 Aug 55 reg: N74048 // Ben Epstein, Trustee for Ben, Leonard and Stanley W. Epstein (Aeronautical Cargo Co.) Miami Beach Florida 29 Dec 55 // Airnews Inc. San Antonio Texas 1 Mar 60 // New Frontier Airlift Corp. Phoenix Arizona 24 Apr 61—purchased for Steward-Davis Jet-Packet program, but no buyers or conversion work carried out. N74048 reg revoked 18 Jan 71. Final Disposition: Scrapped.

10097 / 44-23053/CQ-053 / C-82A-30-FA

Avble: 16 Jan 47; Acc: 30 Jan 47; Del: 11 Feb 47 to USAAF // 316th TCG (TAC) Lawson Field Georgia (detached) 12 Feb 47; assigned 75th TCSq; 316th to Greenville Field South Carolina 25 Aug 47; to 316th MSU GP (TAC) Greenville AFB South Carolina 23 Apr 48 & 7 Oct 49; to Middletown Air Materiel Area (AMC) Olmsted AFB Pennsylvania 4 Jun 49; 316th to Smyrna AFB Tennessee 4 Nov 49; multiple depls to 314th TCG (CNC) Smyrna AFB Tennessee starting 25 Nov 49; assigned 2601st Light Assault SQ; depl to Guantanamo Bay Cuba 28 Feb 50; Smyrna AFB renamed Sewart AFB 25 Mar 50; depl to 314th TCG (CNC) Laurinburg-Maxton Airport North Carolina 20 Apr 50; to 4408th AB SQ (CNC) Lawson AFB Georgia 2 Sep 50 // 375th TCWG (TAC) Greenville AFB South Carolina 10 Mar 51; to Warner-Robins Air Materiel Area (AMC) Robins AFB Georgia 28 Sep 51 for depmnt; depl to Grenier AFB New Hampshire 3 Jan 52; depl to Brownwood Field Texas 13 Mar 52 // 64th TCWG (TAC) Donaldson AFB South Carolina 14 Jul 52 // Wfu to San Antonio Air Materiel Area (AMC) Kelly AFB Texas 14 Jul 53 and stored. Dropped from inventory 1 Jul 54 // Bankers Life & Casualty Co. Chicago Illinois 7 Sep 55 reg: N5111B. Subsequent history unk; might have been exported. De-reg 14 Jul 70. Final Disposition: Unknown (Presumed Scrapped).

10098 / 44-23054/CQ-054 / C-82A-30-FA

Avble: 21 Jan 47; Acc: 7 Feb 47; Del: 17 Feb 47 to USAAF // 316th TCG (TAC) Lawson Field Georgia (detached) 17 Feb 47; assigned 75th TCSq; to 319th AAF BAS (TAC) Lawson Field Georgia 20 Jul 47 & 30 Sep 47; 316th to Greenville Field South Carolina 25 Aug 47; multiple assignments to 316th MSU GP (TAC) Greenville AFB South Carolina starting 16 Jan 48; to Middletown Air Materiel Area (AMC) Olmsted AFB Pennsylvania 6 Apr 49; 316th to Smyrna AFB Tennessee 4 Nov 49; multiple depls to 314th TCG (CNC) Smyrna AFB Tennessee starting 25 Nov 49; assigned 2601st Light Assault SQ; depl to Guantanamo Bay Cuba 28 Feb 50; Smyrna AFB renamed Sewart AFB 25 Mar 50; depl to 314th TCG (CNC) Laurinburg-Maxton Airport North Carolina 24 Apr 50 // 375th TCWG (TAC) Greenville AFB South Carolina 10 Mar 51; to Warner-Robins Air Materiel Area (AMC) Robins AFB Georgia 6 Jul 51 & 14 Nov 51 for depmnt; depl to Grenier AFB New Hampshire 6 Jan 52; depl to Brownwood Field Texas 11 Mar 52 // 64th TCWG (TAC) Donaldson AFB South Carolina 14 Jul 52; assigned 17th TCSq. Minor taxiing accident at Miami Intl. Airport Florida 2 Aug 52, no fatalities. Depl to 435th TCWG (TAC) Miami Intl. Airport Florida 4 Aug 52 // Wfu to San Antonio Air Materiel Area (AMC) Kelly AFB Texas 7 Jul 53 and stored. Dropped from inventory 1 Jul 54 // Samuel C. Rudolph, Nathan Sidell, Charles J. Katz (Joint Venturers) Los Angeles California 10 Aug 55 reg: N7850B // Albert J. Leeward d/b/a Leeward Aeronautical Service Fort Wayne Indiana 17 Aug 55; ownership transferred to Leeward Aeronautical Sales Inc. Fort Wayne Indiana same day; cert of reg not issued until 2 May 57 by which time Leeward was relocated to Miami Florida // Aero Enterprises Inc. Dunlap Indiana 20 Feb 62 // Peter Bercut San Francisco California 14 Feb 62; subsequent history unk. Photographed at Sebring, Florida, in late 1969 appearing extremely derelict as though it had been damaged in a tropical storm. It was covered in mud and debris, and the fabric control surfaces were punctured. Also parked nearby was s/n: 44-23018 (N6246C), both aircraft were still in their USAF liveries with no visible civil markings applied. Reg revoked 1971. Final Disposition: Unknown (Presumed Scrapped).

10099 / 44-23055/CQ-055 / C-82A-30-FA

Avble: 24 Jan 47; Acc: 31 Jan 47; Del: 24 Feb 47 to USAAF. Used as a test aircraft 1950-1953 // 316th TCG (TAC) Lawson Field Georgia (detached) 24 Feb 47; assigned 75th & 37th TCSq; depls to 313th AAF BAS (TAC) Greenville Field South Carolina 16 Mar 47 & 5 May 47; 316th to Greenville Field South Carolina 25 Aug 47; deployment to 47th MSU GP (TAC) Biggs Field Texas 15 Sep 47; multiple assignments to 316th MSU GP (TAC) Greenville AFB South Carolina starting 7 Jan 48. Landing accident at Greenville AFB South Carolina 14 Jan 48, no fatalities. To 4117th AF BAS (AMC) Robins AFB Georgia 7 Apr 48 for depmnt; depl to 37th TCSq (316th) Elmendorf AFB Alaska 2 Jul 48; 316th to Smyrna AFB Tennessee 4 Nov 49; Smyrna AFB renamed Sewart AFB 25 Mar 50; depl to 314th TCG (CNC) Laurinburg-Maxton Airport North Carolina 21 Apr 50 // Fairchild Aircraft Maryland (AMC) for mods 19 Jun 50 // 3203rd MSU GP & 3200th Proof Test GP (APG) Eglin AFB Florida 17 Aug 50 for test duties // Multiple assignments to Warner-Robins Air Materiel Area (AMC) Robins AFB Georgia & San Antonio Air Materiel Area (AMC) Kelly AFB Texas starting 17 Jan 51 for ongoing projects. Had a taxiing accident due to mechanical failure at Kelly AFB Texas 17 Apr 51, no fatalities // Rotational assignments to Boeing Airplane Co. (Wichita) Kansas (AMC) starting 28 May 52 for flying proficiency duties & Oklahoma Air Materiel Area (AMC) Tinker AFB Oklahoma starting 24 Jun 52 for depmnt. Modernized to Group A standard during this period. Had a ground collision at Tinker AFB Oklahoma 16 Feb 53, no fatalities // Wfu to Ogden Air Materiel Area (AMC) Hill AFB Utah 29 Dec 53 and stored. Dropped from inventory 8 Jul 54 // L.B. Smith Aircraft Corp. Miami Florida 19 Sep 55 reg: N2058A // Harry R. Playford (Madden & Playford Aircraft Inc.) St. Petersburg Florida 21 Sep 55; ferried from Ogden, Utah with reg: N6239C but later canx in favor of N2058A; one of five C-82s based at Pinellas Airport, Florida; cert of reg issued 12 Mar 56 // Rodest and Company New York N.Y. 17 Apr 56; aircraft furnished for export by Aero Supply Associates Inc. Miami Florida // Capt. Gustavo Torres Bogota Colombia 3 May 56 reg: HK-930. N2058A reg canx 20 Jun 56. Crashed 17 Jun 58 Paramo de Tarma Venezuela, cause and fatalities unk, nfd. Final Disposition: Accident.

10100 / 44-23056/CQ-056 / C-82A-30-FA

Avble: 31 Jan 47; Acc: 3 Feb 47; Del: 12 Mar 47 to USAAF // Retained at Fairchild Aircraft Maryland (AMC) 13 Mar 47; to Middletown Air Materiel Area (AMC) Olmsted Field Pennsylvania 31 Mar 47 // 4000th AAF BAS (AMC) Patterson Field Ohio 2 Jul 47 // To National Advisory Committee for Aeronautics (NACA) (under AMC) NAS Moffett

Field California 31 Aug 47 for research, development and flight-testing. Permanently to NACA 11 Apr 50. Dropped from inventory 13 Apr 50. Assigned NACA fleet no. 107. Served in flight-test, utility and specialized cargo roles based out of the Ames Research Center at NAS Moffett Field. NACA renamed National Aeronautics & Space Administration (NASA) 29 Jul 58; NASA logos carried on aircraft. Wfu to 2704th Aircraft Storage & Disposition GP (AMC) Davis-Monthan AFB Arizona 7 Feb 61. Earmarked for U.S. Navy then USAF Museum Jun 61 but ntu. Noted at Davis-Monthan Jun 63. Final Disposition: Scrapped.

NASA No.107 is C-82A s/n: 44-23056 (msn: 10100). Note the faded "United States National Advisory Committee for Aeronautics" on the boom from its pre–NASA days (Milo Peltzer Collection).

10101 / 44-23057/CQ-057 / C-82A-30-FA

Avble: 5 Feb 47; Acc: 27 Feb 47; Del: 23 May 47 to USAAF // 62nd TCG (TAC) Bergstrom Field Texas 27 May 47; assigned 8th TCSq; 62nd to McChord Field Washington 7 Aug 47; to Fairchild Aircraft Maryland (AMC) for mods 25 Aug 47; depl to Pope AFB North Carolina 13 Apr 48; multiple assignments to 62nd MSU GP (TAC) McChord AFB Washington starting 28 Aug 48; depl to Elmendorf AFB Alaska 3 Mar 49 // 6th RES SQ (MATS) Westover AFB Massachusetts 13 Mar 50; cvtd to SC-82A; depl to Goose Bay AB Labrador Canada 29 Mar 50; to San Antonio Air Materiel Area (AMC) Kelly AFB Texas 15 May 50; depl to Ernest Harmon AFB Newfoundland Canada 18 Apr 51 // 4th RES SQ (MATS) McChord AFB Washington 1 Dec 51; assigned Flight "C." Had a mid-air collision 3 miles NE Rocky Bar Idaho 18 Jan 52, no fatalities and aircraft landed safely. To 1300th AB WG (MATS) Mt Home AFB Idaho 18 Jan 52 // 43rd RES SQ (MATS) McChord AFB Washington 4 Nov 52 // Aircraft Engineering & Maintenance Co. (AMC) Oakland California 26 Jun 53 on bailment; cvtd back to C-82A standard and modernized to Group A standard // 3rd Air Materiel (Overseas) SQ (MATS) Tinker AFB Oklahoma 1 Dec 53; to San Bernardino Aircraft Repair Depot (AMC) Norton AFB California 5 Jan 54 for depmnt // 568th Air Defense GP (ADC) McGuire AFB New Jersey 17 May 54 // 2nd Fighter-

Interceptor SQ (ADC) McGuire AFB New Jersey 17 May 54 // 519th Air Defense GP (ADC) Suffolk AFB Virginia 11 Jun 54 // 521st Air Defense GP (CAD) Sioux City MAP Iowa 3 Sep 54; to Oklahoma Air Materiel Area (AMC) Tinker AFB Oklahoma 8 Nov 54 // Wfu to 3040th Aircraft Storage SQ (AMC) Davis-Monthan AFB Arizona 7 Mar 55 and stored. Dropped from inventory 1 Aug 55. No records exist of any civil service, presumed scrapped by the USAF. Final Disposition: Scrapped.

10102 / 44-23058/CQ-058 / C-82A-30-FA

Avble: 7 Feb 47; Acc: 24 Feb 47; Del: 23 May 47 to USAAF // 62nd TCG (TAC) Bergstrom Field Texas 27 May 47; 62nd to McChord Field Washington 7 Aug 47; to Fairchild Aircraft Maryland (AMC) for mods 21 Aug 47; depl to Pope AFB North Carolina 13 Apr 48; multiple assignments to 62nd MSU GP (TAC) McChord AFB Washington starting 28 Aug 48; depl to Elmendorf AFB Alaska 8 Mar 49. Had a structural failure at McChord AFB Washington 29 Apr 50, no fatalities. To 325th Fighter (All-Weather) WG (CNC) McChord AFB Washington 5 May 50 // 1st RES SQ (MATS) MacDill AFB Florida 17 May 50; cvtd to SC-82A; to Albrook AFB Panama Canal Zone 29 Aug 50; to San Antonio Air Materiel Area (AMC) Kelly AFB Texas 11 Sep 50 // 27th RES SQ (MATS) Albrook AFB Panama Canal Zone 4 Nov 52 // Wfu to Ogden Air Materiel Area (AMC) Hill AFB Utah 28 Jun 53 and stored. Dropped from inventory 8 Jul 54 // L.B. Smith Aircraft Corp. Miami Florida 19 Sep 55 reg: N2059A. Destroyed by Hurricane Cleo while stored at Miami Intl. Airport Florida 27 Aug 64. Also destroyed were C-82s N2055A (10067) and N5117B (10083). Reg canx 5 Feb 71. Final Disposition: Accident.

10103 / 45-57733/CQ-733 / C-82A-30-FA

Avble: 12 Feb 47; Acc: 27 Feb 47; Del: 23 May 47 to USAAF // 62nd TCG (TAC) Bergstrom Field Texas 27 May 47; assigned 8th TCSq; 62nd to McChord Field Washington 7 Aug 47; to Fairchild Aircraft Maryland (AMC) for mods 25 Aug 47; depl to Pope AFB North Carolina 13 Apr 48; multiple assignments to 62nd MSU GP (TAC) McChord AFB Washington starting 3 Sep 48; depl to Elmendorf AFB Alaska 3 Mar 49; assigned 7th TCSq // 5th RES SQ (MATS) Biggs AFB Texas 10 Mar 50; cvtd to SC-82A; to 5th at Ellington AFB Texas 19 Jul 50; to Sacramento Air Materiel Area (AMC) McClellan AFB California 9 Sep 50; to 415th Technical Training WG (TC) Lowry AFB Colorado 19 Oct 51; to 3605th Navigator Training WG (TC) Ellington AFB Texas 7 Mar 52; to 3605th Observer Training WG (TC) Ellington AFB Texas 2 Jul 52 // San Antonio Air Materiel Area (AMC) Kelly AFB Texas 11 Oct 52 for depmnt // 47th RES SQ (MATS) Ellington AFB Texas 27 Feb 53 // Wfu to Ogden Air Materiel Area (AMC) Hill AFB Utah 25 Jun 53 and stored. Dropped from inventory 8 Jul 54 // Ben W. Widtfeldt & Harry S. McCandless Council Bluffs Iowa 23 Aug 55 reg: N4834V // M&W Aircraft Leasing Council Bluffs Iowa 7 Sep 55. Lease to SkySpray Inc. as an aerial sprayer. Supposed lease to Switzerland reg: HB-AAC but ntu // Ben W. Widtfeldt Phoenix Arizona 25 Mar 59 // George B. Alder Chattanooga Tennessee 11 Jun 59. Operated by Alder in Honduras from 1960 reg: XH-163; Feb 61 re-reg: HR-163 then HR-163P. Lease to Servicio Aereos de Honduras S.A. (SAHSA) Tegucigalpa Honduras 1962 re-reg: HR-SAM, 1963 back to N4834V. Ditched in the ocean off the coast of Lermer, Campeche, Mexico 29 Jul 65 due to fuel exhaustion when bad weather closed the destination airport and surrounding alternate airports. Pilot: Wendell

Levister, copilot Caesar Ortega, and one other crew member uninjured but aircraft w/o. In 2009, Capt Levister himself provided the author with the following intriguing story of N4834V's final flight:

> On a flight from New Orleans we had a cargo consisting of two 450 hp aircraft engines, a few hundred gallons of dope and thinner. Altogether, the cargo weighed approximately 13,000 lb. The aircraft had four wing fuel tanks with a total capacity of 2,100 gallons, which at a fuel burn of approximately 200 gallons per hour would provide for approximately ten hours of flight time, and which added another 13,650 lb to the total aircraft takeoff weight of 55,000 lb. I took off from Lake Front Airport and headed for Guatemala. Crossing the Gulf of Mexico at 10,000 feet and about 3.3 hours into the flight, we passed Merida, Mexico, where I turned southwest to take course for Guatemala City, where we were to deliver some of the cargo, the rest of which would be off-loaded at Tegucigalpa on a following flight. We flew inland towards Guatemala, the weather grew worse, forcing me to cancel my instrument flight plan by radio, and to begin descending to stay visual beneath the building clouds and adverse weather. Approximately 2.3 hours later, at about 7,000 feet, we arrived at the valley where Guatemala City is situated, which was completely closed in by clouds. The valley is surrounded by mountains ranging from 5,000 to 9,000 feet, all of which were topped by clouds, and I was not about to attempt to try and penetrate those clouds on a descent into the valley for an instrument approach to the airport, besides, I had already cancelled my instrument flight plan. Consequently, by radio to the Aurora Airport tower control, I declared an emergency and informed them that I was aborting my original flight plan to land there, and would instead fly to my alternate destination, which was Belize. Taking course for Belize, all the way back across the Yucatan Peninsula (Mexico) and part of Guatemala, southward toward Belize, we were dodging thunderheads as night fell. After two hours wandering around dangerous thunderheads but still flying in the general direction towards Belize, through broken clouds we saw off in the distance, the lights of a fairly large city, which because of the general direction, and the length of time that we had been flying since taking course for Belize, I calculated it to be on the Caribbean coast. Because of the extended time that we had been flying, the fuel situation was becoming critical. Each fuel tank has a red light on the instrument panel that would light up when there was only five minutes of fuel remaining in the particular tank. Of the four tanks, I had three red lights lit up, with the left outboard tank still not lit up. I then switched the fuel valves to feed both engines from that left outboard tank. In order to conserve fuel, I had reduced the power on both of those 2,100 hp Pratt & Whitney engines and at the leanest mixture setting for a slow descent, while we searched for the water. At approximately 5,000 feet, the red light for the left outboard tank lit up, and because both engines had been feeding from that tank, it went dry before the five minute period, and both engines quit. When those rumbling engines died, the silence was shocking! I yelled at my co-pilot to light up the instrument panel, as I worked to get both engines running again. Suddenly both engines restarted with a low rumble, and I immediately added power to slow the aircraft's descent. Now that both engines were running from tanks that were both displaying red lights, it meant that we had but a very short time before we would lose both again. It was then that I decided that it would not be possible to reach that city and circle until we found the airport, and I informed the crew that we were going to ditch and to make ready. The extra crew member who was hitching a ride with us panicked, put on a parachute and went down the ladder to the cargo compartment, where he tried to open the main entrance door to jump out. Fortunately for him, the door which was located just in front of the left engine would not open, as it opened out and the slipstream was too strong. He climbed back up to the flight deck, and standing behind my seat still in a panic, was begging me to open one of the doors so that he could jump. I was so completely absorbed in keeping the aircraft flying until I could put it safely in the water, where ever it was, I swung my elbow back at him to get him from behind me and almost knocked him back down the ladder. He went back down the ladder and went to the rear of the cargo compartment and tried to open one of the paratainer doors. Now knowing that I was going to ditch my aircraft, I wanted to be over solid water when I put it in, and not over a rocky coast line. So I turned the aircraft to the left to put that city off of my right wing tip, which I calculated would take us further out over the ocean, and continued descending. The extra flight crewmember, now very alarmed, climbed back to the flight-deck, and I ordered him to take off the parachute and take the flight engineer's seat. At that moment, the left engine died of fuel starvation, and I further

reduced the power on the right engine to reduce the yaw and drag effect of the windmilling left propeller. With that, I was committed and had to put the aircraft in the water before I lost the still running right engine. At approximately 500 feet I ordered the co-pilot to turn on the landing lights again, which still blinded me but I had to keep them on to be able to finally see the water and put the aircraft in a nose up attitude just before impact. I instructed my crew, that when I yelled "NOW," they were to jettison their hatch and prepare to debark once the aircraft stopped moving. At just a few feet above the water, I finally saw it, yelled "NOW" at the crew, jettisoned my hatch, pulled back the throttle of the still running right engine, and back on the yoke, raising the nose of the aircraft about 25 degrees, touching down on the tail-booms first. The aircraft went in clean and smoothly, no landing gear or flaps deployed. It felt just like a landing on a runway, with very heavy braking, which was the effect of the aircraft rapidly slowing down as it settled into the water. We were safely in the water with no injury to anyone. My faithful co-pilot, who had worked so great with me all through the emergency, froze, gripping the arms of his seat and failed to jettison his hatch. We were standing on the wing, which was just barely above the water, and preparing to inflate the life raft, when we thought that the aircraft was floating. However, we later found out that it was sitting on the sea-bottom, as we were in nine feet of water at low tide. We looked toward the shoreline and saw the lights of a small town, which turned out to be the coastal town of Lerma, Mexico. We heard people yelling at us, and I yelled back in Spanish "Auxilio!" which means "Help!" They called back "Ya viene!" meaning "we're coming!" We were later told that they heard our engine as it quit on impact, saw the landing lights and heard the impact as the aircraft entered the water. They called by phone to the police of the city that we had seen from the air and told them that an aircraft had just landed in the water. Shortly after, we saw vehicles with rotating red beacons rushing up the road towards the small community. Then we heard some outboard motors start up and head towards our downed aircraft. The first one arrived pulling up to the wing, and a large gentleman stepped out of the boat looking around at the three of us and asked, "Captain?" I answered in Spanish "Yo soy" ("I am"). He greeted me in Spanish, "Bienvenido a Campeche, Mexico" meaning "Welcome to Campeche, Mexico." We were rescued. I was commended

Looks of relief on the faces of Captain Wendell Levister (in hatch with scuba mask) and the rescuers the morning after N4834V (msn: 10103) ditched in the ocean off the coast of Lermer, Mexico (Captain Wendell Levister).

by the manufacturer, Fairchild Aviation, as being one of the few pilots that had ever ditched a C-82 without breaking up the aircraft. I had never ditched any aircraft before, but used every skill that I had, and every bit of information that I had learned about how to ditch an aircraft.

Final Disposition: Accident.

10104 / 45-57734/CQ-734 / C-82A-30-FA

Avble: 18 Feb 47; Acc: 27 Feb 47; Del: 23 May 47 to USAAF // 62nd TCG (TAC) Bergstrom Field Texas 27 May 47; assigned 4th & 8th TCSq; 62nd to McChord Field Washington 7 Aug 47; to Fairchild Aircraft Maryland (AMC) for mods 20 Aug 47; multiple depls to Elmendorf AFB Alaska starting 1 Apr 48; multiple assignments to 62nd MSU GP (TAC) McChord AFB Washington starting 20 Oct 48 // 1st RES SQ (MATS) MacDill AFB Florida 14 Feb 50; cvtd to SC-82A; to San Antonio Air Materiel Area (AMC) Kelly AFB Texas 29 Aug 50; depl to Albrook AFB Panama Canal Zone 11 Jun 51 // 2156th RES UT (MATS) MacDill AFB Florida 2 Jul 51; to 306th AB GP (SAC) MacDill AFB Florida 4 Apr 52. Made a forced landing due to onboard fire 1 May 52 at MacDill AFB Florida, no fatalities and minor damage // 809th AB GP (SAC) MacDill AFB Florida 16 Jun 52 // 1707th Training SQ (MATS) Palm Beach Intl. Airport 12 Feb 53 // 46th RES SQ (MATS) Westover AFB Massachusetts 30 Apr 53 // Aircraft Engineering & Maintenance Co. (AMC) Oakland California 18 May 53 on bailment ; cvtd back to C-82A standard and modernized to Group A standard // 1800th AACS WG (MATS) Tinker AFB Oklahoma 6 Jan 54 // San Bernardino Aircraft Repair Depot (AMC) Norton AFB California 7 Jan 54 // 1st AACS Installation & Maintenance SQ (MATS) Tinker AFB Oklahoma 19 Feb 54 // Wfu to Ogden Air Materiel Area (AMC) Hill AFB Utah 15 Sep 54 and stored. Dropped from inventory 9 May 55 // L.B. Smith Aircraft Corp. Miami Florida 19 Sep 55 reg: N2060A // Harry R. Playford (Madden & Playford Aircraft Inc.) St. Petersburg Florida 21 Sep 55; ferried from Ogden, Utah with reg: N6240C but later canx in favor of N2060A; one of five C-82As based at Pinellas Airport, Florida // Royal International Corp. Miami Florida 7 May 57 // The Ohio Oil Co. of Guatemala Puerto Barrios Guatemala 6 Apr 59 reg: TG-OOC-3; subsequent history unk, reg canx 1960. N2060A de-reg 27 Aug 71. Final Disposition: Unknown (Presumed Scrapped).

10105 / 45-57735/CQ-735 / C-82A-30-FA

Avble: 24 Feb 47; Acc: 11 Mar 47; Del: 23 May 47 to USAAF // 62nd TCG (TAC) Bergstrom Field Texas 27 May 47; assigned 8th TCSq; 62nd to McChord Field Washington 7 Aug 47; to Fairchild Aircraft Maryland (AMC) for mods 25 Aug 47; depl to Pope AFB North Carolina 13 Apr 48; multiple assignments to 62nd MSU GP (TAC) McChord AFB Washington starting 1 Jul 48 // 1600th MSU GP (MATS) Westover AFB Massachusetts 31 Mar 49 // 1227th AB GP (MATS) Goose Bay AB Labrador Canada 4 Apr 49; multiple assignments to Middletown Air Materiel Area (AMC) Olmsted AFB Pennsylvania starting 27 Apr 49 // Warner-Robins Air Materiel Area (AMC) Robins AFB Georgia 5 Jan 50 for depmnt // 1226th AB GP (MATS) Ernest Harmon AFB Newfoundland Canada 29 Aug 50 // 6602nd AB WG (NEAC) Ernest Harmon AFB Newfoundland Canada 2 Nov 50; to 6603rd AB GP (NEAC) Goose Bay AB Labrador Canada 29 Jan 52 // 6622nd Air Transport SQ (NEAC) Ernest Harmon AFB Newfoundland Canada 18 Aug 52 // 64th TCWG (TAC) Greenville AFB South Carolina 14 Dec 52 // Wfu to San Antonio Air Materiel

Area (AMC) Kelly AFB Texas 2 Jul 53 and stored. Dropped from inventory 1 Jul 54. No records exist of any civil service, presumed scrapped by the USAF. Final Disposition: Scrapped.

C-82A s/n: 45-57735 (msn: 10105). Note the fin on the nose (National Museum of the United States Air Force).

10106 / 45-57736/CQ-736 / C-82A-30-FA

Avble: 26 Feb 47; Acc: 14 Mar 47; Del: 23 May 47 to USAAF // 62nd TCG (TAC) Bergstrom Field Texas 27 May 47; assigned 4th TCSq; 62nd to McChord Field Washington 7 Aug 47; to Fairchild Aircraft Maryland (AMC) for mods 21 Aug 47; depl to Elmendorf AFB Alaska 1 Apr 48; multiple assignments to 62nd MSU GP (TAC) McChord AFB Washington starting 26 Aug 48; 62nd MSU GP depl to San Bernardino Air Depot California 13 Dec 49 // 314th TCG (CNC) Smyrna AFB Tennessee 13 Dec 49; assigned 2601st Light Assault SQ // Smyrna AFB renamed Sewart AFB 25 Mar 50 // 4th RES SQ (MATS) Hamilton AFB California 10 May 50; cvtd to SC-82A; to Sacramento Air Materiel Area (AMC) McClellan AFB California 2 Nov 50; to Ogden Air Materiel Area (AMC) Hill AFB Utah 2 Jan 51 & 2 May 51; to 78th Fighter-Interceptor WG (ADC) Hamilton AFB California 24 Sep 51 // 2156th RES SQ (MATS) MacDill AFB Florida 15 Nov 51; to 22nd AB GP (SAC) March AFB California 23 Jan 52 // 1707th Training SQ (MATS) Palm Beach Intl. Airport Florida 20 Jul 52 // 4th RES SQ (MATS) Lowry AFB Colorado 9 Sep 52 // 44th RES SQ (MATS) Lowry AFB Colorado 4 Nov 52 // Ogden Air Materiel Area (AMC) Hill AFB Utah 6 Jun 53 for depmnt. Wfu 11 Jun 53 and stored. Dropped from inventory 8 Jul 54 // Ben W. Widtfeldt & Harry S. McCandless Council Bluffs Iowa 23 Aug 55 reg: N4835V // M&W Aircraft Leasing Council Bluffs Iowa 7 Sep 55; Lease to SkySpray Inc. as an aerial sprayer. Supposed lease to Switzerland reg: HB-AAD but ntu // Roberto M. Tribolet Culiacan Mexico Dec 56 reg: XB-ZUZ. N4835V reg canx 13 Dec 56. Leased to Steward-Davis Inc. Aug 58 for a demonstration tour of Latin America. Later photographic evidence shows the horizontal stabilizers removed, which indicates XB-ZUZ may have been a temporary Jet-Packet conversion for the tour // Transcarga S.A. Buenos Aires

Argentina, reg: LV-PNY rsved 4 Jun 59 but ntu, re-reg: LV-GIS 17 Nov 59; in service 1 Apr 60 until 1966; stored at Buenos Aires-Ezeiza Intl. Airport Argentina until bku Aug 67. Final Disposition: Scrapped.

10107 / 45-57737/CQ-737 / C-82A-30-FA

Avble: 5 Mar 47; Acc: 18 Mar 47; Del: 23 May 47 to USAAF // 62nd TCG (TAC) Bergstrom Field Texas 27 May 47; assigned 4th TCSq; 62nd to McChord Field Washington 7 Aug 47; to Fairchild Aircraft Maryland (AMC) for mods 21 Aug 47. Suffered a taxiing accident at Fort Nelson AB Canada 29 Nov 47, no fatalities. Deployments to Elmendorf AFB Alaska 1 Apr 48 & 3 Mar 49; multiple assignments to 62nd MSU GP (TAC) McChord AFB Washington starting 20 Oct 48 // 5th RES SQ (MATS) Selfridge AFB Michigan 12 Apr 50; cvtd to SC-82A; to 56th Fighter-Interceptor WG (CNC) Selfridge AFB Michigan 29 May 50; to San Antonio Air Materiel Area (AMC) Kelly AFB Texas 28 Aug 50; to Warner-Robins Air Materiel Area (AMC) Robins AFB Georgia 19 Jan 51 for depmnt; 5th RES SQ depl to Laurinburg-Maxton Airport North Carolina 7 Aug 51; to 22nd AB GP (SAC) March AFB California 10 Oct 51; to 2750th AB WG (AMC) WPAFB Ohio 18 Dec 51; to 4708th Defense WG (ADC) Selfridge AFB Michigan 3 Apr 52 // 49th RES SQ (MATS) Selfridge AFB Michigan 4 Nov 52 // Wfu to Ogden Air Materiel Area (AMC) Hill AFB Utah 14 Jul 53 and stored. Dropped from inventory 8 Jul 54 // L.B. Smith Aircraft Corp. Miami Florida 19 Sep 55 reg: N2061A // Lineas Aereas del Caribe Ltda. (LIDCA) Barranquilla Colombia Feb 56 reg. HK-914-X; N2061A reg canx 8 Feb 56; reg. HK-914 10 May 56. Crashed 13 Oct 56, cause and fatalities unk, nfd. HK-914 reg canx 13 Oct 56. Final Disposition: Accident.

10108 / 45-57738/CQ-738 / C-82A-FA

Some parts of this IARC indecipherable. Avble: 19 Mar 47; Acc: 31 Mar 47; Del: 21 Apr 47 to USAAF // 310th AAF BAS (TAC) Pope Field North Carolina 21 Apr 47; to 1504th AAF BAS (ATC) Fairfield-Suisun Field California 27 Apr 47 // 316th TCG (TAC) Greenville Field South Carolina 23 Jul 47; assigned 37th TCSq; to 313th AAF BAS (TAC) Greenville AFB South Carolina 10 Aug 47; multiple assignments to 316th MSU GP (TAC) Greenville AFB South Carolina starting 18 Aug 47; to 3203rd MSU GP & 3200th Proof Test GP (APG) Eglin AFB, Florida 10 Dec 48; depl to Guantanamo Bay Cuba 28 Feb 50; Smyrna AFB renamed Sewart AFB 25 Mar 50; depl to 314th TCG (CNC) Laurinburg-Maxton Airport North Carolina 21 Apr 50 // 314th TCG (CNC) Sewart AFB South Carolina 21 Jul 50 // 325th Fighter (All-Weather) WG (CNC) McChord AFB Washington Sep 50 // 4408th AB SQ (CNC) Lawson AFB Georgia Nov 50 // 375th TCWG (TAC) Greenville AFB South Carolina 22 Nov 50; assigned 55th TCSq; to 117th Reconnaissance (Tactical) WG (TAC) Lawson AFB Georgia 27 Dec 50; to Warner-Robins Air Materiel Area (AMC) Robins AFB Georgia 27 Jun 51 & 30 Aug 51 for depmnt. Suffered a minor landing accident at Donaldson AFB South Carolina 27 Sep 51, no fatalities // 64th TCWG (TAC) Donaldson AFB South Carolina 14 Jul 52. Crashed in the United States between Jul and Sep 1952; details on exact location, cause of crash and fatalities unk. Assigned to reclamation 15 Sep 52. Dropped from inventory 13 Oct 52. Final Disposition: Accident.

C-82A Packet s/n: 45-57738 (msn: 10108) on a visit to Matsushima Field, Japan, on May 27, 1947 (United States Air Force).

10109 / 45-57739/CQ-739 / C-82A-FA

Avble: 24 Mar 47; Acc: 31 Mar 47; Del: 25 Apr 47 to USAAF // 62nd TCG (TAC) Bergstrom Field Texas 28 Apr 47; assigned 4th TCSq; to 1377th AAF BAS (ATC) Westover Field Massachusetts 19 May 47; 62nd to McChord Field Washington 7 Aug 47; to Fairchild Aircraft Maryland (AMC) for mods 25 Aug 47; depl to Elmendorf AFB Alaska 1 Apr 48; multiple assignments to 62nd MSU GP (TAC) McChord AFB Washington starting 13 Sep 48 // 314th TCG (CNC) Smyrna AFB Tennessee 13 Dec 49; assigned 2601st Light Assault SQ; Smyrna AFB renamed Sewart AFB 25 Mar 50 // San Antonio Air Materiel Area (AMC) Kelly AFB Texas 26 Jun 50 // 325th Fighter (All-Weather) WG (CNC) McChord AFB Washington 1 Aug 50; to 57th Fighter-Interceptor WG (AAC) Elmendorf AFB Alaska 22 Oct 50; 54th TCSq (Attached) // 375th TCG (CNC) Greenville AFB South Carolina 9 Nov 50. Crashed into the top of Bully Mountain 12 miles NW of Pickens South Carolina 11 Nov 50 while on a nighttime descending approach into Greenville AFB. Killed on impact were pilot: Capt John M. Stuckrath, co-pilot: 1st Lt Robert P. Schmitt, SSgt John D. Bloomer and passenger SSgt Walter O. Lott. The crash set a large part of the impact area on fire, which attracted the attention of local hunters, who rushed to the scene also alerting the Air Force // 4418th Base Complement SQ (CNC) Greenville AFB South Carolina 11 Nov 50 for reclamation and salvage. Dropped from inventory 19 Dec 50. Wreckage remains at the site to this day, the largest piece being part of a main u/c unit. One chunk of debris landed in a tree and over the decades since has become embedded in the trunk as the tree grew around it! Final Disposition: Accident.

10110 / 45-57740/CQ-740 / C-82A-FA

Avble: 25 Mar 47; Acc: 31 Mar 47; Del: 16 Apr 47 to USAAF // On bailment to Fairchild Aircraft (AMC) Maryland for project. Had an engine failure over Hagerstown Field Maryland 27 Jun 47, landed safely, no fatalities // 316th TCG (TAC) Greenville AFB South Carolina 1 Aug 48; 316th MSU GP (TAC) Greenville AFB South Carolina 8 Sep 48

// 60th TCG (AFE) Erbenheim (Wiesbaden AB) Germany 16 Sep 48; to 7160th AB GP (AFE) Erbenheim (Wiesbaden AB) Germany 6 Oct 48; to 7165th AB GP (AFE) Erbenheim (Wiesbaden AB) Germany 22 Dec 48 & 17 Mar 49; to 60th AB GP (AFE) Wiesbaden AB West Germany 1 Jun 49; depl to 513th TCG (AFE) Rhein-Main AB West Germany 22 Sep 49; cvtd to JC-82A on temp special duties for the Berlin Airlift; depl to Rhein-Main AB West Germany 1 Oct 49; back to Wiesbaden AB West Germany 7 Jun 50; to 60th TCG at Rhein-Main AB West Germany 7 Jul 50; depl to 61st TCWG (AFE) Rhein-Main AB West Germany (60th Attached) 7 Apr 51; on loan to Royal Aircraft Establishment Farnborough England 5 Dec 51 // 85th Air Depot WG (AFE) Erding AB, West Germany 7 Nov 52 for depmnt // San Antonio Air Materiel Area (AMC) Kelly AFB Texas 22 May 53 for depmnt. Wfu 24 Jun 53 and stored. Dropped from inventory 1 Jul 54 // U.S. civil owner unk, reg: N75884 // Compania Mexicana de Aviacion S.A. Mexico City Mexico, 1957, reg: XA-LOJ; fitted with Mexicana dorsal fillets // New Frontier Airlift Corp. Phoenix Arizona Oct 1962 reg: N2779 but ntu, reg canx 18 Dec 67; aircraft ferried from Mexico to U.S. 19–23 Dec 67; subsequently stored at Long Beach Airport becoming derelict. Derelict airframe moved off-airport 1970; scrapped by mid–1972. Final Disposition: Scrapped.

C-82A XA-LOJ (msn: 10110) of Compania Mexicana de Aviacion S.A. at Tijuana, Mexico, in an early CMA company livery (Gary Kuhn).

10111 / 45-57741/CQ-741 / C-82A-FA

Avble: 27 Mar 47; Acc: 31 Mar 47; Del: 25 Apr 47 to USAAF // 62nd TCG (TAC) Bergstrom Field Texas 28 Apr 47; assigned 7th TCSq; 62nd to McChord Field Washington 7 Aug 47; to Fairchild Aircraft Maryland (AMC) for mods 21 Aug 47; depl to Pope AFB North Carolina 13 Apr 48; multiple assignments to 62nd MSU GP (TAC) McChord AFB Washington starting 25 Aug 48; depl to Elmendorf AFB Alaska 3 Mar 49 // 61st MSU GP (AFE) Rhein-Main AB West Germany (60th Attached) 25 Oct 49 // 60th TCG (AFE) Wiesbaden AB West Germany 28 Dec 49; to 60th TCWG at Rhein-Main AB West Germany 7 Jul 50 // San Antonio Air Materiel Area (AMC) Kelly AFB 21 Feb 53; to 80th AB

SQ (MATS) Dover AFB Delaware 23 Feb 53; to 3380th Technical Training WG (TC) Keesler AFB Mississippi 12 Jun 53. Wfu to San Antonio Air Materiel Area (AMC) Kelly AFB Texas 25 Jun 53 and stored. Dropped from inventory 1 Jul 54 // Bankers Life & Casualty Co. Chicago Illinois 7 Sep 55 reg: N5110B; subsequent history unk; might have been exported. Listed as scrapped and reg canx reg 8 Oct 70. Final Disposition: Scrapped.

10112 / 45-57742/CQ-742 / C-82A-FA

Avble: 2 Apr 47; Acc: 24 Apr 47; Del: 25 Apr 47 to USAAF // 62nd TCG (TAC) Bergstrom Field Texas 28 Apr 47 // 4000th AAF BAS (AMC) Patterson Field Ohio 2 Jul 47 for experimental and development tests; to Wright Field Ohio 28 Aug 47 // 316th MSU GP (TAC) Greenville Field South Carolina 26 May 48 for storage; 316th TCG (TAC) Greenville Field South Carolina 9 Jul 48; 316th to Smyrna AFB Tennessee 4 Nov 49 // 314th TCG (CNC) Smyrna AFB Tennessee 25 Nov 49; assigned 2601st Light Assault SQ // 60th TCG (AFE) Wiesbaden AB West Germany 12 Jan 50; to 60th TCG at Rhein-Main AB West Germany 7 Feb 50. Crashed in West Germany sometime in early 1950; details on exact location, cause of crash and fatalities unk. Assigned to reclamation 25 Apr 50. Dropped from inventory 20 Oct 50. Final Disposition: Accident.

10113 / 45-57743/CQ-743 / C-82A-FA

Avble: 9 Apr 47; Acc: 24 Apr 47; Del: 31 Jul 47 to USAAF // 609th AAF BAS (PGC) Eglin Field Florida 18 Aug 47 // 611th AAF BAS (PGC) Eglin Field Florida 18 Aug 47 // 605th AF BAS (PGC) Eglin AFB Florida 1 Oct 47 // 62nd TCG (TAC) McChord AFB Washington 20 Oct 47; assigned 4th TCSq; multiple depls to Elmendorf AFB Alaska starting 1 Apr 48; multiple assignments to 62nd MSU GP (TAC) McChord AFB Washington starting 1 Oct 48 // 61th MSU GP (AFE) Rhein-Main AB West Germany (60th Attached) 20 Oct 49 // 60th TCG (AFE) Rhein-Main AB West Germany 27 Oct 49; assigned 10th TCSq; depl to Wiesbaden AB West Germany 26 Jan 50; depl to 61st TCWG (AFE) Rhein-Main AB West Germany (60th Attached) 5 Jun 50. Made a belly crash-landing at Neubiberg AB West Germany 22 Nov 50 due to an engine failure. Pilot: Richard A. Kellogg, no fatalities but aircraft w/o. Assigned to reclamation 26 Nov 50. Dropped from inventory 19 Jan 51. Final Disposition: Accident.

10114 / 45-57744/CQ-744 / C-82A-FA

Avble: 14 Apr 47; Acc: 24 Apr 47; Del: 12 Aug 47 to USAAF // 62nd TCG (TAC) McChord Field Washington 19 Aug 47; assigned 7th TCSq; depl to Fort Defiance Virginia 23 Oct 47; multiple depls to Elmendorf AFB Alaska starting early 48; assigned 7th & 4th TCSq; depl to Pope AFB North Carolina 13 Apr 48; to Sacramento Air Materiel Area (AMC) McClellan AFB California 16 Mar 49; 62nd MSU GP (CNC) McChord AFB Washington 13 Oct 49 // 61st MSU GP (AFE) Rhein-Main AB West Germany (60th Attached) 24 Jan 50 // 60th TCG (AFE) Wiesbaden AB West Germany 1 Mar 50; to 60th TCG at Rhein-Main AB West Germany 7 Jul 50 // San Antonio Air Materiel Area (AMC) Kelly AFB 5 Apr 53 // Aircraft Engineering & Maintenance Co. (AMC) Oakland California 14 Apr 53 on bailment; modernized to Group A standard // 521st Air Defense GP (CAD) Sioux City MAP Iowa 4 Sep 53; to 1739th Ferrying SQ (MATS) Amarillo AFB Texas 14

Sep 53. Departed Norton AFB California for Hill AFB Utah on 21 Sep 54 when around 20 miles out of Norton, over the 6,500-foot-high San Bernardino Mountains, and 9 miles NW of Fawnskin California had an engine failure. With the poor single-engine performance record of the C-82, the aircraft's altitude could not be maintained. Pilot instructor Capt Charles M. Eckstein Jr. ordered the eight other crew and passengers to bail out but was unable to do so himself before the aircraft crashed. Capt Eckstein was killed on impact. The wreckage started a localized forest fire. The eight survivors who bailed out were: Maj James M. Wagner, Capt Charles G. Chapman, Capt C.A. Metzler, 1st Lt Alfred Gathercoal, MSgt J. Marinovich, MSgt Glenn L. McQuigg, A1C Joseph P. Tyron and A2C Eugene E. Dasare. Aircraft assigned to reclamation 22 Sep 54. Dropped from inventory 30 Nov 54. The last military C-82 crash before the USAF retired the type. Parts and fragments of the aircraft can still be found at the wreck site today. Final Disposition: Accident.

10115 / 45-57745/CQ-745 / C-82A-FA

Avble: 21 Apr 47; Acc: 30 Apr 47; Del: 12 Aug 47 to USAAF // 62nd TCG (TAC) McChord Field Washington 19 Aug 47; assigned 7th TCSq; multiple assignments to 62nd MSU GP (TAC) McChord Field Washington starting 16 Sep 47; depl to Fort Defiance Virginia 6 Nov 47; multiple depls to Elmendorf AFB Alaska starting early 48; assigned 4th, 7th & 8th TCSq; depl to Pope AFB North Carolina 13 Apr 48; to 2621st AF BAS (TC) Barksdale AFB Louisiana 12 May 48 // 61st MSU GP (AFE) Rhein-Main AB West Germany (60th Attached) 15 Jan 50 // 60th TCG (AFE) Wiesbaden AB West Germany 18 Jan 50; to 60th TCG at Rhein-Main AB West Germany 7 Jul 50; assigned 10th TCSq; depls to 61st TCWG (AFE) Rhein-Main AB West Germany (60th Attached) 7 Apr 51 & 14 May 51. Minor taxiing accident due to mechanical failure at Kitzingen AB West Germany 10 May 51, no fatalities. To Middletown Air Materiel Area (AMC) Olmsted AFB Pennsylvania 7 Jul 51 for depmnt // San Antonio Air Materiel Area (AMC) Kelly AFB 6 Mar 53; assigned 6603rd AB GP in error; to depmnt 17 Mar 53. Wfu 24 Jun 53 and stored. Dropped from inventory 1 Jul 54 // Leeward Aeronautical Inc. Fort Wayne Indiana 1955–56 reg: unk // Francis L. Duncan Rockville Maryland 1957 reg: unk, for export // Servicos Aereos Cruzeiro do Sul Rio de Janeiro Brazil 8 Oct 57; arrived in Brazil 16 Oct 57. Crashed at Santos-Dumont Airport Rio de Janeiro Brazil 11 Jan 58 while on a training flight that had blind flying screens in place. As the aircraft took off, the instructor pilot raised the u/c but the pilot in training failed to establish an adequate rate of climb and the aircraft hit a barrier at the end of the runway, then ditching into Guanabara Bay. Both pilots were uninjured but the C-82 was damaged beyond repair. Reg: PP-CEH 18 Jul 58. PP-CEH reg canx 18 Jul 58—issued and canceled the same day! Final Disposition: Accident.

10116 / 45-57746/CQ-746 / C-82A-FA

Avble: 23 Apr 47; Acc: 30 Apr 47; Del: 12 Aug 47 to USAAF // 62nd TCG (TAC) McChord Field Washington 19 Aug 47 // Fairchild Aircraft Maryland (AMC) 16 Oct 47 on bailment for project and mods; cvtd with tracked u/c, ff: 1948 // 2750th AB GP (AMC) WPAFB Ohio 8 Feb 49; redes EC-82A tracked u/c prototype 15 Feb 49; to 3203rd MSU GP & 3200th Proof Test GP (APG) Eglin AFB Florida 19 Sep 49 for test and experimental duties of the tracked u/c; cvtd back to C-82A standard 6 Oct 50; to Ogden Air Materiel

Area (AMC) Hill AFB Utah 13 Nov 50 for project duties // Ogden Air Materiel Area (AMC) Hill AFB Utah 16 Apr 52 for project and depot mods. Wfu 21 Jan 53 and stored. Assigned to reclamation 23 Feb 54. Dropped from inventory as surplus 15 Mar 54 and scrapped. Final Disposition: Scrapped.

EC-82A s/n: 45-57746 (msn: 10116) prototype with tracked undercarriage (National Museum of the United States Air Force).

10117 / 45-57747/CQ-747 / C-82A-FA

Avble: 25 Apr 47; Acc: 30 Apr 47; Del: 12 Aug 47 to USAAF // 62nd TCG (TAC) McChord Field Washington 19 Aug 47; assigned 7th TCSq; depl to Fort Defiance Virginia 23 Oct 47; depl to Elmendorf AFB Alaska early 48; depl to Pope AFB North Carolina 13 Apr 48; 62nd MSU GP (TAC) McChord AFB Washington 25 Aug 48 // Fairchild Aircraft Maryland (AMC) 17 Sep 48 on bailment; cvtd with tracked u/c 7 Mar 49 but not redes; retrofitted to standard u/c 27 Aug 49 // 314th TCG (CNC) Smyrna AFB Tennessee 31 Aug 49; assigned 2601st Light Assault SQ; Smyrna AFB renamed Sewart AFB 25 Mar 50 // Ogden Air Materiel Area (AMC) Hill AFB Utah 13 Aug 50 for project and depot mods // 60th TCWG (AFE) Rhein-Main AB West Germany 7 Feb 52 // San Antonio Air Materiel Area (AMC) Kelly AFB Texas 6 Mar 53 for depmnt. Wfu 24 Jun 53 and stored. Dropped from inventory 1 Jul 54 // Guest Aerovias Mexico S.A. Mexico City Mexico, 1955, reg: XA-LIL; the first C-82A to enter civil service // Aerovias Condor Ltda. La Paz Bolivia, 1960, reg: CP-677 // Transportes Aereos Benianos S.A. (TABSA) Bolivia, 1963. Took off from Sasasama Airport Bolivia bound for San Borja Airport Bolivia 15 Mar 70 when it inexplicably crashed in thick jungle around 7 miles from the airport near the Izeze River; all four onboard were killed. A recovery team took ten days, due to becoming lost in the jungle, to reach the crash site on foot in order to retrieve the bodies. Final Disposition: Accident.

10118 / 45-57748/CQ-748 / C-82A-FA

Avble: 30 Apr 47; Acc: 30 Apr 47; Del: 19 Aug 47 to USAAF // 62nd TCG (TAC) McChord Field Washington 21 Aug 47; assigned 7th TCSq; depl to Fort Defiance Virginia

23 Oct 47; depl to Elmendorf AFB Alaska early 48; depl to Pope AFB North Carolina 13 Apr 48; 62nd MSU GP (TAC) McChord AFB Washington 3 Sep 48 // Fairchild Aircraft Maryland (AMC) 1 Oct 48 on bailment for mods; cvtd with tracked u/c 7 Mar 47 // 2750th AB GP (AMC) WPAFB Ohio 8 Mar 49 for test and experimental duties but not redes EC-82A; retrofitted to standard u/c late 1949 but remained at WPAFB until 1 Sep 50// Ogden Air Materiel Area (AMC) Hill AFB Utah 1 Sep 50 for project duties and depot mods. Placed in storage 3 Jan 52. Out of storage for depot mods 4 Mar 52. Wfu 21 Jan 53 and stored. Assigned to reclamation 23 Feb 54. Dropped from inventory as surplus 15 Mar 54 and scrapped. Final Disposition: Scrapped.

EC-82A s/n: 45-57748 (msn: 10118) at Dayton, Ohio, for tracked undercarriage tests (National Museum of the United States Air Force).

10119 / 45-57749/CQ-749 / C-82A-FA

Avble: 5 May 47; Acc: 16 May 47; Del: 19 Aug 47 to USAAF // 62nd TCG (TAC) McChord Field Washington 21 Aug 47; assigned 7th TCSq; depl to Fort Defiance Virginia 23 Oct 47; depl to Elmendorf AFB Alaska early 48; depl to Pope AFB North Carolina 13 Apr 48; 62nd MSU GP (TAC) McChord AFB Washington 9 Oct 48; depl to San Bernardino Air Depot California 12 Oct 48 // Fairchild Aircraft Maryland (AMC) 21 Jan 49 on bailment for mods; cvtd with tracked u/c 7 Mar 49 but not redes; retrofitted to standard u/c 22 Jul 49 // 316th TCG (CNC) Greenville AFB South Carolina 26 Jul 49; 316th to Smyrna AFB Tennessee 4 Nov 49; depl to 314th MSU GP (CNC) Smyrna AFB Tennessee 25 Nov 49 then 314th TCWG 10 Mar 50; assigned 2601st Light Assault SQ; Smyrna AFB renamed Sewart AFB 25 Mar 50; to Mobile Air Materiel Area (AMC) Brookley AFB Alabama 1 Jun 50 // 375th TCWG (CNC) Greenville AFB South Carolina 1 Nov 50; to Warner-Robins Air Materiel Area (AMC) Robins AFB Georgia 11 Aug 51 for depmnt; depls to Brownwood Field Texas 6 Mar 52 & 4 Apr 52 // 64th TCWG (TAC) Donaldson AFB South Carolina 14 Jul 52; assigned 35th TCSq // 6520th Test Support SQ (ARD) (Laurence G.) Hanscom AFB Massachusetts 23 Oct 52; cvtd to EC-82A for test support duties. Had a minor structural failure incident at Patrick AFB Florida 1 Oct 53, no fatalities. To Oklahoma Air Materiel Area (AMC) Tinker AFB Oklahoma 9 Dec 53; modernized to Group A standard // Wfu to Ogden Air Materiel Area (AMC) Hill AFB Utah 17 Nov 54 and stored. Dropped from inventory 9 May 55 // L.B. Smith Aircraft Corp. Miami Florida 19 Sep 55 reg: N2064A // Harry R. Playford (Madden & Playford Aircraft Inc.) St. Petersburg Florida 21 Sep 55; ferried from Ogden, Utah with reg: N6242C but later canx in favor of N2064A; one of five C-82s based at Pinellas Airport, Florida; cert of reg issued 12 Mar 56 // Madden & Playford Aircraft Inc. Miami Florida 15 Aug 56 // Rodest and Company New York N.Y. 15 Aug 56 // Mercantil Colombiana Ltda. Bogota Colombia 3 Sep 56 reg: HK-924. N2064A reg canx 22 Jan 57. W/o in an accident 1958, cause and fatalities unk, nfd. HK-924 reg canx 27 Jun 69. Final Disposition: Accident.

10120 / 45-57750/CQ-750 / C-82A-FA

Avble: 8 May 47; Acc: 16 May 47; Del: 19 Aug 47 to USAAF // 62nd TCG (TAC) McChord Field Washington 21 Aug 47; assigned 7th TCSq; depl to Fort Defiance Virginia 23 Oct 47; depl to Elmendorf AFB Alaska early 48; depl to Pope AFB North Carolina 13 Apr 48; 62nd MSU GP (TAC) McChord AFB Washington 19 Sep 48 // Fairchild Aircraft Maryland (AMC) 19 Oct 48 on bailment for mods; cvtd with tracked u/c 7 Mar 49 but not redes // 314th TCG (CNC) Smyrna AFB Tennessee 22 Mar 49; assigned 2601st Light Assault SQ; multiple assignments to 314th MSU GP (CNC) Smyrna AFB Tennessee starting 17 Jun 49. Retrofitted back to standard u/c late 1949. Smyrna AFB renamed Sewart AFB 25 Mar 50 // Ogden Air Materiel Area (AMC) Hill AFB Utah 13 Aug 50 for project duties and depot mods. Placed in storage 3 Jan 52. Out of storage for depot mods 4 Mar 52. Wfu 21 Jan 53 and stored. Assigned to reclamation 23 Feb 54. Dropped from inventory as surplus 15 Mar 54 and scrapped. Final Disposition: Scrapped.

10121 / 45-57751/CQ-751 / C-82A-FA

Avble: 13 May 47; Acc: 20 May 47; Del: 20 Aug 47 to USAAF // 62nd TCG (TAC) McChord Field Washington 24 Aug 47; assigned 7th TCSq; depl to Fort Defiance Virginia 23 Oct 47; depl to Elmendorf AFB Alaska early 48; depl to Pope AFB North Carolina 13 Apr 48; 62nd MSU GP (TAC) McChord AFB Washington 17 Sep 48 // Fairchild Aircraft Maryland (AMC) 1 Nov 48 on bailment for mods; cvtd with tracked u/c 7 Mar 49 but not redes; retrofitted to standard u/c 23 Jul 49 // 316th TCG (CNC) Greenville AFB South Carolina 26 Jul 49; 316th to Smyrna AFB Tennessee 4 Nov 49 // 314th TCG (CNC) Smyrna AFB Tennessee 25 Nov 49; assigned 2601st Light Assault SQ; 314th MSU GP (CNC) Smyrna AFB Tennessee 27 Jan 50; Smyrna AFB renamed Sewart AFB 25 Mar 50 // Ogden Air Materiel Area (AMC) Hill AFB Utah 21 Aug 50 for project duties and depot mods. Placed in storage 3 Jan 52. Out of storage for depot mods 4 Mar 52. Wfu 21 Jan 53 and stored. Assigned to reclamation 23 Feb 54. Dropped from inventory as surplus 15 Mar 54 and scrapped. Final Disposition: Scrapped.

10122 / 45-57752/CQ-752 / C-82A-FA

Avble: 16 May 47; Acc: 23 May 47; Del: 20 Aug 47 to USAAF // 62nd TCG (TAC) McChord Field Washington 24 Aug 47; assigned 7th TCSq; depl to Fort Defiance Virginia

23 Oct 47; depl to Elmendorf AFB Alaska early 48; depl to Pope AFB North Carolina 13 Apr 48; 62nd MSU GP (TAC) McChord AFB Washington 5 Oct 48 // Fairchild Aircraft Maryland (AMC) for mods 15 Nov 48 on bailment for mods; cvtd with tracked u/c 7 Mar 49 but not redes; retrofitted to standard u/c 23 Aug 49 // 314th TCG (CNC) Smyrna AFB Tennessee 23 Aug 49; assigned 2601st Light Assault SQ. W/o at Smyrna AFB Tennessee 21 Mar 50 when a taxiing C-119B s/n: 48–326 suffered a mechanical failure and collided with the parked aircraft, no fatalities but aircraft "damaged beyond repair." Parked C-82A s/n: 45-57760 also w/o. Assigned to reclamation 24 Mar 50. Dropped from inventory 23 May 50. Final Disposition: Accident.

10123 / 45-57753/CQ-753 / C-82A-FA

Avble: 22 May 47; Acc: 23 May 47; Del: 21 Aug 47 to USAAF // 62nd TCG (TAC) McChord Field Washington 2 Sep 47; assigned 7th TCSq; depl to Fort Defiance Virginia 23 Oct 47; depl to Elmendorf AFB Alaska early 48; depl to Pope AFB North Carolina 13 Apr 48; 62nd MSU GP (TAC) McChord AFB Washington 8 Nov 48 // Fairchild Aircraft Maryland (AMC) 6 Jan 49 on bailment for mods; cvtd with tracked u/c 7 Mar 49 but not redes; retrofitted to standard u/c 31 Aug 49 // 314th TCG (CNC) Smyrna AFB Tennessee 2 Sep 49; assigned 2601st Light Assault SQ; Smyrna AFB renamed Sewart AFB 25 Mar 50 // Ogden Air Materiel Area (AMC) Hill AFB Utah 13 Aug 50 for project duties and depot mods. Placed in storage 3 Jan 52. Out of storage for depot mods 4 Mar 52. Wfu 21 Jan 53 and stored. Assigned to reclamation 23 Feb 54. Dropped from inventory as surplus 15 Mar 54 and scrapped. Final Disposition: Scrapped.

10124 / 45-57754/CQ-754 / C-82A-FA

Avble: 23 May 47; Acc: 28 May 47; Del: 21 Aug 47 to USAAF // 62nd TCG (TAC) McChord Field Washington 24 Aug 47; assigned 7th TCSq; to 62nd MSU GP (TAC) McChord AFB Washington 30 Sep 47 & 28 Sep 48; depl to Fort Defiance Virginia 23 Oct 47; depls to Elmendorf AFB Alaska early 48 & 1 Sep 48; assigned 7th & 8th TCSq; depl to Pope AFB North Carolina 13 Apr 48 // Fairchild Aircraft Maryland (AMC) 13 Dec 48 on bailment for mods; cvtd with tracked u/c 7 Mar 49 but not redes; retrofitted to standard u/c 10 Sep 49 // 314th TCG (CNC) Smyrna AFB Tennessee 13 Sep 49 // 3203rd MSU GP & 3200th Proof Test GP (APG) Eglin AFB Florida 21 Oct 49 for test and experimental duties // Ogden Air Materiel Area (AMC) Hill AFB Utah 30 Aug 50 for project duties and depot mods. Placed in storage 3 Jan 52. Out of storage for depot mods 4 Mar 52. Wfu 21 Jan 53 and stored. Assigned to reclamation 23 Feb 54. Dropped from inventory as surplus 15 Mar 54 and scrapped. Final Disposition: Scrapped.

10125 / 45-57755/CQ-755 / C-82A-FA

Avble: 27 May 47; Acc: 31 May 47; Del: 27 Aug 47 to USAAF // 62nd TCG (TAC) McChord Field Washington 27 Aug 47; assigned 7th TCSq; depl to Fort Defiance Virginia 23 Oct 47; depl to Elmendorf AFB Alaska early 48; depl to Pope AFB North Carolina 13 Apr 48; 62nd MSU GP (TAC) McChord AFB Washington 30 Nov 48 // Fairchild Aircraft Maryland (AMC) 16 Jan 49 on bailment for mods; cvtd with tracked u/c 7 Mar 49 but not redes; retrofitted to standard u/c 19 Sep 49 // 314th TCG (CNC) Smyrna AFB Tennessee 20 Sep 49 // 61st MSU GP (AFE) Rhein-Main AB West Germany (60th Attached) 16 Dec 49 // 60th TCG (AFE) Wiesbaden AB West Germany 21 Dec 49; to 60th TCG at Rhein-Main AB West Germany 7 Jul 50 // San Antonio Air Materiel Area (AMC) Kelly AFB Texas 16 Feb 53 for depmnt. Wfu 24 Jun 53 and stored. Dropped from inventory 1 Jul 54 // FAA Files Missing → Bankers Life & Casualty Co. Chicago Illinois 7 Sep 55 reg: N5109B; subsequent history unk ← FAA Files Missing. Final Disposition: Unknown (Presumed Scrapped).

C-82A s/n: 45-57755 (msn: 10125) with the 60th TCG in Italy during 1950 (Giorgio Salerno Collection via A. Romano).

10126 / 45-57756/CQ-756 / C-82A-FA

Avble: 2 Jun 47; Acc: 2 Jun 47; Del: 25 Aug 47 to USAAF // 62nd TCG (TAC) McChord Field Washington 26 Aug 47; assigned 7th TCSq; depl to Fort Defiance Virginia 23 Oct 47; depl to Elmendorf AFB Alaska early 48 & 1 Sep 48; assigned 7th & 8th TCSq; depl to Pope AFB North Carolina 13 Apr 48; to 62nd MSU GP (TAC) McChord AFB Washington 2 Aug 48 & 20 Dec 48 // Fairchild Aircraft Maryland (AMC) 11 Feb 49 on bailment for mods; cvtd with tracked u/c 7 Mar 49 but not redes; retrofitted to standard u/c 27 Jun 49 // 314th TCG (CNC) Smyrna AFB Tennessee 27 Jun 49 // 60th TCG (AFE) Wiesbaden AB West Germany 20 Dec 49; assigned 10th TCSq; to 60th TCG at Rhein-Main AB West Germany 7 Jul 50; to 85th Air Depot WG (AFE) Rome Italy 9 Mar 51; to 85th at Erding Air Depot West Germany 11 Apr 51. Suffered an engine failure 79 miles South of Ciampino Italy 23 Mar 51, no fatalities. Had a minor ground accident at Marignane Airport France 14 Nov 51, no fatalities // San Antonio Air Materiel Area (AMC) Kelly AFB Texas 4 Mar 53 for depmnt. Wfu 24 Jun 53 and stored. Dropped from inventory 1 Jul 54 // U.S. civil owner unk reg: N75885 // Compania Mexicana de Aviacion S.A. Mexico City Mexico, 1957, reg: XA-LOK; fitted with Mexicana dorsal fillets. Earmarked for export to Bolivia Sep 60, reg: CP-694 but sale canx and reg ntu, but reg was marked on the aircraft prior to cancellation. Photographic evidence shows aircraft with CP-694 markings in 1963 // New Frontier Airlift Corp. Phoenix Arizona Oct 1962 reg: N1799 but ntu; aircraft ferried from Mexico to U.S. 18–19 Aug 67; subsequently stored at Long Beach Airport becoming derelict. Likely scrapped 1970–71; N1799 reg canx 6 Nov 75. Final Disposition: Scrapped.

10127 / 45-57757/CQ-757 / C-82A-FA

Avble: 5 Jun 47; Acc: 5 Jun 47; Del: 25 Aug 47 to USAAF // 62nd TCG (TAC) McChord Field Washington 25 Aug 47; assigned 7th TCSq; depl to Fort Defiance Virginia 23 Oct 47; depl to Elmendorf AFB Alaska early 48; depl to Pope AFB North Carolina 13 Apr 48; 62nd MSU GP (TAC) McChord AFB Washington 6 Oct 48 // Fairchild Aircraft Maryland (AMC) 22 Nov 48 on bailment for mods; cvtd with tracked u/c 7 Mar 47 // 2750th AB GP (AMC) WPAFB Ohio 12 Apr 49; redes EC-82A tracked u/c prototype 27 Apr 49; to 5064th Cold Weather Materiel Testing UT (AAC) Ladd AFB Alaska 25 Jan 50 for test and experimental duties of the tracked u/c; cvtd back to C-82A standard 12 Apr 50 // 314th TCWG (CNC) Stewart AFB Tennessee 15 May 50; assigned 2601st Light Assault SQ // Ogden Air Materiel Area (AMC) Hill AFB Utah 13 Aug 50 for project duties and depot mods. Placed in storage 3 Jan 52. Out of storage for depot mods 4 Mar 52. Wfu 21 Jan 53 and stored. Assigned to reclamation 23 Feb 54. Dropped from inventory as surplus 15 Mar 54 and scrapped. Final Disposition: Scrapped.

10128 / 45-57758/CQ-758 / C-82A-FA

Avble: 10 Jun 47; Acc: 10 Jun 47; Del: 25 Aug 47 to USAAF // 62nd TCG (TAC) McChord Field Washington 2 Sep 47; assigned 7th TCSq; depl to Fort Defiance Virginia 23 Oct 47; depl to Elmendorf AFB Alaska early 48; depl to Pope AFB North Carolina 13 Apr 48; 62nd MSU GP (TAC) McChord AFB Washington 12 Oct 48 // Fairchild Aircraft Maryland (AMC) 1 Dec 48 on bailment for mods; cvtd with tracked u/c 7 Mar 49 but not redes; retrofitted to standard u/c 2 Sep 49 // 314th TCG (CNC) Smyrna AFB Tennessee 8 Sep 49; assigned 2601st Light Assault SQ; to Ogden Air Materiel Area (AMC) Hill AFB Utah 28 Sep 49; 314th MSU GP (CNC) Smyrna AFB Tennessee 31 Jan 50; Smyrna AFB renamed Sewart AFB 25 Mar 50; depl to Laurinburg-Maxton Airport North Carolina 28 Apr 50 // Ogden Air Materiel Area (AMC) Hill AFB Utah 13 Aug 50 for project and depot mods // 60th TCWG (AFE) Rhein-Main AB West Germany 29 Jul 52 // San Antonio Air Materiel Area (AMC) Kelly AFB Texas 29 Apr 53 for depmnt. Wfu 24 Jun 53 and stored. Dropped from inventory 1 Jul 54 // Ukn operator in Mexico, date unk, reg: XB-YOA // Guest Aerovias Mexico S.A. Mexico City Mexico, date unk, reg: XA-LIK // Aerovias Condor Ltda. La Paz Bolivia, 1959, reg: CP-678. Crashed 26 Nov 60 at Santa Cruz Bolivia. Apparently the u/c was raised before the aircraft became airborne due to the first officer mistaking the pilot scratching his beard for the signal to raise the u/c, fatalities unk, nfd. Final Disposition: Accident.

10129 / 45-57759/CQ-759 / C-82A-FA

Avble: 13 Jun 47; Acc: 13 Jun 47; Del: 25 Aug 47 to USAAF // 62nd TCG (TAC) McChord Field Washington 8 Sep 47; assigned 7th TCSq; depl to Fort Defiance Virginia 23 Oct 47; depl to Elmendorf AFB Alaska early 48; depl to Pope AFB North Carolina 13 Apr 48; 62nd MSU GP (TAC) McChord AFB Washington 12 Oct 48 // Fairchild Aircraft Maryland (AMC) 10 Jan 49 on bailment for mods; cvtd with tracked u/c 7 Mar 49 but not redes; retrofitted to standard u/c 31 Aug 49 // 314th TCG (CNC) Smyrna AFB Tennessee 2 Sep 49; assigned 2601st Light Assault SQ; Smyrna AFB renamed Sewart AFB 25 Mar 50 // Ogden Air Materiel Area (AMC) Hill AFB Utah 13 Aug 50 for project duties and depot mods. Placed in storage 3 Jan 52. Out of storage for depot mods 4 Mar 52. Wfu 21 Jan 53 and stored. Assigned to reclamation 23 Feb 54. Dropped from inventory as surplus 15 Mar 54 and scrapped. Final Disposition: Scrapped.

10130 / 45-57760/CQ-760 / C-82A-FA

Avble: 18 Jun 47; Acc: 18 Jun 47; Del: 25 Aug 47 to USAAF // 62nd TCG (TAC) McChord Field Washington 25 Aug 47; assigned 7th TCSq; depl to Fort Defiance Virginia 23 Oct 47; depl to Elmendorf AFB Alaska early 48; depl to Pope AFB North Carolina 13 Apr 48; 62nd MSU GP (TAC) McChord AFB Washington 28 Oct 48 // Fairchild Aircraft Maryland (AMC) 21 Dec 48 on bailment for mods; cvtd with tracked u/c 7 Mar 49 but not redes; retrofitted to standard u/c 10 Sep 49 // 314th TCG (CNC) Smyrna AFB Tennessee 13 Sep 49; assigned 2601st Light Assault SQ; to 314th MSU GP (CNC) Smyrna AFB Tennessee 23 Jan 50. W/o at Smyrna AFB Tennessee 21 Mar 50 when a taxiing C-119B s/n: 48–326 suffered a mechanical failure and collided with the parked aircraft, no fatalities but aircraft later deemed as "damaged beyond repair." Parked C-82A s/n: 45-57752 was w/o immediately. Assigned to reclamation 20 Jun 50. Dropped from inventory 31 Jul 50. Final Disposition: Accident.

10131 / 45-57761/CQ-761 / C-82A-FA

Avble: 24 Jun 47; Acc: 24 Jun 47; Del: 10 Oct 47 to USAF // 62nd TCG (TAC) McChord AFB Washington 14 Oct 47; assigned 8th TCSq; to 62nd MSU GP (TAC) McChord AFB Washington 7 Feb 48 & 16 Dec 48; depl to Pope AFB North Carolina 13 Apr 48; depl to Elmendorf AFB Alaska 1 Sep 48 // Fairchild Aircraft Maryland (AMC) 4 Feb 48 on bailment for mods; cvtd with tracked u/c 7 Mar 49 but not redes; to 2750th AB GP (AMC) WPAFB Ohio 11 Feb 49 for experimental tests of tracked u/c; retrofitted to standard u/c 13 Jun 49 // 314th TCG (CNC) Smyrna AFB Tennessee 14 Jun 49. Had an engine failure near Smyrna AFB Tennessee 28 Jul 49, no fatalities. To 314th MSU GP (CNC) Smyrna AFB Tennessee 5 Aug 49; Smyrna AFB renamed Sewart AFB 25 Mar 50; depl to 316th TCG (CNC) Sewart AFB Tennessee 19 Sep 50 // 375th TCWG (TAC) Greenville AFB South Carolina 26 Jan 51; assigned 57th TCSq. Took off from Campbell AFB Kentucky bound for Fort Sill Oklahoma on 3 Jun 51. En route 3 miles SSW New Boston Texas the C-82A flew into a patch of severe weather resulting in structural failure of a wing sending the aircraft into the ground. Pilot: 1st Lt William Dudick and 7 other crew and passengers killed. Assigned to reclamation 3 Jun 51. Dropped from inventory 1 Nov 51. Final Disposition: Accident.

10132 / 45-57762/CQ-762 / C-82A-FA

Avble: 26 Jun 47; Acc: 26 Jun 47; Del: 21 Oct 47 to USAF // 62nd TCG (TAC) McChord AFB Washington 23 Oct 47; assigned 8th TCSq; depl to Pope AFB North Carolina 13 Apr 48; depl to Elmendorf AFB Alaska 1 Sep 48; 62nd MSU GP (CNC) McChord AFB Washington 20 Jan 49 // Fairchild Aircraft Maryland (AMC) 23 Feb 49 on bailment for mods; cvtd with tracked u/c 7 Mar 49 but not redes; retrofitted to standard u/c 21 Jun 49 // 314th TCG (CNC) Smyrna AFB Tennessee 22 Jun 49 // 61st MSU GP (AFE) Rhein-Main AB West Germany (60th Attached) 16 Dec 49 // 60th TCG (AFE) Wiesbaden AB

West Germany 20 Dec 49; to 60th TCG at Rhein-Main AB West Germany 7 Jul 50; to 7th RES SQ (AFE) Wiesbaden AB West Germany 6 Nov 50; not likely cvtd to SC-82A due to such a short assignment, back to the 60th TCG 8 Nov 50; to 80th Air Depot WG (AFE) Nouasseur AB French Morocco 1 Mar 52 for depmnt // To San Antonio Air Materiel Area (AMC) Kelly AFB Texas 26 Feb 53 for depmnt. Wfu 24 Jun 53 and stored. Dropped from inventory 1 Jul 54 // Unconfirmed Data →History unk from this point. Photographic evidence shows this airframe derelict at Miami Intl. Airport in the late 1960s crudely marked as "N74047" but there's no record to show this registration was ever transferred to this airframe. "N47047" was assigned to C-82A 10056/44-23012. Who applied this reg to this aircraft and why remains a mystery. ← Unconfirmed Data. The airframe was then acquired by the George T. Baker Aviation School Miami Intl. Airport Florida from 1971 to 1974 as an unregistered hulk for technical instruction. Final Disposition: Unknown (Presumed Scrapped).

C-82A s/n: 45-57762 (msn: 10132) derelict in Miami, Florida, in the late 1960s. Its past history is somewhat of a mystery, as no civil records or known registrations seem to exist (John Wegg Collection).

10133 / 45-57763/CQ-763 / C-82A-FA

Avble: 3 Jul 47; Acc: 3 Jul 47; Del: 21 Oct 47 to USAF // 62nd TCG (TAC) McChord AFB Washington 26 Oct 47; assigned 4th TCSq; depl to Elmendorf AFB Alaska 1 Apr 48 // Fairchild Aircraft Maryland (AMC) 31 Aug 48 on bailment for mods; cvtd with tracked u/c 7 Mar 49 but not redes // 314th TCG (CNC) Smyrna AFB Tennessee 15 Mar 49; assigned 2601st Light Assault SQ; to 314th MSU GP (CNC) Smyrna AFB Tennessee 17 Jun 49 & 31 Jan 50. Retrofitted back to standard u/c late 1949. Smyrna AFB renamed Sewart AFB 25 Mar 50; depl to Laurinburg-Maxton Airport North Carolina 26 Apr 50 // Ogden Air Materiel Area (AMC) Hill AFB Utah 13 Aug 50 for project // 54th TCSq (AAC) Elmendorf AFB Alaska 13 Jun 51 // 39th Air Depot WG (AAC) Elmendorf AFB

Alaska 15 Apr 52 // 5039th Maintenance GP (AAC) Elmendorf AFB Alaska 13 Apr 53 for project; to 5025th Maintenance GP (renamed 5039th MNT GP) (AAC) Elmendorf AFB Alaska 1 Jul 53. Had a mechanical failure 50 miles S North Bay Canada 2 Feb 54, no fatalities // Wfu to Ogden Air Materiel Area (AMC) Hill AFB Utah 6 Feb 54 and stored. Dropped from inventory 8 Jul 54 // Whitney-Ben Trading Co. Calexico California 17 Aug 55 reg: N4830V // Truman E. Miley of Roy Utah 17 Aug 55; cvtd to sprayer aircraft 29 May 56 with four 675 U.S. gal tanks in hold and associated spray equipment; all fabric control surfaces re-skinned 29 Oct 56; modified both heat-exchanger tail pipes 16 Apr 57; R-2800-34W engines installed with water-injection 15 May 59; spray equipment removed 26 Jan 60 and cvtd to aerial tanker with four 400 U.S. gal tanks for trials with the U.S. Forest Service but was never called on for any operational service; tank system modified 16 Aug 60 // Big Piney Aviation Inc. Big Piney Wyoming 7 Jan 61; fabric control surfaces re-skinned 18 Jun 62 // Trans-Peruana de Aviacion S.A. Lima Peru Jul 64 reg: OB-T-749. U.S. reg canx 20 Jul 64; subsequent history unk, wfu 1967; noted as bku at Tarapoto Lima. Final Disposition: Scrapped.

Peruvian C-82A Packet OB-T-749 (msn: 10133) of Trans-Peruana De Aviacion while in for maintenance in Miami, Florida, sometime between 1964 and 1967 (Peter J. Marson Collection).

10134 / 45-57764/CQ-764 / C-82A-FA

Avble: 8 Jul 47; Acc: 8 Jul 47; Del: 24 Oct 47 to USAF // 62nd TCG (TAC) McChord AFB Washington 27 Oct 47; assigned 4th TCSq; depls to Elmendorf AFB Alaska 1 Apr 48 & 30 Nov 48; depl to Fort Richardson Alaska 20 Dec 48; 62nd MSU GP (CNC) McChord AFB Washington 28 Jan 49 // Fairchild Aircraft Maryland (AMC) 25 Feb 49 on bailment for mods; cvtd with tracked u/c 7 Mar 49 but not redes; retrofitted to standard u/c 13 Jun 49 // 314th TCG (CNC) Smyrna AFB Tennessee 13 Jun 49 // 61st MSU GP (AFE) Rhein-Main AB West Germany (60th Attached) 16 Dec 49 // 60th TCG (AFE) Wiesbaden AB West Germany 21 Dec 49; to 60th TCG at Rhein-Main AB West Germany 7 Jul 50; assigned 12th TCSq; depl to 61st TCWG (AFE) Rhein-Main AB West Germany (60th Attached) 16 Apr 51. Had a taxiing accident at Landstuhl AB West Germany 9 Aug

52, no fatalities // San Antonio Air Materiel Area (AMC) Kelly AFB Texas 16 Feb 53 for depmnt. Wfu 24 Jun 53 and stored. Dropped from inventory 1 Jul 54 // Smock & Jenner Inc. Cincinnati Ohio 16 Aug 55 reg: N74039 // Ben Epstein, Trustee for Ben, Leonard and Stanley W. Epstein (Aeronautical Cargo Co.) Miami Beach Florida 29 Dec 55 // Henry A. Smith Richmond California 24 May 61 // New Frontier Airlift Corp. Berkeley California 1 May 63—purchased for Steward-Davis Jet-Packet program but no buyers or conversion work carried out. One of eight C-82A derelicts for Fairchild-Hiller Corp. Maryland; reg: N6781A rsved 1967 but ntu. N74039 reg revoked 5 Feb 71. Final Disposition: Scrapped.

10135 / 45-57765/Q-765 / C-82A-FA

Avble: 14 Jul 47; Acc: 14 Jul 47; Del: 23 Oct 47 to USAF // 62nd TCG (TAC) McChord AFB Washington 27 Oct 47; assigned 4th TCSq; depls to Elmendorf AFB Alaska 1 Apr 48 & 30 Nov 48; depl to Fort Richardson Alaska 20 Dec 48. Had a landing accident due to mechanical failure at Elmendorf AFB Alaska 19 Feb 49, no fatalities. To Alaska Air Lines Air Depot (AAC) Elmendorf AFB Alaska 24 Feb 49 for repairs; to 57th MSU GP (AAC) Elmendorf AFB Alaska 13 Jun 49; 62nd MSU GP (CNC) McChord AFB Washington 15 Sep 49 // 61st MSU GP (AFE) Rhein-Main AB West Germany (60th Attached) 20 Oct 49 // 60th TCG (AFE) Wiesbaden AB West Germany 27 Oct 49; to 60th TCG at Rhein-Main AB West Germany 7 Jul 50; depl to 61st TCWG (AFE) Rhein-Main AB West Germany (60th Attached) 9 Apr 51 // San Antonio Air Materiel Area (AMC) Kelly AFB Texas 14 Apr 53 for depmnt. Wfu 24 Jun 53 and stored. Dropped from inventory 1 Jul 54 // Bankers Life & Casualty Co. Chicago Illinois 7 Sep 55 reg: N5108B // Fuzzy Furlong Miami Florida 1959, sold for scrap; de-reg 25 Jan 71. Final Disposition: Scrapped.

10136 / 45-57766/CQ-766 / C-82A-FA

Avble: 18 Jul 47; Acc: 18 Jul 47; Del: 22 Oct 47 to USAF // 62nd TCG (TAC) McChord AFB Washington 22 Oct 47; assigned 4th TCSq. Had a landing accident due to mechanical failure at Lockbourne Field Ohio 22 Oct 47 while on its delivery flight, no fatalities. To 4000th AF BAS (AMC) Patterson Field Ohio 27 Oct 47; to 4136th AF BAS (AMC) Tinker AFB Oklahoma 15 Nov 47; depl to Pope AFB North Carolina 13 Apr 48; multiple assignments to 62nd MSU GP (TAC) McChord AFB Washington starting 22 Jul 48; briefly to Pasadena California 27 Aug 48; depls to Elmendorf AFB Alaska 1 Sep 48 & 6 Jun 49; assigned 8th TCSq // 61st MSU GP (AFE) Rhein-Main AB West Germany (60th Attached) 25 Oct 49 // 60th TCG (AFE) Wiesbaden AB West Germany 27 Oct 49; assigned 10th TCSq; to 60th TCG at Rhein-Main AB West Germany 7 Jul 50. Had a minor taxiing accident at RAF Burtonwood England 15 Aug 50, possibly collided with C-82A s/n: 45-57796, no fatalities // San Antonio Air Materiel Area (AMC) Kelly AFB Texas 7 Mar 53 // 314th TCWG (TAC) Sewart AFB Tennessee 17 Mar 53 // San Antonio Air Materiel Area (AMC) Kelly AFB Texas 12 Apr 53 for depmnt. Wfu 24 Jun 53 and stored. Dropped from inventory 1 Jul 54 // U.S. civil owner unk reg: N75886 // Compania Mexicana de Aviacion S.A. Mexico City Mexico, 1957, reg: XA-LOL; fitted with Mexicana dorsal fillets. Earmarked for export to Bolivia Sep 60, reg: CP-693 but sale canx and reg ntu, but it was marked on aircraft // New Frontier Airlift Corp. Phoenix Arizona Oct 62 reg: N93067 but ntu; assigned N93068 but reg never applied to the aircraft itself; ferried from Mexico to the

U.S. 30–31 Oct 62 // Steward-Davis Inc. Long Beach California 7 Oct 64. Photographic evidence shows the C-82A was stored at Long Beach in Mexicana livery but with Bolivian "CP-693" reg and subsequently became derelict, the engines were eventually removed and sold. Derelict airframe moved off-airport 1970; scrapped by mid–1972. Deregistered 9 Jun 75. Final Disposition: Scrapped.

C-82A XA-LOL (msn: 10136) prior to delivery to Compania Mexicana de Aviacion S.A. It appears the aircraft is covered in oil for preservation purposes (José Villela G.).

10137 / 45-57767/CQ-767 / C-82A-FA

Avble: 23 Jul 47; Acc: 23 Jul 47; Del: 20 Oct 47 to USAF // 62nd TCG (TAC) McChord AFB Washington 26 Oct 47; assigned 8th TCSq; to 1455th AF BAS (ATC) East Base Field Montana 13 Jan 48; depl to Pope AFB North Carolina 13 Apr 48; depls to Elmendorf AFB Alaska 1 Sep 48 & 6 Jun 49; to 5020th AB GP (AAC) Davis AFB Alaska 10 Jun 49; 62nd MSU GP (CNC) McChord AFB Washington 29 Sep 49 // 61st MSU GP (AFE) Rhein-Main AB West Germany (60th Attached) 20 Oct 49 // 60th TCG (AFE) Wiesbaden AB West Germany 29 Oct 49; to 60th TCG at Rhein-Main AB West Germany 7 Jul 50; depl to 61st TCWG (AFE) Rhein-Main AB West Germany (60th Attached) 14 May 51; to 85th Air Depot WG (AFE) Erding AB West Germany 31 Mar 52 for depmnt // San Antonio Air Materiel Area (AMC) Kelly AFB Texas 8 Mar 53 // Aircraft Engineering & Maintenance Co. (AMC) Oakland California 17 Apr 53 on bailment, modernized to Group A standard // 501st Air Defense GP (ADC) O'Hare Int. Airport Illinois 1 Aug 53; to Oklahoma Air Materiel Area (AMC) Tinker AFB Oklahoma 16 Mar 54 & 1 Apr 54; to Northern Air Materiel Area (AMC) Inglewood California 11 Jun 54; to 3345th Technical Training WG (TC) Chanute AFB Illinois 1 Nov 54 // Wfu to 3040th Aircraft Storage SQ (AMC) Davis-Monthan AFB Arizona 18 Feb 55 and stored. Dropped from inventory 1 Aug 55 // Montgomery Construction Co. Grove City Pennsylvania 26 Oct 55 reg: N4962V; all control surfaces re-skinned 21 Dec 55 // Minerales Y Metales S.A. Lima Peru 10 Apr 57 reg: OB-LHF-508. U.S. reg canx 27 Mar 58; lease to Expreso Aereo Peruano S.A. (EAPSA) Lima Peru 14 Jan 59; re-reg: OB-UAD-508. Proposed export to Bolivia 1959 but canx, reg: CP-634 ntu. Abandoned at Chiclayo Airport Peru in 1963; gone by Jul 66; reg canx 28 Aug 73. Final Disposition: Unknown (Presumed Scrapped).

10138 / 45-57768/CQ-768 / C-82A-FA

Avble: 29 Jul 47; Acc: 29 Jul 47; Del: 27 Oct 47 to USAF // 62nd TCG (TAC) McChord AFB Washington 27 Oct 47; assigned 8th TCSq; depl to Pope AFB North Carolina 13 Apr 48; depls to Elmendorf AFB Alaska 1 Sep 48 & 6 Jun 49; to 62nd MSU GP (CNC) McChord AFB Washington 6 May 49 & 29 Sep 49 // 61st MSU GP (AFE) Rhein-Main AB West Germany (60th Attached) 21 Oct 49 // 60th TCG (AFE) Wiesbaden AB West Germany 24 Dec 49; to 60th TCG at Rhein-Main AB West Germany 7 Jul 50 // San Antonio Air Materiel Area (AMC) Kelly AFB Texas 5 May 53 // 1631st AB SQ (MATS) RAF Prestwick Scotland 8 May 53 // 7559th Maintenance Depot GP (AFE) Burtonwood Air Depot England 6 Jan 54. Had an accident around mid–1954 in England; exact location, cause and fatalities are unk. Assigned to reclamation and salvage 20 Jul 54. Dropped from inventory 4 Oct 54. Final Disposition: Accident.

10139 / 45-57769/CQ-769 / C-82A-FA

C-119 prototype. Cvtd on production line as XB-82B with fuselage redesign and upgraded radial engines. ff: 17 Dec 47 as XC-119A (Model 105A) prototype; retained by Fairchild Aircraft Corp. for flight tests through AMC // Avble & Acc for USAF service: 24 May 48; Del: 14 Jun 48 to USAF des C-119A. Redes EC-119A 11 Feb 49 for ECM tests with Fairchild through AMC // 3345th Technical Training WG (TC) Chanute AFB Illinois 18 Jan 51 as a mock-up airframe. Dropped from inventory 2 Dec 51 due to "abnormal deterioration in use." Final Disposition: Scrapped.

C-82A s/n: 45-57769 (msn: 10139) was modified into the XC-119A with a new fuselage design and upgraded engines, among other improvements (National Museum of the United States Air Force).

10140 / 45-57770/CQ-770 / C-82A-FA

Avble: 31 Jul 47; Acc: 31 Jul 47; Del: 20 Oct 47 to USAF // 62nd TCG (TAC) McChord AFB Washington 25 Oct 47; assigned 4th TCSq; multiple depls to Elmendorf AFB Alaska starting 1 Apr 48; to 57th MSU GP (AAC) Elmendorf AFB Alaska 22 Jun 48; assignments to 62nd MSU GP (TAC) McChord AFB Washington 19 Oct 48 & 3 Oct 49; depl to Fort

Richardson Alaska 20 Dec 48. Appears in a 1950 USAF documentary titled *Survival in the Arctic Tundra*, produced as a survival guide for USAF crews // 61st MSU GP (AFE) Rhein-Main AB West Germany (60th Attached) 18 Jan 50 // 60th TCG (AFE) Wiesbaden AB West Germany 18 Jan 50; to 60th TCG at Rhein-Main AB West Germany 31 Jul 50; depl to 61st TCWG (AFE) Rhein-Main AB West Germany (60th Attached) 30 Apr 51 // Assigned 2753rd AST SQ at Pyote in error. San Antonio Air Materiel Area (AMC) Kelly AFB Texas 30 Jan 53 for depmnt. Wfu 24 Jun 53 and stored. Dropped from inventory 1 Jul 54 // Bankers Life & Casualty Co. Chicago Illinois 7 Sep 55 reg: N5107B // Fuzzy Furlong Miami Florida 1959, sold for scrap; de-reg 25 Jan 71. Final Disposition: Scrapped.

10141 / 45-57771/CQ-771 / C-82A-FA

Avble: 7 Aug 47; Acc: 22 Aug 47; Del: 27 Oct 47 to USAF // 62nd TCG (TAC) McChord AFB Washington 27 Oct 47; assigned 8th TCSq; depl to Pope AFB North Carolina 13 Apr 48; depls to Elmendorf AFB Alaska 1 Sep 48 & 27 Jun 49; assignments to 62nd MSU GP (CNC) McChord AFB Washington 11 May 49 & 29 Sep 49 // 61st MSU GP (AFE) Rhein-Main AB West Germany (60th Attached) 20 Oct 49 // 60th TCG (AFE) Wiesbaden AB West Germany 27 Oct 49; to 60th TCG at Rhein-Main AB West Germany 7 Jul 50 // San Antonio Air Materiel Area (AMC) Kelly AFB Texas 13 May 53 // 6603rd AB GP (NEAC) Goose Bay AB Labrador Canada 20 May 53 for mnt // San Antonio Air Materiel Area (AMC) Kelly AFB Texas 26 May 53 for depmnt. Wfu 24 Jun 53 and stored. Dropped from inventory 1 Jul 54 // Leeward Aeronautical Inc. Fort Wayne Indiana 15 Aug 55 reg: N7853B; Albert J. Leeward Miami Florida 23 Feb 56; ownership transferred to Leeward Aeronautical Sales Inc. Miami Florida same day; cert of reg issued 2 May 57 // Francis L. Duncan Rockville Maryland 5 Jun 57 for export // Servicos Aereos Cruzeiro do Sul Rio de Janeiro Brazil 17 Dec 57; arrived in Brazil 23 Dec 57; reg: PP-CEG 28 Aug 58. Wfu 30 Jun 65 and stored at Santos-Dumont Airport Rio de Janeiro Brazil. PP-CEG reg canx 25 Oct 65. Bku Dec 65. N7853B reg canx 23 Nov 70. Final Disposition: Scrapped.

10142 / 45-57772/CQ-772 / C-82A-FA

Some parts of this IARC indecipherable. Avble: 12 Aug 47; Acc: 22 Aug 47; Del: 27 Oct 47 to USAF // 62nd TCG (TAC) McChord AFB Washington 27 Oct 47; assigned 4th TCSq; depls to Elmendorf AFB Alaska 1 Apr 48 & 30 Nov 48; depl to Fort Richardson Alaska 20 Dec 48; to Sacramento Air Materiel Area (AMC) McClellan AFB California 18 Jul 49 for depmnt; to 57th MSU GP (AAC) Elmendorf AFB Alaska 22 Sep 49; to Alaska Air Lines Air Depot (AAC) Elmendorf AFB Alaska 6 Oct 49 for depmnt; 62nd MSU GP (CNC) McChord AFB Washington 24 Oct 49 // 61st MSU GP (AFE) Rhein-Main AB West Germany (60th Attached) 18 Jan 50 & 24 Jul 50; 60th TCG (AFE) Wiesbaden AB West Germany 18 Jan 50; assigned 12th TCSq; depl to 61st TCWG (AFE) Rhein-Main AB West Germany (60th Attached) 23 Jun 50; to Warner-Robins Air Materiel Area (AMC) Robins AFB Georgia 29 Sep 50 for depmnt; to 60th TCG at Rhein-Main AB West Germany 7 Mar 51. Aircraft ran out of fuel 30 miles SW Chaumont France 16 Jan 53. Pilot: Leland D. Albright and five other crew bailed out, the aircraft was destroyed on impact. Assigned to reclamation 16 Jan 53. Final Disposition: Accident.

10143 / 45-57773/CQ-773 / C-82A-FA

Avble: 15 Aug 47; Acc: 22 Aug 47; Del: 27 Oct 47 to USAF // 62nd TCG (TAC) McChord AFB Washington 27 Oct 47; assigned 4th TCSq; multiple depls to Elmendorf AFB Alaska starting 1 Apr 48; depl to Fort Richardson Alaska 20 Dec 48; 62nd MSU GP (CNC) McChord AFB Washington 13 Oct 49 // 60th TCG (AFE) Rhein-Main AB West Germany 3 Feb 50; depl to Wiesbaden AB West Germany 30 Mar 50; depl to 61st TCWG (AFE) Rhein-Main AB West Germany (60th Attached) 30 Apr 51 // San Antonio Air Materiel Area (AMC) Kelly AFB Texas 16 Feb 53 for depmnt. Wfu 28 Jun 53 and stored. Dropped from inventory 1 Jul 54 // Bankers Life & Casualty Co. Chicago Illinois 7 Sep 55 reg: N5106B; subsequent history unk; might have been exported. Listed as scrapped and reg canx 8 Oct 70. Final Disposition: Unknown (Presumed Scrapped).

10144 / 45-57774/CQ-774 / C-82A-FA

Avble: 21 Aug 47; Acc: 26 Aug 47; Del: 27 Oct 47 to USAF // 62nd TCG (TAC) McChord AFB Washington 31 Oct 47; assigned 8th TCSq; to 62nd MSU GP (TAC) McChord AFB Washington 5 Apr 48 & 6 Sep 49 // depl to Elmendorf AFB Alaska 1 Sep 48 & 6 Jun 49; to 1050th MSU GP (HQC) Andrews AFB Maryland 27 Apr 49 for mnt // 60th TCG (AFE) Rhein-Main AB West Germany 14 Oct 49; assigned 12th TCSq; depl to 61st MSU GP (AFE) Rhein-Main AB West Germany (60th Attached) 20 Oct 49. Had a minor taxiing accident at RAF Molesworth England 25 Jun 51, no fatalities // San Antonio Air Materiel Area (AMC) Kelly AFB Texas 25 Feb 53 for depmnt. Wfu 24 Jun 53 and stored. Dropped from inventory 1 Jul 54 // Leeward Aeronautical Sales Inc. Fort Wayne Indiana 1955–56 reg unk // Jose Balbi Montevideo Uruguay 10 Apr 56 reg: CX-AQA // Lorenzo Castelluci Uruguay, 1956 // Aerovias Monder Montevideo Uruguay, 1956 // Fran-

C-82A PP-CEE (msn: 10144) in retirement as the short-lived Hangar's Bar in Rio de Janeiro (Martin Bernsmuller [AeroMuseum]).

cis L. Duncan Rockville Maryland 1957 reg unk, for export // Servicos Aereos Cruzeiro do Sul Rio de Janeiro Brazil 11 Jul 57; arrived in Brazil 20 Jul 57; named *Hercules*; reg: PP-CEE 27 Aug 58. Wfu 30 Jun 65 and stored at Santos-Dumont Airport Rio de Janeiro Brazil; reg canx 29 Oct 65. Entire aircraft transferred to the Barra da Tijuca district in Rio de Janeiro Jul 66 and cvtd into a nightclub named Hangar's Bar. On the menu were such cocktails as "looping," "landing," "departure," "engine trouble," etc. Removed and bku 10 Dec 66. Final Disposition: Scrapped.

10145 / 45-57775/CQ-775 / C-82A-FA

Avble: 25 Aug 47; Acc: 26 Aug 47; Del: 22 Oct 47 to USAF // 62nd TCG (TAC) McChord AFB Washington 28 Oct 47; assigned 8th TCSq; depl to Pope AFB North Carolina 13 Apr 48; depls to Elmendorf AFB Alaska 1 Sep 48 & 6 Jun 49; 62nd MSU GP (CNC) McChord AFB Washington 1 Sep 49 // 61st MSU GP (AFE) Rhein-Main AB West Germany (60th Attached) 20 Oct 49 // 60th TCG (AFE) Wiesbaden AB West Germany 27 Oct 49; to 60th TCG at Rhein-Main AB West Germany 7 Jul 50 // San Antonio Air Materiel Area (AMC) Kelly AFB Texas 10 Apr 53 for depmnt. Wfu 24 Jun 53 and stored. Dropped from inventory 1 Jul 54 // Bankers Life & Casualty Co. Chicago Illinois 7 Sep 55 reg: N5105B // Unconfirmed Data → Aerovias Monder Montevideo Uruguay, 1956, reg: CX-AQB; appears to have been imported back into the U.S. in 1957 and stored ← Unconfirmed Data // Fuzzy Furlong Miami Florida 1959, sold for scrap; de-reg 25 Jan 71. Final Disposition: Scrapped.

10146 / 45-57776/CQ-776 / C-82A-FA

Avble: 28 Aug 47; Acc: 29 Aug 47; Del: 23 Oct 47 to USAF // 62nd TCG (TAC) McChord AFB Washington 31 Oct 47; assigned 4th TCSq; depl to Elmendorf AFB Alaska 1 Apr 48; to 62nd MSU GP (TAC) McChord AFB Washington 19 Sep 48 & 10 Feb 50; to Sacramento Air Materiel Area (AMC) McClellan AFB California 27 Jan 49 for depmnt // 325th Fighter (All-Weather) WG (CNC) McChord AFB Washington 5 May 50 // 1226th AB GP (MATS) Ernest Harmon AFB Newfoundland Canada 19 May 50 // 6602nd AB

C-82A s/n: 45-57776 (msn: 10146). Note the lineup of B-25 Mitchells in the background (National Museum of the United States Air Force).

WG (NEAC) Ernest Harmon AFB Newfoundland Canada 2 Nov 50; multiple assignments to 6603rd AB WG (NEAC) Goose Bay AB Labrador Canada starting 4 Dec 51 // 6622nd Air Transport SQ (NEAC) Ernest Harmon AFB Newfoundland Canada 18 Aug 52 // 64th TCWG (TAC) Donaldson AFB South Carolina 29 Oct 52 // Wfu to San Antonio Air Materiel Area (AMC) Kelly AFB Texas 5 Aug 53 and stored. Dropped from inventory 1 Jul 54 // Bankers Life & Casualty Co. Chicago Illinois 7 Sep 55 reg: N5104B // Fuzzy Furlong Miami Florida 1959, sold for scrap; de-reg 25 Jan 71. Final Disposition: Scrapped.

10147 / 45-57777/CQ-777 / C-82A-FA

Avble: 29 Aug 47; Acc: 29 Aug 47; Del: 23 Oct 47 to USAF // 62nd TCG (TAC) McChord AFB Washington 26 Oct 47; assigned 8th TCSq; depl to Pope AFB North Carolina 13 Apr 48; depls to Elmendorf AFB Alaska 1 Sep 48 & 6 Jun 49; to Sacramento Air Materiel Area (AMC) McClellan AFB California 18 Mar 49; 62nd MSU GP (CNC) McChord AFB Washington 17 Oct 49 // 61st MSU GP (AFE) Rhein-Main AB West Germany (60th Attached) 18 Jan 50 // 60th TCG (AFE) Wiesbaden AB West Germany 18 Jan 50; to 60th TCG at Rhein-Main AB West Germany 7 Jul 50; to 85th Air Depot WG (AFE) Erding AB West Germany 1 Mar 51 for depmnt // San Antonio Air Materiel Area (AMC) Kelly AFB Texas 2 Apr 53 // Aircraft Engineering & Maintenance Co. (AMC) Oakland California 5 May 53 on bailment; modernized to Group A standard // 521st Air Defense GP (CAD) Sioux City MAP Iowa 9 Feb 54; to 3320th Technical Training WG (TC) Amarillo AFB Texas 3 Mar 54 for tranmnt; to Ogden Air Materiel Area (AMC) Hill AFB Utah 24 Jul 54 for tranmnt; depl to 314th TCWG (TAC) Sewart AFB Tennessee 19 Aug 54; to 4901st AB WG (ARD) Kirtland AFB New Mexico 8 Feb 55 for tranmnt // Wfu to 3040th Aircraft Storage SQ (AMC) Davis-Monthan AFB Arizona 14 Mar 55 and stored. Dropped from inventory 1 Aug 55 // FAA Files Missing → Leeward Aeronautical Sales Inc. Miami Florida 9 Mar 56 reg: N7856B // likely to Francis L. Duncan 1957 for export ← FAA Files Missing // Servicos Aereos Cruzeiro do Sul Rio de Janeiro Brazil 19 Aug 57; arrived in Brazil 19 Aug 57; named *Atlas*; reg: PP-CEK 25 Sep 58. Cvtd to Steward-Davis Jet-Packet 1600 with J30-W Jet-Pak. Left main u/c failed to lower due to hydraulic failure on approach to Recife Intl. Airport Brazil 25 Jul 62, no fatalities and aircraft repaired and remained operational until the end of 1971 // Aero Inca Ltda. Bolivia 16 Jun 72; reg: CP-983 1 Jul 72, ferried to Bolivia and stored; reg PP-CEK canx 11 Jul 72. Minor accident at La Paz Bolivia 1 Sep 72, no fatalities and aircraft repaired. Reg to Gonzalo Sanchez de Losada (Aero Inca Ltda. owner) 4 Apr 73; named *Kyle*. Lease to Sociedad Agropecuaria Tohomonoco Ltda. with Tohomonoco marked on aircraft // Lineas Aereas Canedo (LAC) Bolivia 7 Jun 76; named *Mobby-Dick* [sic] with a new red striped livery. On one flight from Santa Cruz up to Cochabamba, company owner and pilot Rolando Canedo Lopez found the aircraft to be very sluggish on take-off, and in the climb, due to a heavy drilling pump which had brought the C-82 up to its maximum weight. On arrival the load sheets were rechecked and it was found the max weight had been 22,000 lb instead of 16,500 lb! // Captain Jose Villaroel Bolivia a/d/b Transportes Aereos Itinez 4 Nov 76. On 27 Jan 77 at San Ramon Airport Bolivia CP-983 was scheduled for take-off carrying 11,000 lb of meat product. A suspected port engine failure during the take-off roll caused the aircraft to veer off the runway but it then continued its take-off along the grass parallel to it. The aircraft barely became airborne when the u/c struck a parked tractor beyond the end of the runway. The C-82 flipped over and crashed on its back at high speed, killing the four crew and two passengers; the pilot was Captain Jose Villaroel himself. Although engine failure was the suspected cause of the crash, it was also found the C-82 was overloaded for the existing conditions, which would have labored the aircraft's climb performance even more. This is both the last crash and last fatal crash of the C-82 aircraft overall. Final Disposition: Accident.

Brazilian C-82A PP-CEK (msn: 10147) was Servicos Aereos Cruzeiro do Sul's only C-82 to be converted to a Jet-Packet 1600. This aircraft later went to Bolivia as CP-983 (Martin Bernsmuller [Aero-Museum]).

10148 / 45-57778/CQ-778 / C-82A-FA

Avble: 8 Sep 47; Acc: 9 Sep 47; Del: 20 Oct 47 to USAF // 62nd TCG (TAC) McChord AFB Washington 26 Oct 47; assigned 8th TCSq; depl to Pope AFB North Carolina 13 Apr 48; depls to Elmendorf AFB Alaska 1 Sep 48 & 9 Jun 49; to Sacramento Air Materiel Area (AMC) McClellan AFB California 18 Mar 49; to 62nd MSU GP (CNC) McChord AFB Washington 31 May 49 & 29 Sep 49 // 61st MSU GP (AFE) Rhein-Main AB West Germany (60th Attached) 25 Oct 49 // 60th TCG (AFE) Rhein-Main AB West Germany 8 Nov 49 // San Antonio Air Materiel Area (AMC) Kelly AFB Texas 3 Apr 53 for depmnt. Wfu 24 Jun 53 and stored. Dropped from inventory 1 Jul 54 // Bankers Life & Casualty Co. Chicago Illinois 7 Sep 55 reg: N5103B; subsequent history unk. Listed as scrapped and reg canx 8 Oct 70 but may have been exported. Final Disposition: Unknown (Presumed Scrapped).

10149 / 45-57779/CQ-779 / C-82A-FA

Avble: 11 Sep 47; Acc: 17 Sep 47; Del: 24 Oct 47 to USAF // 62nd TCG (TAC) McChord AFB Washington 27 Oct 47; assigned 4th TCSq; depls to Elmendorf AFB Alaska 1 Apr 48 & 30 Nov 48; depl to Fort Richardson Alaska 20 Dec 48. Made a crash-landing due to mechanical failure 1 mile S Fort Nelson Canada 23 Dec 48. Pilot: Walter M. Pickett, no fatalities but aircraft deemed as "damaged beyond repair" // 57th MSU GP (AAC) Elmendorf AFB Alaska 24 Dec 48, assigned for reclamation and salvage. Assigned to reclamation 25 Jul 49. Dropped from inventory 20 Sep 49. Final Disposition: Accident.

10150 / 45-57780/CQ-780 / C-82A-FA

Avble: 15 Sep 47; Acc: 22 Sep 47; Del: 27 Oct 47 to USAF // 62nd TCG (TAC) McChord AFB Washington 27 Oct 47; assigned 8th TCSq; depl to Pope AFB North Carolina 13 Apr 48; depls to Elmendorf AFB Alaska 1 Sep 48 & 6 Jun 49; to 62nd MSU GP (CNC) McChord AFB Washington 7 & 29 Sep 49 // 61st MSU GP (AFE) Rhein-Main AB West Germany (60th Attached) 20 Oct 49 // 60th TCG (AFE) Wiesbaden AB West Germany 29 Oct 49; assigned 12th TCSq; to 60th TCG at Rhein-Main AB West Germany 7 Jul 50. Had a belly crash-landing due to mechanical failure at Marignane Airport 13 miles NW Marseille France 17 Jan 53, no fatalities // 73rd Air Depot WG (AFE) Chateauroux-Deols AB France 20 Jan 53 for repairs & depmnt // San Antonio Air Materiel Area (AMC) Kelly AFB Texas 25 Sep 53 // Wfu to Ogden Air Materiel Area (AMC) Hill AFB Utah 6 Feb 54 and stored. Dropped from inventory 8 Jul 54 // FAA Files Incomplete → Owner unk 27 Sep 55 reg N6236C; reg canx 5 Oct 55 ← FAA Files Incomplete. Dispatch Services Inc. Miami Florida, purchase date unk, reg: N54210 24 Oct 55 // Expreso Aereo Panama S.A., Panama 31 Jan 56 reg: HP-219. This company appears to be the parent company to Peru-based Expreso Aereo Peruano, apparently HP-219 reg ntu but photographic evidence shows it applied to aircraft, maybe for ferrying purposes // Compania Aerea Mercantil S.A. (CAMSA) Peru 7 Feb 56 reg: OB-TAI-438 // Expreso Aereo Peruano S.A. (EAPSA) Lima Peru 28 May 56; re-reg: OB-WAE-438 13 Mar 57; re-reg: OB-UAA-438 28 Sep 57. Damaged on landing when left main u/c failed to extend at Puero Barrios, Guatemala 3 Dec 58, aircraft repaired // Empresa Guatemalteca de Aviacion (Aviateca Guatemalteca) Guatemala 19 Feb 59 reg: TG-AYA; had been leased since 1957; served in Guatemala up to 1960; de-reg: 18 Oct 1961 // Air Agency Inc. Miami Florida 27 Mar 61 reg: N74810; sold back into the U.S. via Expreso Aereo Panama S.A., Panama. Lease to Minneapolis-Honeywell Regulator Co. for flight testing of inertial navigation equipment 15 Jun 61 // Esso Standard (Guatemala) Inc. Wilmington Delaware 7 Feb 62; re-reg: N127E 7 Mar 62;

A very rare photograph of C-82A N127E (msn: 10150) flying out of Sharjah, UAE, in January 1968. Shortly afterwards this C-82 and Mecom's Douglas B-23 (N86E) were flown to Athens, Greece, as technical training aids (Jock Manson).

Ex-Mecom Oil Company C-82A N127E (msn: 10150) in use as a ground training aid at Athens, Greece, in April 1973 (John Wegg).

flight-tested with JATO rockets plus engine & avionics upgrades 4 Apr 62 // John W. Mecom Houston Texas 24 Jul 63; nav & avionics upgrade 9 Aug 63; stabilizer wing tips removed date unk. Based out of Aden, Yemen, from 1964 in support of Mecom Oil Co.'s activities in the Middle East. Operations with N127E ceased around early 1968 and the aircraft, along with a derelict Mecom Douglas B-23 reg: N86E (msn: 2745), was flown to Athens, Greece, during this period and stored; de-reg: 6 Sep 72 // Donated to Delta Technical & Business School Athens Greece Apr 74 for use as an instructional airframe in training aircraft technicians. The C-82A remained at the school for over 12 years before being removed in 1986 and bku. Final Disposition: Scrapped.

10151 / 45-57781/CQ-781 / C-82A-FA

Avble: 17 Sep 47; Acc: 26 Sep 47; Del: 27 Oct 47 to USAF // 62nd TCG (TAC) McChord AFB Washington 28 Oct 47; assigned 4th TCSq; depls to Elmendorf AFB Alaska 1 Apr 48 & 30 Nov 48; depl to Fort Richardson Alaska 20 Dec 48; to 62nd MSU GP (CNC) McChord AFB Washington 18 Jul 49 & 13 Oct 49 // 61st MSU GP (AFE) Rhein-Main AB West Germany (60th Attached) 15 Jan 50 // 60th TCG (AFE) Wiesbaden AB West Germany 18 Jan 50; assigned 12th TCSq; to 60th TCG at Rhein-Main AB West Germany 7 Jul 50. Experienced a take-off accident due to mechanical failure at Mezzeh AB Damascus Syria 20 Jan 51. Pilot: Peter C. Reed, no fatalities but aircraft w/o. Assigned to reclamation 22 Jan 51. Dropped from inventory 24 Jul 51. Final Disposition: Accident.

10152 / 45-57782/CQ-782 / C-82A-FA

Avble: 22 Sep 47; Acc: 29 Sep 47; Del: 18 Dec 47 to USAF // 300th AF BAS (AMC) Fairchild Aircraft Maryland 18 Dec 47 // 62nd TCG (TAC) McChord AFB Washington

22 Dec 47. Suffered a take-off accident due to engine failure at Great Falls AFB Montana 16 Feb 48, no fatalities and aircraft repaired // 1455th AF BAS (ATC) Great Falls AFB Montana 17 Feb 48 // 4135th AF BAS (AMC) Hill AFB Utah 4 Mar 48; to Ogden Air Materiel Area (AMC) Hill AFB Utah 25 Aug 49 // 62nd MSU GP (CNC) McChord AFB Washington 29 Aug 49 // 60th TCG (AFE) Rhein-Main AB West Germany 14 Oct 49; depl to 61st MSU GP (AFE) Rhein-Main AB West Germany (60th Attached) 20 Oct 49; depl to Wiesbaden AB West Germany 12 Jan 50; to 80th Air Depot WG (AFE) Nouasseur AB French Morocco 7 Mar 52 for depmnt // San Antonio Air Materiel Area (AMC) Kelly AFB Texas 8 Mar 53; to depmnt 17 Mar 53. Wfu 24 Jun 53 and stored. Dropped from inventory 1 Jul 54 // Bankers Life & Casualty Co. Chicago Illinois 7 Sep 55 reg: N5102B; possibly exported for a period, reg. and operator unk // E.M. Edwards Sacramento California 25 Oct 60 // New Frontier Airlift Corp. Phoenix Arizona 17 Mar 61. Leased to Star Airlines Ltd. of Canada; fabric control surfaces replaced with metal ones 20 Apr 61; cvtd to Steward-Davis Jet-Packet 1600 7 Aug 61; cvtd to Steward-Davis Jet-Packet 1600A 16 Apr 62 with R-2800-85AM2H engines and hydraulic nose wheel steering. Performed a nationwide sales tour transporting the Studebaker Avanti automobile to various U.S. cities for display, flights took place during Apr-May 1962 by Steward-Davis pilot Ted Whaley; aircraft nicknamed *Ol' Ratler* // Tanana Investment Corp. Fairbanks Alaska 11 Jan 63. Leases made to Wien Alaska Airlines Inc., Western Geophysical Co. of America and Sky Van Airways Inc.; radio & nav upgrade 26 Dec 63 // Interior Airways Inc. Fairbanks Alaska 30 Nov 65 // Maurice L. Carlson Anchorage Alaska 14 Nov 73; wfu and stored during the 1970s // Northern Air Cargo Inc. Anchorage Alaska 15 May 81; bku at some point // Darryl G. Greenamyer Inc. Rancho Santa Fe California 13 Jun 88 // Hawkins & Powers Aviation Inc. Greybull Wyoming 16 Jun 95 in dismantled condition // The Pride Capital Group LLC. Deerfield Illinois 1 Sep 05 // Hagerstown Aviation Museum

C-82A Jet-Packet 1600 N5102B (msn: 10152) at Anchorage, Alaska, during April 1968 (Norm Taylor).

Hagerstown Maryland 30 Aug 06; fuselage and minor components stored for museum display. Final Disposition: Preserved.

10153 / 45-57783/CQ-783 / C-82A-FA

Avble: 30 Sep 47; Acc: 30 Sep 47; Del: 13 Nov 47 to USAF // 300th AF BAS (AMC) Fairchild Aircraft Maryland 13 Nov 47 // 316th MSU GP (TAC) Greenville AFB South Carolina 17 Nov 47 // 313th TCG (TAC) Bergstrom AFB Texas 24 Nov 47; to 1377th AF BAS (ATC) Westover AFB Massachusetts 23 Mar 48; to 520th Air Transport SQ (ATC) Westover AFB Massachusetts 2 Jun 48 // 4414th AB SQ (TAC) Bergstrom AFB Texas 13 Oct 48 for storage; depl to 20th TCSq (314th TCG) 22 Nov 48 // 314th TCG (CNC) Smyrna AFB Tennessee 31 Dec 48; assigned 2601st Light Assault SQ; 314th AB GP (CNC) Smyrna AFB Tennessee 3 Mar 49; 314th MSU GP (CNC) Smyrna AFB Tennessee 3 Mar 49; to Mobile Air Materiel Area (AMC) Brookley AFB Alabama 31 Mar 49 for tranmnt // 60th TCG (AFE) Wiesbaden AB West Germany 20 Dec 49; depl to 61st MSU GP (AFE) Rhein-Main AB West Germany 23 Jan 50; to 60th TCG at Rhein-Main AB West Germany 7 Jul 50 // San Antonio Air Materiel Area (AMC) Kelly AFB Texas 21 Apr 53 for depmnt. Wfu 24 Jun 53 and stored. Dropped from inventory 1 Jul 54 // Leeward Aeronautical Inc. Fort Wayne Indiana 15 Aug 55 reg: N7855B; Albert J. Leeward Miami Florida 23 Feb 56; ownership transferred to Leeward Aeronautical Sales Inc. Miami Florida same day; cert of reg issued 2 May 57 // Francis L. Duncan Rockville Maryland 5 Aug 57 for export // Servicos Aereos Cruzeiro do Sul Rio de Janeiro Brazil 27 Oct 58; arrived in Brazil 13 Dec 58; named *Coronel* (as CEL is the Portuguese abbrev. of Colonel); reg: PP-CEL 31 Mar 59. Wfu and stored 15 Dec 69 at Santos-Dumont Airport, Rio de Janeiro. N7855B reg canx 23 Nov 70. Noted engineless 10 Jan 71 // Avimotor Suprimentos Ltda. Rio de Janeiro Brazil 4 Jul 73; retained the basic Cruzeiro livery; lease to Agropecuaria do Jurua Ltda. 7 Nov 73–13 May 74. Suffered a "pancake" landing at Cruz Alta Airport, Parana, Brazil 4 May 74, badly damaged but repaired // FrigoSul Manaus Brazil 20 May 74; still in basic Cruzeiro livery. Aircraft seized by Shell Oil Brazil SA 18 May 76 due to fuel payments not being made, grounded at Manaus Airport (where it remained from 1976 to 2010!) and purchased by Shell through a judicial auction 16 Jun 79 // Aristek Ltda. San Paulo Brazil 10 Dec 79; purchased from Shell Oil Brazil SA but remained at Manaus Airport in Cruzeiro livery, FrigoSul markings and PP-CEL reg. Aircraft abandoned at some point in 1983. Earmarked for display in a Manaus shopping center 5 May 97 but this was denied by local authorities. Dismantled by Brazilian Air Force staff Jan-Apr 2010 with a few parts going to their museum (MUSAL) in Rio de Janeiro and the bulk of the aircraft sold for scrap. Final Disposition: Scrapped.

10154 / 45-57784/CQ-784 / C-82A-FA

Avble: 30 Sep 47; Acc: 30 Sep 47; Del: 14 Nov 47 to USAF // 300th AF BAS (AMC) Fairchild Aircraft Maryland 15 Nov 47 // 313th TCG (TAC) Bergstrom AFB Texas 18 Nov 47 // 4414th AB SQ (TAC) Bergstrom AFB Texas 13 Oct 48 for storage; depl to 20th TCSq (314th TCG) 22 Nov 48 // 314th TCG (CNC) Smyrna AFB Tennessee 24 Feb 49; assigned 20th TCSq; to 314th MSU GP (CNC) Smyrna AFB Tennessee 8 Jul 49 & 14 Nov 49 // 60th TCG (AFE) Wiesbaden AB West Germany 10 Jan 50; to 60th TCG at Rhein-Main AB West Germany 7 Jul 50; on loan to Royal Aircraft Establishment Farnborough England

13 Aug 51; to 85th Air Depot WG (AFE) Erding AB West Germany 19 Nov 51 for depmnt // Assigned 2753rd AST SQ in error. San Antonio Air Materiel Area (AMC) Kelly AFB Texas 28 Jan 53 for depmnt. Wfu 24 Jun 53 and stored. Dropped from inventory 1 Jul 54 // Aerodex Inc. Miami Florida 30 Jun 55 reg: N2048A // L.B. Smith Aircraft Corp. Miami Florida 5 Jul 55 // La Consolidada, S.A. Mexico City Mexico 2 Aug 55 reg: XB-KOI. Fitted with unique panoramic windows on the rear clamshell doors and along the side of the fuselage, likely performed by Steward-Davis, based on drawings from their civil proposals. N2048A reg canx 4 Aug 55. Still in Mexico 1959. Subsequent history unk. Final Disposition: Unknown (Presumed Scrapped).

10155 / 45-57785/CQ-785 / C-82A-FA

Avble: 8 Oct 47; Acc: 16 Oct 47; Del: 17 Nov 47 to USAF // 4000th AF BAS (AMC) Wright Field Ohio 17 Nov 47 for experimental and test duties. Suffered a taxiing accident at Wright Field 14 Nov 47, no fatalities and aircraft repaired // 316th TCG (TAC) Greenville AFB South Carolina 25 Dec 47; 316th MSU GP (TAC) Greenville AFB South Carolina 8 Sep 48 for storage // 60th TCG (AFE) Erbenheim (Wiesbaden AB) Germany 16 Sep 48; to 7160th AB GP (AFE) Erbenheim (Wiesbaden AB) Germany 6 Oct 48. Landing accident due to mechanical failure at Tempelhof AB Germany 14 Dec 48. Pilot: Billy S. Stewart, no fatalities but aircraft extensively damaged. Assigned to 7350th AB GP (AFE) Tempelhof AB Germany 15 Dec 48 for reclamation. Assigned to salvage 22 Jan 49. Dropped from inventory 20 May 49. Final Disposition: Accident.

10156 / 45-57786/CQ-786 / C-82A-FA

Avble: 10 Oct 47; Acc: 16 Oct 47; Del: 19 Nov 47 to USAF // 300th AF BAS (AMC) Fairchild Aircraft Maryland 20 Nov 47 // 313th TCG (TAC) Bergstrom AFB Texas 20 Nov 47; assigned 47th TCSq; 313th MSU GP (TAC) Bergstrom AFB Texas 27 Jan 48; depl to Pope AFB North Carolina 14 Apr 48. Had a ground collision due to mechanical failure 21 Apr 48 at Greenville AFB South Carolina, no fatalities // 4414th AB SQ (TAC) Bergstrom AFB Texas 13 Oct 48 for storage // 4408th AB SQ (TAC) Lawson AFB Georgia 12 Nov 48 // Warner-Robins Air Materiel Area (AMC) Robins AFB Georgia 19 May 49 for depmnt // 314th TCG (CNC) Smyrna AFB Tennessee 17 Oct 49 // 60th TCG (AFE) Wiesbaden AB West Germany 20 Dec 49; to 60th TCG at Rhein-Main AB West Germany 7 Jul 50; to 7150th AB GP (AFE) Wiesbaden AB West Germany 5 Jul 51 // Assigned 2753rd AST SQ in error. San Antonio Air Materiel Area (AMC) Kelly AFB Texas 7 Feb 53 for depmnt. Wfu 24 Jun 53 and stored. Dropped from inventory 1 Jul 54 // Leeward Aeronautical Inc. Fort Wayne Indiana date reg unk // Francis L. Duncan Rockville Maryland 5 Jun 57 for export // Servicos Aereos Cruzeiro do Sul Rio de Janeiro Brazil 27 Oct 58; arrived in Brazil 13 Dec 58; reg: PP-CEJ assigned but ntu. Never entered service, used as a spares source. Bku Jun 60. Final Disposition: Scrapped.

10157 / 45-57787/CQ-787 / C-82A-FA

Avble: 15 Oct 47; Acc: 24 Oct 47; Del: 19 Nov 47 to USAF // 300th AF BAS (AMC) Fairchild Aircraft Maryland 20 Nov 47 // 313th TCG (TAC) Bergstrom AFB Texas 20 Nov 47; assigned 47th TCSq; 313th MSU GP (TAC) Bergstrom AFB Texas 27 Jan 48; depl to Pope AFB North Carolina 14 Apr 48 // 4414th AB SQ (TAC) Bergstrom AFB Texas 13 Oct 48 for storage; depl to 334th TCSq (314th TCG) 22 Nov 48 // 314th TCG (CNC) Smyrna AFB Tennessee 24 Feb 49; assigned 2601st Light Assault SQ // 60th TCG (AFE) Wiesbaden AB West Germany 20 Dec 49; to 60th TCG at Rhein-Main AB West Germany 7 Jul 50 // San Antonio Air Materiel Area (AMC) Kelly AFB Texas 13 Apr 53 for depmnt. Wfu 24 Jun 53 and stored. Dropped from inventory 1 Jul 54. No records exist of any civil service, presumed scrapped by the USAF. Final Disposition: Scrapped.

10158 / 45-57788/CQ-788 / C-82A-FA

Avble: 20 Oct 47; Acc: 29 Oct 47; Del: 26 Nov 47 to USAF // 300th AF BAS (AMC) Fairchild Aircraft Maryland 27 Nov 47 // 313th TCG (TAC) Bergstrom AFB Texas 27 Dec 47; assigned 47th TCSq; depl to Pope AFB North Carolina 20 Apr 48 // 4414th AB SQ (TAC) Bergstrom AFB Texas 13 Oct 48 for storage; depl to 334th TCSq (314th TCG) 19 Nov 48 // 314th TCG (CNC) Smyrna AFB Tennessee 24 Feb 49; multiple assignments to 314th MSU GP (CNC) Smyrna AFB Tennessee starting 17 Mar 49; assignment to 2601st Light Assault SQ 7 Dec 49; Smyrna AFB renamed Sewart AFB 25 Mar 50 // 316th TCG (CNC) Sewart AFB Tennessee 19 Sep 50 // 375th TCWG (CNC) Greenville AFB South Carolina 31 Oct 50; to Warner-Robins Air Materiel Area (AMC) Robins AFB Georgia 28 Sep 51 for depmnt // 64th TCWG (TAC) Donaldson AFB South Carolina 14 Jul 52 // Wfu to San Antonio Air Materiel Area (AMC) Kelly AFB Texas 14 Jul 53 and stored. Dropped from inventory 1 Jul 54 // Bankers Life & Casualty Co. Chicago Illinois 7 Sep 55 reg: N5101B // Carlos Herrera (Servicios Integrales Aeronauticos (SIA) Ltda.) Bogota Colombia 22 Jan 60 reg: HK-583; U.S. reg canx 28 Mar 60 // Servicios Especiales Aereos (SEA) Ltda. Bogota Colombia 18 Apr 61 re-reg: HK-583E. Crashed near Arauca Colombia 10 Jul 71 killing SEA founder and owner Capt Luis Carlos Herrera, nfd. HK-583 reg canx 29 Nov 71. Final Disposition: Accident.

10159 / 45-57789/CQ-789 / C-82A-FA

Avble: 23 Oct 47; Acc: 30 Oct 47; Del: 21 Nov 47 to USAF // 300th AF BAS (AMC) Fairchild Aircraft Maryland 23 Nov 47 // 313th TCG (TAC) Bergstrom AFB Texas 27 Nov 47; assigned 47th TCSq; depl to Pope AFB North Carolina 14 Apr 48 // 4414th AB SQ (TAC) Bergstrom AFB Texas 13 Oct 48 for storage; depl to 334th TCSq (314th TCG) 22 Nov 48. Suffered a landing accident at Sheppard AFB Texas 21 Jan 49, no fatalities // 314th MSU GP (CNC) Smyrna AFB Tennessee 14 Feb 49 for repairs; to Mobile Air Materiel Area (AMC) Brookley AFB Alabama 3 Jun 49 for tranmnt; 314th TCG (CNC) Smyrna AFB Tennessee 4 Nov 49 // 60th TCG (AFE) Rhein-Main AB West Germany 20 Dec 49; assigned 12th TCSq; to 85th Aircraft Maintenance GP (AFE) Erding AB West Germany 23 Jan 50 for depmnt; to 7350th Base Complement SQ (AFE) Tempelhof AB West Germany 15 Jun 50; to 60th TCG at Rhein-Main AB West Germany 7 Jul 50. Had a take-off accident due to weather at Ossun Airfield France 17 May 51, no fatalities. Depl to 61st TCWG (AFE) France (60th Attached) 22 May 51 // San Antonio Air Materiel Area (AMC) Kelly AFB Texas 5 Mar 53 for depmnt. Wfu 24 Jun 53 and stored. Dropped from inventory 1 Jul 54 // Bankers Life & Casualty Co. Chicago Illinois 7 Sep 55 reg: N5100B // Servicios Especiales Aereos (SEA) Ltda. Bogota Colombia 25 Feb 59 reg: HK-777. U.S. reg canx 31 Mar 59. Crashed while making an emergency landing at Cucuta Colombia

20 Dec 61. Onboard as passengers were well-known pilot Capt Santiago Perez Quiroz and Father Bernardo Merino. Capt Perez suffered a head trauma in the crash landing and later died in hospital, nfd. Arauca airport is today named Santiago Perez Quiroz Airport in his honor. Final Disposition: Accident.

10160 / 45-57790/CQ-790 / C-82A-FA

Avble: 24 Oct 47; Acc: 31 Oct 47; Del: 1 Dec 47 to USAF // 313th TCG (TAC) Bergstrom AFB Texas 3 Dec 47; 313th MSU GP (TAC) Bergstrom AFB Texas 24 Feb 48; 4414th AB SQ (TAC) Bergstrom AFB Texas 13 Oct 48 for storage; depl to 20th TCSq (314th TCG) 19 Nov 48 // 314th TCG (CNC) Smyrna AFB Tennessee 24 Feb 49; to 314th MSU GP (CNC) Smyrna AFB Tennessee 23 Mar 49 for repairs & 14 Jun 49 // 60th TCG (AFE) Wiesbaden AB West Germany 20 Dec 49; to 60th at Rhein-Main AB West Germany 7 Jul 50 // San Antonio Air Materiel Area (AMC) Kelly AFB Texas 16 Feb 53 for depmnt. Wfu 24 Jun 53 and stored. Dropped from inventory 1 Jul 54 // Unconfirmed Data → American Airmotive Corp. Miami Florida reg: N75887 // Distribudora Mexicana S.A. Mexico 4 Sep 56 reg: XB-PEJ // Compania Mexicana de Aviacion S.A. Mexico City Mexico, date unk. It's not confirmed if this aircraft ever entered regular service with Mexicana and whether it was a lease or purchase from Distribudora. The registration is only scribbled on the booms and no livery was ever applied, which might indicate it was only used as a spares source. It's also been noted that this C-82 crashed, but no record exists, so it is currently listed as scrapped ← Unconfirmed Data. Noted in a stored and decaying condition in Mexico during 1964 after Mexicana had ceased C-82 operations. Final Disposition: Scrapped.

10161 / 45-57791/CQ-791 / C-82A-FA

Avble: 29 Oct 47; Acc: 26 Nov 47; Del: 5 Dec 47 to USAF // 300th AF BAS (AMC) Fairchild Aircraft Maryland 7 Dec 47 // 316th TCG (TAC) Greenville AFB South Carolina 8 Dec 47; 316th MSU GP (TAC) Greenville AFB South Carolina 8 Sep 48 // 60th TCG (AFE) Asmushausen Germany 14 Sep 48; assigned 12th TCSq; to 7160th AB GP (AFE) Erbenheim (Wiesbaden AB) Germany 6 Oct 48; to 7165th Composite GP (AFE) Erbenheim (Wiesbaden AB) Germany 22 Dec 48 & 17 Mar 49; to 60th at Erbenheim (Wiesbaden AB) Germany 15 Mar 49; to 60th AB GP (AFE) Wiesbaden AB West Germany 1 Jun 49; depl to 513th TCG (AFE) Rhein-Main AB West Germany 19 Sep 49; cvtd to JC-82A on temp special duties for the Berlin Airlift; depl to Rhein-Main AB West Germany 1 Oct 49; back to Wiesbaden AB West Germany 26 Jan 50; to 60th at Rhein-Main AB West Germany 7 Jul 50; to 85th Air Depot WG (AFE) Erding AB, West Germany 13 Jun 51 for depmnt. While in a formation of twelve C-82A aircraft on 28 Jan 52, an engine fire occurred 6 miles WSW Rhein-Main AB West Germany. Pilot: Howard F. O'Neal and 4 other crew members bailed out, but the abandoned aircraft plummeted into a house in the village of Raunheim, killing 3 German civilians—Heinrich Kolb (76 yrs), his daughter Louise Kolb and Irene Kandler (12 yrs), the daughter of a boarder staying in the house. Assigned to reclamation 28 Jan 52. Dropped from inventory 28 May 52. Final Disposition: Accident.

10162 / 45-57792/CQ-792 / C-82A-FA

Avble: 4 Nov 47; Acc: 19 Nov 47; Del: 1 Dec 47 to USAF // 300th AF BAS (AMC) Fairchild Aircraft Maryland 1 Dec 47 // 313th TCG (TAC) Bergstrom AFB Texas 3 Dec 47; assigned 47th TCSq; depl to Pope AFB North Carolina 14 Apr 48 // 4414th AB SQ (TAC) Bergstrom AFB Texas 13 Oct 48 for storage // 4408th AB SQ (TAC) Lawson AFB Georgia 12 Nov 48 // 314th TCG (CNC) Smyrna AFB Tennessee 5 Oct 49; assigned to 2601st Light Assault SQ // 60th TCG (AFE) Wiesbaden AB West Germany 20 Dec 49; to 60th at Rhein-Main AB West Germany 7 Jul 50 // 59th Air Depot WG (AFE) Burtonwood Air Depot England 2 Apr 53 for tranmnt // Wfu to San Antonio Air Materiel Area (AMC) Kelly AFB Texas 3 Aug 53 and stored. Dropped from inventory 1 Jul 54 // Smock & Jenner Inc. Cincinnati Ohio 16 Aug 55 reg: N74044 // Ben Epstein, Trustee for Ben, Leonard and Stanley W. Epstein (Aeronautical Cargo Co.) Miami Beach Florida 29 Dec 55 // Henry A. Smith Richmond California 24 May 61 // New Frontier Airlift Corp. Berkeley California 1 May 63—purchased for Steward-Davis Jet-Packet program, but no buyers or conversion work carried out. One of eight C-82A derelicts for Fairchild-Hiller Corp. Maryland; reg: N6845A rsved 1967 but ntu. N74044 reg revoked 5 Feb 71. Final Disposition: Scrapped.

10163 / 45-57793/CQ-793 / C-82A-FA

Avble: 10 Nov 47; Acc: 26 Nov 47; Del: 4 Dec 47 to USAF // 300th AF BAS (AMC) Fairchild Aircraft Maryland 4 Dec 47 // 316th TCG (TAC) Greenville AFB South Carolina 8 Dec 47; assigned 37th TCSq; depl to Elmendorf AFB Alaska 2 Jul 48; 316th MSU GP (CNC) Greenville AFB South Carolina 31 Jan 49 // 1701st Air Transport GP (MATS) Great Falls AFB Montana 6 Sep 49; briefly to 1701st AB GP (MATS) Great Falls AFB Montana Mar 49. Had a landing accident due to mechanical failure at Tinker AFB Oklahoma 23 Feb 50, no fatalities. To Oklahoma Air Materiel Area (AMC) Tinker AFB Oklahoma 4 Mar 50 for tranmnt and repairs // 6602nd AB WG (NEAC) Ernest Harmon AFB Newfoundland Canada 11 Jan 51 // Middletown Air Materiel Area (AMC) Olmsted AFB Pennsylvania 31 Jan 53 for depmnt // Assigned 6622nd Air Transport SQ (NEAC) in error. Wfu to San Antonio Air Materiel Area (AMC) Kelly AFB Texas 24 Jul 53 and stored. Dropped from inventory 1 Jul 54 // Bankers Life & Casualty Co. Chicago Illinois 7 Sep 55 reg: N5120B // Aviation Facilities Inc. Miami Florida 22 Jan 60 // The Ohio Oil Co. of Guatemala Puerto Barrios Guatemala 7 Dec 60 reg: TG-OOC-5; re-reg: N208M 5 Feb 63 with the Aviation Division of the Ohio Oil Co. of Guatemala Findlay Ohio when the aircraft was imported back into the U.S. // Interior Airways Inc. Fairbanks Alaska 11 Feb 63; N208M reg retd; twin JATO pack installed. Multiple leases to the Western Geophysical Co. of America from Mar 64. Made a belly crash-landing 16 Jan 65 ten miles north of Beaver on the Yukon Flats, Alaska. The flight departed in dark, Arctic weather conditions from Fort Yukon, and upon retracting the u/c there was a total electrical failure resulting in multiple failures of onboard equipment including the radios. The runway they had just departed was blanked out from a snow cloud generated in the prop wash. The crew, including co-pilot Tom Hird, decided to steer a dead-reckoning heading to Fairbanks, climbing to around 8,000 feet. Later the port engine quit, and without electrical power, no feathering of the propeller was possible. The C-82 made a hasty descent onto the Alaskan tundra, the crew flaring the aircraft to the point where the tail booms snapped on contact with the ground. Apart from the broken booms, the aircraft made a textbook belly landing and came to rest in one piece. The three crew were rescued three days later by a USAF helicopter, surviving their time on the tundra with plenty of firewood and one candy bar each for food. The wreck remains at the site to this day (GPS location: N66 28 56.68/W147 13 30.54), but over the years some parts have been removed by passing hunters and souvenir collectors. Final Disposition: Accident.

10164 / 45-57794/CQ-794 / C-82A-FA

Avble: 14 Nov 47; Acc: 28 Nov 47; Del: 4 Dec 47 to USAF // 300th AF BAS (AMC) Fairchild Aircraft Maryland 4 Dec 47 // 316th TCG (TAC) Greenville AFB South Carolina 8 Dec 47; assigned 36th TCSq; 316th MSU GP (TAC) Greenville AFB South Carolina 8 Sep 48. Had a mid-air collision with a bird 8 miles S Phoenix City Alabama 3 Mar 49, no fatalities. 316th to Smyrna AFB 4 Nov 49; depl to Guantanamo Bay Cuba 28 Feb 50; Smyrna AFB renamed Sewart AFB 25 Mar 50; depl to 314th TCG (CNC) Laurinburg-Maxton Airport North Carolina 20 Apr 50; depl to 314th TCG (CNC) Sewart AFB Tennessee 21 Jul 50; assigned 2601st Light Assault SQ // 314th TCG (CNC) Sewart AFB Tennessee 17 Nov 50 // 375th TCWG (TAC) Greenville AFB South Carolina 8 Jan 51; assigned 54th TCSq. Suffered a minor ground accident due to fire at Campbell AFB North Carolina 12 Jul 51, no fatalities. To 301st AB GP (SAC) Barksdale AFB Louisiana 17 Feb 52 for tranmnt // 64th TCWG (TAC) Donaldson AFB South Carolina 14 Jul 52 // Wfu to San Antonio Air Materiel Area (AMC) Kelly AFB Texas 26 Jun 53 and stored. Dropped from inventory 1 Jul 54 // Bankers Life & Casualty Co. Chicago Illinois 7 Sep 55 reg: N5121B // Airparts Inc. Miami Florida 6 Feb 62 // Miami Aircraft Maintenance Inc. Miami Florida 7 Feb 62 // Esso Standard (Guatemala) Inc. Wilmington Delaware 12 Feb 62; re-reg: N128E 7 Mar 62; flight-tested with JATO rockets plus engine & avionics upgrades 4 Apr 62 // John W. Mecom Houston Texas 24 Jul 63; nav & avionics upgrade 9 Aug 63; stabilizer wing tips removed 18 Dec 63. Based out of Aden, Yemen, from 1964 in support of Mecom Oil Co.'s activities in the Middle East. Shot down by Egyptian MiG-21 fighters 20 miles E Alexandria, Egypt, 19 Dec 64 after entering restricted airspace. In what became dubbed as a "Diplomatic Incident Involving Aircraft of U.S. Registry," an inspector from the Civil Aeronautics Board (CAB) and Federal Aviation Agency (FAA) were sent to Egypt to determine the nature and cause of the incident. They established the following chain of events from their investigations:

1. The aircraft was a Fairchild C-82A Packet owned by the Mecom Oil Co. carrying U.S. reg: N128E on both sides of the fuselage. The pilot in command was Hoyt J. Williams (44 yrs) of Mulberry, Texas (or Florida) and his copilot/engineer Kjell Grupp (37 yrs) of Malmo, Sweden. Both held current pilot licenses and medical certificates.
2. The flight was from Amman, Jordan, west to Benghazi, Libya, with the route going through the United Arab Republic (UAR/Egypt), as it was known in 1964, where political tensions existed between it and other Middle Eastern countries. The area around Alexandria in Egypt is a prohibited and militarily sensitive no-fly zone. Commercial airways and air corridors do exist around Alexandria with frequent reminders issued by the UAR about remaining strictly within these airways at all times.

3. Williams filed a VFR flight plan in Amman, intending to fly west along a path that included an unapproved route through the UAR, which as he indicated was Amman—Rosetta (Alexandria)—Marsa Matruh—Benina (Benghazi), but there is no direct airway from Rosetta to Marsa Matruh. It is known he had not flown this particular route before and it appears he was unaware of the sensitive area around Alexandria or any of the UAR NOTAMS issued to pilots about flying these routes. Most importantly, the flight plan was never questioned by anyone at Amman or even forwarded to Cairo controllers for clearance until three hours after the shoot-down!
4. The C-82 Packet departed Amman at 0440Z but was forced to return due to mechanical trouble.
5. They departed again at 0522Z; this time it appears the onboard radio was inoperative as no further contact could be made with the C-82 from any station, including other aircraft in the area! The late departure was forwarded to Cairo and Benghazi, but again, no flight plan or route information was included. Cairo made attempts to determine the route of the aircraft without success.
6. Williams radioed a message (it seems, whether he knew it or not, he could intermittently transmit but could not receive at all), to Cairo Control Center he was entering UAR airspace over Ras Sudr. But since they never received a flight plan, could not establish his intentions, and could not communicate with the aircraft directly, they saw it as an unidentified aircraft coming in from the direction of Israel and dispatched two MiG-21 fighters to intercept.
7. Using internationally recognized hand signals, the MiGs indicated that the C-82 follow them and land at Cairo Intl. Airport. It seems no radio communication was had at all during this time. The C-82 approached Cairo and the MiGs departed the scene, but the Packet only, silently, circled the airport for some time, then flew off to the north toward Alexandria.
8. A second pair of MiG-21 fighters were sent to intercept and again indicated for the aircraft to return to Cairo and land. When the Packet refused to obey, at this point departing the approved flight path, the MiGs fired shots "across the bow" with fatal results. The Packet fell from the sky in a wings-level but inverted position, indicating there was no longer any control from the pilots. It struck the ground at approximately 0917 hrs local time 20 miles east of Alexandria (approx N31 12.00/E030 18.00), sustaining fatal impact damage and a post-crash fire.

Mecom Oil protested the UAR's decision to shoot down an unarmed cargo plane with an obvious U.S. registration, citing it as "reckless and brutal behaviour" on the part of the Egyptian military. Their justification was that certain countries had used subterfuge methods of sneaking reconnaissance planes into UAR airspace and that the aircraft had failed to communicate or obey instructions in any way. UAR controllers stated that the aircraft would have been cleared through their airspace had a flight plan been received. The crash site was visited by the investigators on 23 Dec 64 where they were surprised to see the local police guarding the site had disturbed the wreckage by building a shelter with the rear clamshell doors! At the conclusion of the investigation it was learned, through information provided by the FBI, that Williams had a long and colorful criminal record, he had also spent some time in a mental institution. CAUSE: Using the evidence that could be gathered, the investigation concluded Williams' actions as being the primary cause of the incident and that the UAR was justified in the shoot down. These actions being: 1) Williams filed a VFR flight plan with an unapproved route; 2) the flight plan was not forwarded to the UAR for clearance (this may not actually be Williams fault however); 3) the aircraft had a radio malfunction soon after take-off but Williams elected to continue the flight; 4) Williams entered UAR airspace with a faulty radio, without over-flight clearance and no flight plan submitted; 5) he acted in defiance of repeated instructions to land at Cairo by the intercepting MiGs; 6) Williams appears to have panicked in his defiance and tried to "make a run for it" departing from his flight path with fatal results. Final Disposition: Accident.

A very rare photograph of ill-fated Mecom Oil Company C-82A N128E (msn: 10164) at RAF Khormaksar (Aden International Airport), Yemen, during 1963 (Ray Deacon).

10165 / 45-57795/CQ-795 / C-82A-FA

Avble: 19 Nov 47; Acc: 9 Dec 47; Del: 10 Dec 47 to USAF // 300th AF BAS (AMC) Fairchild Aircraft Maryland 11 Dec 47 // 316th TCG (TAC) Greenville AFB South Carolina 16 Dec 47; 316th MSU GP (TAC) Greenville AFB South Carolina 9 Jul 48 // 4000th AF BAS (AMC) WPAFB Ohio 9 Jul 48 // 2750th AB GP (AMC) WPAFB Ohio 25 Oct 48; cvtd to EC-82A for test and experimental duties; to 3203rd MSU GP & 3200th Proof Test GP (APG) Eglin AFB Florida 1 Dec 48 for further test and experimental work; back to 2750th AB GP 9 Aug 49; cvtd back to C-82A standard 5 Dec 49 // 314th TCG (CNC) Smyrna AFB Tennessee 10 Mar 50; assigned 2601st Light Assault SQ; Smyrna AFB renamed Sewart AFB 25 Mar 50; depl to Laurinburg-Maxton Airport North Carolina 20 Apr 50 // 316th TCG (CNC) Sewart AFB Tennessee 10 Oct 50 // 375th TCWG (TAC) Greenville AFB South Carolina 9 Mar 51; assigned 55th TCSq; to Warner-Robins Air Materiel Area (AMC) Robins AFB Georgia 28 Jun 51 for depmnt; depl to Grenier AFB New Hampshire 6 Jan 52. Moderately damaged while parked at Wheeler-Sack AAF New York 10 Feb 52 when a C-46D Commando (s/n: 44-77508) crashed after take-off. The C-46D was the ninth of seventeen taking-off for an exercise when it made a sharp 60-degree turn soon after leaving the runway and smashed into a row of parked aircraft.

The four crew on the C-46D were killed and five of the 32 paratroopers onboard were injured. Another parked C-82A (s/n: 44-23017) and an L-17B Navion (s/n: 48–1064) were also damaged. To Middletown Air Materiel Area (AMC) Olmsted AFB Pennsylvania 29 Feb 52 for depmnt and repairs // 64th TCWG (TAC) Donaldson AFB South Carolina 12 Aug 52; to Middletown Air Materiel Area (AMC) Olmsted Field Pennsylvania 25 Aug 52 for depmnt // Wfu to San Antonio Air Materiel Area (AMC) Kelly AFB Texas 14 Jul 53 and stored. Dropped from inventory 1 Jul 54 // Bankers Life & Casualty Co. Chicago Illinois 7 Sep 55 reg: N5122B // FAA Files Incomplete → Lewis Consultants Inc. purchase date unk ← FAA Files Incomplete // The Ohio Oil Co. of Guatemala Puerto Barrios Guatemala 23 Dec 60 reg: TG-OOC-4; re-reg: N209M 5 Feb 63 with the Aviation Division of the Ohio Oil Co. of Guatemala Findlay Ohio when the aircraft was imported back into the U.S. // Interior Airways Inc. Fairbanks Alaska 11 Feb 63; N209M reg retd; twin JATO pack installed. Various leases include United Geophysical Corp., Pruhs & Associates, Globe Plumbing & Heating Inc., National Geophysical, Geophysical Service Inc., Western Geophysical Corp. and Richfield Oil Corp. Left boom repaired 8 Dec 65. Wfu 1970s; de-reg: 14 Jun 76. Noted as derelict on a fire dump in Fairbanks Alaska 1973 to 1979. Final Disposition: Scrapped.

10166 / 45-57796/CQ-796 / C-82A-FA

Avble: 21 Nov 47; Acc: 12 Dec 47; Del: 17 Dec 47 to USAF // 300th AF BAS (AMC) Fairchild Aircraft Maryland 17 Dec 47 // 316th TCG (TAC) Greenville AFB South Carolina 22 Dec 47; assigned 37th TCSq. Suffered a mid-air collision 7 miles N Fayetteville North Carolina 7 Jan 48, no fatalities and aircraft repaired. Made a forced landing due to engine failure over Quantico MCAS Virginia 2 Feb 48. Pilot: Joe T. Schindler, no fatalities. No doubt some skillful flying here as a C-82A rarely survived an engine failure to make a successful landing! 316th MSU GP (TAC) Greenville AFB South Carolina 7 Apr 48; to 4117th AF BAS (AMC) Robins AFB Georgia 9 Jun 48 for depmnt // 60th TCG (AFE) Erbenheim (Wiesbaden AB) Germany 14 Sep 48; assigned 11th TCSq; to 7160th AB GP (AFE) Erbenheim (Wiesbaden AB) Germany 6 Oct 48; to 7165th Composite GP (AFE) Erbenheim (Wiesbaden AB) Germany 22 Dec 48 & 17 Mar 49; to 60th AB GP (AFE) Wiesbaden AB West Germany 1 Jun 49; assigned to Middletown Air Materiel Area (AMC) Olmsted AFB Pennsylvania 12 Sep 49; cvtd to JC-82A on temp special duties for the Berlin Airlift alongside four C-82As assigned to the 513th TCG (Special); depl to 61st MSU GP (AFE) Rhein-Main AB West Germany (60th Attached) 19 Jan 50; to 60th at Rhein-Main AB West Germany 24 Jan 50. Minor taxiing accident at RAF Burtonwood England 15 Aug 50, possibly collided with C-82A s/n: 45-57766, no fatalities. Depl to 61st TCWG (AFE) Rhein-Main AB West Germany (60th Attached) 16 Apr 51. Destroyed by a ground fire at Rhein-Main AB West Germany 16 Aug 51. Pilot: Kenneth P. Lacey, no fatalities. Assigned to reclamation 16 Oct 51. Dropped from inventory 16 Apr 52. Final Disposition: Accident.

10167 / 45-57797/CQ-797 / C-82A-FA

Avble: 26 Nov 47; Acc: 31 Dec 47; Del: 15 Jan 48 to USAF // 300th AF BAS (AMC) San Diego California 15 Jan 48 // 313th TCG (TAC) Bergstrom AFB Texas 16 Jan 48; assigned to 47th TCSq; depl to Pope AFB North Carolina 14 Apr 48 // 4414th AB SQ

(TAC) Bergstrom AFB Texas 13 Oct 48. Crash-landed due to engine failure in a field 4 miles N Clinton Louisiana 17 Oct 48. Pilot: Paul E. Blow and three other crew survived; four of the thirty passengers were killed and one seriously injured. The C-82 was part of a seven-plane convoy flying from Biggs AFB, Texas, to Eglin AFB, Florida, when it developed engine trouble. It was decided to make an emergency landing rather than ordering the aircraft to be abandoned, probably due to the proximity of populated areas. A portion of the fuselage was crushed in the crash-landing, resulting in the four deaths and one injury // 3380th Technical Training WG (TC) Keesler AFB Mississippi 23 Oct 48; airframe for study? Assigned to reclamation and dropped from inventory 7 Jan 49. Final Disposition: Accident.

10168 / 45-57798/CQ-798 / C-82A-60-FA

Avble: 5 Dec 47; Acc: 29 Dec 47; Del: 6 Jan 48 to USAF; 300th AF BAS (AMC) // 316th TCG (TAC) Greenville AFB South Carolina 9 Jan 48; assigned 37th TCSq; depl to Elmendorf AFB Alaska 2 Jul 48; to 4127th AF BAS (AMC) McClellan AFB California 14 Sep 48. Suffered some damage due to a mechanical failure at Greenville AFB South Carolina 10 Dec 48, no fatalities and aircraft repaired. To 316th MSU GP (CNC) Greenville

C-82A s/n: 45-57798 (msn: 10168) after crashing on Cornwallis Island during 1950 (United States Air Force).

AFB South Carolina 3 Mar 49; to 1227th AB GP (MATS) Goose Bay AB Labrador Canada 21 Mar 49. Damaged in a forced landing due to running out of fuel 318 miles NW Resolute Bay Canada 24 Mar 49, no fatalities and aircraft repaired // Middletown Air Materiel Area (AMC) Olmsted Field Pennsylvania 21 Apr 49 // 1225th AB GP (MATS) Pepperell AFB Newfoundland Canada 12 Jul 49 // 1226th AB GP (MATS) Ernest Harmon AFB Newfoundland Canada 23 Mar 50. Suffered an engine failure at take-off 11 Apr 50 on Cornwallis Island Northwest Territories Canada. Pilot: Thomas P. Wirth, no fatalities but aircraft w/o. Assigned to reclamation 19 Apr 50. Dropped from inventory 20 Jul 50. Final Disposition: Accident.

10169 / 45-57799/CQ-799 / C-82A-60-FA

Individual Aircraft Record Card (IARC) missing. Known data: Del: 8 Jan 48 to USAF // Assigned TAC // Cvtd to SC-82A. 4th RES SQ (MATS) Lowry AFB Colorado; assigned to Flight "D." Made a forced landing due to engine fire 11 Jul 52 at Quad City Airport Moline Illinois. Pilot: William L. McGeary, no fatalities but the aircraft was w/o when fire engulfed it on the ground once evacuated. Final Disposition: Accident.

SC-82A s/n: 45-57799 (msn: 10169). Note the MATS rescue markings (Robert Stachowiak via Stephen Miller).

10170 / 45-57800/CQ-800 / C-82A-60-FA

Avble: 11 Dec 47; Acc: 31 Dec 47; Del: 8 Jan 48 to USAF // 300th AF BAS (AMC) Fairchild Aircraft Maryland 8 Jan 48 // 62nd TCG (TAC) McChord AFB Washington 11 Jan 48; assigned 4th TCSq; depls to Elmendorf AFB Alaska starting 1 Apr 48 & 30 Nov 48; depl to Fort Richardson Alaska 20 Dec 48; to 62nd MSU GP (CNC) McChord AFB Washington 12 Aug 49 & 29 Sep 49 // 61st MSU GP (AFE) Rhein-Main AB West Germany (60th Attached) 20 Oct 49 // 60th TCG (AFE) Rhein-Main AB West Germany 5 Nov 49 // San Antonio Air Materiel Area (AMC) Kelly AFB Texas 16 Feb 53 for depmnt. Wfu 24 Jun 53 and stored. Dropped from inventory 1 Jul 54 // Bankers Life & Casualty Co. Chicago Illinois 7 Sep 55 reg: N5126B. Subsequent history unk; might have been exported.

10171 / 45-57801/CQ-801 / C-82A-60-FA

Individual Aircraft Record Card (IARC) incomplete. Known data: Avble: unk; Acc: 31 Dec 47; Del: 8 Jan 48 to USAF // 60th TCWG (AFE) Rhein-Main AB West Germany unk-1951; assigned 11th TCSq. Had an engine failure 15 miles WNW Marignane France 2 Oct 50. The pilot had the crew and passengers bail out, but the aircraft was then apparently able to be flown down and landed on one engine. Crashed due to a ground collision in the Mont-Dore (Mt. Dore) region 23 miles SW of Clermont-Farrand, France 13 Nov 51 killing all 36 onboard. The flight took off from Rhein-Main AB, West Germany at 0925Z destined for Bordeaux-Merignac Airport near the west coast of France, where the 32 passengers were to set up a motor pool and postal service. The weight and balance sheet shows the take-off weight was 50,824 lb with 9,600 lb of this the fuel load for the 560-mile direct flight. The weather across the region was marginal with thick cloud and generally limited visibility. A position check was conducted at 1108Z with a controller at Dijon, France, but #7801 did not acknowledge the radio "fix." The arrival at Bordeaux was scheduled for around 1315Z and the aircraft was reported as missing several hours later with an air search subsequently activated. The following day a charred piece of paper identifying one of the passengers was found by French skiers searching in the Mont-Dore region after reports aircraft engine sounds had been heard by locals around the time of the crash. The crash site itself was located the next day below the summit of Mt. Dore by a French military ground party. The aircraft was totally destroyed by a high-velocity impact and consumed further by a post-crash fire. Bodies were strewn around the crash site, by now partly covered by the two days of snowfall since the accident. The burnt twin tails were the only identifying parts of the aircraft left, with "557801" visible on one fin. The following lists the 36 crew and passengers who perished:

Crew	Capt Raphael F. Baird (Pilot)	Cpl Ernest Glingener
	2nd Lt Roy W. Finck (Copilot)	PFC Arthur Graber
	PFC Miles W. Folger	Cpl Jack M. Greathouse
	TSgt Francis F. Fox (Engineer)	PFC Charles L. Gregory
	Sgt Donald E. Griffith (Radio Operator)	
Passengers	PFC Newton M. Benson	Sgt Stanley V. Krushas
	SSgt Merton R. Boardman	Cpl Freddie Lewis
	PFC Samuel S. Bruington Jr. (Postal Sq.)	Sgt Richard W. Lewis
	PFC Joseph M. Calfee	Cpl Judson E. Miller
	PFC William C. Click	SSgt Horace A. Patterson
	Sgt Ramon L. Deken	Sgt Harold R. Powell
	Cpl Leonard R. Del Vecchio	Sgt Vinson Royal
	Cpl Edward DeVilla	Sgt Walter E. Schuette
	Cpl William A. Dickerson	PFC Kenneth Shoemaker
	SSgt John Duke	PFC Frank A. Stanklewicz
	PFC David E. Edie	Sgt Earl C. Sykes Jr.
	TSgt Wilson C. Edmondson	Cpl Cesario Verde
	Capt John J. Fitzgerald (Postal Sq.)	Cpl Charles G. West
	PFC Hubert Johnson, Jr.	

The subsequent USAF investigation established the following facts and made the following conclusions as to the cause of the accident:

1. The pilot planned the flight for 8,000 feet but filed the flight-plan for 6,000 feet and failed to take into account an 8 degree westerly variation to the true heading.
2. En route, the pilot radioed his position as being over Dijon, France, but the controller at Dijon, using four D/F radios, gave #7801's exact position as actually being 23 miles SE from Dijon. The controller tried to radio the actual correct position but #7801 did not acknowledge his calls.
3. The time of the crash, from watches found in the wreckage, was 1205Z.
4. The aircraft was found to be in perfect flying condition right up to the point of impact based on the following: the aircraft struck the mountain peak at a normal flying attitude; both engines were operating as engine switches were "on" and marks left in the terrain by the propellers would indicate both were operating; both CO_2 fire extinguishers were found to be safetied and "off," indicating no pre-crash engine failure or fire; engine mixture, pitch and throttle levers were found to be in the cruise setting; pitot heat switch was "on." The flight instrument panel actually survived the crash intact, so many readings like these could be gathered.
5. The crash occurred at an altitude of 5,600 feet, 400 feet below the assigned altitude. The pilot and copilot's altimeters were found to be set differently, but only slightly (29.41 and 29.44 respectively); the barometric pressure at the time was 29.63, giving an error of around 200 feet. The aircraft was being manually flown in rough weather, so a variation of a further 200 feet, it was concluded, could be expected.
6. It appears the local weather conditions were worse than had been forecast in the pre-flight briefing. The actual conditions in the Clermont-Farrand region at 1200Z was a 6/8 cloud cover with a more northerly wind than had been forecast. Locals later reported, in newspaper accounts, of a thick fog in the region and a raging localized "tempest" over Mont-Dore at the time of the accident.

Cause: Essentially the crew of #7801, only using "time and distance" in calculating their position and progress, failed to take into account, or be cognizant of, a left drift to their correct course, this likely amplified by the stronger than expected northerly winds. Over two hours this put them, unknowingly, around 50 miles south of their intended course toward Bordeaux. The crew's failure to properly use navigational aids in determining exact positions en route and maintain a listening watch on radio frequencies (it appears the Dijon frequency was switched before the controller could relay the correct position, or were they having radio difficulties?), was also a major contributing factor toward the accident. So, oblivious to being off course and 400 feet below their assigned altitude, #7801, it appears, then flew into a localized patch of severe weather in complete white-out conditions. Dealing with the rough air in zero visibility, the pilots then flew completely unawares into the side of Mt. Dore, the impact instantly killing all onboard. The fact the engines were in a cruise setting indicates they had no warning at all of oncoming terrain. As a result of this crash, flight-planning, radio and navigation procedure for pilots was reviewed with the minimum IFR altitudes over the area assigned from 7,000 to 8,000 ft. This crash is the worst military C-82 accident and the worst overall accident of the C-82 Packet aircraft in terms of lives lost. Final Disposition: Accident.

Top and bottom: Two views of ill-fated C-82A Packet s/n: 45-577801 (msn: 10171) taken in Italy on June 14, 1950. This aircraft crashed in France on November 13, 1951, killing all 36 onboard. Note the rippled anti-corrosion paint on the fuselage belly (Giorgio Salerno Collection via A. Romano).

10172 / 45-57802/CQ-802 / C-82A-60-FA

Avble: 17 Dec 47; Acc: 31 Dec 47; Del: 29 Jan 48 to USAF // 300th AF BAS (AMC) Fairchild Aircraft Maryland 1 Feb 48 // 316th TCG (TAC) Greenville AFB South Carolina 30 Jan 48 (early assignment date); multiple assignments to 316th MSU GP (CNC) Greenville AFB South Carolina starting 2 Feb 49 // 3203rd MSU GP & 3201th AB GP (APG) Eglin AFB Florida 13 Jun 49 for experimental and test support duties // 3210th Chemical and Ordnance Test GP (APG) Phillips Field Maryland 6 Jun 51 for test support duties. Had a weather-related accident 20 miles W Rawlins Wyoming 10 Jul 51, no fatalities. Assigned Armament Test Division (APG) 1951 in error. To Ogden Air Materiel Area

(AMC) Hill AFB Utah 10 Jul 51 for tranmnt // Armament Test HQ (ARD) Eglin AFB Florida 24 Apr 52 for test support duties; renamed Air Force Armament Test Center 1 Feb 53. Modernized to Group A standard during 1953 but no mnt center listed in IARC // 6520th Test Support WG (ARD) (Laurence G.) Hanscom AFB Massachusetts 26 Mar 54. Cvtd to EC-82A for test support duties. Had a minor mechanical incident 1 mile E Littleneck Massachusetts 11 May 54, no fatalities // Wfu to Ogden Air Materiel Area (AMC) Hill AFB Utah 7 Dec 54 and stored. Dropped from inventory 9 May 55 // L.B. Smith Aircraft Corp. Miami Florida 19 Sep 55 reg: N2065A // Harry R. Playford (Madden & Playford Aircraft Inc.) St. Petersburg Florida 21 Sep 55; ferried from Ogden, Utah with reg: N6241C but later canx in favor of N2065A; one of five C-82As based at Pinellas Airport, Florida // Royal International Corp. Miami Florida 7 May 57 // The Ohio Oil Co. of Guatemala Puerto Barrios Guatemala 21 Jan 59 reg: TG-OOC-2; subsequent history unk apparently exported, reg canx 1961. N2065A de-reg 15 Sep 71. Final Disposition: Unknown (Presumed Scrapped).

10173 / 45-57803/CQ-803 / C-82A-60-FA

Avble: 26 Dec 47; Acc: 13 Jan 48; Del: 16 Feb 48 to USAF // 300th AF BAS (AMC) Fairchild Aircraft Maryland 16 Feb 48 // 313th TCG (TAC) Bergstrom AFB Texas 18 Feb 48; assigned to 47th TCSq; depl to Pope AFB North Carolina 14 Apr 48 // 4414th AB SQ (TAC) Bergstrom AFB Texas 13 Oct 48 for storage // 4408th AB SQ (TAC) Lawson AFB Georgia 29 Oct 48 // Warner-Robins Air Materiel Area (AMC) Robins AFB Georgia 19 May 49 // 314th TCG (CNC) Smyrna AFB Tennessee 7 Sep 49; assigned 2601st Light Assault SQ // 60th TCG (AFE) Rhein-Main AB West Germany 20 Dec 49; depls to 61st TCWG (AFE) Rhein-Main AB West Germany (60th Attached) 30 Apr 51 & 16 May 51 // San Antonio Air Materiel Area (AMC) Kelly AFB Texas 5 Mar 53 for depmnt. Wfu 24 Jun 53 and stored. Dropped from inventory 1 Jul 54 // Bankers Life & Casualty Co. Chicago Illinois 7 Sep 55 reg: N5127B // Fuzzy Furlong Miami Florida 1959, sold for scrap; de-reg 25 Jan 71. Final Disposition: Scrapped.

10174 / 45-57804/CQ-804 / C-82A-60-FA

Avble: 7 Jan 48; Acc: 22 Jan 48; Del: 2 Feb 48 to USAF // 300th AF BAS (AMC) Fairchild Aircraft Maryland 2 Feb 48 // 313th TCG (TAC) Bergstrom AFB Texas 4 Feb 48; 313th MSU GP (TAC) Bergstrom AFB Texas 24 Mar 48 // 4414th AB SQ (TAC) Bergstrom AFB Texas 13 Oct 48 for storage; depl to 20th TCSq (314th TCG) 22 Nov 48 // 314th TCG (CNC) Smyrna AFB Tennessee 24 Feb 49 // 60th TCG (AFE) Rhein-Main AB West Germany 10 Jan 50 // San Antonio Air Materiel Area (AMC) Kelly AFB Texas 16 Feb 53 for depmnt. Wfu 24 Jun 53 and stored. Dropped from inventory 1 Jul 54 // Bankers Life & Casualty Co. Chicago Illinois 7 Sep 55 reg: N5128B // Fuzzy Furlong Miami Florida 1959, sold for scrap; de-reg 26 Jan 71. Final Disposition: Scrapped.

10175 / 45-57805/CQ-805 / C-82A-60-FA

Avble: 12 Jan 48; Acc: 21 Jan 48; Del: 11 Mar 48 to USAF // 300th AF BAS (AMC) Farmingdale Field New York 11 Mar 48 // 316th TCG (TAC) Greenville AFB South Carolina 12 Mar 48; to 131st AF BAS (ADC) Offutt AFB Nebraska 21 Jun 48 for tranmnt;

C-82A s/n: 45-57804 (msn: 10174) (National Museum of the United States Air Force).

316th MSU GP (CNC) Greenville AFB South Carolina 31 Jan 49 // 1227th AB GP (MATS) Goose Bay AB Labrador Canada 1 Jul 49 // to Warner-Robins Air Materiel Area (AMC) Robins AFB Georgia 13 Feb 50 for depmnt // 6602nd AB WG (NEAC) Ernest Harmon AFB Newfoundland Canada 9 Feb 51. Aircraft lost due to an unk accident at King George IV Lake Newfoundland Canada 21 Sep 51. Pilot: Walter L. Kemp and crew survived. Assigned to salvage 1 Feb 52. Dropped from inventory 16 Apr 52. Final Disposition: Accident.

10176 / 45-57806/CQ-806 / C-82A-60-FA

Avble: 15 Jan 48; Acc: 26 Jan 48; Del: 2 Feb 48 to USAF // 300th AF BAS (AMC) Fairchild Aircraft Maryland 2 Feb 48 // 313th TCG (TAC) Bergstrom AFB Texas 4 Feb 48 // 4414th AB SQ (TAC) Bergstrom AFB Texas 13 Oct 48 for storage // 4408th AB SQ (TAC) Lawson AFB Georgia 5 Nov 48 // 314th TCG (CNC) Smyrna AFB Tennessee 11 Jul 49 // 60th TCG (AFE) Rhein-Main AB West Germany 10 Jan 50; depl to 61st TCWG (AFE) Rhein-Main AB West Germany (60th Attached) 23 Apr 51 // San Antonio Air Materiel Area (AMC) Kelly AFB Texas 7 Apr 53 // Aircraft Engineering & Maintenance Co. (AMC) Oakland California 14 Apr 53 on bailment; modernized to Group A standard // 567th Air Defense GP (ADC) McChord AFB Washington 7 Feb 54; to San Bernardino Aircraft Repair Depot (AMC) Norton AFB California 11 May 54 for tranmnt; to Oklahoma Air Materiel Area (AMC) Tinker AFB Oklahoma 5 Feb 55 for tranmnt // Wfu to 3040th Aircraft Storage SQ (AMC) Davis-Monthan AFB Arizona 24 Feb 55 and stored. Dropped from inventory 1 Aug 55 // Leeward Aeronautical Sales Inc. Miami Florida 9 Mar 56 reg: N56582 // Aero Enterprises Inc. Elkhart Indiana 28 Feb 62 (hull only) // Peter Bercut San Francisco California 14 Feb 62 (hull only). Reg canx 6 Dec 71. Final Disposition: Unknown (Presumed Scrapped).

10177 / 45-57807/CQ-807 / C-82A-60-FA

Avble: 20 Jan 48; Acc: 26 Jan 48; Del: 2 Feb 48 to USAF // 300th AF BAS (AMC) Fairchild Aircraft Maryland 2 Feb 48 // 313th TCG (TAC) Bergstrom AFB Texas 4 Feb 48; assigned 47th TCSq; 313th MSU GP (TAC) Bergstrom AFB Texas 29 Mar 48; depl to Pope AFB North Carolina 14 Apr 48 // 4414th AB SQ (TAC) Bergstrom AFB Texas 13 Oct 48 for storage; depl to 334th TCSq (314th TCG) 19 Nov 48 // 314th TCG (CNC) Smyrna AFB Tennessee 24 Feb 49; assigned 2601st Light Assault SQ // 60th TCG (AFE) Rhein-Main AB West Germany 20 Dec 49; assigned Warner-Robins Air Materiel Area (AMC) in error; to 85th Air Depot WG (AFE) Erding AB, West Germany 31 Mar 52 for depmnt // San Antonio Air Materiel Area (AMC) Kelly AFB Texas 6 Mar 53; to 6603rd AB GP (NEAC) Goose Bay AB Labrador Canada 13 Mar 53 for tranmnt. Wfu 24 Jun 53 and stored. Dropped from inventory 1 Jul 54 // unk U.S. civil owner reg: N75888 // Distribudora Mexicana S.A. Mexico, date unk, reg: XB-PEK // Compania Mexicana de Aviacion S.A. Mexico City Mexico, date unk, reg: XA-MAW, cert of reg 17 May 57; fitted with Mexicana dorsal fillets. Earmarked for export to Bolivia Oct 60, reg: CP-697 but sale canx and reg ntu // New Frontier Airlift Corp. Phoenix Arizona 22 Aug 61 reg: N74127; aircraft ferried to U.S. 28–29 Nov 62; cert of reg issued 9 May 63. Ctvd to Steward-Davis Skytruck Mk. I 1963 with J34-WE Jet-Pak, engine water-injection, horizontal stabilizer tips removed, nose wheel steering and braking system upgrade; ff: 26 Feb 64, engaged in experimental and research testing early 1964 in relation to the new "Skytruck" conversion design. Leased to *Las Vegas Sun* newspaper 28 Feb 64 for carriage of newspapers from Los Angeles to Las Vegas after a fire destroyed their printing machines; the lease

Steward-Davis Skytruck Mk. I N74127 (msn: 10177) testing aerial delivery equipment for the All-American Engineering Co. in Delaware during 1964. The Ford Motor Company later used the film footage shot during the tests for a pick-up truck television commercial (Rebecca Wiant Collection).

was shared with Steward-Davis Jet-Packet 1600 N6887C. For seven months the two aircraft airlifted 16,000 lb of newspapers seven nights a week from Los Angeles to Las Vegas. One of the pilots was Steward-Davis employee Jim Springer, who wrote to his mother during the operation to say, "Well, I have my old job back.... I'm delivering newspapers again." Used for research and development of a "ground proximity delivery system" 5 Aug 64 by the All-American Engineering Co. in Delaware. Tests involved dropping a Ford pick-up from the rear of N74127 as it made low passes along the runway. The test-film was later used in a TV commercial for Ford // Steward-Davis Inc. Long Beach California 18 Aug 64. Cvtd to a Steward-Davis "Flying Repair Station" 8 Sep 64. Crashed 7 Nov 64 on approach 68 miles WNW of Veracruz, Mexico. Killed were pilots Jim Springer (43 yrs) and Cecil John (41 yrs), who were on their way to San Juan, Puerto Rico, to make repairs to a helicopter owned by the governor of Veracruz. They were to stop in Veracruz en route to obtain technical details and expertise before continuing on to San Juan. According to newspaper accounts N74127 was cleared to descend 20 minutes out of Veracruz when it hit a mountain peak named Cofre de Perote (GPS location: N19 29 36.11/W097 08 54.00). It appears the aircraft had entered into clouds as it descended and would have been likely traveling at around 220 to 230mph when it struck the mountain, resulting in a total disintegration of the airframe. The wreckage was located just 200 ft below the summit the following day, with the remains of the two pilots returned to the U.S. for funeral and burial services. Final Disposition: Accident.

10178 / 45-57808/CQ-808 / C-82A-60-FA

Avble: 23 Jan 48; Acc: 30 Jan 48; Del: 16 Feb 48 to USAF // 300th AF BAS (AMC) Fairchild Aircraft Maryland 16 Feb 48 // 313th TCG (TAC) Bergstrom AFB Texas 16 Feb 48; assigned 47th TCSq. Had a minor taxiing accident at Fort Nelson Canada 2 Apr 48, no fatalities. Depl to Pope AFB North Carolina 14 Apr 48 // 4414th AB SQ (TAC) Bergstrom AFB Texas 13 Oct 48 for storage; depl to 334th TCSq (314th TCG) 19 Nov 48 // 314th TCG (CNC) Smyrna AFB Tennessee 24 Feb 49; assigned 2601st Light Assault SQ; 314th MSU GP (CNC) Smyrna AFB Tennessee 13 Sep 49 // 60th TCG (AFE) Rhein-Main AB West Germany 20 Dec 49 // San Antonio Air Materiel Area (AMC) Kelly AFB Texas 2 Mar 53 for depmnt. Wfu 24 Jun 53 and stored. Dropped from inventory 1 Jul 54 // Bankers Life & Casualty Co. Chicago Illinois 7 Sep 55 reg: N5123B. Subsequent history unk; might have been exported. Listed as scrapped and reg canx 8 Oct 70. Final Disposition: Unknown (Presumed Scrapped).

10179 / 45-57809/CQ-809 / C-82A-60-FA

Avble: 27 Jan 48; Acc: 6 Feb 48; Del: 16 Feb 48 to USAF // 300th AF BAS (AMC) Fairchild Aircraft Maryland 16 Feb 48 // 313th TCG (TAC) Bergstrom AFB Texas 17 Feb 48. Had a landing accident due to weather at Cambridge Bay Canada 25 Feb 48, no fatalities. To 1455th AF BAS (ATC) Great Falls AFB Montana 1 Apr 48 for tranmnt; 313th MSU GP (TAC) Bergstrom AFB Texas 5 May 48 // 4121st AF BAS (AMC) Kelly AFB Texas 26 May 48 for depmnt; later transferred to San Antonio Air Materiel Area (AMC) Kelly AFB Texas // 314th TCG (CNC) Smyrna AFB Tennessee 4 Apr 49; to Mobile Air Materiel Area (AMC) Brookley AFB Alabama 3 Sep 49 for tranmnt // 61st MSU GP (AFE) Rhein-Main AB West Germany 16 Dec 49; 60th TCG (AFE) Rhein-Main AB West

Germany 20 Dec 49. Aircraft lost due to an unk accident in Libya in early 1951; exact location, cause and fatalities are unk. To 1603rd AB GP (MATS) Wheelus AFB Libya 12 Jan 51 for salvage. Assigned to salvage and reclamation 10 Jun 51. Dropped from inventory 12 Sep 51. Final Disposition: Accident.

10180 / 45-57810/CQ-810 / C-82A-60-FA

Avble: 2 Feb 48; Acc: 11 Feb 48; Del: 10 Mar 48 to USAF // 300th AF BAS (AMC) Farmingdale Field New York 10 Mar 48 // 316th TCG (TAC) Greenville AFB South Carolina 9 Apr 48; to 1455th AF BAS (ATC) Fort Nelson Field Canada 23 Apr 48 for tranmnt; 1455th renamed 517th Air Transport WG (MATS) Great Falls AFB Montana 1 Jun 48; reassigned 517th AB GP (MATS) Fort Nelson Field Canada 2 Jun 48 for tranmnt // 7165th Composite GP (AFE) Erbenheim (Wiesbaden AB) Germany 22 Feb 49 & 17 Mar 49; 60th TCG (AFE) Erbenheim (Wiesbaden AB) Germany 8 Mar 49; to 60th AB GP (AFE) Wiesbaden AB West Germany 1 Jun 49. Had a minor weather-related incident 45 miles S Braunsuring 11 Jun 49, no fatalities. Depl to 513th TCG (AFE) Rhein-Main AB West Germany 19 Sep 49 on temp special duties for the Berlin Airlift; to 60th at Rhein-Main AFB West Germany 1 Oct 49; to 1603rd AB GP (MATS) Wheelus AFB Libya 23 Oct 50 for tranmnt; depl to 61st TCWG (AFE) Rhein-Main AB West Germany (60th Attached) 10 May 51; to 7150th AB GP (AFE) Wiesbaden AB West Germany 16 Nov 51. Minor ground accident at Rhein-Main AB West Germany 23 Oct 52, no fatalities // Assigned 2753rd Aircraft Storage SQ (AMC) & 6602nd AB GP (NEAC) in error // San Antonio Air Materiel Area (AMC) Kelly AFB Texas 7 Feb 53 for depmnt. Wfu 24 Jun 53 and stored. Dropped from inventory 1 Jul 54 // Leeward Aeronautical Sales Inc. Fort Wayne Indiana 1955–56 reg unk // Francis L. Duncan Rockville Maryland 1957 reg: unk, for export // Servicos Aereos Cruzeiro do Sul Rio de Janeiro Brazil 7 Nov 57; arrived in Brazil 25 Nov 57; reg: PP-CEM 25 Sep 58. Damaged beyond repair while parked at Galeao Intl. Airport Rio de Janeiro Brazil 21 Jun 60 when it was hit by a mechanic taxiing Douglas DC-7C

60th TCG C-82A s/n: 45-57810 (msn: 10180) on the island of Malta during 1950 (Giorgio Salerno Collection via A. Romano).

C-82A PP-CEM (msn: 10180) performing an engine run-up (Sergio Luis dos Santos Collection).

(reg: PP-PDM) of Panair do Brasil, no fatalities. Scrapped at Galeao Dec 60; reg: PP-CEM canx 25 Oct 65. Final Disposition: Accident.

10181 / 45-57811/CQ-811 / C-82A-60-FA

Avble: 5 Feb 48; Acc: 16 Feb 48; Del: 5 Mar 48 to USAF // 300th AF BAS (AMC) Farmingdale Field New York 5 Mar 48 // 313th TCG (TAC) Bergstrom AFB Texas Mar 48; to 1377th AF BAS (ATC) Westover AFB Massachusetts 23 Mar 48; to 1383rd AF BAS (ATC) Goose Bay Labrador Canada 7 Apr 48 for tranmnt // 4414th AB SQ (TAC) Bergstrom AFB Texas 13 Oct 48 for storage // 3800th Air University WG (AU) Maxwell AFB Alabama 13 Nov 48 for tranmnt // 314th TCG (CNC) Smyrna AFB Tennessee 18 Feb 49; assigned 2601st Light Assault SQ; assigned Oklahoma Air Materiel Area (AMC) in error // 60th TCG (AFE) Rhein-Main AB West Germany 20 Dec 49; to 1603rd MSU GP & 1603rd AB GP (MATS) Wheelus AFB Libya 3 Feb 51 for tranmnt; depl to 61st TCWG (AFE) Rhein-Main AB West Germany (60th Attached) 7 Apr 51 // San Antonio Air Materiel Area (AMC) Kelly AFB Texas 1 Apr 53 // Aircraft Engineering & Maintenance Co. (AMC) Oakland California 21 Apr 53 on bailment; modernized to Group A standard // 567th Air Defense GP (ADC) McChord AFB Washington 3 Jan 54; to 2500th AB WG (CNC) Mitchel AFB New York 16 Nov 54 for tranmnt; to Oklahoma Air Materiel Area (AMC) Tinker AFB Oklahoma 9 Feb 55 for tranmnt // Wfu to 3040th Aircraft Storage SQ (AMC) Davis-Monthan AFB Arizona 28 Feb 55 and stored. Dropped from inventory 1 Aug 55. No records exist of any civil service, presumed scrapped by the USAF. Final Disposition: Scrapped.

10182 / 45-57812/CQ-812 / C-82A-60-FA

Avble: 10 Feb 48; Acc: 19 Feb 48; Del: 19 May 48 to USAF // 300th AF BAS (AMC) Fairchild Aircraft Maryland 19 May 48 // multiple assignments to 62nd MSU GP (TAC)

McChord AFB Washington starting 21 May 48; 62nd TCG (TAC) McChord AFB Washington 7 Jun 48; assigned 7th TCSq. Had a landing accident due to mechanical failure at Great Falls AFB Montana 18 Oct 48, no fatalities. To 1701st MSU GP (MATS) Great Falls AFB Montana 21 Oct 48 for repairs; depl to Elmendorf AFB Alaska 3 Mar 49 // 60th TCG (AFE) Rhein-Main AB West Germany 14 Oct 49; depl to 61st MSU GP (AFE) Rhein-Main AB West Germany (60th Attached) 20 Oct 49; depl to 61st TCWG (AFE) Rhein-Main AB West Germany (60th Attached) 12 Apr 51 // Assigned 2753rd Aircraft Storage SQ (AMC) in error. San Antonio Air Materiel Area (AMC) Kelly AFB Texas 8 Feb 53 // Aircraft Engineering & Maintenance Co. (AMC) Oakland California 14 Apr 53 on bailment; modernized to Group A standard // 521st Air Defense GP (CAD) Sioux City MAP Iowa late 53; to 3320th Technical Training WG (TC) Amarillo AFB Texas late 53 for tranmnt; to Oklahoma Air Materiel Area (AMC) Tinker AFB Oklahoma 22 Dec 53, 6 Apr 54 & 17 Feb 55 for tranmnt. Minor ground incident at Scott AFB Illinois 3 Mar 54, no fatalities // Wfu to 3040th Aircraft Storage SQ (AMC) Davis-Monthan AFB Arizona 7 Mar 55 and stored. Dropped from inventory 1 Aug 55 // Leeward Aeronautical Sales Inc. Miami Florida 9 Mar 56 reg: N7857B; cert of reg issued 2 May 57 // Francis L. Duncan Rockville Maryland 5 Sep 57 for export // Cruzeiro do Sul Rio de Janeiro Brazil 1959 reg: PP-CFF. Never entered service, used as a spares source. N7857B reg canx 19 Mar 79. Final Disposition: Scrapped.

10183 / 45-57813/CQ-813 / C-82A-65-FA

Avble: 13 Feb 48; Acc: 23 Feb 48; Del: 10 Mar 48 to USAF // 300th AF BAS (AMC) Farmingdale Field New York 10 Mar 48 // 316th TCG (TAC) Greenville AFB South Carolina 2 Jul 48; assigned 37th TCSq; depl to Elmendorf AFB Alaska 2 Jul 48. Landing accident at Barter Island Alaska 28 Jul 48, no fatalities but aircraft extensively damaged // Aircraft Maintenance (AAC) Ladd AFB Alaska 5 Aug 48, deemed as "damaged beyond repair" // 57th MSU GP (AAC) Elmendorf AFB Alaska 5 Aug 48, assigned to reclamation and salvage; likely bku for spares. Assigned to reclamation 1 Jan 49. Dropped from inventory 1 Feb 49. Final Disposition: Accident.

10184 / 45-57814/CQ-814 / C-82A-65-FA

Avble: 18 Feb 48; Acc: 27 Feb 48; Del: 26 Mar 48 to USAF // 300th AF BAS (AMC) Fairchild Aircraft Maryland 29 Mar 48 // 316th TCG (TAC) Greenville AFB South Carolina 29 Mar 48; assigned 37th TCSq; depl to Elmendorf AFB Alaska 2 Jul 48; to 316th MSU GP (CNC) Greenville AFB South Carolina 9 Feb 49 // 1226th AB GP (MATS) Ernest Harmon AFB Newfoundland Canada 5 Jul 49 // 6602nd AB WG (NEAC) Ernest Harmon AFB Newfoundland Canada 2 Nov 50 // 6622nd Air Transport SQ (NEAC) Ernest Harmon AFB Newfoundland Canada 18 Aug 52; to Rome Air Development Center (ARD) Griffiss AFB New York 10 Sep 52 for tranmnt; to 6603rd AB GP (NEAC) Goose Bay AB Labrador Canada 19 Jan 53 // San Antonio Air Materiel Area (AMC) Kelly AFB Texas 16 Jun 53 for depmnt. Wfu 19 Jun 53 and stored. Dropped from inventory 1 Jul 54 // Aerodex Inc. Miami Florida 30 Jun 55 reg: N2047A // L.B. Smith Aircraft Corp. Miami Florida 5 Jul 55 // Selk Co. North Hollywood California 25 Aug 55; leased to Bedek Aviation Tel Aviv Israel // Trans World Airlines (TWA) Inc. Kansas City Kansas. 14 Apr 56; based at Orly Field, Paris; TWA fleet no. 5551. Large scale overhaul and modification program undertaken at Orly Field, Paris to create a "Flying Repair Station" for servicing TWA's airliner fleet in European sectors. Mods included new Pratt & Whitney R-2800-CB4 radials, Fairchild J44-R Jet-Pak, aircraft systems, flight-deck and radio & nav. systems fully upgraded, cargo hold equipment added for workshop repair capabilities, empty weight at 36,595 lb, weight and balance sheets dated 1 Jan 60. Given a highly polished aluminium finish with red side stripes and TWA logos, it looked like a new aircraft; named *Ontos* (Greek for "thing"); senior TWA pilot from 1957–1972 was Claude Girard. Served TWA briefly in Ethiopia reg: ET-T-12 2 Feb 60 to 17 Jun 60; re-reg: N9701F 1 Mar 60. Cvtd to Steward-Davis Jet-Packet 3400A 1962 with J34-WE-34 Jet-Pak // Steward-Davis Inc. Long Beach California 30 Jan 73. Cvtd to Steward-Davis Jet-Packet 3400B with R-2800-CB16 radials // Briles Wing & Helicopter Inc. Medford Oregon 20 Feb 73, served as a "Flying Repair Station" for helicopter engines and parts mainly into South America. Made the C-82 Packets first and only flight to the South Pacific to deliver a Bell 205 to Australia in 1974 // Ball Bros. Inc. Anchorage Alaska 1 May 78. Suffered hard landing 3 Sep 80 requiring repairs to lower fuselage, completed 19 May 81 // Northern Pacific Transport Inc. Anchorage Alaska 20 Dec 82. Lower fuselage damaged when the u/c retracted during taxiing Jun 83. Leases to Icicle Seafoods and Intl. Seafoods of Alaska Inc. 1985–1986 // Alaska Aircraft Leasing Inc. Anchorage Alaska 1 Apr 87 // The First National Bank of Anchorage Alaska 27 Apr 92 as a repossession from Alaska Aircraft Leasing Inc. // Hawkins & Powers Aviation Inc. Greybull Wyoming 12 Aug 92. Flight-deck & avionics upgrade 17 Dec 92 // D&G Inc. Greybull Wyoming 1 Jan 93, grounded and stored in 2000 // The Pride Capital Group LLC. Deerfield Illinois 1 Sep 05, purchased for auctioning // Hagerstown Aviation Museum Maryland 30 Aug 06. Made the last-ever flight of a C-82 15 Oct 06 returning the aircraft to its birthplace at Hagerstown Airport for display. The pilot on this historic flight was Frank Lamm, an ex-USAF pilot with over 3,000 hours on the C-119 who had this to say to the author about the C-82: "I had never set foot in a C-82 before doing so at Greybull in 2006. This posed no problems as the similarity of the two planes [C-119] made us all feel quite confident." About the cockpit: "The cockpit

C-82A Jet-Packet 3400 N9701F (msn: 10184) at Orly, Paris, during June 1970 (John Wegg).

layout has good points and bad points. Though the C-82 has a lot of floor space, nowhere is there enough room in which to stand up. The forward visibility on take-off and landing is much better on the C-119. I believe the C-82 cockpit is wider than the DC-10 cockpit!" About handling: "On the initial departure out of Greybull, on the take-off roll, when I started to pull back on the yoke to rotate, nothing happened. I yanked harder and the nose finally started to come off the runway and a little help from the trim wheel made it better. What I did notice was the stiffness in the controls, particularly the ailerons." About flying the C-82: "The plane flew very well; however, I would not have enjoyed flying it in a formation for a long length of time." N9701F was the most famous, most recognized, most successful and longest-serving C-82 in civilian service! It remains today on display in Hagerstown with its engines in running order. Final Disposition: Preserved.

Top: C-82A Jet-Packet 3400 N9701F (msn: 10184) at Oakland, California, during November 1973. *Bottom:* C-82A N9701F (msn: 10184) of Briles Wing & Helicopter outside the McDonnell Douglas plant at Long Beach, California, during May 1978 (both photographs, John Wegg).

10185 / 45-57815/CQ-815 / C-82A-65-FA

Avble: 25 Feb 48; Acc: 5 Mar 48; Del: 25 Mar 48 to USAF // 300th AF BAS (AMC) Fairchild Aircraft Maryland 25 Mar 48 // 316th TCG (TAC) Greenville AFB South Carolina 29 Mar 48; 316th MSU GP (TAC) Greenville AFB South Carolina 21 Sep 48; 316th to Smyrna AFB Tennessee 4 Nov 49; depl to Guantanamo Bay Cuba 28 Feb 50; Smyrna AFB renamed Sewart AFB 25 Mar 50; depl to 314th TCG (CNC) Laurinburg-Maxton Airport North Carolina 20 Apr 50; depl to 314th TCG (CNC) Sewart AFB South Carolina 21 Jul 50; assigned 2601st Light Assault SQ; to Sacramento Air Materiel Area (AMC) McClellan AFB California 13 Nov 50 for tranmnt; to 325th Fighter (All-Weather) WG (CNC) McChord AFB Washington 19 Nov 50 // 375th TCWG (TAC) Greenville AFB South Carolina 4 Mar 51; to Warner-Robins Air Materiel Area (AMC) Robins AFB Georgia 11 Aug 51 for depmnt; depl to Grenier AFB New Hampshire 3 Jan 52; to Wright Air Development Center (ARD) WPAFB Ohio 20 Mar 52 for test duties; depl to Brownwood Field Texas 4 Apr 52 // 64th TCWG (TAC) Donaldson AFB South Carolina 14 Jul 52 // Wfu to San Antonio Air Materiel Area (AMC) Kelly AFB Texas 2 Jul 53 and stored. Dropped from inventory 1 Jul 54 // Leeward Aeronautical Inc. Fort Wayne Indiana 15 Aug 55 reg: N7854B; Albert J. Leeward Miami Florida 23 Feb 56; ownership transferred to Leeward Aeronautical Sales Inc. Miami Florida same day; cert of reg issued 2 May 57 // Francis L. Duncan Rockville Maryland 5 Jul 57 for export // Servicos Aereos Cruzeiro do Sul Rio de Janeiro Brazil 24 Dec 57; arrived in Brazil 11 Jan 58; reg: PP-CEI assigned but ntu. Never entered service, used as a spares source. Bku Jun 60. Final Disposition: Scrapped.

10186 / 45-57816/CQ-816 / C-82A-65-FA

Some parts of this IARC indecipherable. Avble: 26 Feb 48; Acc: 9 Mar 48; Del: 5 Apr 48 to USAF // 300th AF BAS (AMC) Fairchild Aircraft Maryland 19 Apr 48 // 316th TCG (TAC) Greenville AFB South Carolina 26 Apr 48; to Sacramento Air Materiel Area (AMC) McClellan AFB California 8 Jul 49 for depmnt; 316th to Smyrna AFB Tennessee 4 Nov 49 // 60th TCG (AFE) Rhein-Main AB West Germany 10 Jan 50; assigned 11th TCSq. Minor taxiing accident at Rhein-Main AFB West Germany 19 May 50, no fatalities. To 59th Air Depot WG (AFE) RAF Burtonwood Air Depot England 10 Jun 52 for depmnt. Suffered a heavy landing accident at RAF Burtonwood England 7 Jun 52 most likely on its arrival flight for depmnt. Pilot: Raymond Moss, no fatalities but aircraft assessed as "damaged beyond repair." Recommended for salvage 26 Jun 52. Assigned to salvage and reclamation 10 Sep 52 and most likely bku for spares. Dropped from inventory 2 Nov 52. Final Disposition: Accident.

10187 / 45-57817/CQ-817 / C-82A-65-FA

Avble: 1 Mar 48; Acc: 12 Mar 48; Del: 2 Apr 48 to USAF // 300th AF BAS (AMC) Fairchild Aircraft Maryland 2 Apr 48 // 319th AF BAS (TAC) Lawson AFB Georgia 2 Apr 48 // 4408th AB SQ (TAC) Lawson AFB Georgia 23 Aug 48 // 314th TCG (CNC) Smyrna AFB Tennessee 25 May 49 // 60th TCG (AFE) Rhein-Main AB West Germany 10 Jan 50; assigned 11th TCSq. Minor taxiing accident at Giebelstadt Field West Germany 16 Apr 52, no fatalities. Mid-air collision with a bird near Rhein-Main AB West Germany 21 Jul

52, no fatalities // San Antonio Air Materiel Area (AMC) Kelly AFB Texas 27 Feb 53 for depmnt. Wfu 24 Jun 53 and stored. Dropped from inventory 1 Jul 54 // Bankers Life & Casualty Co. Chicago Illinois 7 Sep 55 reg: N5124B. Subsequent history unk; might have been exported. Listed as scrapped and reg canx 8 Oct 70. Final Disposition: Unknown (Presumed Scrapped).

10188 / 45-57818/CQ-818 / C-82A-65-FA

Avble: 4 Mar 48; Acc: 22 Mar 48; Del: 30 Apr 48 to USAF // 300th AF BAS (AMC) Fairchild Aircraft Maryland 30 Apr 48 // 316th TCG (TAC) Greenville AFB South Carolina 1 May 48; assigned 37th TCSq. Suffered a weather-related incident near Great Falls AFB Montana 11 Jul 48, no fatalities. To 517th MSU GP (MATS) Great Falls AFB Montana 17 Jul 48 for tranmnt; to 316th MSU GP (TAC) Greenville AFB South Carolina 9 Sep 48 // 60th TCG (AFE) Erbenheim (Wiesbaden AB) Germany 14 Sep 48; assigned 12th TCSq. Had a mechanical failure over the Wiesbaden area Germany 1 Oct 48, no fatalities. To 7210th Aircraft Maintenance GP (AFE) Erding AB Germany 5 Oct 48 & 22 Mar 49 for repairs; to 7160th AB GP (AFE) Erbenheim (Wiesbaden AB) Germany 9 Oct 48; to 7165th Composite GP (AFE) Erbenheim (Wiesbaden AB) Germany 22 Dec 48 & 17 Mar 49; to 60th AB GP (AFE) Wiesbaden AB West Germany 1 Jun 49; depl to 513th TCG (AFE) Rhein-Main AB West Germany 19 Sep 49; cvtd to JC-82A on temp special duties for the Berlin Airlift; to 60th at Rhein-Main AFB West Germany 1 Oct 49; depl to 61st TCWG (AFE) Rhein-Main AB West Germany (60th Attached) 18 Apr 51 // 2753rd Aircraft Storage SQ (AMC) Pyote AFB Texas 30 Jan 53; to 1400th AB GP (MATS) Keflavik Airport Iceland 6 Feb 53 for tranmnt. Appears to have had an accident in Iceland around this date that has deemed the aircraft as "damaged beyond repair." Exact location, cause and fatalities unk. Assigned to reclamation and salvage 4 Oct 54, likely bku for spares. Final Disposition: Accident.

10189 / 45-57819/CQ-819 / C-82A-65-FA

Avble: 10 Mar 48; Acc: 25 Mar 48; Del: 6 May 48 to USAF // 300th AF BAS (AMC) Fairchild Aircraft Maryland 6 May 48 // 316th TCG (TAC) Greenville AFB South Carolina 6 May 48; 316th MSU GP (CNC) Greenville AFB South Carolina 3 Feb 49 // 1700th Air Transport GP (MATS) Kelly AFB Texas 8 Aug 49 // 1701st Air Transport GP (MATS) Great Falls AFB Montana 26 Aug 49; to 1701st AB GP (MATS) Great Falls AFB Montana 12 Oct 49 // 1226th AB GP (MATS) Ernest Harmon AFB Newfoundland Canada 29 May 50 // 6602nd AB WG (NEAC) Ernest Harmon AFB Newfoundland Canada 2 Nov 50 // Mobile Air Materiel Area (AMC) Brookley AFB Alabama 5 Feb 52 for depmnt // Ogden Air Materiel Area (AMC) Hill AFB Utah 16 Apr 53 for mnt. Wfu 30 Apr 53 and stored. Assigned to reclamation 11 Mar 54. Dropped from inventory 14 Apr 54. No records exist of any civil service, presumed scrapped by the USAF. Final Disposition: Scrapped.

10190 / 45-57820/CQ-820 / C-82A-65-FA

Avble: 11 Mar 48; Acc: 29 Mar 48; Del: 23 Apr 48 to USAF // 300th AF BAS (AMC) Fairchild Aircraft Maryland 23 Apr 48 // 4000th AF BAS (AMC) Wright-Patterson AFB Ohio 28 Apr 48 for test duties // to 62nd MSU GP (TAC) McChord AFB Washington 7

Jun 48 & 23 Aug 49; 62nd TCG (TAC) McChord AFB Washington 1 Jul 48; assigned 8th TCSq; depls to Elmendorf AFB Alaska 1 Sep 48 & 6 Jun 49 // 60th TCG (AFE) Rhein-Main AB West Germany 14 Oct 49; assigned 11th TCSq; depl to 61st MSU GP (AFE) Rhein-Main AB West Germany (60th Attached) 20 Oct 49. Made a forced landing due to onboard fire over Rhein-Main AB West Germany 22 May 50. Pilot: Roger P. Larivee, no fatalities but aircraft was "damaged beyond repair." Assigned to reclamation 9 Jun 50. Dropped from inventory 19 Oct 50. Final Disposition: Accident.

C-82A s/n: 45-57820 (msn: 10190) (National Museum of the United States Air Force).

10191 / 45-57821/CQ-821 / C-82A-65-FA

Avble: 17 Mar 48; Acc: 19 Apr 48; Del: 30 Apr 48 to USAF // 300th AF BAS (AMC) Fairchild Aircraft Maryland 30 Apr 48 // 316th TCG (TAC) Greenville AFB South Carolina 1 May 48; assigned 37th TCSq; depl to Elmendorf AFB Alaska 2 Jul 48; 316th MSU GP (CNC) Greenville AFB South Carolina 26 Jan 49 // 3203rd MSU GP & 3201th AB GP (APG) Eglin AFB Florida 17 Jun 49 for experimental and test support duties. Had a landing accident due to mechanical failure at Eglin AFB Florida 9 Jan 51. Pilot: Arthur L. Vaughan, no fatalities but aircraft extensively damaged // To Mobile Air Materiel Area (AMC) Brookley AFB Alabama 2 Mar 51 for repair but assessed as "damaged beyond repair." Assigned to reclamation and salvage 4 Sep 51. Dropped from inventory 19 Feb 52. Final Disposition: Accident.

10192 / 45-57822/CQ-822 / C-82A-65-FA

Avble: 22 Mar 48; Acc: 30 Apr 48; Del: 10 May 48 to USAF // 316th TCG (TAC) Greenville AFB South Carolina 11 May 48; assigned 37th TCSq; depl to Elmendorf AFB Alaska 2 Jul 48; 316th to Smyrna AFB Tennessee 4 Nov 49 // 60th TCG (AFE) Rhein-Main AB West Germany 10 Jan 50 // 1227th AB GP (MATS) Goose Bay AB Labrador Canada 22 Mar 50 // 314th TCG (CNC) Sewart AFB Tennessee 2 Oct 50 // 375th TCWG (TAC) Greenville AFB South Carolina 5 Dec 50; to 4418th Base Complement SQ (TAC) Greenville AFB South Carolina 5 Dec 50; to Warner-Robins Air Materiel Area (AMC)

Robins AFB Georgia 19 Oct 51 for depmnt; depl to Brownwood Field Texas 5 Mar 52 // 64th TCWG (TAC) Donaldson AFB South Carolina 14 Jul 52; assigned 18th TCSq. Had an in-flight structural failure over the Caribbean between Miami Florida and San Juan Puerto Rico 12 Nov 52, no fatalities and aircraft landed safely // Wfu to San Antonio Air Materiel Area (AMC) Kelly AFB Texas 2 Jul 53 and stored. Dropped from inventory 1 Jul 54 // Forca Aerea Brasileira (FAB/Brazilian Air Force) 20 Sep 55 s/n: 2208. Ferried to Brazil Jan 56; No. 2 Grupo de Transporte (2nd Transport Group) Aerea dos Afonsos AB Rio de Janeiro; redes No. 1/1 Grupo de Transporte de Tropa (1st Troop Carrier Group) 22 Jan 58. Wfu 19 Apr 68 and stored. SOC: 25 Nov 70 and sold for scrap. Final Disposition: Scrapped.

10193 / 45-57823/CQ-823 / C-82A-65-FA

Avble: 24 Mar 48; Acc: 26 Apr 48; Del: 11 May 48 to USAF// 300th AF BAS (AMC) Fairchild Aircraft Maryland 11 May 48 // 316th TCG (TAC) Greenville AFB South Carolina 12 May 48; assigned 37th TCSq; depl to Elmendorf AFB Alaska 2 Jul 48. Crashed due to engine failure 2 miles SSW Birds Landing California 2 Sep 49. Pilot: Vess J. Ward Jr. and copilot killed, six other occupants bailed out and survived. Crew reported engine failure about eight minutes prior to crash. Assigned to reclamation 23 Sep 49. Dropped from inventory 4 Jan 50. Final Disposition: Accident.

10194 / 45-57824/CQ-824 / C-82A-65-FA

Avble: 31 Mar 48; Acc: 27 Apr 48; Del: 11 May 48 to USAF// 300th AF BAS (AMC) Fairchild Aircraft Maryland 11 May 48 // 10th MSU GP (TAC) Pope AFB North Carolina 13 May 48; 10th AB GP (TAC) Pope AFB North Carolina 1 Sep 48. Taxiing accident at Cleveland Municipal Airport Ohio 2 Sep 48, no fatalities. To 2471st Air Repair SQ (ADC) O'Hare Intl. Airport Illinois 3 Sep 48 for tranmnt and repairs // 316th MSU GP (CNC) Greenville AFB South Carolina 22 Dec 48; to Warner-Robins Air Materiel Area (AMC) Robins AFB Georgia 4 Jan 49 for depmnt; 316th TCG (CNC) Greenville AFB South Carolina 21 Feb 49; 316th to Smyrna AFB Tennessee 4 Nov 49; depl to Guantanamo Bay Cuba 28 Feb 50; Smyrna AFB renamed Sewart AFB 25 Mar 50; depl to 314th TCG (CNC) Laurinburg-Maxton Airport North Carolina 20 Apr 50 // 1226th AB GP (MATS) Ernest Harmon AFB Newfoundland Canada 12 Jun 50; to 1600th Air Transport WG (MATS) Westover AFB Massachusetts 28 Jun 50 for tranmnt. Assigned 7226th AB GP & 1227th AB GP (NEAC) in error // 6602nd AB WG (NEAC) Ernest Harmon AFB Newfoundland Canada 2 Nov 50; to 6603rd AB WG (NEAC) Goose Bay AB Labrador Canada 16 Mar 52 // 6622nd Air Transport SQ (NEAC) Ernest Harmon AFB Newfoundland Canada 18 Aug 52; to 6603rd AB WG (NEAC) Goose Bay AB Labrador Canada 12 Mar 53 // Wfu to San Antonio Air Materiel Area (AMC) Kelly AFB Texas 24 Jun 53 and stored. Dropped from inventory 1 Jul 54. No records exist of any civil service, presumed scrapped by the USAF. Final Disposition: Scrapped.

10195 / 45-57825/CQ-825 / C-82A-65-FA

Avble: 6 Apr 48; Acc: 30 Apr 48; Del: 11 May 48 to USAF// 300th AF BAS (AMC) Fairchild Aircraft Maryland 11 May 48 // 316th TCG (TAC) Greenville AFB South

Carolina 12 May 48; assigned 37th TCSq; depl to Elmendorf AFB Alaska 2 Jul 48; 316th to Smyrna AFB Tennessee 4 Nov 49; depl to Guantanamo Bay Cuba 28 Feb 50; Smyrna AFB renamed Sewart AFB 25 Mar 50; depl to 314th TCG (CNC) Laurinburg-Maxton Airport North Carolina 20 Apr 50; depl to 314th TCG (CNC) Sewart AFB South Carolina 21 Jul 50; assigned 2601st Light Assault SQ // 375th TCWG (TAC) Greenville AFB South Carolina 3 Mar 51; depl to Brownwood Field Texas 10 Mar 52 // 64th TCWG (TAC) Donaldson AFB South Carolina 14 Jul 52; assigned 35th TCSq. Had a paratroop drop accident over Pope AFB North Carolina 21 Aug 52, details unk. Suffered a minor ground collision incident at Donaldson AFB South Carolina 19 Mar 53, no fatalities // Wfu to San Antonio Air Materiel Area (AMC) Kelly AFB Texas 14 Jul 53 and stored. Dropped from inventory 1 Jul 54 // Bankers Life & Casualty Co. Chicago Illinois 7 Sep 55 reg: N5125B. Subsequent history unk; might have been exported. Listed as scrapped and reg canx 8 Oct 70. Final Disposition: Unknown (Presumed Scrapped).

10196 / 45-57826/CQ-826 / C-82A-65-FA

Avble: 12 Apr 48; Acc: 30 Apr 48; Del: 2 Jul 48 to USAF // 62nd MSU GP (TAC) McChord AFB Washington 6 Jul 48; 62nd TCG (TAC) McChord AFB Washington 16 Jul 48; assigned 4th TCSq; to 4127th AF BAS (AMC) McClellan AFB California 13 Aug 48 for tranmnt; depl to Elmendorf AFB Alaska 30 Nov 48; depl to Fort Richardson Alaska 20 Dec 48. Damaged in an engine failure incident at McChord AFB Washington 9 Apr 49, no fatalities. To 62nd MSU GP (CNC) 11 Apr 49, assessed as "damaged beyond repair." Assigned to reclamation 21 Apr 49. Dropped from inventory 23 Nov 49. Final Disposition: Accident.

10197 / 45-57827/CQ-827 / C-82A-65-FA

Avble: 15 Apr 48; Acc: 14 May 48; Del: 18 Jun 48 to USAF // 414th AF BAS (AMC) Fairchild Aircraft Maryland 14 Jun 48 // multiple assignments to 62nd MSU GP (TAC) McChord AFB Washington starting 15 Jun 48; 62nd TCG (TAC) McChord AFB Washington 1 Jul 48; assigned 4th TCSq; to 2621st AF BAS (TC) Barksdale AFB, Louisiana 3 Sep 48 for tranmnt; multiple depls to Elmendorf AFB Alaska starting 30 Nov 48; depl to Fort Richardson Alaska 20 Dec 48 // 2156th Technical Training UT (MATS) MacDill AFB Florida 30 Mar 50; 2156th RES UT (MATS) MacDill AFB Florida 30 Mar 51; cvtd to SC-82A; to San Bernardino Aircraft Repair Depot (AMC) Norton AFB California 16 Jul 51 for tranmnt; to 2156th RES SQ at Palm Beach Intl Airport Florida 1 May 52 // 1707th Training SQ (MATS) Palm Beach Intl. Airport Florida 20 Jul 52 // 1st RES SQ (MATS) Ramey AFB Puerto Rico 18 Oct 52 // 28th RES SQ (MATS) Ramey AFB Puerto Rico 5 Feb 53 // Wfu to Ogden Air Materiel Area (AMC) Hill AFB Utah 13 Jun 53 and stored. Assigned to reclamation and dropped from inventory 8 Jul 54 // Ben W. Widtfeldt & Harry S. McCandless Council Bluffs Iowa 23 Aug 55 reg: N6233C // Richard S. Lowe Miami Florida 19 Aug 55 // LEBCA International Inc. Miami Florida 31 Aug 55. Subsequent history unk Unconfirmed Data → Some sources quote this aircraft as going to LACE as HK-468, then to Venezuela as YV-C-LBA (see under: 10198/45-57828) and Colombian records show HK-486 as ex-N6233C but with the wrong s/n (45-57817) quoted, but FAA documents don't show an export to Colombia ← Unconfirmed Data. N6233C reg revoked 14 Dec 70. Final Disposition: Unknown (Presumed Scrapped).

10198 / 45-57828/CQ-828 / C-82A-FA

Avble: 21 Apr 48; Acc: 18 May 48; Del: 7 Jun 48 to USAF // 300th AF BAS (AMC) Fairchild Aircraft Maryland 7 Jun 48 // 62nd MSU GP (TAC) McChord AFB Washington 14 Jun 48 & 3 Nov 49; 62nd TCG (TAC) McChord AFB Washington 1 Jul 48; assigned 8th TCSq; depls to Elmendorf AFB Alaska 1 Sep 48 & 6 Jun 49. Minor ground collision incident at McClellan AFB California 24 Jun 49, no fatalities. To Sacramento Air Materiel Area (AMC) McClellan AFB California 28 Jun 49 for depmnt // 4th RES SQ (MATS) March AFB California 21 Mar 50; cvtd to SC-82A; to 22nd Bombardment WG (SAC) March AFB California 18 Oct 50 for tranmnt; to San Antonio Air Materiel Area (AMC) Kelly AFB Texas 7 Jun 51 for tranmnt // 42nd RES SQ (MATS) March AFB California 4 Nov 52 // Aircraft Engineering & Maintenance Co. (AMC) Oakland California 5 Jun 53 on bailment; cvtd back to C-82A standard and modernized to Group A standard // 1st AACS Installation & Maintenance SQ (MATS) Tinker AFB Oklahoma 15 Dec 53 // Wfu to Ogden Air Materiel Area (AMC) Hill AFB Utah 16 Sep 54 and stored. Dropped from inventory 9 May 55 // Ben W. Widtfeldt & Harry S. McCandless Council Bluffs Iowa 23 Aug 55 reg: N6234C // Richard S. Lowe Miami Florida 19 Aug 55 // LEBCA International Inc. Miami Florida 31 Aug 55. Leased to Lloyd Aereo Boliviano (LAB) Cochabamba during 1955 for a 30-day period, reg: CP-614 // Expreso Aereo Peruano S.A. (EAPSA) Peru 13 Mar 57 reg: OB-RAB-458, re-reg: OB-WAG-458; appears to have never been exported or entered service // Lineas Aereas del Colombianas Expresas (LACE) Ltda. Bogota Colombia 17 Apr 57 reg: HK-468; named *Leticia*. N6234C reg canx 6 May 57. Possible short-term lease to Linea Aeropostal Venezolana (LAV) Caracas Venezuela date unk; reg YV-C-LBA marked on tail but LACE markings retained. Unconfirmed Data → Direccion de Aeronautica Civil (DAC) Bolivia 1960 reg.: CP-665 but ntu due to a crash 24 Aug 60 in Bolivia during the aircraft's delivery flight ← Unconfirmed Data. HK-486 reg canx 2 Aug 69. A crash site was discovered during 2005 by a German aviation enthusiast, Hans-Joachim Wirtz, in the Puerto Health area in NW Bolivia. The exact position is 32 miles east of Chive, Bolivia (GPS location: S12 18 30.60/W068 07 24.30) along the Rio Madre de Dios River. Data plates onboard confirm the aircraft as indeed being s/n: 45-57828, but the airframe is devoid of any other form of markings or registration, putting some doubt on its actually being CP-665. An analysis of the wreckage indicates severe impact damage to the entire nose section back to the main entry door and a broken starboard boom behind the trailing edge of the wing. The u/c is down and locked with the struts on both main bogies being straight and appearing to be in good condition. The leading edges of the wings appear undented and straight and the underbelly of the fuselage seems undamaged. It appears the aircraft made an emergency landing on what was at the time a Pampas grassland clearing, making a clean, wheels-down landing, but struck a rut in the ground, completely smashing the nose section in with a subsequent structural failure of the right boom. It seems the crew may have only received minor or no injuries. Many questions remain over this accident, such as the actual civil reg. The remains of a 3,000-ft-long airstrip running out behind the C-82's resting spot suggests an airstrip was there at the time of the crash; however, many contest this claim. In the 50-plus years since the crash, the aircraft has been robbed of all useful parts—engines, flight instruments, onboard equipment, seats, fuselage skin, and even the wire that makes up the control cables, leaving, for the most part, an empty shell. Final Disposition: Accident.

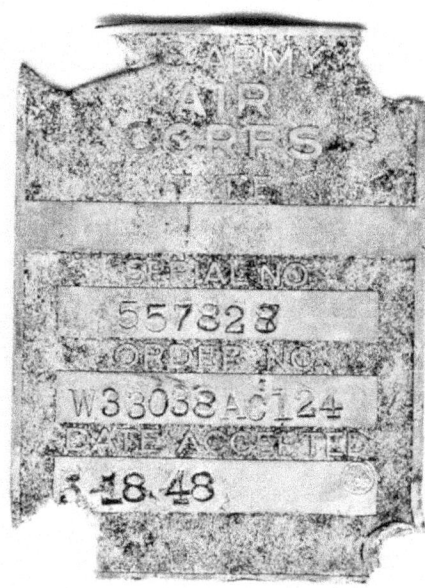

Top: Data-plates for C-82A s/n: 45-57828 (msn: 10198), showing those for the manufacturer (*left*) and the one applied by the United States Air Force upon delivery (*right*). *Bottom:* C-82A s/n: 45-57828 as found in a Bolivian rain forest during 2005 (three photographs, Hans-Joachim Wirtz).

What remains of the flight-deck on C-82A s/n: 45-57828 after many decades in a Bolivian rain forest (Hans-Joachim Wirtz).

10199 / 45-57829/CQ-829 / C-82A-FA

Avble: 27 Apr 48; Acc: 21 May 48; Del: 3 Jun 48 to USAF // 300th AF BAS (AMC) Fairchild Aircraft Maryland 3 Jun 48 // multiple assignments to 62nd MSU GP (TAC) McChord AFB Washington starting 7 Jun 48; 62nd TCG (TAC) McChord AFB Washington 23 Jun 48; assigned 7th & 4th TCSq; depls to Elmendorf AFB Alaska 3 Mar 49 & 3 Oct 49 // 7th RES SQ (MATS) Wiesbaden AB West Germany 17 Apr 50; cvtd to SC-82A; to 60th AB GP (AFE) Wiesbaden AB West Germany 27 Nov 50 for tranmnt // 9th RES SQ (MATS) Wiesbaden AB West Germany 20 Feb 51 // 69th RES SQ (MATS) Wiesbaden AB West Germany 4 Nov 52; to 69th RES SQ at Furstenfeldbruck AB West Germany 23 Mar 53 // 84th RES SQ (MATS) Furstenfeldbruck AB West Germany 16 May 53 // To San Antonio Air Materiel Area (AMC) Kelly AFB Texas 5 Sep 53 for storage // To Ogden Air Materiel Area (AMC) Hill AFB Utah 29 Sep 53 for depmnt. Wfu 1953 and stored. Dropped from inventory 8 Jul 54 // Ben W. Widtfeldt & Harry S. McCandless Council Bluffs Iowa 23 Aug 55 reg: N6235C // Richard S. Lowe Miami Florida 19 Aug 55 // LEBCA International Inc. Miami Florida 31 Aug 55 // Lineas Aereas del Colombianas Expresas (LACE) Ltda. Bogota Colombia 26 Sep 56 reg: HK-426; named *Arauca* // Lilia Lizcano de Herrera Bogota Colombia 6 Oct 59; later to Servicios Especiales Aereos (SEA) Ltda. Bogota Colombia. Wfu early 70s; N6235C reg canx 14 Dec 70; HK-426 reg canx 2 Nov 73. Derelict at El Dorado Intl. Airport Bogota Colombia from 1973. Scrapped, along with several other derelict aircraft, when the airport expanded with a new runway in 1997. Final Disposition: Scrapped.

10200 / 45-57830/CQ-830 / C-82A-FA

Avble: 14 May 48; Acc: 24 May 48; Del: 16 Jun 48 to USAF // 1st RES SQ (AAC) Fort Richardson Alaska 15 Jun 48; cvtd to SC-82A // 10th RES SQ (AAC) Elmendorf AFB Alaska 16 Jun 48 // 54th TCSq (AAC) Elmendorf AFB Alaska 30 Nov 48; cvtd back to C-82A standard // 57th AB GP (AAC) Elmendorf AFB Alaska 12 Mar 49; to 57th MSU GP (AAC) Elmendorf AFB Alaska 4 Aug 49; to 57th Fighter WG (AAC) Elmendorf AFB Alaska 9 May 50; 54th TCSq (Attached) // 39th Air Depot WG (AAC) Elmendorf AFB Alaska 3 May 50 for depmnt // 54th TCSq (AAC) Elmendorf AFB Alaska 19 May 50. Had a landing accident due to mechanical failure at Elmendorf AFB Alaska 1 Apr 51, no fatalities // 39th Air Depot WG (AAC) Elmendorf AFB Alaska 4 Apr 52 for depmnt and project duties // To Ogden Air Materiel Area (AMC) Hill AFB Utah 19 Nov 52 for depmods. Wfu 21 Jan 53 and stored. Assigned to reclamation and dropped from inventory 8 Jul 54 // Samuel C. Rudolph, Nathan Sidell, Charles J. Katz (Joint Venturers) Los Angeles California 29 Sep 55 reg: N6247C // Albert J. Leeward d/b/a Leeward Aeronautical Service Fort Wayne Indiana 17 Aug 55 (paper sale made prior to acquisition from the Air Force); ownership transferred to Leeward Aeronautical Sales Inc. Fort Wayne Indiana same day; cert of reg not issued until 7 May 57 by which time Leeward was relocated to Miami Florida // Francis L. Duncan New York, N.Y. 2 May 57, for export to Brazil // Servicos Aereos Cruzeiro do Sul Rio de Janeiro Brazil 12 Aug 57; arrived in Brazil 24 Aug 57; named *Centauro*. Soon after taking off from Val de Cans Airport, Belem, Brazil on 16 Jan 58 the aircraft had a port engine fire. While attempting to return, the C-82, losing altitude, hit trees and crashed 5 miles NW of the airport, killing the 3 crew members: Captain Edison Ribeiro do Couto, copilot Celio Augusto Fanti, and radio-navigator Benedito Pereira Alves. Reg: PP-CEF 18 Jul 58; PP-CEF reg canx 18 Jul 58—issued and canceled the same day! N6247C reg canx 27 Oct 70. Final Disposition: Accident.

10201 / 45-57831/CQ-831 / C-82A-FA

Avble: 3 May 48; Acc: 27 May 48; Del: 16 Jun 48 to USAF // 1st RES SQ (AAC) Fort Richardson Alaska 15 Jun 48; cvtd to SC-82A // 10th RES SQ (AAC) Elmendorf AFB Alaska 16 Jun 48 // 57th AB GP (AAC) Elmendorf AFB Alaska 1 Apr 49; cvtd back to C-82A standard; to San Bernardino Air Depot (AMC) Norton AFB California 31 Aug 49 for depmnt; 57th Fighter WG (AAC) Elmendorf AFB Alaska 9 May 50; 54th TCSq (Attached); renamed 57th Fighter-Interceptor WG Sep 50. Suffered a landing accident due to weather at Kenai Airport Alaska 21 Jul 50. Pilot: Ralph V. Korhnak, no fatalities but aircraft assessed as "damaged beyond repair." Assigned to reclamation & salvage and dropped from inventory 30 Oct 50. Final Disposition: Accident.

10202 / 45-57832/CQ-832 / C-82A-FA

Avble: 20 May 48; Acc: 27 May 48; Del: 8 Jul 48 to USAF // assigned 316th TCG (TAC) in error. Multiple assignments to 62nd MSU GP (TAC) McChord AFB Washington starting 12 Jul 48; 62nd TCG (TAC) McChord AFB Washington 26 Jul 48; assigned 4th

& 7th TCSq; depls to Elmendorf AFB Alaska 30 Nov 48 & 3 Mar 49; depl to Fort Richardson Alaska 20 Dec 48 // 1800th AACS WG (MATS) Tinker AFB Oklahoma 23 Dec 49 // 1850th AACS SQ (MATS) Tinker AFB Oklahoma 30 Dec 49; to 3520th Combat Crew Training WG (ATC) Wichita AFB Kansas 10 Nov 51 for tranmnt; to 6501st Support SQ (MATS) Wichita AFB Kansas 10 Nov 51 // 3rd Air Materiel (Overseas) SQ (MATS) Tinker AFB Oklahoma 30 Jan 53; to 807th AB GP (SAC) March AFB California 15 May 53 for tranmnt // Wfu to Ogden Air Materiel Area (AMC) Hill AFB Utah 17 Jun 53 and stored. Assigned to reclamation and dropped from inventory 8 Jul 54 // L.B. Smith Aircraft Corp. Miami Florida 1 Sep 55 reg: N2054A // Donald B. Sittman & Alfred E. Merhige Miami Florida 27 Aug 55. FAA Files Incomplete → Dispatch Services Inc. Miami Florida, Purchased for export, date unk, reg: N54211 // Expreso Aereo Panama S.A., Panama 31 Jan 56 reg: HP-220. This company appears to be the parent company to Peru-based Expreso Aereo Peruano, HP-220 reg ntu but may have been used for ferrying purposes // Rutas Aereas del Peru S.A. (RAPSA) 28 May 56 reg: OB-RAA-439, ntu and export canx, remained in U.S. // Expreso Aereo Peruano S.A. (EAPSA) Lima Peru 12 Nov 56; re-reg: OB-WAF-439 13 Mar 57; re-reg: OB-UAB-439 28 Sep 57 // Empresa Guatemalteca de Aviacion (Aviateca Guatemalteca) Guatemala 13 Nov 58 reg: TG-AVA ← FAA Files Incomplete. Skidded off the runway when brakes applied after landing at San Francisco Mt., La Libertad, Guatemala 29 Nov 58; aircraft collided with a parked tractor and was w/o by a fire, still apparently in Peruvian markings, fatalities unk, nfd. OB-UAB-439 reg canx 17 Jan 59. N2054A reg canx 12 Mar 71. Final Disposition: Accident.

C-82A Packet (msn: 10202), probably photographed in the United States while being readied for export to Peru marked as OB-RAA-439 (Peter J. Marson Collection).

10203 / 48-568/CQ-568 / C-82A-FA

Avble: 25 May 48; Acc: 28 May 48; Del: 27 Jul 48 to USAF // 316th TCG (TAC) Greenville AFB South Carolina 29 Jul 48; to 316th MSU GP (CNC) Greenville AFB South Carolina 9 Feb 49 // 1701st Air Transport WG (MATS) Great Falls AFB Montana 6 Sep 49 // Warner-Robins Air Materiel Area (AMC) Robins AFB Georgia 6 Jan 50 for depmnt

// 7th RES SQ (MATS) Wiesbaden AB West Germany 17 Nov 50; cvtd to SC-82A // 9th RES SQ (MATS) Wiesbaden AB West Germany 20 Feb 51; to RAF Manston England 1 Apr 51; to RAF Sculthorpe England 30 Jul 51; to 85th Air Depot WG (AFE) Erding AB, West Germany 1 Feb 52 // 67th RES SQ (MATS) RAF Sculthorpe England 4 Nov 52 // Wfu to Ogden Air Materiel Area (AMC) Hill AFB Utah 25 Aug 53 and stored. Dropped from inventory 8 Jul 54 // L.B. Smith Aircraft Corp. Miami Florida 19 Sep 55 reg: N2062A; reg: N6237C rsvd but ntu // Lineas Aereas del Caribe Ltda. (LIDCA) Barranquilla Colombia Feb 56 reg: HK-915-X; N2062A reg canx 8 Feb 56; reg: HK-915 22 May 56. W/o in accident prior to 1965, cause and fatalities unk, nfd. HK-915 reg canx 11 Jun 69. Final Disposition: Accident.

10204 / 48-569/CQ-569 / C-82A-FA

Avble: 28 May 48; Acc: 23 Jun 48; Del: 19 Jul 48 to USAF // 316th TCG (TAC) Greenville AFB South Carolina 19 Jul 48; 316th to Smyrna AFB Tennessee 4 Nov 49; depl to Guantanamo Bay Cuba 28 Feb 50; Smyrna AFB renamed Sewart AFB 25 Mar 50; depl to 314th TCG (CNC) Laurinburg-Maxton Airport North Carolina 20 Apr 50; depl to 2601st Light Assault SQ (314th) (CNC) Sewart AFB Tennessee 21 Jul 50; to 78th Fighter-Interceptor WG (CNC) Hamilton AFB California 24 Nov 50; to San Antonio Air Materiel Area (AMC) Kelly AFB Texas 29 Jan 51 // 375th TCWG (TAC) Greenville AFB South Carolina 9 Mar 51; to Warner-Robins Air Materiel Area (AMC) Robins AFB Georgia 12 Oct 51 for depmnt; depl to Grenier AFB New Hampshire 10 Jan 52; depl to Brownwood Field Texas 11 Mar 52 // 64th TCWG (TAC) Donaldson AFB South Carolina 14 Jul 52 // Aircraft Engineering & Maintenance Co. (AMC) Oakland California 21 Jul 53 on bailment; modernized to Group A standard // 567th Air Defense GP (ADC) McChord AFB Washington 6 Jan 54. Made a belly crash-landing due to an engine failure 1 mile N Yelm, Washington 14 Feb 54. Pilot: Raymond E. Costello, no fatalities but aircraft w/o. Assigned to reclamation and salvage 14 Feb 54. Dropped from inventory 14 Apr 54. Final Disposition: Accident.

10205 / 48-570/CQ-570 / C-82A-FA

Avble: 8 Jun 48; Acc: 24 Jun 48; Del: 16 Jul 48 to USAF // 316th TCG (TAC) Greenville AFB South Carolina 16 Jul 48; assigned 75th TCSq. Suffered an in-flight engine failure resulting in a crash landing 11 miles SW Portsmouth Ohio 12 Nov 48. Pilot: Johnnie R. Godwin, no fatalities // 332nd MSU GP (TAC) Lockbourne AFB Ohio 16 Nov 48; assessed as "damaged beyond repair." Assigned to reclamation and salvage 13 Apr 49. Dropped from inventory 4 May 49. Final Disposition: Accident.

10206 / 48-571/CQ-571 / C-82A-FA

Avble: 14 Jun 48; Acc: 24 Jun 48; Del: 21 Jul 48 to USAF // 316th TCG (TAC) Greenville AFB South Carolina 22 Jul 48; 316th to Smyrna AFB Tennessee 4 Nov 49; depl to Guantanamo Bay Cuba 28 Feb 50; Smyrna AFB renamed Sewart AFB 25 Mar 50; depl to 314th TCG (CNC) Laurinburg-Maxton Airport North Carolina 20 Apr 50; depl to 2601st Light Assault SQ (314th) (CNC) Sewart AFB Tennessee 21 Jul 50 // 375th TCWG (TAC) Greenville AFB South Carolina 13 Mar 51; to Warner-Robins Air Materiel Area

(AMC) Robins AFB Georgia 6 Sep 51 for depmnt; depl to Grenier AFB New Hampshire 3 Jan 52; depl to Brownwood Field Texas 10 Mar 52 // 64th TCWG (TAC) Donaldson AFB South Carolina 14 Jul 52 // Wfu to San Antonio Air Materiel Area (AMC) Kelly AFB Texas 7 Aug 53 and stored. Dropped from inventory 1 Jul 54 // Forca Aerea Brasileira (FAB/Brazilian Air Force) 20 Sep 55 FAB s/n: 2210. Ferried to Brazil Jan 56; No. 2 Grupo de Transporte (2nd Transport Group) Aerea dos Afonsos AB Rio de Janeiro; redes No. 1/1 Grupo de Transporte de Tropa (1st Troop Carrier Group) 22 Jan 58. Wfu 19 Apr 68 and stored. SOC: 3 Sep 73 and sold for scrap. Final Disposition: Scrapped.

10207 / 48-572/CQ-572 / C-82A-FA

Avble: 18 Jun 48; Acc: 30 Jun 48; Del: 16 Jul 48 to USAF // 316th TCG (TAC) Greenville AFB South Carolina 8 Sep 48; 316th MSU GP (CNC) Greenville AFB South Carolina 26 Jan 49 // 1227th AB GP (MATS) Goose Bay AB Labrador Canada 21 Mar 49; to Middletown Air Materiel Area (AMC) Olmsted AFB Pennsylvania 30 Apr 49. Crashed during take-off run at Isachsen Weather Station, Ellef Ringnes Is. Arctic Canada 20 May 49. Pilot: Gerald D. McCrea, no fatalities but aircraft w/o. Fuselage subsequently used as a storehouse on the island but its ultimate fate is unknown. Some inner wing parts remain at the site today. Assigned to reclamation 27 May 49. Dropped from inventory 31 Oct 49. Final Disposition: Accident.

10208 / 48-573/CQ-573 / C-82A-FA

Avble: 23 Jun 48; Acc: 30 Jun 48; Del: 23 Jul 48 to USAF // 316th TCG (TAC) Greenville AFB South Carolina 27 Jul 48. Cvtd to a Packet Pressroom for the purposes of promoting the USAF to the public at air shows. The cargo hold was outfitted with desks, typewriters and lamps for the traveling media to use as a mobile newsroom. A nose motif was painted on the forward fuselage with the words "nose for news" underneath. Msn: 10213 (48–578) was another conversion; both were in use for a period during 1948–1949. 316th to Smyrna AFB Tennessee 4 Nov 49; depl to Guantanamo Bay Cuba 28 Feb 50; Smyrna AFB renamed Sewart AFB 25 Mar 50; depl to 314th TCG (CNC) Laurinburg-Maxton Airport North Carolina 20 Apr 50; depl to 2601st Light Assault SQ (314th) (CNC) Sewart AFB Tennessee 21 Jul 50; to 3800th Air University WG (AU) Maxwell AFB Alabama 1 Sep 50 for tranmnt // 375th TCWG (TAC) Greenville AFB South Carolina 13 Mar 51; to Warner-Robins Air Materiel Area (AMC) Robins AFB Georgia 28 Sep 51 for depmnt; depl to Brownwood Field Texas 8 Mar 52 // 64th TCWG (TAC) Donaldson AFB South Carolina 14 Jul 52 // Wfu to San Antonio Air Materiel Area (AMC) Kelly AFB Texas 5 Aug 53 and stored. Dropped from inventory 1 Jul 54 // Forca Aerea Brasileira (FAB/Brazilian Air Force) 20 Sep 55 s/n: 2209. Ferried to Brazil Jan 56; No. 2 Grupo de Transporte (2nd Transport Group) Aerea dos Afonsos AB Rio de Janeiro; redes No. 1/1 Grupo de Transporte de Tropa (1st Troop Carrier Group) 22 Jan 58. Wfu 19 Apr 68 and stored. SOC: 3 Sep 73 and sold for scrap. Final Disposition: Scrapped.

10209 / 48-574/CQ-574 / C-82A-FA

Avble: 29 Jun 48; Acc: 12 Jul 48; Del: 20 Jul 48 to USAF // 316th TCG (TAC) Greenville AFB South Carolina 1 Sep 48; briefly to 316th MSU GP (TAC) Greenville AFB

South Carolina 8 Sep 48. Had an in-flight mechanical failure 20 miles NW Fayetteville North Carolina 7 Apr 49, no fatalities. 316th to Smyrna AFB Tennessee 4 Nov 49; multiple depls to 314th TCG (TAC) Smyrna AFB Tennessee starting 25 Nov 49; assigned 2601st Light Assault SQ; depl to Guantanamo Bay Cuba 28 Feb 50; Smyrna AFB renamed Sewart AFB 25 Mar 50; depl to 314th TCG (CNC) Laurinburg-Maxton Airport North Carolina 20 Apr 50 // 375th TCWG (TAC) Greenville AFB South Carolina 9 Mar 51; to Warner-Robins Air Materiel Area (AMC) Robins AFB Georgia 27 Jun 51 for depmnt // 54th TCSq (AAC) Elmendorf AFB Alaska 6 Dec 51. Had a structural failure during take-off at Elmendorf AFB Alaska 20 Mar 52, no fatalities. Minor ground accident at Elmendorf AFB Alaska 21 Mar 52, no fatalities. Had a taxiing accident upon landing at Sparrevohn Mount AFS Alaska 22 Apr 52, no fatalities // 39th Air Depot WG (AAC) Elmendorf AFB Alaska 25 Jan 53 // 5039th Maintenance GP (AAC) Elmendorf AFB Alaska 13 Apr 53 for depmnt; to 5039th Air Base WG (AAC) Elmendorf AFB Alaska 21 Apr 53 for special missions; to 5025th Maintenance GP (renamed 5039th MNT GP) (AAC) Elmendorf AFB Alaska 16 Dec 53 for depmnt, modernized to Group A standard. Wfu to 5039th Aircraft Repair SQ (AAC) Elmendorf AFB Alaska 12 Aug 55. Assigned to reclamation 16 Nov 55 and stored // Robert G. Sholton Anchorage Alaska 15 Dec 55 reg.: N4753C // Northern Air Cargo Inc. Anchorage Alaska 22 Apr 70; avionics upgrade 24 Feb 78; structural repairs to fuselage and wings 9 Jun 79. Suffered a belly-landing accident 26 Jun 84. Avionics upgrade 20 Jul 84; wfu 1 Jan 85 // Darryl G. Greenamyer Inc. Rancho Santa Fe California 13 Jun 88 // USAF Museum WPAFB Dayton Ohio 30 Jun 88; aircraft currently displayed at McChord AFB Air Museum Tacoma Washington State from 1993; de-reg: 17 Mar 05. Final Disposition: Preserved.

C-82A N4753C (msn: 10209) of Northern Air Cargo Inc. at Anchorage, Alaska, during September 1969 (Norm Taylor).

10210 / 48-575/CQ-575 / C-82A-FA

Avble: 7 Jul 48; Acc: 15 Jul 48; Del: 29 Jul 48 to USAF // 316th TCG (TAC) Greenville AFB South Carolina 1 Aug 48; 316th MSU GP (CNC) Greenville AFB South Carolina 26

Jan 49 // 2152nd RES UT (MATS) Ernest Harmon AFB Newfoundland Canada 28 Feb 49, cvtd to SC-82A // 6th RES SQ (MATS) Ernest Harmon AFB Newfoundland Canada 25 Apr 49; assigned Flight "B"; to San Antonio Air Materiel Area (AMC) Kelly AFB Texas 28 May 51 & 25 May 52. Minor landing accident at Andrews AFB Maryland 12 Apr 52, no fatalities // 52th RES SQ (MATS) Ernest Harmon AFB Newfoundland Canada 4 Nov 52; to San Antonio Air Materiel Area (AMC) Kelly AFB Texas 6 Feb 53 // Wfu to Ogden Air Materiel Area (AMC) Hill AFB Utah 7 Jun 53 and stored. Dropped from inventory 8 Jul 54 // L.B. Smith Aircraft Corp. 19 Sep 55 reg: N2063A // Rodest & Company New York N.Y. 8 Feb 56 // Vagon Volante De Colombia Ltda. (Wagon Wheel of Colombia Ltd.) Barranquilla Colombia 28 May 56 reg: HK-913X. Crashed in Funza Bogota while on final approach to Bogota Intl. Airport Colombia 22 Nov 56 with over 8,800 lb of cargo onboard. Fatalities unk, aircraft w/o. FAA reg N2063A canx 15 Feb 57. Final Disposition: Accident.

10211 / 48-576/CQ-576 / C-82A-FA

Avble: 12 Jul 48; Acc: 21 Jul 48; Del: 5 Aug 48 to USAF // 316th TCG (TAC) Greenville AFB South Carolina 5 Aug 48; 316th to Smyrna AFB Tennessee 4 Nov 49; Smyrna AFB renamed Sewart AFB 25 Mar 50; depl to 314th TCG (CNC) Laurinburg-Maxton Airport North Carolina 20 Apr 50; depl to 2601st Light Assault SQ (314th) (CNC) Sewart AFB Tennessee 7 Jul 50 // 375th TCWG (TAC) Greenville AFB South Carolina 6 Mar 51; to Warner-Robins Air Materiel Area (AMC) Robins AFB Georgia 13 Oct 51 for depmnt // 64th TCWG (TAC) Donaldson AFB South Carolina 14 Jul 52 // Wfu to San Antonio Air Materiel Area (AMC) Kelly AFB Texas 7 Jul 53 and stored. Dropped from inventory 1 Jul 54 // Forca Aerea Brasileira (FAB/Brazilian Air Force) 20 Sep 55 s/n: 2211. Ferried to Brazil Jan 56; No. 2 Grupo de Transporte (2nd Transport Group) Aerea dos Afonsos AB Rio de Janeiro; redes No. 1/1 Grupo de Transporte de Tropa (1st Troop Carrier Group) 22 Jan 58. Wfu 19 Apr 68 and stored. SOC: 3 Sep 73 and sold for scrap. Final Disposition: Scrapped.

10212 / 48-577/CQ-577 / C-82A-FA

Avble: 15 Jul 48; Acc: 26 Jul 48; Del: 31 Aug 48 to USAF // Multiple assignments to 62nd MSU GP (TAC) McChord AFB Washington starting 2 Sep 48; 62nd TCG (TAC) McChord AFB Washington 3 Sep 48; assigned 7th TCSq; depl to Elmendorf AFB Alaska 3 Mar 49; 62nd MSU GP depl to San Bernardino Air Depot California 13 Dec 49 // 314th TCG (CNC) Smyrna AFB Tennessee 23 Dec 49; assigned 2601st Light Assault SQ // 316th TCG (CNC) Smyrna AFB Tennessee 6 Feb 50; depl to Guantanamo Bay Cuba 28 Feb 50; Smyrna AFB renamed Sewart AFB 25 Mar 50; depl to 314th TCG (CNC) Laurinburg-Maxton Airport North Carolina 20 Apr 50; depl to 2601st Light Assault SQ (314th) (CNC) Sewart AFB Tennessee 21 Jul 50; to 54th TCSq (AAC) Elmendorf AFB Alaska 21 Sep 50; depl to 314th TCWG (CNC) Sewart AFB Tennessee 30 Oct 50 // 375th TCWG (TAC) Greenville AFB South Carolina 13 Mar 51; to Warner-Robins Air Materiel Area (AMC) Robins AFB Georgia 7 Sep 51 for depmnt; depl to Grenier AFB New Hampshire 3 Jan 52; depl to Brownwood Field Texas 11 Mar 52 // 64th TCWG (TAC) Donaldson AFB South Carolina 14 Jul 52 // Wfu to San Antonio Air Materiel Area (AMC) Kelly AFB Texas 7 Jul 53 and stored. Dropped from inventory 1 Jul 54 // Forca Aerea Brasileira (FAB/Brazilian Air Force) 20 Sep 55 s/n: 2206. Ferried to Brazil Jan 56; No. 2 Grupo de Transporte (2nd Transport Group) Aerea dos Afonsos AB Rio de Janeiro; redes No. 1/1 Grupo de Transporte de Tropa (1st Troop Carrier Group) 22 Jan 58. Wfu 19 Apr 68 and stored. SOC: 3 Jul 73 and sold for scrap. Final Disposition: Scrapped.

Photographed just after retirement in 1967 is Brazilian C-82A Packet s/n: 2206 (msn: 10212). Note the split black & white painted booms and parachute emblem on the tail (via José de Alvarenga).

10213 / 48-578/CQ-578 / C-82A-FA

Avble: 21 Jul 48; Acc: 28 Jul 48; Del: 6 Aug 48 to USAF // 316th TCG (TAC) Greenville AFB South Carolina 6 Aug 48. Cvtd to a Packet Pressroom for the purposes of promoting the USAF to the public at air shows. The cargo hold was outfitted with desks, typewriters and lamps for the traveling media to use as a mobile newsroom. A nose motif was painted on the forward fuselage with the words "nose for news" underneath. Msn: 10208 (48-573) was another conversion; both were in use for a period during 1948–1949. To 316th MSU GP (CNC) Greenville AFB South Carolina 3 Feb 49; 316th to Smyrna AFB Tennessee 4 Nov 49 // 314th TCG (CNC) Smyrna AFB Tennessee 25 Nov 49; assigned 2601st Light Assault SQ; 316th depl to Guantanamo Bay Cuba 28 Feb 50; Smyrna AFB renamed Sewart AFB 25 Mar 50; 314th depl to Laurinburg-Maxton Airport North Carolina 20 Apr 50; to Sacramento Air Materiel Area (AMC) McClellan AFB California 19 Nov 50 // 375th TCWG (TAC) Greenville AFB South Carolina 15 Jan 51; to Warner-Robins Air Materiel Area (AMC) Robins AFB Georgia 12 Sep 51 for depmnt; depl to Brownwood Field Texas 14 Mar 52 // 64th TCWG (TAC) Donaldson AFB South Carolina 14 Jul 52 // To Middletown Air Materiel Area (AMC) Olmsted AFB Pennsylvania 22 May 53 for depmnt // Wfu to San Antonio Air Materiel Area (AMC) Kelly AFB Texas 10 Sep 53 and stored. Dropped from inventory 1 Jul 54 // Forca Aerea Brasileira (FAB/Brazilian Air Force) 20 Sep 55 s/n: 2207. Ferried to Brazil Jan 56; No. 2 Grupo de Transporte (2nd Transport Group) Aerea dos Afonsos AB Rio de Janeiro; redes No. 1/1 Grupo de Transporte de Tropa (1st Troop Carrier Group) 22 Jan 58. Wfu 19 Apr 68 and stored. SOC: 25 Sep 70 by civil sale // Amazonia Transporte, Industria E Comercio Belem Brazil 5 Oct 70 reg: PT-DNZ. Crashed while on approach for landing at Maraba, Brazil 28 Oct 70 when it hit a hill at Ponta Norte, Serra dos Carajas. Four crew onboard killed and aircraft destroyed. Reg canx 14 Jul 71. Final Disposition: Accident.

C-82A s/n: 48-578 (msn: 10213) as the Packet Pressroom for the use of news media at United States Air Force air shows. Note the "nose for news" artwork on the aircraft nose (National Museum of the United States Air Force).

10214 / 48-579/CQ-579 / C-82A-FA

Avble: 26 Jul 48; Acc: 30 Jul 48; Del: 31 Jul 48 to USAF // 62nd MSU GP (TAC) McChord AFB Washington 2 Sep 48; 62nd TCG (TAC) McChord AFB Washington 3 Sep 48; assigned 7th TCSq; depl to Elmendorf AFB Alaska 3 Mar 49. Minor taxiing accident at Alberta Municipal Airport Canada 12 Apr 49, no fatalities. Suffered a landing accident 10 Aug 49 at McChord AFB Washington. Pilot: Dick H. Ormand Jr., no fatalities but aircraft badly damaged. To 62nd MSU GP (CNC) 12 Aug 49; assessed as "damaged beyond repair." Assigned to reclamation and salvage 17 Oct 49. Dropped from inventory 14 Feb 50. Final Disposition: Accident.

10215 / 48-580/CQ-580 / C-82A-FA

Avble: 30 Jul 48; Acc: 6 Aug 48; Del: 1 Sep 48 to USAF // 62nd TCG (TAC) McChord AFB Washington 7 Sep 48; assigned 4th TCSq; depls to Elmendorf AFB Alaska 30 Nov 48 & 17 Aug 49; depl to Fort Richardson Alaska 20 Dec 48; to 57th MSU GP (AAC) Elmendorf AFB Alaska 15 Sep 49. Had a landing accident due to mechanical failure at Elmendorf AFB Alaska 31 Oct 49, no fatalities. To Alaska Air Lines Air Depot (AAC) Elmendorf AFB Alaska 1 Nov 49 likely for repairs; to 5039th Air Depot WG (AAC) Elmendorf AFB Alaska 1 Dec 49 for depmnt // 325th Fighter (All-Weather) WG (CNC) McChord AFB Washington 5 May 50; to 54th TCSq (AAC) Elmendorf AFB Alaska 26 Sep 50 // 375th TCWG (TAC) Greenville AFB South Carolina 9 Nov 50; to Warner-Robins Air Materiel Area (AMC) Robins AFB Georgia 27 Jun 51 for depmnt; depl to Grenier AFB New Hampshire 3 Jan 52; depl to Brownwood Field Texas 10 Mar 52 // 64th TCWG (TAC) Donaldson AFB South Carolina 14 Jul 52 // Wfu to San Antonio Air Materiel Area (AMC) Kelly AFB Texas 2 Jul 53 and stored. Dropped from inventory 1 Jul

54 // Forca Aerea Brasileira (FAB/Brazilian Air Force) 20 Sep 55 s/n: 2204. Ferried to Brazil Jan 56; No. 2 Grupo de Transporte (2nd Transport Group) Aerea dos Afonsos AB Rio de Janeiro; redes No. 1/1 Grupo de Transporte de Tropa (1st Troop Carrier Group) 22 Jan 58. Wfu 19 Apr 68 and stored. SOC: 25 Nov 70 and used for fire training at Escola de Aeronautica (EAer/Air Force School) then sold for scrap. Final Disposition: Scrapped.

10216 / 48-581/CQ-581 / C-82A-FA

Avble: 6 Aug 48; Acc: 19 Aug 48; Del: 31 Aug 48 to USAF // Briefly to 62nd MSU GP (TC) McChord AFB Washington 2 Sep 48; 62nd TCG (TAC) McChord AFB Washington 3 Sep 48; assigned 4th TCSq; depls to Elmendorf AFB Alaska 30 Nov 48 & 17 Aug 49; depl to Fort Richardson Alaska 20 Dec 48; 62nd MSU GP (CNC) McChord AFB Washington 21 Nov 49 // 316th TCG (CNC) Smyrna AFB Tennessee 6 Feb 50; depls to 2601st Light Assault SQ (attached 314th TCG) (CNC) Smyrna AFB Tennessee 6 Feb 50 & 21 Jul 50; depl to Guantanamo Bay Cuba 28 Feb 50; Smyrna AFB renamed Sewart AFB 25 Mar 50; 314th depl to Laurinburg-Maxton Airport North Carolina 21 Apr 50 // 54th TCSq (AAC) Elmendorf AFB Alaska 21 Sep 50 // 375th TCWG (TAC) Greenville AFB South Carolina 13 Mar 51; to Warner-Robins Air Materiel Area (AMC) Robins AFB Georgia 6 Sep 51 for depmnt; to Fairchild Aircraft Maryland (AMC) 5 Nov 51 // 39th Air Depot WG (AAC) Elmendorf AFB Alaska 11 Dec 51; assignments to 54th TCSq (AAC) Elmendorf AFB Alaska 12 Dec 51 & 15 Oct 52. Moderate landing accident at Sparrevohn Mount AFS Alaska 4 Mar 52, no fatalities // 5039th Air Transport GP (AAC) Elmendorf AFB Alaska 1 Mar 53 // 5039th Air Base WG (AAC) Elmendorf AFB Alaska 13 Apr 53; to 5039th Maintenance GP (AAC) Elmendorf AFB Alaska 14 Apr 53 for depmnt; to 5025th Maintenance GP (renamed 5039th MNT GP) (AAC) Elmendorf AFB Alaska 29 Jul 53 for depmnt, modernized to Group A standard. To 5039th Aircraft Repair SQ (AAC) Elmendorf AFB Alaska 13 Apr 55 for depmnt. Wfu to 5039th Aircraft Repair SQ (AAC) Elmendorf AFB Alaska 15 Aug 55. The last C-82A to be retired from active USAF service.

Northern Air Cargo Inc. C-82A N4752C (msn: 10216) at Anchorage, Alaska, during August 1973 (John Wegg).

Assigned to reclamation 16 Nov 55 and stored // Robert G. Sholton Anchorage Alaska 15 Dec 55 reg.: N4752C; major avionics upgrade 17 Feb 62 // Northern Air Cargo Inc. Anchorage Alaska 22 Apr 70; structural repairs made to fuselage 26 Jan 74. Repairs made to aircraft 17 Jul 77 after a belly-landing accident 25 Jun 77. Avionics upgrades 24 Feb 78 & 24 Jun 84. Wfu 1 Jan 85 // Darryl G. Greenamyer Inc. Rancho Santa Fe California 13 Jun 88 // USAF Museum WPAFB Dayton Ohio 30 Jun 88; de-reg: 16 Aug 88. Refurbished after 2010 with recovered flight control surfaces, undercarriage servicing, sheet metal repairs, complete repaint and interior and flight-deck refurbishment. Final Disposition: Preserved.

10217 / 48-582/CQ-582 / C-82A-FA

Avble: 10 Aug 48; Acc: 20 Aug 48; Del: 14 Sep 48 to USAF // 62nd TCG (TAC) McChord AFB Washington 16 Sep 48; assigned 8th TCSq; depl to Elmendorf AFB Alaska 3 Mar 49; to 62nd MSU GP (CNC) McChord AFB Washington 15 Aug 49. Crashed 5 miles NE McCleary Washington 29 Sep 49 as a result of a navigation error made during a training flight. Pilot: Burton A. Reeves plus two others onboard killed. To 62nd MSU GP (CNC) 30 Sep 49 for disposal. Assigned to reclamation 17 Oct 49. Dropped from inventory 10 Nov 49. Final Disposition: Accident.

10218 / 48-583/CQ-583 / C-82A-FA

Avble: 13 Aug 48; Acc: 23 Aug 48; Del: 13 Sep 48 to USAF // 62nd TCG (TAC) McChord AFB Washington 20 Sep 48; assigned 7th TCSq; depl to Elmendorf AFB Alaska 3 Mar 49; to 62nd MSU GP (TAC) McChord AFB Washington 15 Aug 49 & 13 Oct 49; 62nd MSU GP depl to San Bernardino Air Depot California 13 Dec 49 // 314th TCG (CNC) Smyrna AFB Tennessee 13 Dec 49; assigned 2601st Light Assault SQ // 316th TCG (CNC) Smyrna AFB Tennessee 6 Feb 50; depl to Guantanamo Bay Cuba 28 Feb 50; Smyrna AFB renamed Sewart AFB 25 Mar 50; depl to 314th TCG (CNC) Laurinburg-

Brazilian C-82A s/n: 2203 (msn: 10218) at Fort Worth, Texas, February 13, 1960 (Gary Kuhn Collection).

Maxton Airport North Carolina 24 Apr 50 // 314th TCWG (CNC) Sewart AFB Tennessee 19 Jul 50 // 375th TCWG (TAC) Greenville AFB South Carolina 22 Jan 51; assigned 55th TCSq; to Warner-Robins Air Materiel Area (AMC) Robins AFB Georgia 27 Sep 51 for depmnt; depl to Grenier AFB New Hampshire 3 Jan 52; depl to Brownwood Field Texas 7 Mar 52. Had a drop mishap (with C-82A s/n: 44-23047) near Gatesville Texas 28 Mar 52, no fatalities // 64th TCWG (TAC) Donaldson AFB South Carolina 14 Jul 52 // Wfu to San Antonio Air Materiel Area (AMC) Kelly AFB Texas 26 Jun 53 and stored. Dropped from inventory 1 Jul 54 // Forca Aerea Brasileira (FAB/Brazilian Air Force) 20 Sep 55 s/n: 2203. Ferried to Brazil Jan 56; No. 2 Grupo de Transporte (2nd Transport Group) Aerea dos Afonsos AB Rio de Janeiro; redes No. 1/1 Grupo de Transporte de Tropa (1st Troop Carrier Group) 22 Jan 58. Wfu 19 Apr 68 and stored. SOC: 3 Sep 73 and sold for scrap. Final Disposition: Scrapped.

10219 / 48-584/CQ-584 / C-82A-FA

Avble: 19 Aug 48; Acc: 30 Aug 48; Del: 16 Sep 48 to USAF // 62nd TCG (TAC) McChord AFB Washington 20 Sep 48; assigned 4th TCSq; depls to Elmendorf AFB Alaska 30 Nov 48 & 17 Aug 49; depl to Fort Richardson Alaska 20 Dec 48; 62nd MSU GP (CNC) McChord AFB Washington 21 Nov 49 // 314th TCG (CNC) Smyrna AFB Tennessee 13 Feb 50; assigned 2601st Light Assault SQ // 316th TCG (CNC) Smyrna AFB Tennessee 13 Feb 50; depl to Guantanamo Bay Cuba 28 Feb 50; Smyrna AFB renamed Sewart AFB 25 Mar 50; depl to 314th TCG (CNC) Laurinburg-Maxton Airport North Carolina 24 Apr 50 // 314th TCG (CNC) Sewart AFB Tennessee 12 Jul 50 // 375th TCWG (TAC) Greenville AFB South Carolina 7 Feb 51; to 117th Reconnaissance (Tactical) WG (TAC) Lawson AFB Georgia 1 Mar 51; to Warner-Robins Air Materiel Area (AMC) Robins AFB Georgia 29 Sep 51 for depmnt; depl to Brownwood Field Texas 4 Mar 52 // 64th TCWG (TAC) Donaldson AFB South Carolina 14 Jul 52; depl to Elmendorf AFB Alaska 1 Oct 52 // Wfu to San Antonio Air Materiel Area (AMC) Kelly AFB Texas 26 Jun 53 and stored.

C-82A Packet with s/n: 2200 (msn: 10219) just after delivery to the Forca Aerea Brasileira during 1956 (via José de Alvarenga).

Dropped from inventory 1 Jul 54 // Forca Aerea Brasileira (FAB/Brazilian Air Force) 20 Sep 55 initial s/n: 2065, photographic evidence shows "2065" marked on the aircraft prior to delivery, later changed to s/n: 2200. Ferried to Brazil Jan 56; No. 2 Grupo de Transporte (2nd Transport Group) Aerea dos Afonsos AB Rio de Janeiro; redes No. 1/1 Grupo de Transporte de Tropa (1st Troop Carrier Group) 22 Jan 58. Wfu 19 Apr 68 and stored. SOC: 27 Jul 70 by civil sale // Amazonia Transporte, Industria E Comercio Belem Brazil 8 Jul 70 reg: PT-DLP. Belly landed at Belem do Para Brazil 11 Jun 71. Noted as under repair at Belem 1972 but probably never returned to service; wfu and stored Jan 74; bku at Belem Oct 74. Final Disposition: Accident.

10220 / 48-585/CQ-585 / C-82A-FA

Avble: 24 Aug 48; Acc: 31 Aug 48; Del: 27 Sep 48 to USAF // 62nd TCG (TAC) McChord AFB Washington 1 Oct 48; assigned 4th TCSq; depls to Elmendorf AFB Alaska 30 Nov 48 & 17 Aug 49; depl to Fort Richardson Alaska 20 Dec 48; 62nd MSU GP (CNC) McChord AFB Washington 21 Nov 49 // 314th TCG (CNC) Smyrna AFB Tennessee 6 Feb 50; assigned 2601st Light Assault SQ // 316th TCG (CNC) Smyrna AFB Tennessee 6 Feb 50; depl to Guantanamo Bay Cuba 28 Feb 50; Smyrna AFB renamed Sewart AFB 25 Mar 50; depl to 314th TCG (CNC) Laurinburg-Maxton Airport North Carolina 20 Apr 50 // 314th TCG (CNC) Sewart AFB Tennessee 7 Jul 50 // 375th TCWG (TAC) Greenville AFB South Carolina 20 Dec 50; to 4418th Base Complement SQ (TAC) Greenville AFB South Carolina 20 Dec 50; to Warner-Robins Air Materiel Area (AMC) Robins AFB Georgia 18 Oct 51 for depmnt. Taxiing accident at Robins AFB Georgia 4 Feb 52, no fatal-

C-82A s/n: 45-585 (msn: 10220) showing to good effect the belly paratainer doors (National Museum of the United States Air Force).

ities. Depl to Brownwood Field Texas 6 Apr 52 // 64th TCWG (TAC) Donaldson AFB South Carolina 14 Jul 52; depl to Elmendorf AFB Alaska 1 Oct 52 // Wfu to San Antonio Air Materiel Area (AMC) Kelly AFB Texas 2 Jul 53 and stored. Dropped from inventory 1 Jul 54 // Forca Aerea Brasileira (FAB/Brazilian Air Force) 20 Sep 55 s/n: 2202. Ferried to Brazil Jan 56; No. 2 Grupo de Transporte (2nd Transport Group) Aerea dos Afonsos AB Rio de Janeiro; redes No. 1/1 Grupo de Transporte de Tropa (1st Troop Carrier Group) 22 Jan 58. Wfu 19 Apr 68 and stored. SOC: 25 Nov 70. Gate guardian at Escola de Aeronautica (EAer/Air Force School) nicknamed "Sapao" (soap suds). Transferred to Museu Aeroespacial (MUSAL) Campos dos Afonos AB Rio de Janeiro Brazil 16 Jul 86 for preservation and display. Currently stored outside in a badly deteriorated condition. Final Disposition: Preserved (At the time of writing, its future was in doubt).

10221 / 48-586/CQ-586 / C-82A-FA

Avble: 14 Sep 48; Acc: 29 Sep 48; Del: 4 Oct 48 to USAF // 62nd TCG (TAC) McChord AFB Washington 5 Oct 48; assigned 7th TCSq; depl to Elmendorf AFB Alaska 3 Mar 49; 62nd MSU GP (CNC) McChord AFB Washington 13 Oct 49 // 314th TCG (CNC) Smyrna AFB Tennessee 7 Nov 49; assigned 2601st Light Assault SQ // Smyrna AFB renamed Sewart AFB 25 Mar 50 // 33rd Fighter-Interceptor WG (CNC) Otis AFB Massachusetts 28 Jun 50 // 375th TCWG (CNC) Greenville AFB South Carolina 22 Nov 50; to 4418th Base Complement SQ (TAC) Greenville AFB South Carolina 3 Jan 51; depl to 433rd TCWG (TAC) Greenville AFB South Carolina 1 Feb 51; to Warner-Robins Air Materiel Area (AMC) Robins AFB Georgia 11 Aug 51 for depmnt; depl to Grenier AFB New Hampshire 3 Jan 52; depl to Brownwood Field Texas 15 Mar 52 // 64th TCWG (TAC) Donaldson AFB South Carolina 14 Jul 52; depl to Elmendorf AFB Alaska 1 Oct 52; to Oklahoma Air Materiel Area (AMC) Tinker AFB Oklahoma 10 Jan 53 // Wfu to San Antonio Air Materiel Area (AMC) Kelly AFB Texas 26 Jun 53 and stored. Dropped from inventory 1 Jul 54 // Forca Aerea Brasileira (FAB/Brazilian Air Force) 20 Sep 55 s/n: 2201. Ferried to Brazil Jan 56; No. 2 Grupo de Transporte (2nd Transport Group) Aerea dos Afonsos AB Rio de Janeiro; redes No. 1/1 Grupo de Transporte de Tropa (1st Troop Carrier Group) 22 Jan 58. Wfu 19 Apr 68 and stored. SOC: 2 Aug 68 and sold for scrap. Final Disposition: Scrapped.

10222 / 48-587/CQ-587 / C-82A-FA

Avble: 20 Sep 48; Acc: 30 Sep 48; Del: 18 Oct 48 to USAF. The last C-82A to be built and delivered // 62nd MSU GP (TAC) McChord AFB Washington 22 Oct 48 & 12 Aug 49; 62nd TCG (TAC) McChord AFB Washington 8 Nov 48; depl to Elmendorf AFB Alaska 3 Mar 49; 62nd MSU GP depl to San Bernardino Air Depot California 13 Dec 49 // 314th TCG (CNC) Smyrna AFB Tennessee 23 Dec 49; assigned 2601st Light Assault SQ; Smyrna AFB renamed Sewart AFB 25 Mar 50 // 4th Fighter-Interceptor WG (CNC) Langley AFB Virginia 28 Jun 50; to 363rd Reconnaissance (Tactical) WG (CNC) Langley AFB, Virginia 2 Sep 50; 4th FI WG to New Castle Airport Delaware 24 Sep 50 // 375th TCWG (CNC) Greenville AFB South Carolina 14 Nov 50; assigned 55th TCSq. Had a minor ground accident at Lawson AFB Georgia 30 Nov 50, no fatalities. To 117th Reconnaissance (Tactical) WG (TAC) Lawson AFB Georgia 26 Jan 51; to Warner-Robins Air Materiel Area (AMC) Robins AFB Georgia 24 Oct 51 for depmnt; depl to Brownwood

Field Texas 17 Mar 52 // 64th TCWG (TAC) Donaldson AFB South Carolina 14 Jul 52; depl to Elmendorf AFB Alaska 21 Oct 52 // Wfu to San Antonio Air Materiel Area (AMC) Kelly AFB Texas 2 Jul 53 and stored. Dropped from inventory 1 Jul 54 // Forca Aerea Brasileira (FAB/Brazilian Air Force) 20 Sep 55 s/n: 2205. Ferried to Brazil Jan 56; No. 2 Grupo de Transporte (2nd Transport Group) Aerea dos Afonsos AB Rio de Janeiro; redes No. 1/1 Grupo de Transporte de Tropa (1st Troop Carrier Group) 22 Jan 58. Wfu 19 Apr 68 and stored. SOC: 2 Aug 68 and sold for scrap. Final Disposition: Scrapped.

135–49496 / 45-25436 / C-82N-1-NT

Acc: 22 Oct 45; Avble: 24 Oct 45; Del: 25 Oct 45 to USAAF // 4000th AAF BAS (ATSC) Wright Field Ohio 25 Oct 45 // 319th AAF BAS (TAC) Lawson Field Georgia 11 Sep 46; to ground instructional airframe 12 Sep 46. Dropped from inventory as salvage 8 Jul 47. Final Disposition: Scrapped.

135–49497 / 45-25437 / C-82N-1-NT

Acc: 28 Nov 45; Del: 5 Dec 45; Avble: 11 Dec 45 to USAAF // 1st Air Force Bolling Field District of Columbia 12 Dec 45 // Fairchild Aircraft Maryland (AMC) 6 Feb 1946 // 4120th AAF BAS (AMC) Freeman Field Indiana 19 Mar 46; to ground instructional airframe // 4105th AAF BAS (AMC) Davis-Monthan Field Arizona 17 Jun 46 for storage under "museum status." Dropped from inventory as salvage 3 Aug 49. Final Disposition: Scrapped.

C-82N s/n: 45-25437 (msn: 135-49497). Note the odd positioning of the tail number (National Museum of the United States Air Force).

135–49498 / 45-25438 / C-82N-1-NT

Acc: 19 Dec 45; Avble: 21 Dec 45; Del: 26 Dec 45 to USAAF // 4121st AAF BAS (ATSC) San Antonio Air Materiel Center Kelly Field Texas 29 Dec 45 // 3704th AAF BAS (TC) Keesler Field Mississippi 18 Dec 46; to ground instructional status 30 Dec 46. Redes as ZC-82N 1948 // 3380th Technical Training WG (TC) Keesler AFB, Mississippi 28 Aug 48 // 3750th Technical Training WG (TC) Sheppard AFB Texas 24 Sep 49. Dropped from inventory as salvage 4 Oct 51. Final Disposition: Scrapped.

135–49499/135–50495 CANCELED CONTRACT FOR 997 C-82N-NT AIRFRAMES. USAAF S/N: 45-25439/45-26435.

Appendix I: Civil Registration to Serial Number Cross-References

The * indicates registrations reserved but not taken up

CC-	**CHILE**	HK-583	10158/45-57788
CC-CAE	10045/44-23001	HK-777	10159/45-57789
CC-CRA-0507*	10059/44-23015	HK-906	10063/44-23019
CC-CRA-0507	10071/44-23027	HK-913X	10210/48-575
CC-CRB-0508	10045/44-23001	HK-914	10107/45-57737
		HK-915	10203/48-568
CP-	**BOLIVIA**	HK-918	10091/44-23047
CP-614	10198/45-57828	HK-924	10119/45-57749
CP-634*	10137/45-57767	HK-930	10099/44-23055
CP-665*	10198/45-57828		
	(not confirmed)	**HP-**	**PANAMA**
CP-677	10117/45-57747	HP-219	10150/45-57780
CP-678	10128/45-57758	HP-220	10202/45-57832
CP-693*	10136/45-57766		
CP-694*	10126/45-57756	**LV-**	**ARGENTINA**
CP-697*	10177/45-57807	LV-GIS	10106/45-57736
CP-772*	unk.	LV-PNY*	10106/45-57736
CP-983	10147/45-57777	LV-PRP*	10045/44-23001
CP-1036*	unk.	LV-PRU*	10052/44-23008
		LV-PRV*	10051/44-23007
CX-	**URUGUAY**	LV-PRW*	10056/44-23012
CX-AQA	10144/45-57774		
CX-AQB	10145/45-57775	**N**	**UNITED STATES**
		N127E	10150/45-57780
ET-	**ETHIOPIA**	N128E	10164/45-57794
ET-T-12	10184/45-57814	N136E	10025/44-22981
		N1799*	10126/45-57756
HB-	**SWITZERLAND**	N2047A	10184/45-57814
HB-AAB*	10075/44-23031	N2048A	10154/45-57784
HB-AAC*	10104/45-57733	N2054A	10202/45-57832
HB-AAD*	10106/45-57736	N2055A	10067/44-23023
		N2056A	10063/44-23019
HK-	**COLOMBIA**	N2057A	10091/44-23047
HK-426	10199/45-57829	N2058A	10099/44-23055
HK-468	10198/45-57828	N2059A	10102/44-23058
	(not confirmed)	N2060A	10104/45-57734

N2061A	10107/45-57737	N6233C	10197/45-57827
N2062A	10203/48-568	N6234C	10198/45-57828
N2063A	10210/48-575	N6235C	10199/45-57829
N2064A	10119/45-57749	N6236C	10150/45-57780
N2065A	10172/45-57802	N6237C*	10203/48–568
N208M	10163/45-57793	N6238C*	10091/44-23047
N209M	10165/45-57795	N6239C*	10099/44-23055
N2779*	10110/45-57740	N6240C*	10104/45-57734
N4752C	10216/48-581	N6241C*	10172/45-57802
N4753C	10209/48–574	N6242C*	10119/45-57749
N4828V	10085/44-23041	N6243C	10074/44-23030
N4829V	10073/44-23029	N6244C	10025/44-22981
N4830V	10133/45-57763	N6245C	10055/44-23011
N4832V	10070/44-23026	N6246C	10062/44-23018
N4833V	10075/44-23031	N6247C	10200/45-57830
N4834V	10104/45-57733	N6769A*	10087/44-23043
N4835V	10106/45-57736	N6781A*	10134/45-57764
N4962V	10137/45-57767	N6782A*	10052/44-23008
N5095V	10071/44-23027	N6845A*	10162/45-57792
N5100B	10159/45-57789	N6850A*	10075/44-23031
N5101B	10158/45-57788	N6856A*	10056/44-23012
N5102B	10152/45-57782	N6857A*	10076/44-23032
N5103B	10148/45-57778	N6862A*	10061/44-23017
N5104B	10146/45-57776	N6887C	10059/44-23015
N5105B	10145/45-57775	N6985C	10090/44-23046
N5106B	10143/45-57773	N6989C	10059/44-23015
N5107B	10140/45-57770	N6990C	10045/44-23001
N5108B	10135/45-57765	N6996C	10049/44-23005
N5109B	10125/45-57755	N6997C	10050/44-23006
N5110B	10111/45-57741	N6998C	10053/44-23009
N5111B	10097/44-23053	N6999C	10077/44-23033
N5112B	10095/44-23051	N74038	10061/44-23017
N5113B	10094/44-23050	N74039	10134/45-57764
N5114B	10093/44-23049	N74041	10076/44-23032
N5115B	10092/44-23048	N74042	10081/44-23037
N5116B	10089/44-23045	N74043	10087/44-23043
N5117B	10083/44-23039	N74044	10162/45-57792
N5118B	10078/44-23034	N74046	10052/44-23008
N5119B	10069/44-23025	N74047	10056/44-23012
N5120B	10163/45-57793	N74048	10096/44-23052
N5121B	10164/45-57794	N74127	10177/45-57807
N5122B	10165/45-57795	N74810	10150/45-57780
N5123B	10178/45-57808	N75398	10006/44-22962
N5124B	10187/45-57817	N75399	10048/44-23004
N5125B	10195/45-57825	N75884	10110/45-57740
N5126B	10170/45-57800	N75885	10126/45-57756
N5127B	10173/45-57803	N75886	10136/45-57766
N5128B	10174/45-57804	N75887	10160/45-57790
N53228	10080/44-23036	N75888	10177/45-57807
N54210	10150/45-57780	N7849B	10084/44-23040
N54211	10202/45-57832	N7850B	10098/44-23054
N56582	10176/45-57806	N7851B	10082/44-23038
N5903V*	10080/44-23036	N7852B	10057/44-23013

Appendix I: Cross-References

N7853B	10141/45-57771	**TG-**	**GUATEMALA**
N7854B	10185/45-57815	TG-ATA	10006/44-22962
N7855B	10153/45-57783	TG-AVA	10202/45-57832
N7856B	10147/45-57777	TG-AXA	10078/44-23034
N7857B	10182/45-57812	TG-AYA	10150/45-57780
N7884C	10057/44-23013	TG-AZA	10069/44-23025
N8009E	10071/44-23027	TG-DAC-79	10094/44-23050
N93067*	10136/45-57766	TG-OOC-2	10172/45-57802
N93068	10136/45-57766	TG-OOC-3	10104/45-57734
N9701F	10184/45-57814	TG-OOC-4	10165/45-57795
NC8855	10060/44-23016	TG-OOC-5	10163/45-57793
OB-	**PERU**	**VR-**	**YEMEN**
OB-LHF-508	10137/45-57767	VR-ABD*	10025/44-22981
OB-RAA-439	10202/45-57832	**XA- XB-**	**MEXICO**
OB-RAB-458*	10198/45-57828	XA-LIK	10128/45-57758
OB-T-479	10028/44-22984	XA-LIL	10117/45-57747
OB-T-749	10133/45-57763	XA-LIW	10093/44-23049
OB-TAI-438	10150/45-57780	XA-LIY	10092/44-23048
OB-UAA-438	10150/45-57780	XA-LIZ	10095/44-23051
OB-UAB-439	10202/45-57832	XA-LOJ	10110/45-57740
OB-UAD-508	10137/45-57767	XA-LOK	10126/45-57756
OB-UAE-528	10069/44-23025	XA-LOL	10136/45-57766
OB-UAF-531	10051/44-23007	XA-MAW	10177/45-57807
OB-WAC-479	10028/44-22984	XB-KOI	10154/45-57784
OB-WAE-438	10150/45-57780	XB-PEJ	10160/45-57790
OB-WAF-439	10202/45-57832	XB-PEK	10177/45-57807
OB-WAG-458*	10198/45-57828	XB-YOA	10128/45-57758
PP-	**BRAZIL**	XB-ZUZ	10106/45-57736
PP-CEE	10144/45-57774	**XH- HR-**	**HONDURAS**
PP-CEF	10200/45-57830	XH-139	10048/44-23004
PP-CEG	10141/45-57771	XH-143-P	10094/44-23050
PP-CEH	10115/45-57745	XH-163	10104/45-57733
PP-CEI	10185/45-57815	HR-163	10104/45-57733
PP-CEJ	10156/45-57786	HR-163P	10104/45-57733
PP-CEK	10147/45-57777	HR-SAM	10104/45-57733
PP-CEL	10153/45-57783	**YV-**	**VENEZUELA**
PP-CEM	10180/45-57810	YV-C-LBA	10198/45-57828
PP-CFF	10182/45-57812		
PP-DLP	10219/48–584		
PP-DNZ	10213/48–578		

Appendix II: C-82 Retirement Bases/ Civil Sales and NACA Assignments

Kelly AFB, Texas
San Antonio Air Materiel Area
Final Reclamation and Salvage Instructions 25 Feb 1955
75 assignments—3 scrapped, 12 MAP to Brazil, 60 civil sales

S/N	WFU	DFI	Sold	Disposition
44-23007	26 Jun 53	1 Jul 54	unk.	Civil sale OB-UAF-531.
44-23008	26 Jun 53	1 Jul 54	16 Aug 55	Civil sale N74046.
44-23012	7 Jul 53	1 Jul 54	16 Aug 55	Civil sale N74047.
44-23013	7 Jul 53	1 Jul 54	10 Aug 55	Civil sale N7852B.
44-23017	26 Jun 53	1 Jul 54	16 Aug 55	Civil sale N74038.
44-23025	8 Jul 53	1 Jul 54	7 Sep 55	Civil sale N5119B.
44-23032	2 Jul 53	1 Jul 54	16 Aug 55	Civil sale N74041.
44-23034	2 Jul 53	1 Jul 54	7 Sep 55	Civil sale N5118B.
44-23037	7 Jul 53	1 Jul 54	16 Aug 55	Civil sale N74042.
44-23038	26 Jun 53	1 Jul 54	10 Aug 55	Civil sale N7851B.
44-23039	14 Jul 53	1 Jul 54	7 Sep 55	Civil sale N5117B.
44-23040	9 Sep 53	1 Jul 54	10 Aug 55	Civil sale N7849B.
44-23043	14 Jul 53	1 Jul 54	16 Aug 55	Civil sale N74043.
44-23045	2 Jul 53	1 Jul 54	7 Sep 55	Civil sale N5116B.
44-23048	26 Jun 53	1 Jul 54	7 Sep 55	Civil sale N5115B.
44-23049	7 Jul 53	1 Jul 54	7 Sep 55	Civil sale N5114B.
44-23050	2 Jul 53	1 Jul 54	7 Sep 55	Civil sale N5113B.
44-23051	5 Aug 53	1 Jul 54	7 Sep 55	Civil sale N5112B.
44-23052	7 Jul 53	1 Jul 54	16 Aug 55	Civil sale N74048.
44-23053	14 Jul 53	1 Jul 54	7 Sep 55	Civil sale N5111B.
44-23054	7 Jul 53	1 Jul 54	10 Aug 55	Civil sale N7850B.
45-57735	2 Jul 53	1 Jul 54	n/a	Scrapped.
45-57740	24 Jun 53	1 Jul 54	unk.	Civil sale N75884.
45-57741	25 Jun 53	1 Jul 54	7 Sep 55	Civil sale N5110B.
45-57745	24 Jun 53	1 Jul 54	unk.	Civil sale PP-CEH.
45-57747	24 Jun 53	1 Jul 54	unk.	Civil sale XA-LIL.
45-57755	24 Jun 53	1 Jul 54	7 Sep 55	Civil sale N5109B.
45-57756	24 Jun 53	1 Jul 54	unk.	Civil sale N75885.
45-57758	24 Jun 53	1 Jul 54	unk.	Civil sale XB-YOA.
45-57762	24 Jun 53	1 Jul 54	unk.	Civil sale unk. owner.
45-57764	24 Jun 53	1 Jul 54	16 Aug 55	Civil sale N74039.
45-57765	24 Jun 53	1 Jul 54	7 Sep 55	Civil sale N5108B.

S/N	WFU	DFI	Sold	Disposition
45-57766	24 Jun 53	1 Jul 54	unk.	Civil sale N75886.
45-57770	24 Jun 53	1 Jul 54	7 Sep 55	Civil sale N5107B.
45-57771	24 Jun 53	1 Jul 54	15 Aug 55	Civil sale N7853B.
45-57773	28 Jun 53	1 Jul 54	7 Sep 55	Civil sale N5106B.
45-57774	24 Jun 53	1 Jul 54	unk.	Civil sale CX-AQA.
45-57775	24 Jun 53	1 Jul 54	7 Sep 55	Civil sale N5105B.
45-57776	8 Aug 53	1 Jul 54	7 Sep 55	Civil sale N5104B.
45-57778	24 Jun 53	1 Jul 54	7 Sep 55	Civil sale N5103B.
45-57782	24 Jun 53	1 Jul 54	7 Sep 55	Civil sale N5102B.
45-57783	24 Jun 53	1 Jul 54	15 Aug 55	Civil sale N7855B.
45-57784	24 Jun 53	1 Jul 54	30 Jun 55	Civil sale N2048A.
45-57786	24 Jun 53	1 Jul 54	unk.	Civil sale PP-CEJ.
45-57787	24 Jun 53	1 Jul 54	n/a	Scrapped.
45-57788	14 Jul 53	1 Jul 54	7 Sep 55	Civil sale N5101B.
45-57789	24 Jun 53	1 Jul 54	7 Sep 55	Civil sale N5100B.
45-57790	24 Jun 53	1 Jul 54	unk.	Civil sale N75887.
45-57792	3 Aug 53	1 Jul 54	16 Aug 55	Civil sale N74044.
45-57793	24 Jul 53	1 Jul 54	7 Sep 55	Civil sale N5120B.
45-57794	26 Jun 53	1 Jul 54	7 Sep 55	Civil sale N5121B.
45-57795	14 Jul 53	1 Jul 54	7 Sep 55	Civil sale N5122B.
45-57800	16 Feb 53	1 Jul 54	7 Sep 55	Civil sale N5126B.
45-57803	24 Jun 53	1 Jul 54	7 Sep 55	Civil sale N5127B.
45-57804	24 Jun 53	1 Jul 54	7 Sep 55	Civil sale N5128B.
45-57807	24 Jun 53	1 Jul 54	unk.	Civil sale N75888.
45-57808	24 Jun 53	1 Jul 54	7 Sep 55	Civil sale N5123B.
45-57810	24 Jun 53	1 Jul 54	unk.	Civil sale PP-CEM.
45-57814	19 Jun 53	1 Jul 54	30 Jun 55	Civil sale N2047C.
45-57815	2 Jul 53	1 Jul 54	15 Aug 55	Civil sale N7854B.
45-57817	24 Jun 53	1 Jul 54	7 Sep 55	Civil sale N5124B.
45-57822	2 Jul 53	1 Jul 54	20 Sep 55	MAP Brazil s/n: 2208.
45-57824	24 Jun 53	1 Jul 54	n/a	Scrapped.
45-57825	14 Jul 53	1 Jul 54	7 Sep 55	Civil sale N5125B.
48-571	7 Aug 53	1 Jul 54	20 Sep 55	MAP Brazil s/n: 2210.
48-573	5 Aug 53	1 Jul 54	20 Sep 55	MAP Brazil s/n: 2209.
48-576	7 Jul 53	1 Jul 54	20 Sep 55	MAP Brazil s/n: 2211.
48-577	7 Jul 53	1 Jul 54	20 Sep 55	MAP Brazil s/n: 2206.
48-578	10 Sep 53	1 Jul 54	20 Sep 55	MAP Brazil s/n: 2207.
48-580	2 Jul 53	1 Jul 54	20 Sep 55	MAP Brazil s/n: 2204.
48-583	26 Jun 53	1 Jul 54	20 Sep 55	MAP Brazil s/n: 2203.
48-584	26 Jun 53	1 Jul 54	20 Sep 55	MAP Brazil s/n: 2200.
48-585	2 Jul 53	1 Jul 54	20 Sep 55	MAP Brazil s/n: 2202.
48-586	26 Jun 53	1 Jul 54	20 Sep 55	MAP Brazil s/n: 2201.
48-587	2 Jul 53	1 Jul 54	20 Sep 55	MAP Brazil s/n: 2205.

Hill AFB, Utah

Ogden Air Materiel Area
39 assignments—9 scrapped, 30 civil sales

S/N	WFU	DFI	Sold	Disposition
44-22962	2 Apr 54	8 Jul 54	29 Sep 55	Civil sale N75398.
44-22981	12 May 53	8 Jul 54	28 Sep 55	Civil sale N6244C.

S/N	WFU	DFI	Sold	Disposition
44-23004	2 Aug 54	9 May 55	29 Sep 55	Civil sale N75399.
44-23011	27 May 53	8 Jul 54	29 Sep 55	Civil sale N6245C.
44-23018	7 May 53	8 Jul 54	29 Sep 55	Civil sale N6246C.
44-23019	18 Jan 54	8 Jul 54	19 Sep 55	Civil sale N2056A.
44-23023	15 Jun 53	8 Jul 54	19 Sep 55	Civil sale N2055A.
44-23026	22 Sep 53	8 Jul 54	23 Aug 55	Civil sale N4832V.
44-23029	9 Aug 53	8 Jul 54	22 Aug 55	Civil sale N4829V.
44-23030	9 Jun 53	8 Jul 54	29 Sep 55	Civil sale N6243C.
44-23031	14 Jan 54	8 Jul 54	23 Aug 55	Civil sale N4833V.
44-23041	22 Jun 53	8 Jul 54	9 Aug 55	Civil sale N4828V.
44-23047	28 May 53	8 Jul 54	19 Sep 55	Civil sale N2057A.
44-23055	29 Dec 53	8 Jul 54	19 Sep 55	Civil sale N2058A.
44-23058	28 Jun 53	8 Jul 54	19 Sep 55	Civil sale N2059A.
45-57733	25 Jun 53	8 Jul 54	23 Aug 55	Civil sale N4834V.
45-57734	15 Sep 54	9 May 55	19 Sep 55	Civil sale N2060A.
45-57736	11 Jun 53	8 Jul 54	23 Aug 55	Civil sale N4835V.
45-57737	14 Jul 53	8 Jul 54	19 Sep 55	Civil sale N2061A.
45-57746	21 Jan 53	15 Mar 54	n/a	Scrapped.
45-57748	21 Jan 53	15 Mar 54	n/a	Scrapped.
45-57749	17 Nov 54	9 May 55	19 Sep 55	Civil sale N2064A.
45-57750	21 Jan 53	15 Mar 54	n/a	Scrapped.
45-57751	21 Jan 53	15 Mar 54	n/a	Scrapped.
45-57753	21 Jan 53	15 Mar 54	n/a	Scrapped.
45-57754	21 Jan 53	15 Mar 54	n/a	Scrapped.
45-57757	21 Jan 53	15 Mar 54	n/a	Scrapped.
45-57759	21 Jan 53	15 Mar 54	n/a	Scrapped.
45-57763	6 Feb 54	8 Jul 54	17 Aug 55	Civil sale N4830V.
45-57780	6 Feb 54	8 Jul 54	27 Sep 55	Civil sale N6236C.
45-57802	7 Dec 54	9 May 55	19 Sep 55	Civil sale N2065A.
45-57819	30 Apr 53	14 Apr 54	n/a	Scrapped.
45-57827	13 Jun 53	8 Jul 54	23 Aug 55	Civil sale N6233C.
45-57828	16 Sep 54	9 May 55	23 Aug 55	Civil sale N6234C.
45-57829	Late 53	8 Jul 54	23 Aug 55	Civil sale N6235C.
45-57830	21 Jan 53	8 Jul 54	29 Sep 55	Civil sale N6247C.
45-57832	17 Jun 53	8 Jul 54	1 Sep 55	Civil sale N2054C.
48-568	25 Aug 53	8 Jul 54	19 Sep 55	Civil sale N2062A.
48-575	7 Jun 53	8 Jul 54	19 Sep 55	Civil sale N2063A.

Davis-Monthan AFB, Arizona
3040th Aircraft Storage Squadron
14 assignments—2 scrapped, 12 civil sales

S/N	WFU	DFI	Sold	Disposition
44-23001	16 Feb 55	1 Aug 55	9 Jan 56	Civil sale N6990C.
44-23005	17 Feb 55	1 Aug 55	9 Jan 56	Civil sale N6996C.
44-23006	21 Feb 55	1 Aug 55	9 Jan 56	Civil sale N6997C.
44-23009	7 Mar 55	1 Aug 55	9 Jan 56	Civil sale N6998C.
44-23015	16 Mar 55	1 Aug 55	9 Jan 56	Civil sale N6989C.
44-23027	21 Feb 55	1 Aug 55	9 Jan 56	Civil sale N5095V.
44-23033	21 Feb 55	1 Aug 55	9 Jan 56	Civil sale N6999C.
44-23046	14 Mar 55	1 Aug 55	9 Jan 56	Civil sale N6985C.

S/N	WFU	DFI	Sold	Disposition
44-23057	7 Mar 55	1 Aug 55	n/a	Scrapped.
45-57767	18 Feb 55	1 Aug 55	26 Oct 55	Civil sale N4962V.
45-57777	14 Mar 55	1 Aug 55	9 Mar 56	Civil sale N7856B.
45-57806	24 Feb 55	1 Aug 55	9 Mar 56	Civil sale N56582.
45-57811	28 Feb 55	1 Aug 55	n/a	Scrapped.
45-57812	7 Mar 55	1 Aug 55	9 Mar 56	Civil sale N7857B.

Other Retirement Locations

11 aircraft—8 scrapped, 3 civil sales

Pope AFB, North Carolina

S/N	WFU	DFI	Sold	Disposition
43-13202	21 Oct 48	21 Oct 48	n/a	Scrapped (XC-82).

Wright Field, Ohio

S/N	WFU	DFI	Sold	Disposition
44-22959	31 Jul 46	31 Jul 46	n/a	Scrapped.

Lawson AFB, Georgia

S/N	WFU	DFI	Sold	Disposition
44-22961	4 Oct 49	14 Oct 49	n/a	Scrapped.

Davis-Monthan AFB, Arizona

S/N	WFU	DFI	Sold	Disposition
44-23056	7 Feb 61	n/a	n/a	Scrapped (ex–NASA).
45-25437	17 Jun 46	3 Aug 49	n/a	Scrapped (C-82N).

Lawson Field, Georgia

S/N	WFU	DFI	Sold	Disposition
45-25436	12 Sep 46	8 Jul 47	n/a	Scrapped (C-82N).

Keesler AFB, Mississippi

S/N	WFU	DFI	Sold	Disposition
45-25438	30 Dec 46	4 Oct 51	n/a	Scrapped (C-82N).

Chanute AFB, Illinois

S/N	WFU	DFI	Sold	Disposition
45-57769	18 Jan 51	2 Dec 51	n/a	Scrapped (XC-119A).

Hagerstown, Maryland

S/N	WFU	DFI	Sold	Disposition
44-23036	30 Jan 57	30 Jan 57	30 Jan 57	Civil sale N53228.

Elmendorf AFB, Alaska

S/N	WFU	DFI	Sold	Disposition
48-574	12 Aug 55	16 Nov 55	15 Dec 55	Civil sale N4753C.
48-581	15 Aug 55	16 Nov 55	15 Dec 55	Civil sale N4752C.

NACA Assignments

32 assignments—30 destroyed, 2 civil sales.

S/N	Assigned	DFI	Disposition
44-22963	22 Jun 50	29 Jun 50	Tested to destruction.
44-22966	22 Jun 50	26 Aug 50	Tested to destruction.
44-22967	22 Mar 50	29 Mar 50	Tested to destruction.
44-22968	20 Mar 50	30 Mar 50	Tested to destruction.
44-22969	15 Feb 50	24 Feb 50	Tested to destruction.
44-22970	6 Apr 50	11 Apr 50	Tested to destruction.
44-22971*	29 Mar 50	5 Apr 50	Tested to destruction.
44-22972	13 Mar 50	29 Mar 50	Tested to destruction.
44-22973	11 Apr 50	16 May 50	Tested to destruction.
44-22974	20 Mar 50	30 Mar 50	Tested to destruction.
44-22975	6 Apr 50	11 Apr 50	Tested to destruction.
44-22976	31 Mar 50	7 Apr 50	Tested to destruction.
44-22977	20 Mar 50	30 Mar 50	Tested to destruction.
44-22978	4 Apr 50	19 Apr 50	Tested to destruction.
44-22979	23 Mar 50	25 May 50	Tested to destruction.
44-22980	29 Mar 50	7 Apr 50	Tested to destruction.
44-22982	31 Mar 50	3 Apr 50	Tested to destruction.
44-22983	4 Apr 50	12 Apr 50	Tested to destruction.
44-22984	10 May 50	10 May 50	Civil sale OB-T-479.
44-22985	20 Mar 50	30 Mar 50	Tested to destruction.
44-22986	9 May 50	25 May 50	Tested to destruction.
44-22987	20 Mar 50	30 Mar 50	Tested to destruction.
44-22988	3 Apr 50	11 Apr 50	Tested to destruction.
44-22989	29 Mar 50	7 Apr 50	Tested to destruction.
44-22990	22 Jun 50	29 Jul 50	Tested to destruction.
44-22991	15 Feb 50	6 Mar 50	Civil sale no registration.
44-22992	15 Feb 50	23 Mar 50	Tested to destruction.
44-22993	15 Feb 50	6 Mar 50	Tested to destruction.
44-22997	15 Feb 50	24 Feb 50	Tested to destruction.
44-22998	16 Feb 50	24 Feb 50	Tested to destruction.
44-23000	15 Feb 50	24 Feb 50	Tested to destruction.
44-23002	20 Mar 50	30 Mar 50	Tested to destruction.

*Airframe also used as a test-bed for jet engine thrust reverse tests.

Appendix III: Unknown Identities and Dispositions

Scrapped by the USAF

These are the 14 C-82A airframes that were never sold to a civil operator and so are listed as supposedly scrapped by the USAF. Several may have had subsequent civil histories, but no connections have as yet been established.

44-23057	Davis-Monthan AFB, Arizona.
45-57735	Kelly AFB, Texas.
45-57746	Hill AFB, Utah, ex-tracked u/c.
45-57748	Hill AFB, Utah, ex-tracked u/c.
45-57750	Hill AFB, Utah, ex-tracked u/c.
45-57751	Hill AFB, Utah, ex-tracked u/c.
45-57753	Hill AFB, Utah, ex-tracked u/c.
45-57754	Hill AFB, Utah, ex-tracked u/c.
45-57757	Hill AFB, Utah, ex-tracked u/c.
45-57759	Hill AFB, Utah, ex-tracked u/c.
45-57787	Kelly AFB, Texas.
45-57811	Davis-Monthan AFB, Arizona.
45-57819	Hill AFB, Utah.
45-57824	Kelly AFB, Texas.

Unknown Initial U.S. Registrations

Several known foreign registrations and operators have no known U.S. civil identities. Given the civil history of the C-82, it would seem no direct USAF foreign civil sales were ever made, so temporary U.S. registrations must have been applied.

44-22984	Exported to Peru as OB-T-479, fate unk.
44-23007	Exported to Peru as OB-UAF-531. Apparently owned by Ben Epstein.
45-57745	To Leeward Aeronautical Sales Inc. Exported to Brazil as PP-CEH.
45-57747	Exported to Mexico as XA-LIL.
45-57758	Exported to Mexico as XB-YOA.
45-57774	To Leeward Aeronautical Sales Inc. Exported to Uruguay as CX-AQA, then to Brazil as PP-CEE.
45-57786	To Leeward Aeronautical Sales Inc. Exported to Brazil as PP-CEJ.
45-57810	To Leeward Aeronautical Sales Inc. Exported to Brazil as PP-CEM.

Possible Export Dispositions

These are C-82 aircraft that were possibly exported to Latin America, but no records exist to show any kind of export had taken place. It may transpire, however, that most, if not all, were simply scrapped in the U.S.

44-23053	Bankers Life & Casualty Co. as N5111B, exported?
45-57741	Bankers Life & Casualty Co. as N5110B, exported?
45-57755	Bankers Life & Casualty Co. as N5109B, exported?
45-57773	Bankers Life & Casualty Co. as N5106B, exported?
45-57778	Bankers Life & Casualty Co. as N5103B, exported?
45-57800	Bankers Life & Casualty Co. as N5126B, exported?
45-57808	Bankers Life & Casualty Co. as N5123B, exported?
45-57817	Bankers Life & Casualty Co. as N5124B, exported?
45-57825	Bankers Life & Casualty Co. as N5125B, exported?

Unknown Identities, Final Dispositions and Mysteries

CP-634	Bolivian reservation ntu, C-82 s/n unk.
CP-772	Bolivian reservation ntu, C-82 s/n unk.
CP-1036	Bolivian reservation ntu, C-82 s/n unk.
44-23011	N6245C. Peter Bercut, fate unk. but listed as "destroyed."
44-23013	N7884C. Steward-Davis Inc. Speculatively might have been cut up for the movie *The Flight of the Phoenix* (1965), but generally its fate is unk.
44-23018	N6246C. Peter Bercut, fate unk. but listed as "destroyed."
44-23025	N5119B. Exported to Peru as OB-UAE-528, fate unk.
44-23030	N6243C. Peter Bercut, fate unk. but listed as "destroyed."
44-23034	N5118B. Exported to Guatemala as TG-AXA, fate unk.
44-23038	N7851B. Peter Bercut, fate unk. but listed as "destroyed."
44-23048	N5115B. Exported to Mexico as XA-LIY, fate unk.
44-23051	N5112B. Exported to Mexico as XA-LIZ, fate unk.
44-23054	N7850B. Peter Bercut, fate unk.
45-57734	N2060A. The Ohio Oil Co. as TG-OOC-3, fate unk.
45-57767	N4962V. Exported to Peru as OB-UAD-508, fate unk.
45-57784	N2048A. Exported to Mexico as XB-KOI, fate unk.
45-57802	N2065A. The Ohio Oil Co. as TG-OOC-2, fate unk.
45-57827	N6233C. To LEBCA Intl., fate unk., has been quoted as HK-468.
45-57762	No known history after retirement by the USAF, but it then turns up at Miami Intl. Airport, Florida, in the late 1960s stored with a batch of New Frontier Airlift Corp. C-82s and incorrectly marked as "N74047," a reg correctly belonging to 44-23012. The airframe later went to the George T. Baker Aviation School.
45-57806	N56582. Purchased by Leeward Aeronautical Sales Inc. in 1956, but sold in 1962 as a hull only. How or why this came about is unknown.

U.S. Registration Batch Gaps

N4831V	Never assigned within C-82 batch: N4828V/N4835V.
N74040	Never assigned to C-82 batch: N74038/N74048. To an F-51D Mustang.
N74045	Never assigned to C-82 batch: N74038/N74048. To an F-51D Mustang.

Appendix IV: Conversions and Unique Packets

Jet-Packet/Skytruck Conversions

MSN/S/N	Civil Reg	In Service	Jet-Pak Standard
10045/44-23001	N6990C	1958–1970s	Jet-Packet 1600.
10059/44-23015	N6887C	1958–1970	Jet-Packet 1600.
10071/44-23027	N5095V	1957–1987	Jet-Packet 3200.
10073/44-23029	N4829V	1963–1964	Jet-Packet 3400.
10090/44-23046	N6985C	1963–1971	Jet-Packet 3400.
10147/45-57777	PP-CEK	1958–1972	Jet-Packet 1600.
10152/45-57782	N5102B	1961–1987	Jet-Packet 1600.
10177/45-57807	N74127	1961–1964	Skytruck Mk. I.
10184/45-57815	N9701F	1963–2000	Jet-Packet 3400.

Skypallet Conversion

MSN/S/N	Civil Reg	In Service	Operator
10085/44-23041	N4828V	n/a	Steward-Davis Inc.

Flying Repair Station Conversions

MSN/S/N	Civil Reg	In Service	Operator
10059/44-23015	N6887C	1965–1970	Steward-Davis Inc.
10177/45-57807	N74127	1964	Steward-Davis Inc.
10184/45-57814	N9701F	1956–1973	TWA Inc.
	N9701F	1973–1978	Briles Wing & Helicopter Inc.

Aerial Sprayer/Tanker Conversions

MSN/S/N	Civil Reg	In Service	Operator
10045/44-23001	N6990C	1958	Steward-Davis Inc.
10048/44-23004	N75399	1957	Air Cargo Equipment Inc.
10070/44-23026	N4832V	1956	United-Heckathorn Corp./SkySpray Inc.*
10073/44-23029	N4829V	1956–1962	United-Heckathorn Corp./SkySpray Inc.* (cvtd Aerial Fire Tanker 1957–1958).
10075/44-23031	N4833V	1956	M&W Aircraft Leasing/SkySpray Inc.*
10080/44-23036	N53228	1957–1961	Master Equipment Co.

MSN/S/N	Civil Reg	In Service	Operator
10085/44-23041	N4828V	1956–1961	Master Equipment Co.
10103/45-57733	N4834V	1956	M&W Aircraft Leasing/SkySpray Inc.*
10106/45-57736	N4835V	1956	M&W Aircraft Leasing/SkySpray Inc.*
10133/45-57763	N4830V	1956–1964	Big Piney Aviation Inc. (cvtd Aerial Fire Tanker 1960–1964).

*Known collectively as the Hayward Packets due to the aircraft being based at Hayward Airport, California, during spraying operations.

Unique Packets

MSN/S/N	Civil Reg	In Service	Unique Feature
10060/44-23016	NC8855	1946	United Flying Mail Car.
10208/48-573	n/a	1948	Packet Pressroom.
10213/48-578	n/a	1948	Packet Pressroom.
10110/45-57740	XA-LOJ	1957–1962	Mexicana Dorsal Fillets.
10126/45-57756	XA-LOK	1957–1962	Mexicana Dorsal Fillets.
10136/45-57766	XA-LOL	1957–1962	Mexicana Dorsal Fillets.
10177/45-57807	XA-MAW	1956–1961	Mexicana Dorsal Fillets.

Appendix V: Attrition

Accidents: Air or ground accidents in which the airframe is destroyed or deemed as "damaged beyond repair." There were no combat losses for the C-82.

USAAF (1946–1947):	8
USAF (1947–1954):	45
Military Accidents Subtotal:	53
U.S. civil operators (1956–1965):	9
South American civil operators (1956–1977):	23
(Includes 2 ex–Brazilian AF).	
Civil Accidents Subtotal:	32

85

Tested to Destruction: Airframes retired for testing. Refers here to C-82 aircraft assigned for crash tests with the NACA. 32 were assigned, but 2 not used in testing were sold to other civil interests.

30

Scrapped: Airframes retired from service and/or broken up.

USAF (XC-82, C-82N, XC-119A):	5
USAF (C-82A, including NASA aircraft):	17
Brazilian Air Force:	9
Military Scrapped Subtotal:	31
U.S. civil operators:	48
South American civil operators:	21
(Includes 1 ex–NACA).	
Greek owned (ex–N127E):	1
Civil Scrapped Subtotal:	70

101

Preserved: Existing airframes, whole or partial, in museums or private collections.

Complete and preserved airframes:	4
Incomplete/derelict airframes:	4
(Includes 1 ex–NACA, 1 ex–Brazilian AF).	

8

Total: **224**

Appendix VI: Accidents

Date	MSN/S/N	Operator	Location/Cause of Loss
18 Jul 1946	10008/44-22964	USAAF	Offutt Field, Nebraska. Landing accident, no fatalities
17 Sep 1946	10039/44-22995	USAAF	Miami Airport, Florida. Landing accident due to mechanical failure, no fatalities.
30 Sep 1946	10043/44-22999	USAAF	Pope Field, North Carolina. Landing accident, no fatalities.
4 Nov 1946	10064/44-23020	USAAF	Bergstrom Field, Texas. Taxiing accident, no fatalities.
13 Dec 1946	10066/44-23022	USAAF	Pope Field, North Carolina. Take-off accident, no fatalities.
2 May 1947	10088/44-23044	USAAF	Keesler Field, Mississippi. Taxiing accident, no fatalities.
11 May 1947	10072/44-23028	USAAF	10 miles SE Austin, Texas. Crash-landed on belly due to engine failure, no fatalities.
14 Aug 1947	10004/44-22960	USAAF	1.5 miles NW Cormey, Ohio. Crash landing following engine failure, no fatalities.
9 Dec 1947	10038/44-22994	USAF	11 miles NNE Eglin AFB, Florida. Engine failure, crew bailed out, no fatalities.
1 Mar 1948	10047/44-23003	USAF	Mobile, Alabama. In-flight mechanical failure, crew bailed out, no fatalities.
28 Jul 1948	10183/45-57813	USAF	Barter Island, Alaska. Landing accident, no fatalities.
13 Aug 1948	10009/44-22965	USAF	40 miles NE Gadsden, Alabama. Engine failure, crew bailed out, no fatalities.
17 Oct 1948	10167/45-57797	USAF	4 miles N Clinton, Louisiana. Crash landing following engine failure, 34 onboard—4 killed, 1 injured.
12 Nov 1948	10205/48-570	USAF	11 miles SW Portsmouth, Ohio. Crash landing following engine failure, no fatalities.
14 Dec 1948	10155/45-57785	USAF	Tempelhof AB, West Germany. Landing accident due to mechanical failure, no fatalities.
16 Dec 1948	10086/44-23042	USAF	10 miles S Greenville, South Carolina. Crashed due to engine failure, crew killed.
23 Dec 1948	10149/45-57779	USAF	1 mile S Fort Nelson, Canada. Crash-landed due to mechanical failure, no fatalities.
14 Jan 1949	10054/44-23010	USAF	1 mile N Haineth, North Carolina. In-flight mechanical failure, 3 crew killed.
1 Mar 1949	10079/44-23035	USAF	State of Para, Brazil. Ran out of fuel due to bad weather, crew bailed out, no fatalities.
9 Apr 1949	10196/45-57826	USAF	McChord AFB, Washington. Engine failure, no fatalities.
20 May 1949	10207/48-572	USAF	Isachsen Weather Station, Ellef Ringnes Is., Arctic Canada. Crashed on take-off, no fatalities.

Appendix VI: Accidents 305

Date	MSN/S/N	Operator	Location/Cause of Loss
14 Jul 1949	10058/44-23014	USAF	WPAFB, Ohio. Crash landing following engine failure, all crew killed.
10 Aug 1949	10214/48-579	USAF	McChord AFB, Washington. Landing accident, no fatalities.
2 Sep 1949	10193/45-57823	USAF	2 miles SSW Birds Landing, California. Crashed due to engine failure, 8 onboard—6 bailed out, 2 killed.
29 Sep 1949	10217/48-582	USAF	5 miles NE McCleary, Washington. Navigational error, 3 crew killed.
4 Nov 1949	10040/44-22996	USAF	7 miles S Bossier City, Louisiana. Crashed on take-off, crew killed.
Early 1950	10112/45-57742	USAF	West Germany. Cause and fatalities unk.
21 Mar 1950	10122/45-57752	USAF	Smyrna AFB, Tennessee. Parked, hit by taxiing aircraft, no fatalities. 45-57760 also w/o.
21 Mar 1950	10130/45-57760	USAF	Smyrna AFB, Tennessee. Parked, hit by taxiing aircraft, no fatalities. 45-57752 also w/o.
11 Apr 1950	10168/45-57798	USAF	Cornwallis Island, NWT, Canada. Engine failure at take-off, no fatalities.
22 May 1950	10190/45-57820	USAF	Rhein-Main AB, West Germany. Forced landing due to onboard fire, no fatalities.
21 Jul 1950	10201/45-57831	USAF	Kenai Airport, Alaska. Landing accident due to weather, no fatalities.
31 Jul 1950	10065/44-23021	USAF	2 miles W Tallahassee, Florida. Crash-landed on belly due to engine failure, no fatalities.
3 Aug 1950	10060/44-23016	USAF	Cheyenne MAP, Wyoming. Forced landing following engine failure, no fatalities.
11 Nov 1950	10109/45-57739	USAF	12 miles NW Pickens, South Carolina. Terrain collision at night, 3 crew & 1 passenger killed.
17 Nov 1950	10068/44-23024	USAF	Donaldson AFB, South Carolina. Taxiing accident due to mechanical failure, no fatalities.
22 Nov 1950	10113/45-57743	USAF	Neubiberg AB, West Germany. Crash-landed on belly due to engine failure, no fatalities.
Early 1951	10179/45-57809	USAF	Libya. Cause and fatalities unk.
9 Jan 1951	10191/45-57821	USAF	Eglin AFB, Florida. Landing accident due to mechanical failure, no fatalities.
20 Jan 1951	10151/45-57781	USAF	Mezzeh AB, Damascus, Syria. Take-off accident due to mechanical failure, no fatalities.
3 Jun 1951	10131/45-57761	USAF	3 miles SSW New Boston, Texas. Structural failure due to weather, 8 killed.
16 Aug 1951	10166/45-57796	USAF	Rhein-Main AB, West Germany. Destroyed by a ground fire, no fatalities.
21 Sep 1951	10175/45-57805	USAF	King George IV Lake, Newfoundland, Canada. Cause unk, no fatalities.
13 Nov 1951	10171/45-57801	USAF	Mt Dore, Clermont-Farrand, France. Hit mountain in bad weather due to navigational error. 36 killed.
28 Jan 1952	10161/45-57791	USAF	6 miles WSW Rhein-Main AB, West Germany. Engine fire, crew bailed out, 3 on ground killed.
7 Jun 1952	10186/45-57816	USAF	RAF Burtonwood, England. Heavy landing accident no fatalities.
11 Jul 1952	10169/45-57799	USAF	Quad City Airport, Illinois. Forced landing due to engine fire, destroyed by fire, no fatalities.

Appendix VI

Date	MSN/S/N	Operator	Location/Cause of Loss
Jul–Sep 1952	10108/45-57738	USAF	Continental U.S. Cause and fatalities unk.
16 Jan 1953	10142/45-57772	USAF	30 miles SW Chaumont, France. Fuel starvation, crew bailed out.
Feb 1953	10188/45-57818	USAF	Keflavik Airport, Iceland. Cause and fatalities unk.
14 Feb 1954	10204/48-569	USAF	1 mile N Yelm, Washington. Crash landed due to engine failure, no fatalities.
Mid-1954	10138/45-57768	USAF	England. Cause and fatalities unk.
21 Sep 1954	10114/45-57744	USAF	9 miles NW Fawnskin, California. Crashed due to engine failure, 9 onboard—1 killed, 8 bailed out.
unk.	10048/XH-139	SAHSA	Trujillo Airport, Honduras. Crashed on take-off, fatalities unk.
unk.	10091/HK-918	LAC	Colombia. Cause and fatalities unk.
unk.	10203/HK-915	LIDCA	Colombia. Cause and fatalities unk.
8 Aug 1956	10070/N4832V	Boothe Leasing Corp.	Boca Raton Airport, Florida. Loss of control due to engine failure. 5 killed.
13 Oct 1956	10107/HK-914	LIDCA	Colombia. Cause and fatalities unk.
22 Nov 1956	10210/HK-913X	Vagon Volante De Colombia	Funza—Bogota, Colombia. Crashed on final approach, fatalities unk.
30 Oct 1957	10093/XA-LIW	TAMSA	Near Campeche, Mexico. Crashed after take-off. 3 killed.
1958	10119/HK-924	Mercantil Colombiana	Colombia. Cause and fatalities unk.
11 Jan 1958	10115/PP-CEH	SACI	Santos-Dumont Airport, Brazil. Crashed on training flight, 2 onboard, no fatalities.
16 Jan 1958	10200/PP-CEF	SACI	5 miles NW Val de Cans Airport, Belem, Brazil. Engine fire, 3 killed.
6 Feb 1958	10006/TG-ATA	Aviateca	La Aurora Intl. Airport, Guatemala. Engine failure after take-off, forced landing, fatalities unk.
17 Jun 1958	10099/HK-930	Capt. Gustavo Torres	Colombia. Cause and fatalities unk.
29 Nov 1958	10202/TG-AVA	Aviateca	La Libertad, Guatemala. Landing accident, fatalities unk.
3 Jun 1960	10063/HK-906	Aerovias Helices	Barranquilla, Colombia. Cause and fatalities unk.
21 Jun 1960	10180/PP-CEM	SACI	Galeao Intl. Airport, Brazil. Parked—hit by taxiing DC-7C, no fatalities.
24 Aug 1960	10198/CP-665	DAC	Near Puerto Heath, Bolivia. Emergency landing, fatalities unk.
26 Nov 1960	10128/CP-678	Aerovias Condor	Santa Cruz, Bolivia. u/c retraction before airborne, fatalities unk.
20 Dec 1961	10159/HK-777	SEA	Cucuta, Colombia. Emergency landing, 4+ onboard, 1 later died.
11 Mar 1962	10051/OB-UAF-531	EAPSA	Peru. Cause and fatalities unk.
3 Aug 1964	10073/N4829V	M&F Inc.	Granite Mt. Airport, Alaska. Undershot runway, no fatalities.
27 Aug 1964	10067/N2055A	L.B. Smith Aircraft Corp.	Miami Intl. Airport, Florida. Destroyed on ground by Hurricane Cleo, no fatalities.
27 Aug 1964	10083/N5117B	L.B. Smith Aircraft Corp.	Miami Intl. Airport, Florida. Destroyed on ground by Hurricane Cleo, no fatalities.

Appendix VI: Accidents

Date	MSN/S/N	Operator	Location/Cause of Loss
27 Aug 1964	10102/N2059A	L.B. Smith Aircraft Corp.	Miami Intl. Airport, Florida. Destroyed on ground by Hurricane Cleo, no fatalities.
7 Nov 1964	10177/N74127	Steward-Davis	Cofre de Perote, Veracruz, Mexico. Hit mountain flying in cloud, 2 killed.
19 Dec 1964	10164/N128E	John W. Mecom	20 miles E Alexandria, Egypt. Shot down by Egyptian MiGs, 2 killed.
16 Jan 1965	10163/N208M	Interior Airways	10 miles N Beaver, Alaska. Electrical and engine failure, no fatalities.
29 Jul 1965	10103/N4834V	George B. Alder	Near Lermer, Mexico. Forced ditching due to fuel starvation, no fatalities.
15 Mar 1970	10117/CP-677	TABSA	7 miles from Sasasama Airport, Bolivia. Cause unk., 4 killed.
28 Oct 1970	10213/PT-DNZ	Amazonia	Ponta Norte, Brazil. Crashed into hill while on landing approach. 4 killed.
11 Jun 1971	10219/PT-DLP	Amazonia	Belem do Para, Brazil. Belly landed, fatalities unk.
10 Jul 1971	10158/HK-583E	SEA	Near Arauca, Colombia. Cause unk., 1+ killed.
27 Jan 1977	10147/CP-983	Transportes Aereos Itinez	San Ramon, Bolivia. Engine failure at take-off, 6 killed.

Appendix VII: Existing Aircraft

MSN/S/N	Present Location	Present Status
10035/44-22991	Walter Soplata Collection, Newbury, Ohio, USA.	*Fuselage only* in a poor and derelict condition. Wings and booms scrapped.
10050/44-23006	Pima Air & Space Museum, Tucson, Arizona, USA.	*Complete airframe* with an above average exterior but interior stripped, unrestored. Displayed outside. Ex-N6997C.
10152/45-57782	Hagerstown Aviation Museum, Hagerstown, Maryland, USA.	*Fuselage only* in a derelict condition, wings and booms also derelict and stored. Ex-N5102B.
10071/44-23027	Hagerstown Aviation Museum, Hagerstown, Maryland, USA.	*Fuselage only* in a derelict condition, wings and booms also derelict and stored. Ex-N8009E.
10184/45-57814	Hagerstown Aviation Museum, Hagerstown, Maryland, USA.	*Complete airframe* and in excellent condition. Made the last C-82 flight in 2006. Engines maintained in running condition. Reg: N9701F.
10209/48–574	McChord AFB Museum, Tacoma, Washington State, USA.	*Complete airframe* in an above average condition but displayed outside. Ex-N4753C.
10216/48–581	USAF Museum, Wright-Patterson AFB, Dayton, Ohio, USA.	*Complete airframe* in an excellent and restored condition. Ex-N4752C.
10220/48–585	Museu Aerospacial (MUSAL), Campos dos Afonos AB, Rio De Janeiro, Brazil.	*Complete airframe* but in a very poor condition and displayed outside. Rust damaged beyond restoration. Ex-2202.

Appendix VIII:
Civil C-82A Checklist

Obtained from a C-82A at Long Beach, California,
dating from 1963

C-82 CHECK LIST

GENERAL EXTERIOR OF AIRCRAFT
1. Gear pins & chocks in position.
2. Check Form 1 and 1A.
3. Gear Handle "DOWN".
4. Mags & radios "OFF".
5. Battery switch "ON".
6. APP "ON".
7. Booster pumps "ON".
8. Pitot covers "REMOVED".
9. External control locks "REMOVED".
10. Check struts for proper inflation (Main struts 4½ inches, nose strut.
11. Check CO_2 discharge indicators.
12. Landing gear pins "REMOVED".

GENERAL INTERIOR OF AIRCRAFT
1. Check anti-icing fluid quantity.
2. Check hydraulic fluid level, spare fluid and switch "ON".
3. Master radio switch "ON".
4. Loading jacks safetied "UP", clamshell doors safetied "CLOSED".
5. Check for safety of all emergency levers.
6. Check for flap emergency extension levers.
7. Briefing kit.
8. Necessary emergency equipment.
9. Flashlights: 2 required.
10. Escape hatch closed and secured.

BEFORE STARTING ENGINES
1. Booster pumps "OFF".
2. Seats, Rudder pedals and belts adjusted.
3. Parking brake "SET" (1000 lb pressure).
4. Engineers report: Fuel and Oil quantity Caps checked and secure.
5. Mixture "IDLE CUT OFF".
6. Throttles, 1000-1200 RPM POSITION.
7. Props "HIGH RPM".
8. OUTBOARD tanks "ON".
9. Carburetor heat "COLD".
10. Blowers "LOW".
11. Fuel-oil shut-off switch "NORMAL".
12. Cowl flaps "OPEN".
13. Generators "ON".
14. Inverters "OFF".
15. Check circuit breakers.
16. Air speed selector, "STATIC AND SAFTIED".
17. Prop anti-icing "CHECKED AND OFF".
18. Pitot heat "CHECKED AND OFF".
19. Check alarm bell.
20. Heating system "OFF".
21. Landing gear sequence switch "NORMAL".
22. Hydraulic pressure switch "MANUAL", then "AUTOMATIC".
23. Auto pilot power seitch "OFF".
24. Check fuel and Oil quantity gages.
25. Check manifold pressure.
26. Check all warning and gear lights.
27. Controls "UNLOCKED".

STARTING ENGINES
1. Right engine clear Fire Guard.
2. Master ignition switch on.
3. Engine starter.
4. Booster pump on.
5. Ignition switch.
6. Mixture auto rich.
7. Oil pressure with in 30 seconds.
8. Spare invertor on then off.
9. Check vacuum.
10. Start left engine.
11. Invertor to main.

BEFORE TAXI
1. Radio on.
2. Check operation of heat exchanger dump lights.
3. Gyros set and uncaged.
4. Torque meter heater on if required.
5. Engine to 700 RPM.
6. Check mags for grounding.
7. Check purdge valves.
8. Check operation of cross flow valves both engines.
9. Taxi when oil pressure is normal.

ENGINE RUN-UP
1. Nose wheel centered.
2. Parking brakes on.
3. Temperatures & Pressures
   Fuel pressure 21-23
   Oil Temp 40 Minimum
   CHT 120 minimum
   Hydraulic pressure 1000 psi
4. Engine to 1700 5.
5. Check volatages.
6. Exercise props.
7. Blowers high at 1700 RPM
8. 2000 RPM wait for 30 seconds.
9. Check carburator heat 35° rise
10. Blowers low.
11. Check feathering 200 RPM drop.
12. Check mags at field barometsic pressure.

C-82 CHECK LIST

BEFORE TAKE-OFF
1. Controls "UNLOCKED" and check for free movement.
2. Gyros "SET" and "UNCAGED".
3. Mixtures "AUTO RICH".
4. Props "HIGH RPM".
5. Carburetor heat "COLD".
6. Outboard tanks "ON".
7. Wing flaps as desired.
8. Auto pilot "OFF".
9. Pitot heat and anti-icing "ON" if required.
10. Astro dome "CLOSED".
11. IFF "ON".
12. Windows "CLOSED".
13. Cowl flaps "CLOSED TRAIL".
14. Booster pumps "ON EMERGENCY".
15. Trim tabs "SET".

TAKE-OFF AND CLIMB
1. 53.5" Hg, 2800 RPM (at sea level).
2. Gear "UP".
3. Flaps "UP" (above 300 feet).
4. Climb power 41.5", 2600 RPM (Maximum continuous).
5. Booster pumps "OFF" at 1000 feet, check fuel pressure.
6. Auxiliary power plant "OFF" (after 5 Min).
7. Check main buss and load meters.

CRUISE
1. Cruising power setting.
2. Cowl flaps "CLOSED" (check CHT).
3. Mixture as required.
4. Altimeter set to regional setting.
5. Shift blowers each odd hour for ten minutes.

CRUISING DESCENT
1. Mixture "AUTO-RICH".
2. Blowers "HIGH".
3. Check hydraulic pressure and quantity.
4. Altimeter "SET" to field pressure.
5. Selectors on fullest gas tanks.
6. Carburetor heat as required.
7. Auto pilot "OFF".
8. Hydraulic switch "AUTOMATIC".
9. Parking brakes "OFF".
10. Paratainer doors "CLOSED".
11. Radar Dome "UP".
12. Trailing Antenna "IN".
13. Auxiliary power plant "ON".

BEFORE LANDING
1. Airspeed 130 MPH.
2. Blowers "LOW".
3. Landing gear handle "DOWN".
4. Props to 2400 RPM.
5. Visual check, green light, no horn.
6. Booster pumps "EMERGENCY".
7. Cowl flaps "TRAIL".
8. Wing flaps as required.

AFTER LANDING
1. Props high RPM.
2. Cowl flaps open.
3. Booster pumps "OFF".
4. Wing heat "OFF".
5. Pitot heat "OFF".
6. IFF "OFF".
7. Wing flaps "UP".
8. All unnecessary radios "OFF".

SECURING AIRCRAFT (Daily Post Flight Check)
1. Nose wheel "CENTERED".
2. Parking brakes "ON".
*3. Check mags at field barometric pressure
*4. Idle Mixture and speed check.
*5. Ignition switch check (700 RPM).
*6. Check idle at 450 RPM.
7. 1200 RPM for 1 minute.
8. Mixture "IDLE CUT OFF", RIGHT ENGINE FIRST (Check vacuum).
9. Ignition and master switches "OFF".
10. Inverters "OFF".
11. All radios "OFF".
12. Battery switch "OFF".
13. Flight controls "LOCKED".
14. Chocks "IN PLACE".
15. Brakes "OFF".
16. Gear pins "IN PLACE".
17. Complete Form 1 and 1A.
18. APP "OFF".

SINGLE ENGINE CHECK LIST
1. Throttle "CLOSED".
2. Mixture "OFF".
3. Feather propeller.
4. Fuel selector "OFF".
5. Fuel & Oil shut-off switch "OFF".
6. Ignition "OFF".
7. Cowl flap "CLOSED".
8. Propeller full high pitch position.
9. Generator "OFF".
10. APP "ON".
11. Wing heat selector to good engine.

Author's Collection.

Postscript: Sebring C-82 Packets

Just before this book went to press new information came to light thanks to motorsport writer Jeff Allison concerning the C-82 Packets stored at Sebring Airport/Raceway in Florida. Connecting dates and a few identities, it was discovered that these aircraft were owned by Leeward Aeronautical Sales Inc. who were using Sebring as a storage yard prior to selling the Packets to U.S. and South American customers.

As listed below, six unsold, and decaying, C-82As were left by 1959 with all being sold to Aero Enterprises Inc. in 1962 then Peter Bercut a short time later. Two are known to have remained by 1969 and FAA records list all as eventually "destroyed."

N56582 is listed in FAA records as "hull only" and one photo from Sebring shows a C-82 with a crushed flight-deck. Likely, N56582 was the aircraft involved in a fatal accident at Sebring concerning a ground crewman taking a Packet for a high-speed joyride – his flight-deck colliding with the wing of a parked C-82. See also: Leeward Aeronautical Sales Inc. & Aero Enterprises Inc. in the Civil Operators Section.

```
N56582 10176 / 45-57806    N6246C 10062 / 44-23018
N6243C 10074 / 44-23030    N7850B 10098 / 44-23054
N6245C 10055 / 44-23011    N7851B 10082 / 44-23038
```

Car racing at Sebring Raceway, Florida during 1960. Visible in the background is C-82A N7850B (msn: 10098). Spectators often used these dilapidated wrecks as viewing stands (Jeff Allison).

Bibliography

Military histories used Individual Aircraft Record Cards (IARC) and 16mm microfilm reels obtained from the Smithsonian Institution, National Air & Space Museum (NASM), Washington, D.C., and the Air Force Historical Research Agency (US-AFHRA), Maxwell AFB, Montgomery, Alabama.

Civil histories used N-number records obtained from the Aircraft Registration Branch, Federal Aviation Administration (FAA), Oklahoma City, Oklahoma.

Primary References

The Packeteer. Steward-Davis Inc. Newsletter. June 1957.
USAAF Pilot's Flight Operating Instructions: C-82 Packet. 1945 Edition.
USAF/AFSC Report: Flight Test Evaluation of C-82 Jet-Packet 1600. November 1961.
USAF Flight Handbook. T.O. NO. 1C-82A-1: C-82A. 1954 Edition.

Books

Brooks, Peter W. *The World's Airliners*. London: Putnam, 1962.
Chakko, Gp. Capt. Jacob. *Memoirs*. Privately published, 1999.
Jane's All the World's Aircraft. Volume years 1961 to 1968. London: Haymarket Publishing Group.
Lloyd, Alwyn T. *Fairchild C-82 Packet and C-119 Flying Boxcar*. Shepperton, UK: Aerofax (Midland Publishing), 2005.
Mitchell, Kent A. *Fairchild Aircraft 1926–1987*. Santa Ana, CA: Narkiewicz-Thompson, 1997.
White, Graham. *R-2800: Pratt & Whitney's Dependable Masterpiece*. Shrewsbury, UK: Airlife, 2001.
Yenne, Bill. *The History of the U.S. Air Force*. Lincoln, NE: Bison Books, 1984.

Articles

Meal, Xavier. "The Thing Is Still Alive." *Aeroplane Monthly Magazine* (April 1999).
Mitchell, Kent A. "The Fairchild C-82 Packet." *The American Aviation Historical Society (AAHS) Journal* (Spring 1999).
Stone, Irving. "Design Analysis of the Fairchild C-82 Packet." *Aviation Magazine* 44, Nos. 8 & 9 (August & September 1945).

Index

Numbers in *bold italics* indicate pages with illustrations

Aero Enterprises 125, 312
Air Defense Command (ADC) 71, 72, 81–82
Air Materiel Command (AMC) 82–86
Air Rescue Service (USAF) 89, 93–95
Aircraft Engineering & Maintenance Co. 38–40, 107
airframe structure 17–19
Allison, Jeff 312
Arnold, General Henry H. 7
Assembly Operation 74
Aviation Facilities 127

Banker's Life & Casualty 127–128
Bercut, Peter 140, 312
Berlin Airlift, The 10, 74–77
The Big Lift (film) 77
block numbers 30–31
Boutelle, Richard S. 7
Brazilian Air Force 108, *109*, 295
Briles Wing & Helicopter 130

C-82A series 32, *33*, 312
C-82N series 37, *289*, 290
cargo capacity 24, 27–28, *47*
Coldspot Operation 78
Combine Operation 73
Comet Project 73
communications equipment 23
crew numbers 20
Cruzeiro do Sul (Brazil) 114–115

Davis-Monthan AFB, Arizona 13, 111, 296–297
Duncan, Francis L. 132

EC-82A conversions 33, *34*, 35
electrical system 22
engines 21
Epstein, Ben 128

Fairchild, Sherman 5
Fairchild Aircraft Company 5–7, 17, 131
Far North Flying Service 131–132
55th Strategic Reconn Group 72
flight controls 20–21
flight-deck *19*, *20*, *24*, *66*, *275*
The Flight of the Phoenix (film) 13, 16, 57–70, 143, 181, 196, *197*, *200*, 201
fuel system 22

Greenamyer, Darryl 130–131
Group A upgrades 39, *40*

Hagerstown Aviation Museum 133
Hawkins & Powers Aviation 15, 133
Haylift Operation 10, 77–78
Hill AFB, Utah 111, 295–296
Honduran Air Force 110, *162*, 163
hydraulic system 22

Interior Airways 134, *244*

JC-82A conversions 35,
Jet-Packet 1600 53, 301
Jet-Packet 3200 *44*, 53–54, 301
Jet-Packet 3400 54–55, 301

Kelly AFB, Texas 111, 294–295

landing gear 21
Lawa Goudvelden (Surinam) 49–50, *53*, 125, 143
L.B. Smith Aircraft Corp. 13
LEBCA International 135
Leeward Aeronautical Sales 135–136
Levister, Wendell 215–218

M&W Aircraft Leasing 136
Master Equipment Co. 137
McChord AFB, Washington 98
Mecom Oil Co. 134, 137, 242–243, 250–252
Mexicana Airlines 120–121, *222*, 302
Military Air Transport Service (MATS) 10, 35, 72, 92–95
mission requirements: air ambulance 26; cargo 24–25; glider tow 27; troop transport 26
Model 78 7, 17

National Advisory Committee for Aeronautics (NACA) 13, *14*, 111, 137, *138*, 213, *214*
National Aerospace & Space Administration (NASA) 139, *214*
New Frontier Airlift Corp. 48–51, 143–144
91st Strategic Reconn Group 72
Northern Air Cargo (NAC) 14, 139
Northshore Goldfields Ltd. 49–50, 127, 139

oil system 22
onboard equipment 23
Operation Haylift (film) 210
oxygen system 22

Packet Pressroom 282, *283*, 279, 302
Portrex Operation 78
production line 7–10, 32–33

Redhead Project 78
Rhein-Main AB, West Germany 75–76, 104–106
Rivaereo Co. (Chile) 51, 116
Royal Aircraft Establishment (RAE) 108
Rudolph, Samuel C. 50, 141–142

SC-82A conversions *35*, 36
search & rescue squadrons 10, 35–36, 89, 93–95
Sebring Raceway *312*
serial numbers 29–31
Sholton, Robert G. 139, 141
60th Troop Carrier Group 72, 74–76, 104–105
64th Troop Carrier Group 72, 99
62nd Troop Carrier Group 71, 72, 98–99
Skypallet *56*, 57, 301
Skytruck Mk. I *55*, 301
Smith, Henry A. 48, 133–134, 143
specifications (detailed) 27–29
Steward, Herb 41, 43, 143
Steward-Davis 13, 41–53, 143–144
Strategic Air Command (SAC) 71, 72, 96–97

Tactical Air Command (USAF) 72, 97–104
Thayer, Bob 51–53, 65
Thieboldt, Armand J. 7
314th Troop Carrier Group 72, 100–101
375th Troop Carrier Group 72, 103
316th Troop Carrier Group 71, 72, 101–102
313th Troop Carrier Group 72, 100
tracked undercarriage 37–38, *39*, *225*, *226*
Trans World Airlines (TWA) 145, 265–267
Troop Carrier Groups 10, 71–79
type certificate (AR-15) 43, 46–47

Umbrella Operation 78
United Airlines 145–146, 184

United Flying Mail Car 145–146, *184*, 302
United Heckathorn 146
United States Air Forces (all namesakes) 7, 10–13, 71

Vittles Operation *see* The Berlin Airlift

Westinghouse jet engines 41–48
Wiesbaden AB, West Germany 75–76, 104
XC-82 prototype *6*, *7–8*, 9, 32, *151*
XC-82B *see* XC-119A prototype
XC-119A prototype 12, *13*, *36*, 37, *236*

Yukon Operation 74

ZC-82N conversion 37, 289–290

www.ingramcontent.com/pod-product-compliance
Lightning Source LLC
Chambersburg PA
CBHW081539300426
44116CB00015B/2685